The Reorganized
Natio... ...ealth Se...

The Reorganized National Health Service

Fifth edition

Ruth Levitt

Lecturer, writer and researcher
on health and public policy

Andrew Wall

Senior Fellow
Health Services Management Centre
University of Birmingham
UK

John Appleby

Senior Lecturer
Department of Health Policy and Practice
University of East Anglia
UK

CHAPMAN & HALL
London · Glasgow · Weinheim · New York · Tokyo · Melbourne · Madras

Published by Chapman & Hall, 2–6 Boundary Row, London SE1 8HN, UK

Chapman & Hall, 2–6 Boundary Row, London SE1 8HN, UK

Blackie Academic & Professional, Wester Cleddens Road, Bishopbriggs, Glasgow G64 2NZ, UK

Chapman & Hall GmbH, Pappelallee 3, 69469 Weinheim, Germany

Chapman & Hall USA, 115 Fifth Avenue, New York, NY 10003, USA

Chapman & Hall Japan, ITP-Japan, Kyowa Building, 3F, 2–2–1 Hirakawacho, Chiyoda-ku, Tokyo 102, Japan

Chapman & Hall Australia, 102 Dodds Street, South Melbourne, Victoria 3205, Australia

Chapman & Hall India, R. Seshadri, 32 Second Main Road, CIT East, Madras 600 035, India

Distributed in the USA and Canada by Singular Publishing Group Inc., 4284 41st Street, San Diego, California 92105

First edition 1976, revised and reprinted July 1976, second edition 1977, revised and reprinted 1979, third edition 1984, reprinted 1989, fourth edition 1992, reprinted 1994, fifth edition 1995.

©1976, 1977 Ruth Levitt; 1984 Ruth Levitt and Andrew Wall; 1992 Ruth Levitt and Andrew Wall; 1995 Ruth Levitt, Andrew Wall and John Appleby

Typeset in 10/12 Times by Florencetype Ltd, Stoodleigh, Devon
Printed in Great Britain by T.J. Press (Padstow) Ltd, Padstow, Cornwall

ISBN 0 412 62100 2   1 56593 420 2 (USA)

A catalogue record for this book is available from the British Library

♾ Printed on permanent acid-free text paper, manufactured in accordance with ANSI/NISO Z39.48–1992 and ANSI/NISO Z39.48–1984 (Permanence of Paper).

Contents

Preface

The National Health Service is a proud British achievement, the expression of a sustained commitment to the ideal of providing effective health care as a public service to all who need it. Despite the NHS's many successes and its continuing ability to offer much that is excellent, the shortcomings of the service demonstrate, as time passes, how difficult it is to attain this simple-sounding goal, either efficiently or fairly.

To many people watching the NHS recently, the word 'reorganization' has acquired a disconcertingly familiar ring. The succession of changes imposed upon its policies and practices has become so bewildering that even those who work in the service confess to feeling confused. There is no doubt, too, that a growing sense of unease is shared by staff and public, who feel sceptical about the supposedly beneficial effects of these repeated attempts at reform and worried that the NHS may be reformed out of existence.

The purpose of this new edition is to explain, in clear terms, what has been happening and why, from the origins to the present day. We have told the story in plain English, translating jargon and decoding initials, and hope readers will find the book helpful, whether they read from the start or refer to particular topics.

We acknowledge with thanks the use of copyright material quoted from HMSO and other sources.

Ruth Levitt
Andrew Wall
John Appleby
London, Bath and Birmingham
March 1995

Selected abbreviations

ACAS	Advisory, Conciliation and Arbitration Service
ACC	Association of County Councils
ACHCEW	Association of Community Health Councils for England and Wales
ADL	Association of District Councils
AIDS	Acquired immune deficiency syndrome
ALA	Association of Local Authorities
AMA	Association of Metropolitan Authorities
ASC	Action for Sick Children (formerly NAWCH)
ASH	Action on Smoking and Health
BDA	British Dental Association
BMA	British Medical Association
BSI	British Standards Institution
BTS	Blood Transfusion Service
BUPA	British United Provident Association
CDSC	Communicable Diseases Surveillance Centre
CE	Chief Executive
CEPOD	Confidential Enquiry into Perioperative Deaths
CHC	Community health council
CIP	Cost improvement programme
CMDS	Core minimum data set
	Community contract minimum data set
COHSE	Confederation of Health Service Employees (see UNISON)
CPN	Community psychiatric nurse
CSO	Central Statistical Office
CSSD	Central sterile services department
CT	Computerized tomography
D&C	Dilatation and curettage
DGH	District general hospital
DGM	District general manager
DH	Department of Health
DHA	District health authority

DHSS	Department of Health and Social Security
DMC	District medical committee
DMO	District medical officer
DMU	Directly managed unit
DN	District nurse
DoH	Department of Health
DPH	Director of Public Health
DRG	Diagnosis related group
DSS	Department of Social Security
EBS	Emergency Bed Service (London)
ECR	Extra-contractual referral
EFL	External financing limit
EL	Executive letter
ENB	English National Board for Nursing, Midwifery and Health Visiting
ENT	Ear, nose and throat
FCE	Finished consultant episode
FHS	Family health services
FHSA	Family health services authority (formerly FPC)
FPA	Family Planning Association
FPC	Family practitioner committee (now FHSA)
GDC	General Dental Council
GDP	General dental practitioner
	Gross domestic product
GDS	General dental services
GHS	General household survey
GIFT	Gamete intra-fallopian transfer
GM	General manager
GMC	General Medical Council
GMP	General medical practitioner
GMS	General medical services
GMSC	General Medical Services Committee
GPFH	General practice fundholder
HA	Health authority
HAA	Hospital Activity Analysis
HAS	Health Advisory Service
HC	Health circular
HCHS	Hospital and community health services
HES	Hospital episode system
HFEA	Human Fertilisation and Embryology Authority
HIPE	Hospital Inpatient Enquiry
HIV	Human immuno-deficiency virus
HMO	Health maintenance organization (USA)
HRG	Healthcare related groups / Healthcare resource group
HSC	Health and Safety Commission

Selected abbreviations

HSI	Health service indicator
HVA	Health Visitors Association
IBD	Interest bearing debt
ICD	International Classification of Diseases
ICU	Intensive care unit
IPR	Individual performance review
IVF	In vitro fertilization
JCC	Joint consultative committee
LoS	Length of stay
MDS	Minimum data set
MDU	Medical Defence Union
MIT	Minimally invasive therapy
MMR	Measles, mumps and rubella (vaccine)
MRC	Medical Research Council
MRI	Magnetic resonance imaging
MSF	Manufacturing, Science and Finance (technical staff trade union)
NALGO	National and Local Government Officers' Union (see UNISON)
NAO	National Audit Office
NCEPOD	National Confidential Enquiry into Perioperative Deaths (formerly CEPOD)
NCT	National Childbirth Trust
NHS	National Health Service
NHSAR	National Health Service Administrative Register
NHSME	National Health Service Management Executive (now National Health Service Executive)
NUPE	National Union of Public Employees (see UNISON)
OECD	Organization of Economic Cooperation and Development
OPCS	Office of Population Censuses and Surveys
P&T	Professional and technical
PAC	Public Accounts Committee
PACT	Prescription analysis and cost tabulation
PAS	Patient administration system
PDC	Public dividend capital
PES	Public Expenditure Survey
PHLS	Public Health Laboratory Service
PPP	Private Patients Plan
PRP	Performance related pay
PSS	Personal social services
QA	Quality assurance
QALY	Quality adjusted life year
R&D	Research and development
RAWP	Resource Allocation Working Party
RCCS	Revenue consequences of capital schemes

RCN	Royal College of Nursing
RGM	Regional general manager
RHA	Regional health authority
SHA	Special health authority
SHARE	Scottish Health Authorities Revenue Equalization
SHHD	Scottish Home and Health Department
SIFTR	Service increment for teaching and research
SMR	Standardized mortality ratio
TQM	Total quality management
UGM	Unit general manager
UKCC	United Kingdom Central Council for Nursing, Midwifery and Health Visiting
UNISON	Public sector union, formerly NALGO/NUPE/COHSE
WHO	World Health Organization
WTE	Whole time equivalent

Ministers of Health and Secretaries of State

MINISTERS OF HEALTH

1919–21	Dr Christopher Addison
1921–22	Sir Alfred Mond
1922–23	Sir Arthur Griffith-Boscawen
1923	Neville Chamberlain
1923–24	Sir William Joynson-Hicks
1924	John Wheatley
1924–29	Neville Chamberlain
1929–31	Arthur Greenwood
1931	Neville Chamberlain
1931–35	Sir E. Hilton-Young
1935–38	Sir Kingsley Wood
1938–40	Walter Elliot
1940–41	Malcolm MacDonald
1941–43	Ernest Brown
1943–45	Henry Willink
1945–51	Aneurin Bevan
1951	Hilary Marquand
1951–52	Harry Crookshank
1952–55	Ian Macleod
1955–57	Robin Turton
1957	Dennis Vosper
1957–60	Derek Walker-Smith
1960–63	Enoch Powell
1963–64	Anthony Barber
1964–68	Kenneth Robinson

SECRETARIES OF STATE FOR SOCIAL SERVICES

1968–70	Richard Crossman
1970–74	Sir Keith Joseph
1974–76	Barbara Castle
1976–79	David Ennals
1979–81	Patrick Jenkin
1981–87	Norman Fowler
1987–88	John Moore

SECRETARIES OF STATE FOR HEALTH

1988–90	Kenneth Clarke
1990–92	William Waldegrave
1992	Virginia Bottomley

1

Background to today's National Health Service

This first chapter explores the beginnings of the NHS by looking at certain key events of the previous century and subsequently which provide important clues about why the NHS was originally created in its particular form and why it has been subject to progressively more frequent reforms. The basic elements of the NHS are the hospital services, the community-based services and the family practitioner services. Their separate origins will be traced to 1948 when the NHS began and will be followed through subsequent developments, in particular the 1974 and 1982 reorganizations, the Griffiths proposals for general management and the most recent major reforms set out in the White Papers *Working for Patients* [1] and *Caring for People* [2] which were incorporated into the National Health Service and Community Care Act in 1990. Later chapters will address these changes in more detail as well as the latest health care priority directions contained in the White Paper *The Health of the Nation* [3].

HEALTH SERVICES BEFORE 1948

Developments up to 1870

The concept of public responsibility for the health of individuals can be traced back at least as far as 1834 when the Poor Law Amendment Act was passed. This established that the parish workhouses should have sick wards where the inmates could be treated when they became ill. However, the health of the community had long been neglected, and it also became necessary for the workhouses to admit to their wards sick paupers living in the parish, since so many were dying in their homes, being unable to obtain any medical care for themselves. By 1848 the demand for institutional care was so great that the sick wards had become entirely devoted to sick paupers. The Public Health Act of that year acknowledged for the first time some State responsibility for the health of the nation through its creation of a central organizing body called the General Board of Health. The Board was able to achieve very few reforms because it did not possess the powers necessary to counter the vested interests of the Boards of Guardians who were the local managers of the institutions concerned.

By 1851 the first links between workhouses and the voluntary hospitals were beginning to be forged. The origins of this second group of hospitals represent a complete contrast to the workhouses. They emerged from the philanthropy and altruism of the well-to-do, and the moral obligations of religious and charitable bodies, whereas the workhouses had developed in the eighteenth century to cope with the problems of poverty and destitution. The voluntary hospitals were built and financed through donations and sub-scriptions and attracted the services of skilled doctors who, acting on their social conscience, treated the patients often without payment. These hospitals became selective in their admissions, leaving all but acute cases to be dealt with by the workhouses. The workhouses themselves sometimes subscribed to nearby voluntary hospitals so that they could transfer their more compli-cated and acute cases to them. In this way, ill-health became divided to mirror the social status of the two types of hospitals, but the load was not evenly shared – in 1861 there were estimated to be 50 000 sick paupers in the workhouses and 11 000 patients in the voluntary hospitals. The Metro-politan Poor Act of 1867 represents a further landmark in health care provision as it obliged local authorities within London to provide separate institu-tional care for tuberculosis, smallpox, fevers and insanity. One year later, another Poor Law Amendment Act established the same provision in the provinces.

Developments from 1870 to 1919

By the 1870s the workhouses, isolation hospitals and asylums together with the voluntary hospitals could be described as a public service through which people had access to hospital care when they became ill. Conditions were often appalling by modern standards and medicine had few effective tools for alleviating disease; most of the activity involved care rather than treatment, and care that was sometimes harshly and unwillingly distributed. It is possible that the stimulus to alter this inadequate state of affairs only came after the experience of war.

The Crimean War (1854–6) demonstrated how inadequate the organization and supply of health care was. Florence Nightingale's administrative and professional reforms arose from her experiences in the Crimea. Later, the recruitment of soldiers for the Boer War (1899–1902) revealed a poor standard of general health in working men. It scarcely improved on arrival in South Africa: for every death from combat there were at least four from typhoid and other fevers. The Army's Committee on Physical Deterioration reported that 48% of recruits had to be rejected on physical grounds alone. Its recommendations were the basis for the establishment of the School Medical Service in 1907.

In addition, the beginning of the twentieth century began a new era in effective medical care with discoveries that put diagnostic, therapeutic and pathology efforts on a much more scientific footing. It was clear that the nineteenth-century hospitals could not ensure a healthy fighting force were there to be another war, so interest moved for the first time towards preventive methods of health care. But this did not happen rapidly, for it depended on having general practitioners who could deal with the huge unmet demand for health education and care in the community.

In comparison with famous specialists in the voluntary hospitals who were able to build up large private practices, the general practitioners in the parishes derived much of their income from the capitation fees paid to them on contract by the friendly societies, trade unions and similar associations, in return for the provision of treatment and medicines to the members. Most of the wage-earning population, including a large proportion of the middle class, received their medical care in this way, through the payment of a flat-rate contribution to their association. The benefits were only available to the wage earner – wives, children, the old and the disabled had to rely on out-patient departments and dispensaries of the voluntary hospitals or go without. In 1911, through the British Medical Association, the doctors put pressure on the Prime Minister, Lloyd George, to protect their interests and, with the passing of the National Health Insurance Act, they were successful in changing the administrative control of their work to new insurance committees, on which they were represented. The Act made lower-paid workers compulsorily insured for the services of a general practitioner and fixed the fee that the doctor could receive for every person on his list. However, this still left the majority of the population without any improvements in their general practitioner services.

Some local authorities had achieved considerable advances in public and environmental health, but since they could not be compelled to provide many health services at all, substantial differences in the amount and quality of their provision emerged across the country. In 1905, the Minority Report of the Poor Law Commission came out strongly in favour of intervention by central government in tackling poverty and ill-health. The Government chose to act indirectly, through the provision of old age pensions and unemployment benefits rather than by improving the health care system itself. The Ministry of Reconstruction, which was set up towards the end of the First World War, continued to approach this problem indirectly by proposing that a Ministry of Health should be established to take on all the functions of the Local Government Board and the work of the National Health Insurance Commission.

Developments from 1919 to 1942

The new Ministry of Health was established in 1919 but it only devoted a small part of its time and efforts to health service administration, since the duties transferred to it from the Local Government Board were so numerous. Nevertheless, a radical stimulus to the provision of a nationally organized, comprehensive health service was provided in the Dawson Report [4]. It recommended a number of objectives including domiciliary services from doctors, pharmacists and local health authority staff; primary health centres with beds under the control of general practitioners, diagnostic facilities, out-patient clinics, dental, ancillary and community services; secondary health centres for specialist diagnosis and treatment; supplementary services for infectious and mental illnesses; teaching hospitals with medical schools; the promotion of research; standardized clinical records; and the establishment of a single authority to administer all medical and allied services with medical representation and local medical committees. Although this report was published in 1920, it identified the issues which continue to be central to most of the debate on the organization of the health services.

Then, in 1926, the Royal Commission on National Health Insurance stated that the ultimate solution would lie in the direction of divorcing the medical service entirely from the insurance system and reorganizing it, together with other public health activities, as a service to be supplied from the general public funds. The need for greater co-ordination between the various parts of the system was only slowly and partially met, as for instance through the Local Government Act, 1929, which transferred to the local authorities all the responsibilities of the Poor Law Boards of Guardians and, in addition, permitted them to provide the full range of hospital treatment. There was no compulsion, however, so great variations in standards existed. Some local authorities actively worked towards providing modern buildings with good equipment and the beginnings of specialist care, while others continued to have crowded, dark and understaffed wards in their old workhouse buildings.

The next important stimulus to reform in the scheme of health care did not come until 1939 when, as part of the wartime measures, the Government set up the Emergency Medical Service. This made the Minister of Health responsible for the treatment of casualties, and thus enabled the central department to direct the day-to-day work of the voluntary and local authority hospitals for the first time. In return, the Government took over the financial burden of this provision which, until that time, had been met by patients' contributions, local authority rates and the funds of the voluntary hospitals. Many prefabricated buildings were erected to create more beds and to compensate for those destroyed by enemy bombings. Out-patient departments, operating theatres and X-ray departments were set up and, through the local co-operation of medical and administrative staff, a much more effective scheme of care began to develop. Special centres grew up to deal with specific types of injury, and the blood transfusion service became a nationally organized effort that could cope far better with the demands of the war emergency. This 'national hospital service' was very quickly formed without any statutory change in ownership or management, and showed, for the first time, albeit under the pressure of war, what sort of developments could arise from central leadership and co-ordination.

In 1941 Ernest Brown, the Minister of Health, announced that the Government had commissioned an independent inquiry into the state of all the country's hospitals and their ability to provide adequate facilities. These hospital surveys confirmed that there were great inequalities of provision, that many of the public's needs were not being properly met and, above all, that without thorough co-ordination of effort there would be insufficient improvement [5]. Although the findings were hardly disputed there was a considerable divergence of views on the best way to finance the necessary reforms and on the question of whether central government should assume ownership and control of the existing hospitals.

THE CREATION OF THE NATIONAL HEALTH SERVICE

In 1942 the Beveridge Report was published, and it made far-reaching recommendations that formed the basis for the post-war system of social welfare services [6]. But, in addition it took as its central assumption the idea that a comprehensive system of health care was essential to any scheme for improving living standards. To Sir William Beveridge, the term 'comprehensive' meant medical treatment available for every citizen, both in the home and in hospital, provided by general practitioners, specialists, dentists and opticians, nurses and midwives, and the provision of surgical appliances and rehabilitation services. He thought these should be available to all citizens as and when they needed them.

The Coalition Government announced in 1943 that it accepted the need for a comprehensive scheme of health care, and it started negotiations with a number of bodies. The first plan envisaged a unified health service with one administrative unit taking full responsibility for local provision. The units would be administered by regional local government or by joint local and health authorities. The hospitals would be partially taken into national ownership and general practitioners would be full-time salaried employees. The British Medical Association was outraged at these proposals which it saw as originating from the influence of the National Association of Local Government Officers and the Society of Medical Officers of Health, so it withdrew from the discussions and progress was temporarily halted.

Later, in 1943, Henry Willink replaced Ernest Brown as Minister of Health and set about devising a scheme that would be acceptable to the various interest groups. In 1944 he published a White Paper, *A National Health Service* [7], which described a system of administration with the central responsibility vested in the Ministry of Health, to be advised by an appointed Central Health Services Council. Local organizations would be based on joint local authority areas which would in turn be advised by local versions of the Central Health Services Council. They would take over the local authority hospitals and would determine the financial compensation to be paid for the participation of the voluntary hospitals boards in the public scheme. General practitioners would be under contract to a central medical board with local committees and would be paid, as in the National Health Insurance System, on a per capita basis, unless they worked from a health centre provided by the local authority, in which case they would receive a salary. The central board would be able to regulate the distribution of practices all over the country. Although this plan failed to satisfy the varying interests, several of its proposals were retained in the final legislation.

The Government was indecisive, and discussions dragged on for fifteen months until a revised version was drawn up. This differed from the White Paper in proposing a two-tiered administrative structure in the form of regional and local planning authorities, in which ownership and administration of the hospitals was to remain with the local authorities and voluntary hospital boards. Instead of the central medical board of the White Paper, a series of local committees, similar to the existing local insurance committees of the National Health Insurance system, was proposed. This plan, therefore, dropped the idea of joint administration of the hospital and local authority services (which was not raised again until 1968), but it did establish the idea of regional and local levels of management. It did not tackle the problem of doctors' remuneration, and the principle of health centre practice was relegated to 'experimental' status. These last points have been of continuing controversy in the health service, but in this case meant that Willink had to drop the idea of a fully integrated service in order to meet the negotiating demands of as many groups as possible.

Although the Labour Party conference of 1944 decided in favour of a full-time salaried service based on regional local government, Aneurin Bevan, as Minister of Health in the 1945–51 Government, did not include these points in his White Paper. In fact he adopted much of the detail worked out for earlier plans and held few discussions before the White Paper was published. The BMA was suspicious of his intentions and organized a campaign of its members to boycott co-operation with the Government.

In March 1946 the National Health Service Bill [8] was published, and its main new point was the proposed nationalization of all hospitals under appointed Regional Hospital Boards, with local responsibility delegated to Hospital Management Committees. Teaching hospitals were to be separately administered under Boards of Governors with a direct link to the Ministry of Health. There were, however, still a great many details to be worked out in the time between the passing of the Act in November 1946 and the 'appointed day', 5 July 1948, when the National Health Service would come into effect. The BMA resumed discussions early in 1947, since it realized that its action could no longer prevent the arrangements from going ahead, but, in fact, the legislation ensured that the medical profession would have a voice on all statutory committees. Accounts of these negotiations disagree on the part played by Aneurin Bevan in reaching the final compromises. Although some observers hold that he did not contribute many original points to the substance of the Act, it seems clear that he was particularly skilful in exploiting the splits within the BMA and in getting the National Health Service underway with widespread enthusiasm among the staff and institutions concerned.

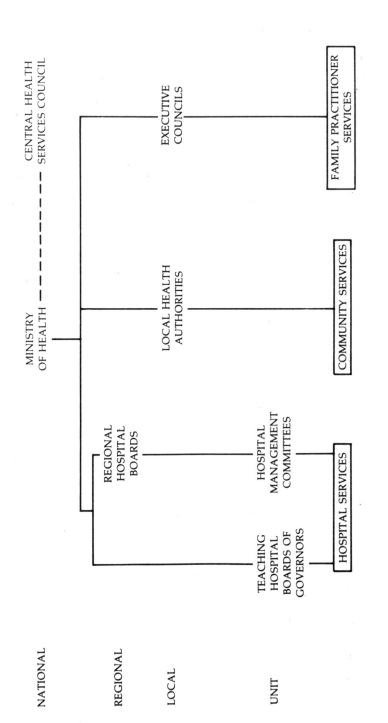

Figure 1.1 The National Health Service 1948–74.

How the new National Health Service worked

Although patients received broadly unchanged services at the point of delivery just before and just after 5 July 1948, the creation of the National Health Service did represent a radical change in the relationship between the individual citizen and the State, and it established a firm government commitment to developing and improving the country's system of health care. In the words of the 1946 Act, the aim was to promote 'the establishment in England and Wales of a comprehensive health service designed to secure improvement in the physical and mental health of the people of England and Wales and the prevention, diagnosis and treatment of illness' [9]. The principles of freedom and choice were upheld in that all people were entitled to use the service, yet they still had the opportunity to go to doctors outside the service. Equally, doctors would have no interference in their clinical judgement and were free to take private patients while participating in the service. The achievement of the Act was to make benefits available to everyone free of charge, on the basis of need, thus ending the former restrictions of provision to those who were insured or those who could afford private treatment.

The Minister of Health was made personally responsible to Parliament for the provision of all hospital and specialist services on a national basis, and for the Public Health Laboratory Service, the Blood Transfusion Service and research concerned with the prevention, diagnosis and treatment of illness. He had indirect responsibility for the family practitioner and local authority health services. The Central Health Services Council and its professional Standing Advisory Committees were established to advise the Minister on the discharge of his duties, and to keep developments in the service under review. The 14 Regional Hospital Boards (subsequently 15) were each focused on a university with a medical school, and teaching hospitals were separately administered by Boards of Governors. Hospital Management Committees were appointed to run the non-teaching hospitals on a day-to-day basis. The local health authorities were the county councils and the borough councils. Through their health committees they provided community and environmental health services, including maternal and child welfare, health visiting, home nurses, vaccination and immunization, care and after-care for mental illness and mental subnormality patients and the maintenance of health centres. Some of these had already been their responsibility before 1948, while others had been provided by a variety of agencies. Executive Councils were established (usually to match the local health authorities) to administer the family practitioner services; these received their finance directly from the Ministry of Health (Figure 1.1).

The Act also recognized the contribution that voluntary organizations could make in the field of health care by absorbing some of their activities into the NHS and giving financial aid to others operating outside the NHS. The school medical service continued to be run by the local education authorities and provided medical and dental inspections for children in state schools and a child guidance service. The Industrial Health Service was organized by the Ministry of Labour mainly through the factory inspectorate. The armed forces retained their own health service quite separate from the NHS.

The problems of the NHS

Just as the final form of the NHS in 1948 represented a compromise between the demands of several interest groups, so the problems that the service encountered between 1948 and 1974 were a reflection of this inability to meet the original hopes for a fully unified and comprehensive health service, hopes that had been expressed as far back as the beginning of the century. For example, when compulsory payments by patients were introduced for some parts of the service, and when the weekly NHS contribution was established, the idea of a free service for all was breached. A more important problem was, however, that the demand for NHS care rose very rapidly and resources were often insufficient to meet it. The uneven distribution of services that had existed before 1948 was not eradicated by the creation of the NHS, so many inequalities between regions were maintained. Because the administrative structure, with its bias towards hospital matters, had the strongest influence on policy-making in the central department, there was inadequate local liaison between hospital and community staff, with the result that services for the acutely ill tended to improve more rapidly, while the needs of the chronically ill and disabled were comparatively neglected.

In 1953, the Minister of Health set up a committee to inquire into the costs of the NHS, and its report (the Guillebaud Report) [10], published three years later, although acknowledging some deficiencies in the service, did not see structural alterations as a necessary measure at that time. One member of the committee, Sir John Maude, stated his reservations about this conservative position. He had identified for himself the weakness of the NHS as being its division into three parts, operated by three sets of bodies having no organic connection with each other; their separate funding from central and local government sources underlined the weakness. The divisions caused preventive medicine, general practice and hospital practice to overlap, while the predominance of the hospital service had the effect of pushing general practice and social medicine into the background. Maude's view was that if local government administration and finance could be reorganized adequately then it might be possible to transfer the local responsibility of the NHS to them, thus arranging for a truly unified service.

The beginnings of reform

The first notable mention of a plan to unify the health service was made in the Porritt Report [11], which was compiled independently of the Ministry of Health by representatives of the medical profession. Its suggestion for local NHS administration under Area Health Boards, although not worked out in detail, at least indicated that the medical profession accepted in principle the need for unification. However, the Gillie Report (1963) [12] rejected unification of admin-istration in favour of much greater efforts to develop the role of general practitioners. It suggested that family doctors alone could effectively co-ordinate the resources of hospital and community care on behalf of their patients, in relation to individual family and working conditions.

During this period, several other reports appeared and further Acts of Parliament were passed in relation to the NHS. They can be seen, in retro-spect, to have reflected the problems being encountered in trying to overcome the deficiencies of the tripartite structure and represent tentative moves towards greater integration. The Cranbrook Report (1959) [13], for example, was critical of the division between local authority and hospital maternity services. The Mental Health Act, 1959, radically altered the legislation on mental illness, reducing the grounds for compulsory admission and detention in mental hos-pitals. This coincided with the use of several new drugs leading to quicker and more effective psychiatric treatment, which could more often be given on an out-patient basis. Mental hospitals began to discharge more patients back into the community and, in 1961, Enoch Powell, the Minister of Health, predicted that half of these hospitals would be closed in ten years' time. Although his time-scale was wrong, progressively more mental hospital patients have been discharged, but not always with appropriate support.

In 1962, Powell published *A Hospital Plan for England and Wales* [14], which formulated the need for new hospitals in the light of projected population growth and the demand for hospital facilities in the coming ten years. It approved the development of district general hospitals for population units of about 125 000 people. The Bonham-Carter Report in 1969 [15] on the functions of the district general hospital developed this concept in more detail, emphasizing the need to plan hospital and community health services jointly. In 1967, the Salmon Report [16] published detailed recommendations for developing the senior nursing staff structure and the status of the profession in hospital management. The first report on the organization of doctors in hospitals was published in 1967 (known as the Cogwheel Report) [17] and it proposed speciality groupings that would arrange clinical and administrative medical work more sensibly. These reports will be discussed in detail in later chapters, but are mentioned here to indicate the variety of efforts involved in trying to reduce the disadvan-tages of the tripartite structure. There was a growing acknowledgement of the complexity of the organization and the corresponding need for effective management.

PREPARATION FOR REORGANIZATION

The necessity for a fundamental reorganization of the service had not, however, become the subject of general discussion even though the administrative struc-ture had remained unchanged for 20 years and the various reports mentioned above had pointed out some of the serious faults that had arisen. The NHS in England and Wales was then composed of 15 Regional Hospital Boards, 36 Boards of Governors, 336 Hospital Management Committees, and 134 Executive Councils administering the services of 20 000 general practitioners while 175 local health authorities ran the community services.

The First Green Paper

The task of reorganizing these elements was first officially tackled on 6 November 1967 when Kenneth Robinson, the Minister of Health, stated in the House of Commons that he had begun a full and careful examination of the administrative structure of the NHS, not only in relation to the present, but looking twenty years ahead. He followed this in July 1968 with the publication of *The Administrative Structure of Medical and Related Services in England and Wales* [18], now known as the First Green Paper. He took as his central theme the unification of health services in an area under one new body called the Area Board. This would replace the Regional Hospital Boards, Boards of Governors, Hospital Management Committees and Executive Councils, and take over certain functions previously held by the local health authorities. There would be 40 to 50 Area Boards in direct contact with the Ministry of Health, and their boundaries would be related to those of local government, serving populations of between 750 000 and 2 to 3 million.

These proposals were launched in anticipation of the reforms which might result from two inquiries that were being held at that time. The first was by the Committee on Local Authority and Allied Personal Social Services (chaired by Frederick Seebohm) [19], which recommended, later in 1968, that all personal social services should be unified, including those administered by local authority health departments, in new, single local authority departments with their own committee of elected representatives, and the appointment of directors of social services trained in social work or social administration.

The second inquiry was by the Royal Commission on Local Government in England [20], whose report, published in 1969, recommended the creation of new local authority areas under unitary authorities and grouped into eight provinces each with its own provincial council. The Commission's scheme aimed to loosen the grip of central government over the control of planning and management in local affairs through fuller participation by communities in their public services. It saw the new unitary authorities as being eminently suitable to take charge of the health services along the lines suggested in the First Green Paper for ending the tripartite divisions, but with the added advantage of being able to co-ordinate the health services with the social services reorganized by the Seebohm proposals. The significant stumbling block of finance was acknowledged by the Commission – the cost of each authority's health services would be far too great for the current rating system to bear – but it was hoped that new sources of finance for local government would in any case be worked out.

The Layfield Committee's report on local government finance [21] was not able to resolve this question. Of the three proposed reforms, the First Green

Paper, the Seebohm Report and the Royal Commission's Report, only the Seebohm recommendations were accepted, and the Government implemented them in the Social Services Act, 1970.

The Second Green Paper

In 1968, Richard Crossman succeeded Kenneth Robinson to become the first Secretary of State for Social Services in the new Department of Health and Social Security. He published *The Future Structure of the National Health Service* [22], known as the Second Green Paper, in February 1970, which reflected some of the criticisms received about the First Green Paper, as well as Crossman's own ideas.

In it he stated that the Government had already decided on three important factors: that the new health authorities would be independent of local government and directly responsible to the central department; that the public health and personal social services would continue to be the responsibility of local government; that the boundaries of the new health authorities would match those of local government. This scheme for the reorganization suggested more health authorities than the first attempt – 90 instead of 40 or 50 – but it inserted Regional Health Councils between them and the Department of Health and Social Security (DHSS). These bodies were to take charge of hospital and specialist planning. Crossman intended to publish a White Paper that summer so that the Bills for health and local government reform could be put before Parliament early in 1972, permitting elections for the new local authorities [23] and appointments for the new health authorities to be completed in 1973, so that they could take over in 1974.

The Consultative Document

The General Election of June 1970 did not, however, return the Labour Party to power, so future plans for the health service awaited the decision of the new Conservative Government's Secretary of State, Sir Keith Joseph. Almost one year later, in May 1971, he issued a Consultative Document [24] to directly interested parties only, without officially publishing it. Two months were allowed for comment so that the legislation could be prepared to come into force on 1 April 1974, the date already set by the local government reforms embodied in the Conservative White Paper *Local Government in England* [25].

The Consultative Document rejected much of the Second Green Paper's plan but retained the proposal to incorporate local authority health services into the duties of the new area authorities and to match health and local authorities' boundaries. Sir Keith Joseph's scheme brought hospitals, health centres and community nursing services under the new health authorities; occupational health service provision was left with the Department of Employment and Productivity, but there was no decision on whether to take over the School Health Service from the Department of Education and Science. The major new feature was the proposal for a strong regional tier of authority to be responsible for planning, finance and building, with the power to direct the area health authorities.

Efficient management was the skill thought to be desirable among the membership of authorities, so professional representatives as such would not be necessary. The consumer's view would be voiced on Community Health Councils, established outside the chain of authority. Social services would remain with the local authorities, and general practitioner services would be administered separately from the new authorities, retaining their distinct source of finance. Clinical teaching services would also be separate and organized on a regional basis.

The Consultative Document also announced that two 'expert studies' had been commissioned by the DHSS; Brunel University's Health Service Organization Research Unit carried out work on the detailed management arrangements for the new authorities and their staff with particular emphasis on role relationships [26]. The management consultants, McKinsey & Co. Inc., were also brought in to conduct trials with a few hospital management committees. At the same time they advised on internal reorganization at the DHSS itself.

Final legislative steps

The sequence of the final procedure to establish the reorganization of the NHS involved publication of the Government's White Paper, *National Health Service Reorganisation: England* [27], in August 1972, followed by the National Health Service Reorganisation Bill in November 1972. After parliamentary debate, the National Health Service Reorganisation Act, 1973 was given Royal Assent on 5 July 1973 (i.e. exactly 25 years after the original 'appointed day') [28]. The first phase of the investigations by the Study Group on the management arrangements was completed in February 1972, but the final report, *Management Arrangements for the Reorganised National Health Service* [29], known as the Grey Book, did not appear until the end of 1972, after the White Paper had been published. The Working Party on Collaboration produced its first report in 1973. These reports contained the fruits of the Brunel and McKinsey studies.

The DHSS started issuing a new series of circulars in 1972 to the existing health authorities and to members of the newly created 'shadow' authorities, detailing preparations for the reorganization, and a news sheet called *NHS Reorganisation News*, but, apart from these, information was sparse and public debate of the complicated issues involved was rare. People working in the NHS began to realize that there would be a period of considerable uncertainty in relation to the jobs they might expect to obtain and the speed at which all the new appointments would be made. The National Health Service Staff Commission was appointed in 1972 to handle all the arrangements relating to recruitment and transfer of staff, and it was also made responsible for protecting the interests of staff under the new arrangements.

The publication of the Grey Book provided the skeleton of the new organization, describing the Regional and Area Health Authorities, the District Management Teams, and outlining job descriptions for some of the new posts at all levels (Figure 1.2). For those unfamiliar with the particular style of language that it employed, the Grey Book was a puzzling document from which to develop a grasp of the implications of the reorganization. The main problem was also that preparations had to be made at speed in order to meet the deadline of 1 April 1974, and this discouraged thorough discussions of the impending changes. The Grey Book contained proposals which could be altered as a result of consultation, but the enforced haste transformed the proposals into official edicts in the minds of many people. DHSS circular HRC(73)3 [30] in fact amended some of the Grey Book's statements, and the representations of certain professional groups against parts of the Grey Book continued to be discussed throughout 1974.

By June 1973 it had become clear that the programme of new staff appointments could not be completed by the following April, so the reorganized NHS would have to be launched with all but the most senior staff lacking formal contracts of employment. Although the need for a reorganization of the NHS was hardly disputed, and, although this particular version of the reorganization was widely supported, it is probably true that many staff working in the NHS and in outside, but related, bodies were not in a position fully to understand the thinking behind the preparations for 1974. The administrative arrangements were not as complete as the staff would have desired, but it is clear that the majority of their patients, as the focus of their efforts, were probably quite unaware that any reorganization was taking place.

Yet on the very date at which the new NHS came into being, changes in its structure were already being planned. In February 1974, a Labour Government had replaced the Conservatives and the new administration was compelled to proceed with the reorganization timed for the coming April even though the design was not of its making. The new Secretary of State, Barbara Castle, acknowledged the problems being encountered by the staff in implementing the reorganization, but she was also determined to influence its development immediately. She set out her proposals in a consultative paper entitled *Democracy in the National Health Service* [31], and changes largely concerned with health authority membership were announced in July 1975.

REASONS FOR CREATING THE AREA HEALTH AUTHORITIES

In order to understand why it was thought necessary to establish a tier of authority at area level for the integrated administration of the NHS, it is helpful to return briefly to the criticisms that were being made about the NHS during the 1960s; the key arguments can be found in the Porritt Report and the two Green Papers. The theme running through them was that despite its considerable achievements, the NHS was not organized in such a way that the three

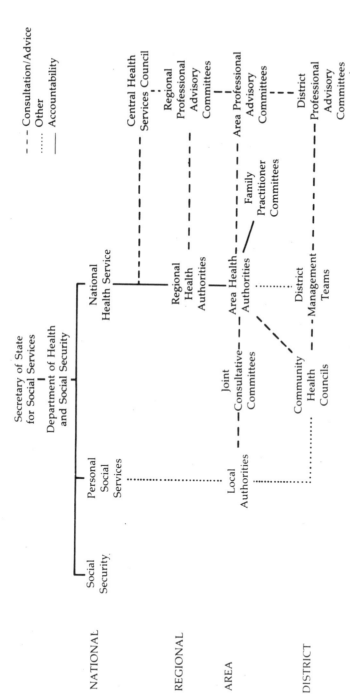

Figure 1.2 The Reorganized National Health Service 1974.

Source: *Management Arrangements for the Reorganised National Health Service* (1974) HMSO.

arms of the service could work efficiently and co-operatively. Without better dovetailing, satisfactory standards of patient care could not be assured because the poor liaison between hospitals, community services and general practitioners too often led to unacceptable delays and unnecessary suffering on the part of many patients.

The Medical Services Review Committee was appointed in the autumn of 1958 under the chairmanship of Sir Arthur Porritt with representatives from the Royal Colleges of Physicians, Surgeons, Obstetricians and Gynaecologists, the Society of Medical Officers of Health, the College of General Practitioners and the British Medical Association. Their report, published four years later, can reasonably be taken as the expression of the opinion of the medical profession at that time, and its unequivocal conclusion was that 'one administrative unit should become the focal point for all the medical services of an appropriate area, and that doctors and other personnel in all branches of the Service should be under contract with this one authority' [32], and that 'the full advantages of the preventive and personal health services and their effective integration with the family doctor and hospital services can only be achieved by transferring both services and staff to the Area Health Boards' [33].

But this view illustrates only part of what the NHS is intended to do. In fact, it is not only concerned with the delivery of care to patients but is also required to allocate and reallocate resources, and these two functions are not the same – they are, rather, interdependent. If the NHS was simply concerned with the day-to-day treatment and prevention of illness, arguments about a reorganization would have focused on ensuring closer co-operation between all the staff involved in these activities. The additional emphasis given to 'management' of the services [34] indicates that it is also obliged to plan for the future. The DHSS's internal reorganization was intended to enable better planning and the improved delegation of its authority.

In his foreword to the White Paper of 1972, the Secretary of State wrote of the reorganization: 'It is about administration, not about treatment and care' [35]. The significance of the new authorities at area level now becomes clearer. The DHSS and the RHAs had to concentrate on strategic planning, whether nationally or regionally, while the Districts were concerned with the day-to-day delivery of health care. Only the Area Health Authorities were in a position to do some of both activities, and, as such, it may be helpful to regard them as having been the embodiment of an 'integrated' service. Put another way, if each part of the new structure had a clear precedent in the pre-1974 organization, critics could have expressed the opinion that the reorganization had simply given new names to all the old jobs and committees without really altering very much. But with the reorganization, although many of its features were not wholly new, an exact ancestor of the Area Health Authorities is difficult to identify. In that sense, their existence could be said to have represented a focus for the hope that the administrative rearrangement would prove to be a successful attempt to improve both the management and the delivery of health care.

Boundaries of the new authorities

The NHS reorganization was planned in the context of the new arrangements for local authority personal social services and the reorganization of local government. Both these reforms set down new geographical boundaries for their respective spheres of administration, facts which could not be ignored by the health service. Therefore another important element in the debate about the NHS was the administrative boundaries that the new area authorities would observe. The First Green Paper, which was published in advance of the report from the Royal Commission on Local Government, did not specify boundaries of the area authorities, but did entertain the possibility that health and local government services could be jointly administered. However, the Second Green Paper favoured the separate administration of health services, but within the same geographical areas as were defined for local authorities.

The question is, what boundaries are most suitable for decentralized administration of the NHS: should they reflect the incidence of ill-health or should they conform to existing boundaries of complementary agencies? The answer depends on the previous point about whether administration of the NHS is concerned with delivery of care to people or strategic planning of available resources. If provision of services is the primary purpose, then organization should take account of the distribution and relative prevalence of disease. However, if realistic planning is the aim, then coterminosity with local authority boundaries (i.e. identical boundaries) should take precedence. Few people would be happy to state a preference between these options, and the creation of Area Health Authorities with the same boundaries as local government, although emphasizing the planning function, also underlined recognition of the need for close collaboration between all parts of the health service and the staff of other agencies [36].

Inequalities

Epidemiological studies have demonstrated that ill-health is associated with a number of social factors such that urban areas of declining employment with a high degree of overcrowding, low standards of housing and low wages are those with higher mortality rates. Yet the pattern of health service provision has been a patchwork, essentially unrelated to population and mortality rates from particular diseases; this is partly what is meant by 'regional inequalities'. However, the difficulty of altering the balance of local services to handle local needs (which was the job of the Area Health Authorities) should not be underestimated. The historical pattern of distribution of resources and the comparative rigidity of financial allocation because of established revenue expenditure commitments has made substantial changes slow and difficult to achieve.

The failure of the tripartite structure to iron out regional inequalities arose partly because the interdependence of hospital and community facilities was not properly understood. The hospital service worked through numbers of hospital beds and supporting services per 1000 population. Thus the Porritt report recommended a ratio of 8 beds to 1000 population distributed on the basis of 3.4 acute beds, 0.6 maternity beds, 1.6 psychiatric beds, 2.0 geriatric beds and 0.2 beds for other categories, including infectious diseases [37].

But it gradually became evident to the Ministry of Health that the quantity of beds and accompanying hospital services alone could not achieve policy goals: if the community health services were poorly staffed or badly equipped to receive patients back from hospital, then the episodes of both acute and chronic illness in the population would not decline. Indeed, a pamphlet on the reorganization issued by the Office of Health Economics stated that 'the regions themselves have little epidemiological significance' [38], implying that, although the NHS is concerned with the provision of health care, the reorganization had very slender demonstrable links with this duty – it had more to do with administrative convenience. The DHSS would not have shared this view and would have maintained that, through the Area Health Authorities and the rest of the new management structure, improvements in both health care and the future planning of the NHS resources would be more effectively managed, because the interests of administration and health care coincided.

Area Health Authorities

Ninety Area Health Authorities were set up in England, and their boundaries in most cases were identical with those of the metropolitan districts and non-metropolitan counties established by the Local Government Act, 1972, which came into effect on the same day as the reorganized health service, 1 April 1974. The populations served by AHAs ranged from ¼ million to over 1 million. Nineteen Areas with teaching hospitals were designated AHA(T). The Grey Book had identified a preferred size of community, for which the full range of personal health and social services could be provided, at about ¼ million. There were as a result 34 single-district Areas, 23 Areas divided into two Districts, 16 into three Districts, 11 into four Districts, 3 into five Districts and 6 into six Districts.

The chairman of each AHA was appointed by the Secretary of State and paid a part-time salary. Membership of the AHA included local authority, university and professional nominees. Local authority membership was increased to one-third by the Secretary of State, Barbara Castle, in 1975. As far as possible, members were nominated not as representatives for any particular group, but as generalists so that they could make decisions on behalf of the community at large. This attempt to remove partisanship from authorities was not entirely successful, given the often strong views held by local authority nominees who were almost invariably county or district councillors, and the likely professional view of the two doctors and one nurse also appointed to AHAs.

A distinctive feature of the duties of AHAs was their dual responsibility for planning and providing services. They not only provided 'comprehensive' health services including hospitals, community and domiciliary care, but also studied the health needs of the area and found out where provision fell below required standards. Each AHA determined policies for provision and found the best way of putting them into effect with the resources allocated to it by the RHA. In addition, the AHA gave special attention to planning and providing services in conjunction with the matching local authority or authorities. The day-to-day executive responsibilities were delegated to the Area Team of Officers (ATO), to individual officers at area level, to the District Management Teams (DMTs) and individual District officers. The activities handled in the Districts (in other than single-district Areas) were the basic services associated with the district hospital, the community health services formerly run by the local authority health departments, and the school health service. The Area Team of Officers had to co-ordinate the work of the DMTs, but it also had to advise the AHA on developing area-wide policies, informing them of particular local needs and circumstances to be taken into consideration.

It is clear that if AHAs were to function as an effective link in the chain of delegated authority, much depended on the ATO's ability to moderate policies handed down from the Region in a manner that was sensitive to District circumstances, and that was respectful of the DMTs' sphere of authority. The DMT and ATO officers were on the same managerial level, so the ATO could not give orders to the DMT nor be held accountable for their work. It was (in all but single-district Areas) the DMT and not the ATO which was responsible for the actual operation of health care services. The role of the ATO in relation to the Districts was a monitoring one, which meant that the Area Officers could persuade their counterparts in the Districts to conform to policies, and could interpret AHA intentions to them. But if they were not satisfied with the outcome they had to refer the issue to the AHA for a decision about what action might be taken. In the case of the relationship between the ATO and the Regional Team Officers, each set of officers was accountable to its own authority, so in no sense did a manager-subordinate relationship exist between them. Regional Officers could give advice and guidance to their counterparts on the ATO and persuade them to act in particular ways, but, if they were dissatisfied with the Area Officers' performance, their recourse was only to the RHA, which had to decide what to do.

THE ROYAL COMMISSION ON THE NHS

The 1974 reorganization took nearly two years to be implemented. Many staff, unused to such major organizational change, found it difficult to meet the challenges of the new system. Furthermore, the years 1975 and 1976 were notable for industrial disputes among hospital medical staff, first the consultants, followed by the junior staff. In 1976 Barbara Castle attempted to restrict private practice facilities (described in Chapter 9). All of this was demanding of administrators' time.

Arising from a general sense that the new reorganization was not proving as successful as planned, in May 1976 Barbara Castle asked Sir Alec Merrison, Vice Chancellor of Bristol University, to chair a Royal Commission on the NHS with the following terms of reference: 'To consider in the interests both of the patients and of those who work in the National Health Service, the best use and management of the financial and manpower resources of the National Health Service' [39]. Such a wide-ranging brief provided the opportunity for the first comprehensive review of the NHS since the Guillebaud Report of 1956. The 16 members of the Royal Commission were drawn from a wide variety of interests. They took three years to deliberate at a cost of £918 000.

Evidence was sought from a variety of sources, including six specially commissioned studies. Just as the incoming Labour Government of 1974 inherited a reorganization not of its own making, the new Conservative Government elected in May 1979 was obliged to deal with a Royal Commission not of its creation. The main conclusion of the Royal Commission when it reported in July 1979 was that 'we need not be ashamed of our health service and that there are many aspects of it of which we can be justly proud' [40]. Nevertheless the Royal Commission was critical of certain aspects of the management of the NHS, saying that there were too many tiers, too many administrators of all disciplines, a failure to make swift decisions and a consequent waste of money. In the light of the Government's reaction, which was surprisingly prompt, it is worth stressing that, although the Royal Commission had made recommendations on a wide range of matters, it was the management of the NHS which emerged as the crucial issue.

The new Government's views were contained in a publication entitled *Patients First* [41] published in December 1979. This document, somewhat slender in contrast to the volumes published by the Royal Commission, was devoted to the subject of structural change. The Government was concerned that over the five years since 1974 the new organization had not provided the 'best framework for the effective delivery of care to patients' [42]. *Patients First*, a consultative paper, suggested that there should be greater delegation so that decisions were made nearer the patients, that District Health Authorities (DHAs) should be set up, thus removing the Area tier; that the professional consultative machinery should be simplified; that functional management should make way for unit management based on hospitals; and that the planning system should be streamlined. Discussion on whether Community Health Councils (CHCs) should continue was invited. *Patients First* did not offer a blueprint for the future and was nervous of wholesale upheaval, in the light of the considerable cost of the 1974 reorganization – said to be in excess of £9 million. Regions would be responsible for making the arrangements, but were to stand back as far as possible to allow the new DHAs to thrive.

Districts were to be drawn up according to certain criteria. First, social geography, a concept based on the idea of a natural community supported by well-established centres of population and linked transport patterns. Interestingly, local government boundaries, even after the 1974 reorganization, had not always been sensitive to these considerations. The significance of the district general hospital (DGH) and its catchment area was re-established as a reasonable basis for organizing health care. Self-sufficiency of services was another reason, leaving coterminosity with local authorities as desirable, but not a necessary criterion. This marked a significant turning away from one of the guiding principles of the 1974 reorganization.

Patients First set a limit of four months for consultation and the Government's intentions were duly published in July 1980 in the circular HC(80)8 *Health Services: Structure and Management* [43]. This circular largely endorsed the proposals of *Patients First*, but, following the widespread and somewhat unexpected support for CHCs, confirmed their continuing existence for the time being. The holding of consultant contracts at District level recommended by *Patients First* had been challenged and was left unresolved.

THE 1982 REORGANIZATION

The timetable for the second reorganization allowed two years, and, in due course, 1 April 1982 was confirmed as the change-over day, with a completion of the total exercise by the end of 1983. This was achieved. But why had this second upheaval been necessary? Major new legislation always needs a running-in period, but the 1974 reorganization was remarkable in that even before it had been completely implemented there was widespread dissatisfaction with the new arrangements. By 1976 the Secretary of State acknowledged the state of affairs by setting up the Royal Commission. That such a costly and large-scale reorganization of a public service could so quickly seem to be unsatisfactory to most people was remarkable, even at a time when such legislative changes were typical.

Some of the reasons for failure could be said to be practical, but others were a result of reliance on faulty concepts. The theme of the 1974 reorganization was planning. It had been seen as necessary because of the inability of the tripartite service to meet the needs of the community. Planning would be facilitated by an integrated NHS coterminous with local authorities. Areas were set up with explicit responsibility for providing strategic plans for their Districts, which in turn were to be more concerned with the day-to-day running of the service. But this scheme of things was unrealistic. Districts were, in practice, just as likely to have the ideas about future demands as Areas, particularly since these ideas often arose out of the frustrations encountered in day-to-day activity. The difference over planning between Area and Districts developed into the difference between theoretical assumptions of need, based on an analysis of statistics together with the views of professional advisers on the one hand, and practical proposals for improvements based on daily experience on the other.

This difference of viewpoint was exacerbated by the coterminosity issue. Common boundaries with county councils (or in metropolitan counties, with district councils) may seem sensible, but many of these boundaries were arbitrary and did not reflect the organization of medical services that had been in existence for nearly half a century. The traditional DGH catchment area often ignored local authority boundaries. AHA members found it difficult to think strategically, and by degrees became more and more remote from the everyday working of the NHS. They found their role unsatisfying, particularly when they observed District Management Teams managing the services with little reference to them.

If the concepts underpinning planning were found to be suspect, those concerning the relationships between managers were even worse. The Area Health Authority was served by two sets of chief officers, the Area Team of Officers (ATO) and the District Management Team (DMT). The DMT were not managerially accountable to the ATO but could be monitored by them. This was resented. Some attempts were made to sort out the roles more satisfactorily, but it was clear that the relationship would always be prone to strain, not least because the ATO had easier access to the AHA and particularly the chairman. But even within Districts reorganization had caused problems. During the late 1960s considerable efforts were made by personnel officers and support service managers – catering and domestic in particular – to develop their roles. The 1974 reorganization encouraged this process and District appointments on relatively high grades began to be made. Given the practical nature of some of these services, local hospital support service managers felt somewhat over-supervised. Furthermore, they were often directly accountable to a District officer, making control by the local hospital administrator more difficult.

The new structure could not operate without a considerable increase in staff: the Government admitted in 1977 that 16 700 extra staff, particularly administrative and clerical, had been recruited because of reorganization. All these factors contributed to a climate in which ideas from the Royal Commission and *Patients First* were welcomed. Even Area members and officers supported their own demise.

The failure of the 1974 reorganization has often been blamed on the management consultants McKinsey, and on the Health Services Organisation Research Unit at Brunel University, who had both contributed significantly to the pre-1974 discussions. To be accurate, the final arrangements contained in the Grey Book represented some compromise of their ideas. For instance, McKinsey did not support the duplication of functions at every level of management, and yet professional pressure brought that about. The Brunel Unit had always campaigned for clarity of role relationships, and the ambiguities of the District/Area relationships could scarcely be said to be their fault.

CHANGES SINCE 1982

The 1974 reorganization was conducted according to nationally agreed rules, whereas in 1982 each Region was left to make its own arrangements. Although minimum upheaval had been advocated by *Patients First,* and subsequently by the Secretary of State, this was not the case in most Regions where many Area and District chief officers lost their jobs only to be reappointed in neighbouring Districts. As in 1974, the cost in human and money terms was considerable.

The first two years of the 1982 reorganization were beset by doctrinal discussions, particularly around the issue of privatization. The Government, faced with an ever-escalating bill for the health services, was seeking ways of shedding some of the costs. Proposals included encouraging patients to use private hospitals and nursing homes, with consequent incentives for more of such establishments to be set up. There was also pressure for health authorities to contract-out such support services as domestic, laundry and catering to private firms [44].

Financial and manpower cuts in 1983 caused considerable unrest. The Government was critical of the quality of management in the NHS, a recurring theme throughout the 1980s. There had been a general impatience with consensus management (managing by mutual consent), which had been seen by many, particularly doctors, as an excuse to procrastinate. As no one member of a District Management Team was clearly given responsibility for taking action, the accusation carried some weight. Accordingly, the Secretary of State set up a team led by Roy Griffiths, Managing Director of Sainsbury's, to advise him privately. The Secretary of State thought well enough of the report, prepared over a six-month period, to publish it in October 1983 [45] as the *NHS Management Inquiry.*

Griffiths identified a lack of drive in the NHS, and he and his team said this was because at each level of management no one person was accountable for action. Consensus management had led to delays in decision making and a lowest common denominator which allowed difficult decisions to be avoided. Professional and functional managers had been given too much scope, without being held sufficiently accountable for advancing the aims of the organization. Griffiths's advice was to appoint General Managers at Unit, District and Regional level, possibly for a fixed tenure, who would be responsible for improving the efficiency of the organization.

At DHSS and government level the Griffiths proposals were even more radical, suggesting that the Secretary of State should set up a Health Service Supervisory Board with a Management Board accountable to it. The Supervisory Board would be responsible for determining the objectives and direction of the health service, for approving the overall budget and resource allocation, for making strategic decisions and for monitoring performance. The Secretary of State would chair the board, and other members would include the Minister of State (Health), the Permanent Secretary of the DHSS, the Chief Medical Officer and the Chairman of the Management Board. The Management Board would be the executive arm of the Supervisory Board, having particular responsibility for implementation of policies, for giving leadership to management in the NHS, for controlling performance and for achieving consistency and drive over the long term. The Chairman of the Management Board would be vested with executive authority derived from the Secretary of State. He or she would also be responsible for consultation, particularly with Regional chairmen. Griffiths proposed that the Chairman of the Management Board should come from outside the NHS and the civil service.

A month after the publication of the Griffiths proposals, the Secretary of State wrote to chairmen of health authorities asking for reactions to the proposals by 9 January 1984. He confirmed his determination to appoint General Managers. In June of the same year Circular HC(84)13 [46] was issued confirming the implementation of the Griffiths proposals forthwith.

The Griffiths proposals stimulated considerable debate, particularly because they appeared to question traditional responsibilities of health authority members and staff. It was not clear whether the Secretary of State saw the proposals as heralding major changes in organizational relationships within health authorities or whether he simply wanted the NHS to work in more action-centred ways. Furthermore, Griffiths's proposals for the DHSS offered fundamental changes in the headquarters' working arrangements.

Although the Secretary of State had claimed the 1982 reorganization would allow DHAs to manage their affairs with little interference from above, he was nevertheless anxious to ensure more effective decision making. Griffiths's response was to propose clearer definitions of responsibility with fewer ambiguous lines of accountability, both within the NHS and DHSS as well as between them. Linking this advice to measures for enhancing effective budgetary management gave the Secretary of State the basis for expecting the NHS to do a better overall job and to offer better value for money.

The initial antagonism, particularly from doctors and nurses, largely evaporated. What was first seen as a simplistic diagnosis of a complex problem was later realized to be a reasonable basis for changes aimed at greater effectiveness, tighter control and less ambiguity of purpose. Nevertheless, the Government remained unhappy with ever-increasing financial demands, and, as a result, even more radical reforms emerged with two White Papers, *Working for Patients* [47] in January 1989 and *Caring for People* [48] in November 1989. These were followed by a revised set of health targets contained in the 1992 White Paper, *The Health of the Nation* [49], yet further reorganizations of the intermediate (Regional) tier of management and a review of the role and functions of the NHS Management Executive and the Department of Health (these latter reforms are discussed in Chapter 3).

WORKING FOR PATIENTS

The White Paper *Working for Patients* promoted radical change for the NHS at all management levels and dramatic alteration to the economic and cultural environment in which the NHS had operated hitherto (a summary of the White Paper's main proposals appears on page 26). But what provoked yet another review of the NHS so soon after the Griffiths proposals had introduced general management principles in 1985? The reasons were probably a mixture of dogma and pragmatism. By the autumn of 1987 financial problems in the NHS were leading to cuts in services and closures of facilities on a serious scale. These were damaging to the Conservative Government's reputation, particularly only months after the general election in which they had made the future of the NHS a major issue.

The financial pressures were not a direct result of government policy; they arose from growing public expectations, advances in medical technology and an ageing population, factors that together continued to put more demands on the system than it could meet. The new Government was concerned to point out that it was aware of this and was increasing the revenue money for the NHS. But this occurred in the context of its desire to reduce total public expenditure and to challenge radically the fundamental assumptions underlying the creation of the welfare state after the Second World War, which had up to then been supported by governments of all parties.

The Conservative Government's aim was to limit the apparently insatiable demand for health care by dismantling comprehensive state provision which, it believed, encouraged unnecessary use and inefficiency. The Government's sense of unease about the NHS was not new. In 1974, the incoming Labour Government had also known that all was not well. But a repeat of the lengthy deliberations and politically controversial proposals of the Royal Commission on the NHS was not sought by the Prime Minister, Margaret Thatcher.

The seemingly simple claim that all public sector organizations had become over-staffed and inefficient was well received, and, in this climate, support for a review of the workings of the NHS was readily forthcoming, though the Prime Minister never issued the terms of reference of this investigation. It was clear that from January 1988 the NHS had become a major preoccupation of the Government. During the next few months many different interests offered the government advice but those who advocated, however eloquently, a higher level of expenditure were disregarded.

More influential were those (particularly the American economist Alain Enthoven [50]) who urged that the NHS should be subjected to the discipline of the market economy, which would encourage greater financial efficiency and less government intervention. They suggested that competition between providers of health care would not only improve patients' choices but also give health authorities and individual hospitals more incentive to work efficiently and become more flexible and adaptable to a discerning market. It was argued that once patients were given the opportunity to 'buy' health care, standards would rise and sensitivity to the consumer would increase. For this to occur effectively, the large bureaucratic organization would have to be dismantled. 'Small is beautiful' was a pervasive idea through the 1970s and 1980s.

The Government also suspected that doctors and managers – not usually seen as allies – both had vested interests in influencing public opinion to demand more resources for the NHS, thereby distracting attention from many inefficiencies they had been unwilling to eliminate. In fact managers had been

---

WORKING FOR PATIENTS

- Introduction of weighted capitation to distribute money voted by Parliament for the NHS to Regions and on to Districts;
- charges for the use and acquisition of capital, including interest and depreciation;
- GP practice budgets for large practices who wished to purchase a selected range of health care for their patients;
- in place of the traditional demand-led drug expenditure, 'indicative prescribing amounts' for GPs to control drug costs;
- audit of the NHS accounts to be carried out by the independent Audit Commission;
- separation of 'providing' and 'purchasing' functions in the NHS; the so-called internal market;
- extension of hospital clinical budgeting (the Resource Management Initiative) to over 260 acute units by the end of 1991/2;
- creation of NHS Trust units with greater freedoms to set pay levels, borrow for capital projects, etc.;
- changes in the composition of health authority and family practitioner committee (FPC – renamed FHSA: Family Health Service Authorities) membership – no local authority or trade union representatives; 'boards' to resemble private sector companies with executive and non-executive directors;
- FHSAs to be accountable to Regions;
- devolved management, together with stronger lines of accountability from top to bottom in the NHS;
- consultants' management service to be taken into account in their meritorious service and distinction awards; managers to have more say in merit awards;
- consultants' contracts to be more detailed; trusts to hold and negotiate their consultants' contracts;
- medical audit to be extended throughout the NHS;
- one hundred new consultants to be appointed over three years;
- tax relief on private medical insurance for elderly people.

Source: Appleby, J. (1992) *Financing Health Care in the 1990s*, Open University Press, Buckingham.

---

exposed to repeated government attempts to improve their efficiency. In 1982, Rayner scrutinies (named after Sir Derek Rayner, then Deputy Chairman of Marks & Spencer and an adviser to the Prime Minister) had been introduced to investigate aspects of NHS managerial and administrative practice. Performance indicators were employed in 1983. These demonstrated differences between Districts for such measures as length of stay and cost per case, and continued to be refined throughout the decade as a means of challenging doctors and managers to improve their effectiveness. Cost improvement programmes were introduced in 1985; these encouraged health authorities to fund developments from the efficiency savings they themselves achieved. At the personal level, the introduction of Individual Performance Review in 1986, coupled with Performance Related Pay for the most senior managers, aimed to stimulate managers to be more achievement-minded.

These changes were also inspired by the political culture of the day, which sought to challenge the old presumption of professional autonomy. Doctors had been conspicuously half-hearted about introducing effective peer review through medical audit, and a key proposal in *Working for Patients* was an insistence on establishing medical audit as a matter of urgency.

The White Paper marked a significant change in overall approach to the NHS, more radical than anything previously proposed by any government. The publicity given to the launch of the document itself cost over £1.4 million, and indicated the Government's intention of leaving nothing to chance. This was followed up by spending further large sums of money to explain the reforms to the general public, which was criticized by the Opposition and from within the NHS. The initial response to the White Paper was negative, but the proposals had been imperfectly understood. The NHS professions launched a vigorous attack but the managers were less hostile, given the heavily managerial content of the proposed reforms. Even Conservative members of the then Social Services (now Health) Select Committee of the House of Commons were against some of the proposals and dubious about the accelerated timetable for change. Notwithstanding this scepticism, which was also reflected in public opinion polls, the Government proceeded to publish the Bill. After a relatively uneventful course through Parliament, it received the Royal Assent as the National Health Service and Community Care Act on 29 June 1990.

In this legislation, the Government's first concern was to allay fears that the whole NHS was to be dismantled. The Prime Minister's introduction to the White Paper had reiterated the principle that the NHS would continue to provide a 'comprehensive' service free at the point of use and financed mainly from general taxation, even though the manner in which this service was to be managed had to be changed. At the top of the organization a Policy Board was created, superseding the previous Supervisory Board, whose purpose had remained vague. Accountable to the Policy Board was the NHS Management Executive. The membership of this group, led by the Chief Executive, included career civil servants and NHS managers together with one or two outsiders brought in for their special knowledge. Similarly the Policy Board combined those with special knowledge of the NHS and those with experience of other industries and organizations.

The NHS's inability to make appropriate decisions was one of the main precipitating causes of the introduction of general management in 1985, but those reforms alone could not cure the problem while there were still health authorities with between fifteen and twenty members, some of whose political or professional special interests could work against the prompt and rigorous consideration of managerial issues. The broadly representative nature of health authorities was therefore replaced by something nearer the style of commercial and industrial concerns. These authorities were reconstituted in 1990 with an executive and a non-executive component usually of equal numbers, with the Chair holding the balance. This was a radical departure from the former relationship between the officers and members. The appointment of the non-executives was the responsibility of the Secretary of State for the Regions and the Regions for the Districts. In turn the non-executive members appointed the executives, although the Regional or District General Manager had to be a member of the executive and take part in the appointment of his or her executive colleagues.

The need to establish a separation between purchasers and providers in order to set up the necessary (if not sufficient) requirements of a market and the desire to release the NHS from excessive bureaucracy led to the creation of Trusts: these elements of the organization were allowed to 'opt out' of local health authority management and pursue their own direction within the overall framework of the NHS, free to operate their own 'market' for patient care and to pay their staff at rates unconstrained by national agreements. The Trusts had their own boards of management who could raise money more freely than allowed by Treasury procedures for the NHS as a whole. Trusts were initially one of the most contentious of the White Paper's proposals. The Secretary of State approved an initial group of 56 Trusts in December 1990. By 1994, virtually all hospital and community units in the UK had become Trusts.

One important disincentive to improving performance in the NHS was the financial deficit that arose if a health authority treated more patients than its yearly revenue budget could sustain. To overcome this, *Working for Patients* proposed that money should in effect follow patients wherever they were treated, so Districts became funded on their resident population, paying for patients wherever they were treated. The vast bulk of treatments were covered by contracts between Districts and providers negotiated before the start of each financial year. In the case of treatments provided outside prearranged contracts – extra-contractual referrals (ECRs) – such as emergencies (road accidents in another part of the country, for instance), the District from which the patient originated was expected to pay on presentation of a bill from the treating District. Non-emergency ECRs were paid for at the District's discretion and required providers to notify Districts before treatment commenced. Contracts, ECRs and the whole process of billing and setting prices for treatments have proved to be a significant time-consuming burden for purchasers and providers, and have highlighted significant gaps in the information needed for the operation of the new health care market. These issues are discussed in later chapters.

While Districts were made the main public sector purchasers, responsible for the bulk of spending in the NHS, some GPs were given the opportunity to hold their own budgets (deducted from their local District allocations) to buy a selected range of care and treatment for their own patients. This gave GP fund-holders power to influence hospital provision and has altered the relative power of general practice and hospital medicine. Historically, consultants in hospitals had been more influential in determining funding priorities; now GPs could use their purchasing leverage to negotiate price reductions and improvements in service delivery and quality from providers. It is also the case that while fundholders had acquired added financial muscle, non-fundholders also enjoyed greater authority over providers and, indeed, their local Districts, due to their traditional role as gatekeepers in the NHS and as the principal agents acting on behalf of patients: Districts' contractual plans and providers' incomes are dependent on their local GPs' referral decisions.

In the past, GPs were generally largely ignored by their Districts and regarded as inferiors by their consultant colleagues. Now, they began to be wooed by both sides – particularly fundholders with some money spare towards the end of the financial year by providers who had 'overperformed' on their District contracts. The GP fundholding scheme has developed from a comparatively insignificant add-on to the reforms in general, since the first practices joined in 1991 (then covering 7% of the population, in 1994 this had grown to over 30%), and has proved (out of proportion to the financial aspect involved) to be a significant and contentious aspect of the reforms.

The implementation of the Act – intrinsically an evolutionary rather than a revolutionary reform – took place in an atmosphere of unease and uncertainty. Some feared that the NHS was being severed from its traditional accountability to the public, because the new authorities might resist the demands of local people much more easily. The introduction of a market for patient care, which the Government claimed would improve efficiency, was seen by some as undermining comprehensive provision and convenience to patients. The GP fundholding scheme has, on the one hand, led to savings in prescribing costs, but has also exposed – and to some extent formalized – inequalities in access to care in the NHS [51]. The separation of purchaser from provider, while on the one hand allowing the potential for more rational planning of services, makes supply more fragmented by building more rigid demarcation lines between providers, across which patients may have difficulty moving.

It is worth re-emphasizing the evolutionary nature of the reforms outlined in *Working for Patients*. The White Paper was far from a 'blueprint' for change. At the heart of the reforms was a mixture of inherent uncertainty and financial and managerial empowerment – the market – but operating in the context of a public service with all the multiple (and often conflicting) objectives that such a service attempts to meet. How the NHS has grappled with the ongoing implementation of the White Paper and its progress on the continuous path of reorganization is discussed in subsequent chapters.

CARING FOR PEOPLE

The second White Paper, *Caring for People*, was intended to sort out growing confusion over responsibility for those patients with continuing needs, such as the elderly, the physically and mentally handicapped and those people with mental illness. *Caring for People* attempted to distinguish more clearly between 'social' care and 'health' care – the former tended to be provided by local authority Social Services departments and the latter by the NHS, although there were overlaps.

The White Paper allocated particular responsibility to Social Services departments of local authorities who, instead of being the principal providers of
residential care, were made the facilitators, ensuring that care was provided. Here
again, the principle of separating purchasing from provision was introduced. It
was intended to allow for more of a 'mixed economy', encompassing statutory
authorities, charitable and for-profit agencies. In order to ensure that clients had
more choice, a process of assessment was needed, taking into account not only
the person's level of dependency but also their financial and domestic circumstances. Good case management was therefore a fundamental requirement.

Widening opportunities for the private and charitable sectors also increased
the need for effective monitoring of standards of provision, so the powers of
the Social Services Inspectorate had to be increased to ensure good practice by
Social Services departments. Because there had to be an individual budget for
each assessed person, the method of providing income support had to be
reformed. The Government also accepted that the consequences for care in the
community of the policy of emptying large mental hospitals could not be ignored,
and Social Services departments and health authorities had to plan an integrated
programme of discharge arrangements, helped by a special allocation from government paid to the Regional Health Authorities. Joint financing arrangements
(discussed in Chapter 7) continued to encourage health and local authorities to
plan together.

Caring for People was welcomed in general, as the long-awaited government
response to the Griffiths community care proposals published nearly two years
earlier; but one year thereafter, late in 1990, the Secretary of State announced
that the changes would have to be brought in more slowly and that 1 April
1991 was to be the starting not the finishing date. This slowing down of implementation arose less from the Secretary of State's ambivalence than from the
problems caused for the government by the new funding arrangements for local
authorities – the community charge or poll tax. It was felt that immediately
raising the financial burden on local authorities by introducing new methods
of supporting dependent people in the community would strain the electorate's
patience with the government too far.

The provision of care for sick and dependent people has been subject to major
changes in the early 1990s. The separation of the purchasing function from the
provision of services, first in the NHS and increasingly in social services, has been
unpopular and often misunderstood. Nevertheless, this separation, with its
increased emphasis on needs on the one hand and efficiency on the other, is being
introduced in other developed countries (see Chapter 14). Certainly the concept
marks a more radical change than the NHS had ever faced before.

THE HEALTH OF THE NATION

The third White Paper, *The Health of the Nation* [52], was published in July
1992 and followed consultations initiated by a Green Paper published a year

earlier. The aim of the White Paper was to provide a new national strategy focused on health rather than health care, unlike the reforms in *Working for Patients* and *Caring for People*. The White Paper was designed to be the start of a continuous process of target setting, monitoring and reviewing of a health strategy across the UK which addressed a rolling programme for key areas of concern in health. Five areas were initially selected, on the basis that they represented major causes of premature death or avoidable mortality, that there existed effective interventions and that it was possible to set targets and monitor progress towards them. The five areas were:

- coronary heart disease
- cancers
- mental illness
- HIV/AIDS and sexual health
- accidents.

For each of these areas targets were set to be achieved by the end of the century. For example, the targets for coronary heart disease (which accounts for around 26% of all deaths) were set to produce a reduction in death rates by 40% for those under 65 and a 30% reduction for those over 65.

While the *Health of the Nation* addressed some of the criticisms that previous reforms had been overly concerned with 'process', organization and managerial structures, the White Paper was not without its detractors. The process of choosing the target areas was criticized for ignoring economic issues: many medical interventions are effective, but are they always cost effective (given all the other calls on scarce resources)? Although the White Paper was generally welcomed for grappling with setting targets, some felt that the targets were perhaps under-ambitious, mere continuations of existing trends in the patterns of mortality and morbidity. Moreover, given the well-established link between wealth and health, the lack of any strategic goals associated with the alleviation of poverty and low pay was a particular criticism. Nevertheless, *The Health of the Nation* represented significant recognition of the role of preventive medicine and health promotion, and with its emphasis on 'healthy alliances', an important step towards cross-sectoral work between government departments, local authorities, the independent sector and individuals themselves.

CONCLUSION

This chapter has described the background to the creation of the NHS on the 'appointed' day of 5 July 1948 and subsequent changes in its organization. Half a century later it still endures, in all its complexity, having grown enormously and having 'reinvented' itself in response to changing government policies, health needs, medical advances and the public's expectations of medical care. While reorganizations are not new to the NHS, the advent of *Working for Patients* and other policy changes in recent years has prescribed a major new direction for the NHS, invoking changes which affect every part of the service. Chapter 2 takes a closer look at these.

NOTES

1. DoH (January 1989) *Working for Patients*, HMSO, London, (Cm. 555).
2. DoH (November 1989) *Caring for People*, HMSO, London, (Cm. 849).
3. DoH (July 1992) *The Health of the Nation*, HMSO, London, (Cm. 1986).
4. Ministry of Health, Consultative Council on Medical and Allied Services (1920) *Interim Report on the Future Provision of Medical and Allied Services* (Chairman, Lord Dawson), HMSO, London.
5. Ministry of Health *Hospital Survey*, HMSO, London, 1945 and 1946. (Separate reports on the ten areas of England and Wales.)
6. Parliament (1942) *Social Insurance and Allied Services*. Report by Sir William Beveridge, HMSO, London (Cmnd. 6404).
7. Ministry of Health and Department of Health for Scotland (1944) *A National Health Service*, HMSO, London (Cmnd. 6502).
8. *National Health Service Bill*, HMSO, London, 1946 (Cmnd. 6761).
9. *The National Health Service Act, 1946*, HMSO, London, 1946 (9 and 10 Geo. 6 Chapter 81 Part I Section I. (1)).
10. Ministry of Health (1956) *Report of the Committee of Enquiry into the Cost of the National Health Service* (Chairman, C.W. Guillebaud), HMSO, London (Cmnd. 9663).
11. Medical Services Review Committee (1962) *A Review of the Medical Services in Great Britain* (Chairman, Sir A. Porritt), Social Assay, London.
12. Ministry of Health. Central Health Services Council. Standing Medical Advisory Committee (1963) *The Field Work of the Family Doctor* (Chairman, Dr Annis Gillie), HMSO, London.
13. Ministry of Health (1959) *Report of the Maternity Services Committee* (Chairman, Earl of Cranbrook), HMSO, London.
14. Ministry of Health (1962) *A Hospital Plan for England and Wales*, HMSO, London (Cmnd. 1604).
15. Department of Health and Social Security and Welsh Office. Central Health Services Council (1969) *The Functions of the District General Hospital*, Report of the Committee (Chairman, Sir Desmond Bonham-Carter), HMSO, London.
16. Ministry of Health and Scottish Home and Health Department (1966) *Report of the Committee on Senior Nursing Staff Structure* (Chairman, B. Salmon), HMSO, London.
17. Ministry of Health (1967) *First Report of the Joint Working Party on the Organisation of Medical work in Hospitals* (Chairman, Sir G. Godber), HMSO, London.
18. Ministry of Health (1968) *The Administrative Structure of Medical and Related Services in England and Wales*, HMSO, London.
19. *Report of the Committee on Local Authority and Allied Personal Social Services* (Chairman, F. Seebohm), HMSO, London, 1968 (Cmnd. 3703).
20. *Report of the Royal Commission on Local Government in England, 1966–1969* (Chairman, Lord Redcliffe-Maud), HMSO, London, 1969 (Cmnd. 4040).
21. Local Government Finance *Report of the Committee of Enquiry* (Chairman, F. Layfield Q.C.), HMSO, London, 1976 (Cmnd. 6453).

22. Department of Health and Social Security (1970) *The Future Structure of the National Health Service*, HMSO, London. In Wales there was a separate publication: Welsh Office (1970) *The Reorganisation of the Health Service in Wales*, HMSO, Cardiff.
23. *Reform of the Local Government in England*, HMSO, London, 1970 (Cmnd. 4276).
24. Department of Health and Social Security (1971) *National Health Service Reorganisation: Consultative Document*, DHSS, London. In Wales, there was a separate publication: Welsh Office (1971) *Consultative Document: National Health Service Reorganisation in Wales*, Welsh Office, Cardiff.
25. *Local Government in England, Government Proposals for Reorganisation*, HMSO, London, 1971 (Cmnd. 4584).
26. The fruits of Brunel University's HSORU's work are contained in two books: *Hospital Organisation*, Heinemann, London, 1973 and *Health Services*, Heinemann, London, 1978.
27. *National Health Service Reorganisation: England*, HMSO, London, 1972 (Cmnd. 5055). In Wales there was a separate publication: *National Health Service Reorganisation in Wales*, HMSO, Cardiff, 1972 (Cmnd. 5057).
28. *The National Health Service Reorganisation Act, 1973*, HMSO, London, 1973 (Eliz. II Chapter 32).
29. Department of Health and Social Security (1972) *Management Arrangements for the Reorganised National Health Service*, HMSO, London. In Wales there was a separate publication: Welsh Office (1972) *Management Arrangements for the Reorganised National Health Service in Wales*, HMSO, Cardiff.
30. DHSS Circular HRC(73)3 *Management Arrangements for the Reorganised NHS*, January 1973.
31. Department of Health and Social Security (1974) *Democracy in the National Health Service*, HMSO, London. In Wales there was a separate paper: Welsh Office (1974) *Making Welsh Health Authorities More Democratic*, HMSO, Cardiff.
32. Medical Services Review Committee (1962) *A Review of the Medical Services in Great Britain* (Chairman, Sir A. Porritt), Social Assay, London.
33. Ibid., p. 23, para. 88.
34. For example, through the publication of the 'Grey Book' which became known, in some circles, as 'the bible'.
35. *National Health Service Reorganisation: England*, HMSO, London, 1972 (Cmnd. 5055), p.v.
36. The Report of the Royal Commission on Local Government emphasized that all the needs of a locality should be considered when deciding on boundaries. The difficulties that have resulted since 1974, because in reality the boundaries of AHAs and Districts were not coterminous with local authority boundaries in several places, cannot be ignored.
37. Op. cit., *A Review of the Medical Services in Great Britain*, p. 99, para. 367.
38. *The NHS Reorganisation*, Office of Health Economics, London, 1974.
39. *Royal Commission on the National Health Service*, HMSO, London, 1979 (Cmnd. 7615).
40. Ibid., p. 27., para. 3.23.
41. Department of Health and Social Security and Welsh Office *Patients First*, HMSO, London, December 1979.
42. Ibid., para. 1.
43. DHSS Circular HC(80)8 *Health Services: Structure and Management*, July 1980.

44. DHSS Circular HC(83)18 *Health Services Management: Competitive Tendering in the Provision of Domestic, Catering and Laundry Services*, September 1983.

45. The *NHS Management Inquiry*, under the chairmanship of Roy Griffiths, was commissioned by the Secretary of State in February 1983 to give advice 'on the effective use and management of manpower and related resources' by June 1983. Originally, no report was intended, but this attracted considerable criticism leading to a change of mind by the Secretary of State. On 6 October a report was sent to the Secretary of State in the form of a letter. It was published two weeks later.

46. DHSS Circular HC(84)13 *Health Services Management: Implementation of the NHS Management Inquiry*, June 1984.

47. Op. cit., *Working for Patients*.

48. Op. cit., *Caring for People*.

49. Op. cit., *The Health of the Nation*.

50. Enthoven, A. (1985) *Reflections on the Management of the NHS*, Nuffield Provincial Hospitals Trust, Occasional Paper 5. NPHT, London. This essay by the American economist Professor Alain Enthoven was the origin of the central policy of *Working for Patients*, the internal market. Ten years after its publication and five years after the White Paper it makes illuminating reading.

51. Although there have been no systematic and comprehensive evaluations of the GP fundholding scheme, certain benefits, such as reductions in prescribing costs, appear to have resulted. However, the scheme has also created (or at least exposed) problems concerning equity of access (cf. Whitehead, M. *Is it Fair? Evaluating the Equity Implications of the NHS Reforms*, in Robinson, R. and Le Grand, J. (1994) *Evaluating the NHS Reforms*, King's Fund Institute/Policy Journals, London.)

52. Op. cit., *The Health of the Nation*.

2

The new health care economy

The reforms embodied in *Working for Patients* and the subsequent NHS and Community Care Act of 1990 included a somewhat disparate set of changes and reorganizations. However, the central plank of the reforms was the introduction of a new economic environment for the NHS. From April 1991 the rudiments of a competitive market for health services began and the NHS started a process of adjusting to these new concepts, ideas and motivations. This chapter gives an overview of the new health care market as it was originally envisaged, key processes in its operation and how it has developed over the last few years.

INTERNAL MARKET, MANAGED COMPETITION, SOCIAL MARKET . . .?

The idea of introducing types of competitive forces into public services was not new. Since the early 1980s, a central thrust of government policy has been the preference for market solutions to public service problems. The most common of these has been privatization – involving the entire transfer of public sector organizations or industries to the private sector. National utilities such as British Telecom, British Gas and the regional electricity boards, and firms such as Cable and Wireless and British Airways have all been sold into private (mainly institutional) hands through the issue of shares.

Although some suggested, before the publication of *Working for Patients*, that the NHS was to be treated in a similar way, the reforms, in fact, proposed a new variant of the competition theme: an internal market. This term, derived from the work of the American economist Alain Enthoven [1], proved confusing however. It suggested a form of interdepartmental competition within a closed NHS system. In working out the practical applications of Enthoven's idea, it was clear that the word 'internal' was misleading. The policies contained in *Working for Patients* were explicit, that competition was to be encouraged, not only between NHS providers but also between the public and private health care sectors. Indeed, such innovations as capital charges (see Chapter 7) were introduced specifically to create comparable financial obligations for both the NHS and private sector health care providers.

The language used to describe this competitive system for the NHS became politically sensitive. *Working for Patients* contained no reference to the word 'market'. Subsequently, of course, ministers and others began to run out of euphemisms for what could, in the end, only be described as a market. Terms such as 'social market', 'quasi market' and 'managed competition' [2] were all coined in attempts to distinguish the NHS reforms from more traditional markets because of their widely perceived unsuitability for health care. Contortions over the vocabulary not only reflected politicians' discomfort at being accused of privatizing the NHS, but also indicated that the changes themselves were proving difficult to put into plain words. Although the NHS was not to be treated like British Telecom or British Gas, the 1990 NHS Act did deliberately create buyers and sellers of health care, but obliged them to operate within strict constraints. For example, there are detailed rules about public sector sellers such as NHS trusts borrowing money or making profits. This is indeed a market, but one in which government control, regulation and constraint are unusually dominant.

Because few, if any, markets for any commodity or service strictly conform to the economist's model of perfect competition [3], the straightforward term 'market' is good enough to describe the NHS's so-called 'internal market'; this chapter expands on its organization and operation.

THE PURCHASER–PROVIDER SEPARATION

At the heart of the market is the separation of two functions previously carried out within one organizational entity (the District Health Authority): the purchasing and providing of health care services (Chapters 4 and 5 describe in more detail these arrangements as they affected Districts and Units). Separation is crucial to the operation of a market. This essential dichotomy was not so straightforward for the NHS however. Although Districts were reconstituted as the main public sector purchasers, GPs were, for the first time, to be given an opportunity to also act as purchasers – although in a more limited way – through the GP fundholding scheme (see Chapter 4).

The separation of functions did not happen overnight. In 1991, in the first year of the reforms, most NHS services were still managed by Districts, albeit at arm's length. Attempts to maintain managerial distance between the purchasing and providing sides of Districts' responsibilities were not always easy. Moreover, as long as Districts were still managerially accountable for their directly managed units, the new health care market could not operate. In recognition of this, and the fact that many units needed time to build up management skills in personnel and accounting, the first two years (1991–3) of the reforms were officially dubbed a period of 'steady state'. Only 56 units in England were awarded trust status by the Secretary of State in the first year.

By 1994, virtually all directly managed units had become trusts and the separation needed by the market was complete (see Chapter 5).

Before *Working for Patients* was published, some advocated a more radical purchaser/provider split in which the public would be direct purchasers of their own care using vouchers distributed by government, and NHS providers would be private enterprises responding solely to market signals [4]. This did not happen, but the separation imposed between purchasers and providers was unique to the NHS reforms (although subsequently emulated, for example, by the BBC through its 'Producer Choice' initiative). Elsewhere in the public sector the introduction of market forces has been more direct and in some senses simpler, where 'purchasers' before and after are the paying public and privatization is limited to the supply of services. For the NHS, the introduction of market forces did not involve abandoning the 'agency relationship' – in which Districts and GPs, acting on behalf of the population, merely (*sic*) redefined their roles in relation to providers and created competition between NHS providers, and between NHS providers and private health care providers. The public were thus protected from a direct market, although the new functions, roles and motivations of providers and purchasers did change the form of the agency relationship.

While the split between purchasers and providers was strongly emphasized at the early stages of the reforms, by 1993 ministers and the NHS Management Executive (NHSME – later to become the NHS Executive) were starting to talk about 'mature relationships' and 'partnerships' and co-operation between purchasers and providers [5]. In a speech to the Royal College of Physicians in 1993, Brian Mawhinney, the Minister for Health, said, 'The purchaser–provider relationship cannot simply be restricted to formal negotiations . . . It has to be constant and ongoing. Both must realize that it is not a contest about who wins or loses in the contracting negotiation process. A dialogue needs to be developed in which purchasers and providers jointly work to achieve their objectives.' [6].

HEALTH CARE NEEDS ASSESSMENT

In theory, the starting point for the new health care market is the assessment by Districts of their population's health care needs. It is this assessment which should then be a major determinant of their purchasing decisions for their resident populations. Within Districts, the Directors of Public Health and their staff are responsible for the epidemiological assessment of health care needs.

The task of assessing needs has proved enormous, and many Districts have found it very difficult to integrate this properly with other tasks such as drawing up and negotiating contracts and the essential priority setting they must undertake, given constraints on their budgets. One of the few published studies to examine the process of needs assessment reported a great range of interpretations and actions on the part of Districts. At one extreme, some contracts managers dismissed the activity altogether as a waste of time. Others thought it kept Directors of Public Health occupied while the rest of the District got on with the real job of setting and placing contracts. One of the conclusions of the study was that progress and attitudes to needs assessments seemed to be linked to the financial position of Districts: those who were struggling financially were less likely to view needs assessment as useful [7].

Support for Districts and their public health departments in their needs assessment role has been somewhat poor compared with the investment in some other areas of the reforms. In 1991, the NHSME published guidance on needs assessment which defined the concept of 'need' (the ability to benefit from health care) and outlined a proposed series of reviews of epidemiologically-based assessments of health needs for various conditions and diseases [8]. The NHSME also set up a clearing house to disseminate details of local assessments. Other initiatives included setting up the UK Clearing House for Information on the Assessment of Health Outcomes at the Nuffield Centre in Leeds; commissioning a series of *Effective Health Care Bulletins* on various illnesses and conditions and the funding of the Cochrane Centre at Oxford [9]. All these initiatives were interlinked and aimed to promote and disseminate the use of information on medical and cost effectiveness.

The publication of the *Health of the Nation* White Paper in the summer of 1992 [10] provided a greater focus for needs assessments as it set out specific health targets. In practice these targets required interpretation and modification at local level. Although the *Health of the Nation* proposed boundaries to the theoretically limitless work of assessing needs, and while some Districts made good progress with the task (and the integration of assessments with other purchasing functions) this area of Districts' work – even though widely welcomed – remains underdeveloped.

CONTRACTING FOR HEALTH CARE

Although the NHS has for many years contracted for a wide range of services, the reforms greatly increased the significance and scope of this activity. Contracting embodies the bridge between purchasers and providers: contracts state details of service provision, prices, service quality, contractual periods and so on. It was decided early on that the contracting process was not a legalistic or adversarial exercise but 'an opportunity to discuss and agree how improvements to patient care can be secured and over what time' [11]. NHS contracts were therefore differentiated from legal documents which could be contested in the courts. Instead, contractual disagreements and disputes between NHS purchasers and providers were in the first instance to be dealt with by the Region and ultimately resolved by the Secretary of State, whose ruling would be binding.

Guidance issued by the NHSME in 1990 also stipulated that all providers, including trusts and those directly managed by Districts, would need to be covered by contracts, and that the latter should be treated no differently than the former in contract negotiations, monitoring or other functions [12]. Although the Department of Health and the NHSME issued a wide range of guidance notes on contracts and the contracting process – from the way providers should cost and price their services to the 'form' of contracts – purchasers and providers were given the freedom to specify and negotiate their own contracts. This was in recognition of the difficulty of laying down a single, definitive form of contract which would suit all local circumstances; a 'good' contract for one purchaser/provider might be too detailed or under-specified by another pair. Variations in providers' ability to generate detailed costings (and hence prices), and variations in purchasers' ability to carry out some of the detailed needs assessment work to support contracts, led to an enormous variety in the forms of contracts, their content and their degree of detail. The block contract (and its variants, such as the block contract with ceilings and floors on activity/funding), in which entire services or facilities are specified, is most popular. Figure 2.1 shows the general forms of contracts.

The first year of the reforms, and to a large extent the second, produced contracts between purchasers and providers which essentially catalogued current patterns of service delivery. This was not surprising given that the main

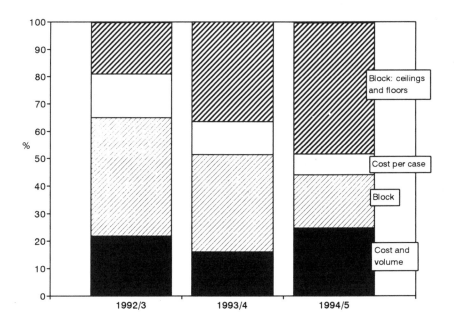

Figure 2.1 Forms of contracts by value: 1992/3 to 1994/5 (District Health Authorities).

Source: Appleby, J. (1994) *Developing Contracting: A National Survey of District Health Authorities, Boards and NHS Trusts* (Research Paper No. 15), NAHAT, Birmingham.

factors influencing purchasers' contracting decisions were the preferences of their local GPs, existing referral patterns and the proximity of services to their local resident population [13].

Extra-contractual referrals

Although contracts (generally lasting a year) cover the majority of the activities carried out by providers, important contractual 'gaps' are dealt with in a different way. 'Extra-contractual referrals' (ECRs) can arise if a patient is referred by a GP or is admitted as an emergency to a provider which does not have a contract with the patient's district of residence. In the former case, called an elective ECR, the provider must seek approval for treatment (and payment) from the patient's district of residence before admission. Districts have the discretion to refuse the referral. This happens if the District is running low on the funds it has set aside to pay for ECRs, or if it feels the patient can receive comparable care within a contract already set up by the District. In the case of emergency ECRs, Districts are obliged to pay providers on receipt of a bill.

Although ECRs generally constitute 2% or 3% of Districts' or providers' total contracted activity, ECRs have generated a disproportionate amount of administrative work, because Districts have had to develop systems for processing ECR requests, and providers have had to produce a comprehensive set of prices at the beginning of each financial year, along with price lists for those procedures GP fundholders are allowed to buy.

MANAGING THE MARKET

While Districts and GP fundholders act as purchasers of health care and NHS trusts and others act as providers, exchanging contracts to supply activity and money respectively, they do so according to rules laid down by government and in an economic environment managed by the NHSE and the Department of Health. Although all markets are subject to regulation of one sort or another – from consumer protection laws to government licensing – the health care market created by the reforms is ultimately in the control of the Secretary of State.

Ministers have extensive powers to intervene and dictate the workings of the market, from authorizing the creation (and dissolution) of trusts and GP fundholding practices to setting health care priorities (and, through managerial accountability, ensuring that these are followed). In addition, of course, the Secretary of State plays a key role in limiting the financial boundary of the market in terms of the total funding of the NHS. In practice, the Secretary of State devolves much of this power to other levels within the NHS and, in any case, given the underlying ideology of the reforms, tends to encourage decisions to be taken at the lowest appropriate level within the market. Hence, the *Health of the Nation* may lay down a national direction in terms of health targets but these are interpreted by Districts to fit in with local circumstances and needs.

Yet paradoxically, NHS purchasers and providers must comply with very many rules proscribing and limiting their autonomy. On the supply side of the market, trusts are free to determine their own management structures, but each trust board is accountable to the Secretary of State. Trusts are also free to determine the range and type of services they provide, but, where a service must be provided locally, a trust must provide it if it is the only unit able to do so. Trusts are able to borrow money (to fund capital schemes for example), but only within an agreed limit (laid down by the Department of Health). Trusts are also obliged to set prices for their services according to rules which stipulate that prices must equal costs (and costs include running costs, depreciation of assets and a set return on those assets). Further pricing rules prevent cross-subsidization (overcharging for one service to subsidize another) and charging different prices for the same service provided to different purchasers.

On the demand side of the market, purchasers are also subject to restrictions and regulations. District purchasers are required to meet certain efficiency targets each year from their contracts. These targets are set by the NHSE and are monitored by a standard measure of efficiency – the efficiency index [14]. Districts must also account for their actions, through the usual managerial channels, to their Region and ultimately to the Secretary of State. GP fund-holders are restricted under the fundholding scheme as to the type of care and treatment they are allowed to buy for their patients.

One of the most significant and wide-ranging examples of the powers of the Secretary of State to intervene in the market and overrule local autonomy occurred when, in 1991, Virginia Bottomley appointed Sir Bernard Tomlinson (Professor of Pathology and former Chairman of the Northern Region) to head an inquiry into London's health services. Tomlinson's recommendations (which are detailed below) included major hospital closures and mergers, together with a reorganization of the capital's primary care services. Although there are good grounds for arguing that the London situation is unique, in fact many other urban centres are undergoing this method of change rather than letting the market determine the pattern of health care provision. Apart from the numerous rules controlling market activity and one-off interventions, such as the Tomlinson inquiry, the issue of how the new health care market is managed has not been clearly resolved. Although the eight new Regional Offices proposed in October 1993 to replace the fourteen English Regions have market management as part of their responsibilities, exactly how they are to carry out this task is also unclear (Chapter 3 has a fuller description of this reorganization).

BEYOND *WORKING FOR PATIENTS*

Unlike previous reorganizations, *Working for Patients* did not provide a 'blue-print' for change. Rather, the reforms and, in particular, the changes concerning the introduction of competition, set the NHS on a new path and were more concerned with means than ends: the presumption being that the particular 'means' proposed by the reforms would inevitably lead to the 'ends' specified by *Working for Patients*: greater efficiency and more patient choice. Conclusive evidence for this association between means and ends remains to be gathered. Meanwhile, in some areas the reforms have spurred or created a number of further 'mini-reorganizations' and rapid changes which are worth noting.

Reconfiguring providers

As finance ministers across Europe attempting to control exchange rates in the early 1990s discovered, markets can be powerful and swift forces for change. The new NHS market, despite its constraints (particularly in the first two years of the reforms) began to build up pressure for change very quickly. One of the clearest examples of this occurred in London.

It was clear, even as early as 1991 (and after nearly a hundred years of organizations such as the King's Fund College arguing for change in London's health services [15]), that the market in London was going to produce some dramatic changes in the capital's health services as purchasers started to transfer their contracts away from the generally high-cost London hospitals. In addition, changes in medical care suggested that by the end of the century there would be a surplus of beds in London of between 2000 and 7000.

Apart from the political agenda of the reforms being seen to be responsible for the closure of hospitals, there was also a widespread perception that London's primary care services were inadequate and that the market might not respond to this latter concern. It was not just about primary care provision, there was also a concern that the many individual decisions made by purchasers might not add up to the best overall decision for London. Therefore, although Tomlinson's recommendations, published in October 1992, included the advice that a number of London's acute hospitals should close or merge – which were also the changes the market was indicating – the intervention by Tomlinson was based on a planned and orderly change in services. In this way it was felt that the issue of community and primary care provision, the protection of centres of excellence and the protection of local services for local people would be sure to be addressed positively. Tomlinson also recommended that there needed to be substantial changes in primary care [16]. The Secretary of State responded in *Making London Better* published in February 1993 [17]. In essence, all of Tomlinson's recommendations were accepted, and through the specialist London Implementation Groups headed by Sir Tim Chessells, Chair of North East Thames RHA, a planned agenda for change was pursued.

Evolving purchasing

The second example of organizational change occurring largely as a result of the reforms, but not part of the original policy, are various realignments on the purchaser side of the market. In 1990 there were 192 District Health Authorities in England, a figure which had remained virtually unchanged since the creation of Districts in 1974. By April 1994, the number had fallen to 130 as a result of mergers. Why was this? One reason for this 'merger mania' was that many Districts were considered too small to carry enough financial clout with their providers. While it may be true that there was a perception of inadequate purchaser leverage, it is not clear that this was true (although perceptions and actuality are often indistinguishable as far as markets and the behaviour of market actors are concerned [18]). In addition to actual mergers, a number of collaborative purchasing agencies have been set up.

A change that is attributable perhaps more to the culture of the reforms than the reforms themselves is the merger of DHAs and Family Health Service Authorities (FHSAs) – this may also relate to the foregoing District mergers, as there are fewer FHSAs than DHAs. Such mergers, while advocated by many before the reforms, have also been spurred on by the more central role in purchasing decisions played by both fundholding and non-fundholding GPs. Finally, a variety of other models of purchasing have begun to emerge since 1991 involving collaborations and partnerships. These have included setting up 'multifunds' or groups of GP fundholding practices (some have involved over 70 GPs) purchasing jointly where they feel they benefit, but otherwise acting independently; 'total fundholding' experiments have also arisen in which a small number of GP fundholders work together with an expanded budget covering all health care for their patients. Alternatives to fundholding, involving much closer collaboration between GPs and their local District Health Authority in determining purchasing priorities, have also emerged (see Chapter 4).

Reconfigurations arising since the implementation of the reforms on purchaser and provider sides of the market can be viewed simply as the effects of the reforms. However, many of these effects are significant innovations in organizational, managerial and, most probably, in health and health care terms and were not envisaged in the original reform White Paper and subsequent legislation. It is this capacity to promote and stimulate rather than prescribe change which makes the reforms of *Working for Patients* stand out from previous reorganizations.

CONCLUSION

Two main issues emerge from this review of the market changes introduced by the 1990 NHS Act. First, although the new market can be characterized as highly regulated and constrained, it is a competitive market none the less. Second, in setting up this market, *Working for Patients* provided a new direction for the NHS rather than a blueprint for change. From this point of view the changes were evolutionary, and they have, in some instances, been rapidly initiated and implemented. This has stimulated considerable ongoing reorganization throughout the NHS as purchasers and providers test their scope to operate within the market's regulations and rules, learn new roles and behaviours and adapt to new incentives.

44 *The new health care economy*

NOTES

1. Enthoven A. (1985) *Reflections on the Management of the National Health Service*, Occasional Paper 5, Nuffield Provincial Hospitals Trust, London. Alain Enthoven's 1985 recommendations for an internal market for the NHS were not in fact his first preference. Rather, he felt that the emerging Health Maintenance Organizations (HMOs) appearing in the US during the 1980s provided a better system of health care, which would not only produce more efficient care but greater patient choice. The market/competitive model adopted by the UK reforms was one removed from the HMO concept in which (among other things) the public choose their own HMO and pay a subscription (either through an insurance scheme or directly) for defined medical cover.
2. The term 'social market' was coined by the former Chief Executive of the NHS, Sir Duncan Nichol; 'quasi market' was a term used by the School for Advanced Urban Studies at the University of Bristol; 'managed competition' had its origins in the US.
3. The classic economist's model of perfect competition includes such criteria as perfect knowledge, numerous consumers and producers and 'rational' economic behaviour, such as profit maximization, etc.
4. Advocates of these policies included right-wing think tanks, such as the Institute of Economic Affairs and the Adam Smith Institute.
5. NHSME (1993) *Purchasing for Health: A Framework for Action* (Speeches by the Minister for Health, Brian Mawhinney, and NHS Chief Executive, Sir Duncan Nichol), NHSME, London.
6. Ibid, p. 24–5.
7. Freemantle N., Watt I., Mason J. (1993) Developments in the Purchasing Process in the NHS Towards an Explicit Policy of Rationing. *Public Administration*, 1993, Winter, **71**, pp. 535–48.
8. DoH (1991) *Assessing Health Care Needs*, Project Paper, DoH, London. In addition, the Department set up the Central Health Monitoring Unit, following a recommendation in the Acheson Report, *Public Health in England* (DHSS (1988), HMSO, London (Cmnd. 289)). The CHMU publish epidemiological overviews of various illnesses and patient groups. Their first publication covered the health of the elderly.
9. The *Effective Health Care Bulletin* series has covered a diverse range of topics including the medical and economic effectiveness of glue ear, depression and osteoporosis.
10. DoH (1992) *The Health of the Nation*, HMSO, London (Cm. 1986).
11. EL(90)MB/24 NHSME An Executive Letter from the Chief Executive of the NHS to the service outlining: *Contracts for Health Services: Operating Contracts* (1990) NHSME, HMSO, London.
12. Ibid., p. 5, para. 2.8.
13. Appleby J., Smith P., Ranade W., Little V., Robinson R. (1994) *Monitoring Managed Competition*, in Robinson R. and Le Grand J. (eds) *Evaluating the NHS Reforms*, King's Fund Institute, London.
14. The efficiency index was a relatively crude measure of technical efficiency, and was calculated by dividing the change from one year to the next of a weighted sum of activity (in-patients, day cases, out-patients, etc.) by the annual change in real spending to produce this activity. The index has been widely criticized within the

NHS as failing to capture the full range of service provision and quality of provision, and also leading to perverse incentives.

15. King's Fund (1994) *London Monitor* No. 1, King's Fund Institute, London.
16. DoH (1992) *Report of the Inquiry into London's Health Service, Medical Education and Research* (the Tomlinson Report), HMSO, London.
17. DoH (1993) *Making London Better*, Department of Health, London.
18. An example of this is the economist's notion of 'contestability': markets do not have to have numerous competing providers for competition to exist, but merely the perception by providers already in the market that new providers could enter the market and compete. Hence, a provider who was in reality a monopolist may well behave in a competitive way if they think their market is contestable.

3

Central Government and the National Health Service

This chapter examines the role of ministers and civil servants in the Department of Health and the NHS Executive and their relationships with the professional and managerial staff of the NHS. Also examined is the history and background of Regional Health Authorities and, in particular, recent changes in their role and functions.

THE FUNCTIONS OF GOVERNMENT DEPARTMENTS

Governments need departments which will transform their laws and policies into action, and thus enable the balance of political power to have its influence on the life of the country. In the United Kingdom each government department is headed by a politician who is called either a Minister or a Secretary of State. He or she is appointed by the Prime Minister who determines how long the minister shall hold that office. If the Prime Minister changes or the Government is voted out of office, the political heads of departments also change. However, the permanent staff of the department, the civil servants, numbering around 4500 in the Department of Health, continue their work irrespective of alterations in political leadership, and often spend most of their working lives in one ministry. Although the Secretary of State is the statutory head of the department, he or she is assisted by junior ministers who are themselves Members of Parliament and are also appointed to ministerial office by the Prime Minister.

There may be substantial differences between civil servants and politicians over what they want the department to achieve and, in particular, over the time-scale for achievement. Ministers will usually want to establish a number of specific changes in the work of the department during their time of office, to follow the policies of their own party and the views of their fellow MPs. On the other hand, civil servants, because of their more extended association with the department, are able to envisage long-term programmes for change.

Although the civil service is free from overt political party domination, it would be naïve to assume that civil servants do not have value systems of their own which may be different from those of their ministers. Those important but nebulous factors, personality and style, influence the relationship: the result can be anywhere on the continuum from close and trusting co-operation to icy formality and deadlock.

Whatever the result, it will influence the department's achievements. A key figure in this is the most senior civil servant, the Permanent Secretary, who is generally in day-to-day contact with the Secretary of State. He or she, on behalf of the Secretary of State, is responsible for the overall management and control of all aspects of the department's administration, a person on whom the Secretary of State depends in order to be in touch with the department's activities.

THE ROLE OF HEALTH MINISTERS

The Secretary of State's goals for the department can sometimes conflict with the priorities of the Cabinet. It is his or her function to argue specifically for the policies and funds the department requires. The Prime Minister and the Cabinet, on the other hand, will expect the Secretary of State to take a wider political role, contributing to and supporting the Government on matters beyond departmental responsibilities and also be active in Parliament generally and in the party organization. So the person who holds the position of Secretary of State has to seek a balance between these factors which will, ideally, enable them to be successful in the department as an innovator and administrator and in the Government as a politician.

Because government departments have greatly expanded their activities, policy preparation increasingly has to be done by civil servants, and the minister may at best only be able to choose between policies determined by senior officials, without knowing the details of departmental and other views on the subject. Although this can lead to an undesirable degree of delegation, it is the inevitable consequence of the sheer volume of work being handled in a department. The minister may call in a group of policy advisers from outside the civil service who can, with the junior ministers, constitute a countervailing influence to the civil servants.

This was the intention, for example, when the Secretary of State, Norman Fowler, asked Roy Griffiths, in 1983, to examine the workings of the NHS. After the general election in 1987, the Government's NHS Review intentionally paid particular attention to opinion outside both the civil service and the NHS itself. This prompted one of the main criticisms of the resulting proposals: that they had been too heavily influenced by those whose knowledge of the NHS was slight, but who had an ideological axe to grind.

What does it mean to say that the Secretary of State is constitutionally accountable to Parliament? Formally, he or she must see that the NHS is run in accordance with statute, in line with government policies, and that its operation is reasonably efficient. But such a generalization poses questions. It clearly is impossible for the Secretary of State to be held personally responsible for the actions of individual staff in the NHS. Nevertheless, this convention of accountability still remains, and ministers are expected to be able to answer parliamentary questions on any aspect of the NHS.

THE DEPARTMENT OF HEALTH

When the Ministry of Health was first formed in 1919, it had responsibility for roads, national insurance, planning, environmental health and local government as well as the health services, but, over the years, these other duties were transferred elsewhere. In 1951, local government housing passed to the new Ministry of Housing and Local Government and, with this, came the loss of a seat in the Cabinet and a considerable reduction of staff at the Ministry of Health.

The origins of the social security ministry go back to 1916 when a Ministry of Pensions was set up. This was amalgamated with the Ministry of National Insurance, set up in 1944, and in 1966 these two joined the National Assistance Board to form a new Ministry of Social Security. In 1968, Richard Crossman, Lord President of the Council and Leader of the House of Commons, was involved with the Prime Minister, Harold Wilson, in planning the restructuring of certain government ministries that would further consolidate the total number of spending departments. The new Department of Health and Social Security (DHSS) was created in this way, with the seat in the Cabinet restored (although Enoch Powell was, as Minister for Health, a member of the Cabinet in 1962).

The first Secretary of State for Social Services, as the head of the new department was now called, was Richard Crossman himself. However, the merger did little to alter the organizations of the two ministries since their functions and methods of working were different. Their workload steadily increased with the reforms of the health service and significant changes in social security legislation. By the 1980s this had necessitated not only a Secretary of State but also two Ministers of similar status, one specializing in health and the other in social security matters, each with a Permanent Secretary. By 1988, it was decided that any advantages of this linkage in one government department were now minimal, so the DHSS was split once more and given its own Secretary of State for Health. The first incumbent was Kenneth Clarke, who had served as the Minister for Health during the 1984 Griffiths changes. The outgoing Secretary of State at the head of the old DHSS, John Moore, became Secretary of State for Social Security.

The organization of the Department of Health

In 1970 the Government ordered a study of the DHSS that would make recommendations for a reorganization of the health side of the DHSS itself. This was carried out by a review team under the guidance of a steering committee. The team was composed of civil servants and of management consultants from the firm McKinsey. Their eight-volume report was published in June 1972 and implemented, without alteration, in December of that year. The DHSS was reorganized into five main divisions: Services Development, Regional Liaison, Finance, Personnel and Works, with Top of the Office made up of each divisional head. There were subdivisions within each main division and, overall, the organization was supported by professional advisors: doctors, nurses, dentists and social workers. Further discussion on the inside working of the DHSS was initiated in 1976 with particular reference to the Department's relationship to the NHS itself.

Yet another enquiry was undertaken by the civil service to prepare for the implementation of the Griffiths proposals in 1983. Griffiths criticized the Department's lack of strategic direction and its poor sense of managerial values. As a consequence of his recommendations, a top-level ministerially-led Supervisory Board was set up to oversee health policy, with an executive Management Board accountable to it. This broad division between policy making and policy implementation was reiterated in 1989 when the Supervisory Board was reconstituted as the Policy Board and the Management Board became the NHS Management Executive (NHSME).

Shortly after the implementation of the reforms, it was again thought necessary to change these new management entities, and, in October 1993, *Managing the New NHS* [1] was published by the Department of Health, outlining a reorganized central executive, announcing the rundown of Regional Health Authorities (and the creation of replacement Regional Offices) and the formal merger of District and Family Health Service Authorities, among other things. These most recent changes are first set in context in a description of the roles and constitution of the NHS Policy Board and the NHSME (many of the tasks and responsibilities of these two groups have been retained following *Managing the New NHS*).

The Policy Board

The Policy Board was originally constituted with 14 members: three ministers, two RHA chairmen, the Permanent Secretary, the Chief Executive, the Chief Medical Officer and Chief Nursing Officer (both appointed in a personal capacity), a leading clinician from the NHS and four people from major industries. The Board was explicitly charged to concern itself not with managerial issues but rather with producing advice for the Secretary of State (who takes the chair) on the overall pattern and balance of policies for the NHS, and with assessing the effectiveness of the implementation of these policies. The Board needed to make sure that health policies did not contradict each other or have unintended results; *Working for Patients* [2] was criticized in just these terms, that its proposals were inadequately analysed and would tend to fragment patient care instead of increasing the efficiency of its delivery.

The work of the Policy Board was somewhat detached from the NHS itself and it had a difficult remit, caught between satisfying its political masters on the one hand and influencing managerial constructive action on the other, although its key task each year was to set objectives for the NHSME. The NHSME's predecessor, the Management Board, had difficulty persuading the departmental civil servants to adopt a new approach to management. The first chairman, Victor Paige, left suddenly for reasons that have never been fully explained, while the second, Sir Len Peach, seconded from IBM, was not asked to serve a second term although he had been popular with the NHS itself.

There was a marked change following the appointment of Duncan Nichol, whose title changed to Chief Executive when the NHSME came into existence in July 1989. As Regional General Manager for the Mersey Region, he had held a non-executive seat on the Management Board. Appointed in January 1989, he consolidated his position by progressively replacing members of the NHSME, introducing more people from outside the civil service. By 1990 the NHSME had 11 people under the chairmanship of the Chief Executive. Nichol appointed an NHS manager as Deputy Chief Executive with particular responsibility for implementing the 1990 reforms. The other members were directors of operations and planning, personnel, finance (held by a person seconded from commerce), information, estates, and research and development. To these were added a director of family practitioner services, which had been brought under the NHSME to integrate primary and secondary care, and nursing and medical directors, who were the Department's deputy medical and nursing officers.

The NHS Management Executive

The role of the NHSME was to act as an organization within the Department, to carry out tasks allocated by the Secretary of State and, in particular, to concentrate on leading the NHS in the directions specified by government policy. This required the NHSME to set objectives for the NHS and to monitor the results. The NHSME had not only to look forward to what should happen but also to assess past performance. Its objectives for 1990/91 included goals to be worked towards over the next five years, as well as tasks to be completed within the year. The long-term aims included better integration of primary and secondary care and the development of more specific outcome measures, to show Parliament and the country as whole what was being achieved in terms of patient care. Short-term objectives included waiting-list management, eliminating financial deficits by April 1991, beginning the NHS and Community Care Act's operations and improving communications throughout the NHS.

The Deputy Chief Executive's job of maintaining the momentum for the implementation of the 1990 Act's reforms centred on one of the hardest challenges ever faced by the Department. The time-scale was short, and the NHSME had to balance the Secretary of State's clear decision not to prescribe too much detail with a readiness to give at least some guidance, so that the task could be completed within nine months of the Act receiving Royal Assent. No fewer than 34 separate project groups were set up in the Department; the leaders of these often ventured out into the NHS in various parts of the country to encourage local managers. This was very different from the conventionally remote style in which civil servants had tended to work. The Chief Executive did much to foster a sense of common purpose by using the Regional General Managers as envoys. Without this new approach the changes could not have been introduced so rapidly and relatively successfully, despite considerable opposition from NHS professionals and the public.

By April 1991, the main thrust of implementing the changes was over. This, together with the proposed move to Leeds in 1992, led to a review of the functions and organization of the NHSME [3]. This in turn followed an internal report on the workings of the whole Department [4]. The review found that the NHSME needed a clearer focus with a more explicit managerial style. First, it needed to be corporate and integrated, thus overcoming the tendency of individual directorates to take an independent line, which might conflict with moves elsewhere. One way of creating this more co-operative way of working is for task groups to be set up with membership from several different directorates. Such an approach is often found in large organizations and is known as matrix management. There was a recognition that the effect of the 1990 reforms had been to increase the numbers of staff, now standing at 1600 in the NHSME alone; a return to a leaner workforce would be both practical (given the reluctance of many of the NHSME's staff to transfer to Leeds) and politically desirable to combat criticism that the 1990 reforms were requiring more and more administrative and managerial staff.

The NHSME inevitably had been closely concerned with leading the implementation of *Working For Patients*. This done, they could now consider longer term issues. In this respect they were challenging the traditional role of the other part of the Department, concerned with policy. However, the unambiguous part of the NHSME's function was, and remains, to ensure good management throughout the NHS and to monitor the performance of the health authorities and, in order to achieve these objectives, it was decided the NHSME needed to be reconstituted. At the head remained the Chief Executive supported by six Directors together with Medical and Nursing Directors, either of whom could be head of one of the other directorates. Research and development had always been rather under-regarded in the Department, but in 1990 a new Director was appointed and his contribution has been enhanced on the new Executive through a role that includes responsibility for new ideas as well as commissioning research throughout the Department and the NHS itself.

The Director of Health Care and Medical Director's post included three main elements. First, responsibility for developmental work; for instance the promotion of a more integrated approach to care across the boundaries of primary and secondary care. Second, the Directorate was concerned with needs assessment to ensure that policies of the NHS were related to what was needed rather than being merely reactive to public demand. The third responsibility was for medical manpower. It would have been more logical to give this task to the Personnel Director but professional politics determined otherwise.

In keeping with the overall approach to management brought about after the implementation of general management in the mid-1980s, the NHSME included a Director of Performance Management, working closely with the Regions to ensure the implementation of national strategies and that health authorities were being effective. This was a further step towards constructing a clear line of authority between the NHSME and health authorities, which inevitably diminished their traditional autonomy. The danger was that top-down authority would stifle bottom-up initiatives and lead to a stultifying conformity.

The Directorate for Finance and Corporate Information linked costs and activity and was the NHSME's voice in negotiations with the Treasury. NHS Trusts were monitored from this Directorate on the grounds that this was largely a financial task. This Directorate was also responsible for management information and health statistics.

The setting up of NHS trusts was seen as a prelude to the disbanding of the central wage bargaining system through the Whitley Councils (see Chapter 12). By 1991, however, the initial enthusiasm for local pay bargaining had waned and the NHSME still thought it necessary to have a Personnel Director with responsibilities for pay and conditions as well as for manpower planning and training. Lastly, the Director for Corporate Affairs provided a backup service for the Executive itself with responsibility for communications and public relations, and had the particular task of ensuring that the Executive related effectively to the rest of the Department and to the NHS as a whole. To enable this to happen, a network of regional officers based in seven 'Outposts' was appointed.

No longer on the NHSME was the Director for Estates, despite the large land holdings and other assets (worth over £18 billion in 1990) with 46 000 acres in public ownership. Agencies with their own chief executives have been set up for this and for Procurement. NHS Superannuation has also been separated.

The introduction of the NHSME into the Department of Health brought about a new style of working, creating an articulate group of people willing to go out and about explaining government policy in a way that, at times, makes them resemble party publicists. The NHSME still required the co-operation of the rest of the civil servants to ensure that government policy was well rooted in expert opinion and was implementable, but the transfer of the NHSME to Leeds, in 1992, may have made the divisions between it and the civil servants even more marked. The move has other consequences: some saw it as the first step to the setting up of an 'NHS Corporation' outside direct government control, an attempt to 'depoliticize' health policy. But this is to misunderstand the importance that governments of all parties attach to health care as a cornerstone of their public policy. It is unlikely that the responsibilities governments are given by the community could be entirely shifted to a semi-autonomous organization. The NHS is almost totally funded through taxation, so governments would be unwilling to relinquish involvement in the allocation and use of resources they provide out of the public purse.

Though the NHSME is responsible for action, it could not work in a vacuum. The NHSME and its supporting Divisions were part of a wider organization that included administrators and professionals in the Health and Social Services (HSS) and Central Resource Management Divisions of the Department. The HSS Divisions, formerly known as the Policy Group, were responsible to ministers for the development of national policies and priorities. Within the group there were subdivisions charged with seeing that all aspects of patient care were covered and that there were no gaps in services. The remit of the HSS Divisions extended to developing policies for local authority social services departments, and, not for the first time, *Caring for People* called for policies to take a view of people's needs across the whole spectrum of care.

Professional advice is particularly important to developing policies, and the Department employs a wide range of medical and other professional experts to keep in touch with the latest views in the NHS in order to contribute informed opinions. These experts in the civil service have been criticized from time to time for being out of touch with day-to-day problems, but they have the advantage of being detached from the type of parochial self-interest that some of those working in the NHS may be susceptible to.

The tradition of involving professional opinion and advice in the work of the Department is also maintained through advisory machinery. The National Health Service Act, 1946, established the Central Health Services Council to advise the Minister on any matters relating to the service that were either referred to it or that it thought it should consider. Significant reports published under its auspices were the Bradbeer report (1954) [5] on administration, the Platt report (1959) [6] on children in hospital and the Bonham-Carter report (1969) [7] on the functions of District General Hospitals. The Council was disbanded by the Health Services Act, 1980.

The Chief Medical Officer produces an annual report *On the Health of the Nation*, which draws the government's attention to trends in sickness and hazards to health. While it is an independent view, it may well be tempered with a perception of what will be acceptable to the Government of the day. The standing of the Chief Medical Officer is considerable, as this post carries responsibilities in other ministries such as the Department of Social Security, the Home Office and the Department of Education and Science. In addition the Chief Medical Officer advises the Ministry of Agriculture, Fisheries and Food and the Department of the Environment.

Other Divisions in the Department of Health include those responsible for the safety of medicines, and the overseeing of those pharmaceutical, dental and optical services that are the responsibility of Family Health Services Authorities. The Social Services Inspectorate has the task of seeing local authority social services departments maintain the standards set by government. The Chief Nursing Officer heads a division of nurse civil servants covering the whole range of nursing and midwifery.

The Functions and Manpower Review

By 1993 the Secretary of State was under increasing pressure to cut the cost of the Department and to simplify the role of Regions, possibly merging them with the Outposts set up to support NHS trusts. Proposals by Kate Jenkins, a member of the Policy Board and previously associated with the Government's proposals for contracting out civil service functions, and by Alan Langlands, the NHSME's Deputy Chief Executive (who became the Chief Executive in 1994), considered streamlining the higher levels of the NHS by employing agencies for certain functions.

In the event, the recommendations of the Jenkins–Langlands review that were accepted and implemented by the Secretary of State did not involve a move towards an agency at arm's length from government, or the formal separation of the Department of Health and the NHS through the creation of an English National Health Authority (both of which were options looked at by the review team). Rather, *Managing the New NHS*, published in October 1993, set out three main changes in the organization and management of the NHS: mergers of District Health Authorities and Family Health Service Authorities; the abolition of the 14 statutory Regional Health Authorities in England and a streamlining of the NHS Management Executive (renamed the NHS Executive).

In part, these changes arose not just from a desire to curb increases in management costs and personnel (and thus direct more resources to direct patient care) but also from the feeling that a number of issues arising from the reforms of *Working for Patients* represented 'unfinished business'. For example, in 1991, there were around 190 Districts in England. By April 1994, mergers had reduced this to just over 100, with many Districts consolidating themselves with their local FHSAs, not just in terms of boundaries, but in their working relationships as well (see Chapter 4). *Managing the New NHS* supported this change by setting out a timetable to deal with the statutory issues associated with the full merger of Districts with FHSAs (see Chapter 4 for more detail). In addition, it was felt that the existing management arrangements were less than ideal in terms of effective oversight of both purchasers and providers.

The structure of the NHS existing in 1993 is shown in Figure 3.1. Figure 3.2 shows the new structure arising from *Managing the New NHS*. The new Regions were established on 1 April 1994; the target date for legislation formally abolishing Regional Health Authorities and enabling Districts and FHSAs to merge was set for 1 April 1996.

The NHS Executive and Policy Board

Following the functions and manpower review, the NHS Management Executive – now renamed the NHS Executive (NHSE) – took on a division between its central, national role and a new role at local level undertaken by Regional Offices which replaced the Regional Health Authorities (see below). The role of the NHS Executive at the centre – with an emphasis as the 'headquarters'

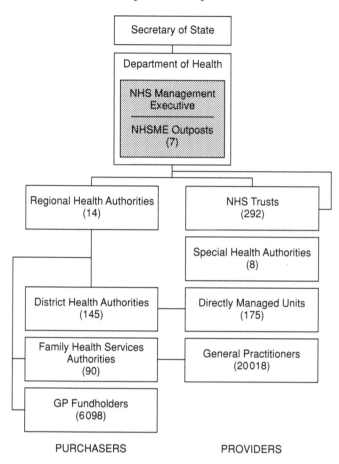

Figure 3.1 Structure of the NHS (England) 1993.

Source: *Managing the New NHS: Consultation Document* (1994) Department of Health.

of the NHS, with a board that includes the Regional Directors of the eight new Regions – largely resembles its previous roles and functions. These include the responsibility for implementing the Government's policies for the NHS and the provision of support and advice to ministers. The Secretary of State, Virginia Bottomley, envisaged the role of the new Executive as strategic rather than operational – although its effective extension into the intermediate tier previously occupied by the Regional Health Authorities gives it some clear operational tasks.

The Policy Board has also retained most of its essential functions, acting as an advisory panel to the Secretary of State, for example. Overall, the Policy Board is now expected to support NHS central management by working closely with the new Regional Directors. Following the demise of the Regions

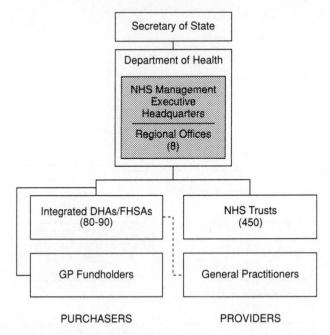

Figure 3.2 New structure of the NHS from 1995/6.

Source: *Managing the New NHS: Consultation Document* (1994), Department of Health.

(see below), it was decided to add eight non-executive directors to the Board who would to some extent represent the eight new Regions. The role of these new directors is to provide a communications bridge between the Secretary of State and the chairs of health authorities and trusts. They are also responsible for advising on the appointment and reappointment of chairmen and non-executives in each of their Regions, and for acting as 'mentors' to the chairs in their areas.

The Regions

The abolition of the 14 Regions and the creation of 8 Regional Offices, incorporating the former NHSME Outposts, will formally occur in 1996 through legislation enacted by Parliament. In legislative terms the abolition of Regional Health Authorities is fairly straightforward. Work on establishing the new regional tier began in 1994 with, for example, the appointment of the new Regional Directors and the realignment of old RHA boundaries. Figure 3.3 and Figure 3.4 show the old and new regional boundaries respectively.

Historically, Regions have existed in one form or another since the creation of the NHS in 1948. Then, the NHS in England was divided into 13 Regional Hospital Boards (RHBs) with, as their name implied, responsibility for hospitals.

*Based on the boundaries of FHSAs reporting to each RHA

Figure 3.3 Regional Health Authority boundaries: 1993.

Source: *Managing the New NHS: Consultation Document* (1994), Department of Health.

In 1959 one Region (South-West Metropolitan) was split in two, creating 14 Regions. After the 1974 reorganization, the RHBs became Regional Health Authorities (RHAs) with a wider remit, including responsibility for overall planning of clinical services and employment of senior medical staff. They retained responsibility for planning and undertaking major capital works and allocating money to their Area Health Authorities. The new RHAs were run by a chairman and members appointed by the Secretary of State.

*Based on boundaries of FHSAs

Figure 3.4 Areas covered by the NHS Executive Regional Offices.

Source: *Managing the New NHS: Consultation Document* (1994), Department of Health.

During the 1980s the monitoring responsibilities of RHAs were further emphasized. In 1982 formal Regional reviews of Districts were introduced, following the abolition of the Areas. The final change to the Regions, prior to their effective abolition in 1994, occurred with the passing of the NHS and Community Care Act, 1990. As with other authorities affected by the Act, Regions were reconstituted along the lines of private businesses with a Board of executive and non-executive directors. The chairman of the Board and the five non-executive directors (who had to include a chairman of a Family Health

Service Authority and someone connected with a local medical school) were appointed by the Secretary of State. The roles of the Regions now included a further emphasis on performance monitoring, setting performance criteria and evaluation of the effectiveness and management of the process of change embodied by the reforms of *Working for Patients.*

However, there were feelings that Regions did not fit easily into the changes introduced by *Working for Patients* and, particularly, the subsequent changes arising from the White Paper. At the time of *Working for Patients,* there had been some suggestion that the regional or intermediate tier of management should disappear altogether, but the Department of Health and the NHSE were less than keen to take on the administrative task of overseeing all 450 trusts, reviewing business plans, allocating external financing limits, dealing with GP fundholder allocations and all the other necessary functions of the NHS. An intermediate tier (of some sort) also provided a managerial buffer between local trusts and purchasers and the 'head office' which ministers were keen to retain.

The Jenkins–Langlands review of 1993 provided the Secretary of State with a new model for the intermediate tier of management, reducing the number of English Regions from fourteen to eight (each headed by a Regional Director, accountable directly to the Chief Executive of the NHS and sitting alongside the Chief Executive on the NHS Management Board), combining the old NHSME Outposts and detailing a revamped set of responsibilities more in tune with the reforms of *Working for Patients.* These included managing the performance of purchasers and providers; ensuring compliance with the regulatory framework of the internal market; arbitrating in contractual disputes between purchasers and providers; approving GP fundholder applications and budgets; developing the role of purchasers and contributing to the centre's work on policy and resources. The exact nature of these tasks and how they were to be performed (how, for example, are Regional Offices to 'regulate the market'?) were not spelt out by *Managing the New NHS,* but have been subject to further scrutiny by the Department during 1994.

The creation of Regional Offices has raised the issue of centralization in the NHS [8]. Although the reorganization was premised on the basis of devolution of power and decision making, in reality it appears to have strengthened the centre's grip on the periphery. Not only are the new Regional Directors directly accountable to the Chief Executive of the NHS (and not, as previously, to the Regional management boards which included nominal local representation), but all the employees of the new Regions are civil servants (not NHS employees as before). Moreover, the Department has made it clear that it now sees the NHS as having just two management tiers, central and local.

ACCOUNTABILITY

Apart from the political accountability to Parliament of the Secretary of State for Health and the accountability of the party in power to the electorate through general elections, in a public service there are various ways in which the people responsible for running that service are held accountable by the community at large. First, the Permanent Secretary and the NHS Chief Executive are formally designated as Accounting Officers and have to report to Parliament for the proper expenditure of public money. They are required to appear before the Public Accounts Committee (which has an all-party membership of 15 MPs) to answer points brought up by the Comptroller and Auditor General, who is an independent officer of Parliament. They may also have to answer criticisms publicized by the Audit Commission, which in 1990 took on the responsibility for NHS audit (see Chapter 7). Following the Functions and Manpower Review, the Department may consider extending the accounting officer role downwards. The abolition of the Regions and the lack of non-executive directors in the new Regional Offices could be seen as a strengthening of central control, and perhaps a tightening of the accountability chain (with Regional Directors accountable to the Chief Executive).

Another instrument of review is the Health (formerly Social Services) Committee, a Select Committee of the House of Commons made up of MPs from government and opposition parties. It hears evidence from departmental officials and also from those working in or concerned with the NHS, and provides critical assessments to the House of Commons. Originally seen by some as a way of giving backbench MPs a minor role in the policy process, Select Committees have grown in influence and do not shirk from criticizing received views nor from adopting cross-party opinions.

As monitoring of central government has grown more rigorous, so has that of the NHS itself. Following the 1982 reorganization, a system of ministerial reviews was set up. Initially, each Regional Chairman was summoned to meet one of the ministers annually. From 1989 this was changed to become a more detailed investigation by the NHSME Chief Executive of the Regional General Manager, assessing the performance of the Region over the last 12 months, comparing it with the objectives that had been agreed, and at the same time examining the plans and the resources likely to be available for the coming year. This review was confirmed formally in a letter to the Regional General Manager, which effectively became a contract for Regional performance. As well as these links between the centre and the Regions, other meetings were encouraged, such as the so-called 'bilaterals' where, for example, a Regional Director of Finance met with his or her counterpart on the NHSME. The effective abolition of the Regions and the direct accountability of the Regional Directors to the Chief Executive has changed this system of corporate contract review at the regional level. However, for the time being at least, such a system remains in place at the next level down in terms of purchasers – Family Health Service Authorities, District Health Authorities and GP fundholders. These arrangements will be reviewed as part of the legislation formerly abolishing Regions (see above).

There are other ways in which national monitoring of the NHS takes place. The Health Advisory Service (HAS) was set up by Richard Crossman in 1969 following the report on mismanagement and cruelty to mentally handicapped patients at Ely Hospital in Wales [9]. Originally, the HAS operated through four teams, but this has been altered so that reviews of service for mentally handicapped people are now undertaken by the Development Team for the Mentally Handicapped, leaving the HAS to look at services for the elderly, the mentally ill and, more recently, services for abusers of drugs and other substances. HAS reports were initially confidential but are now published. Health authorities are expected to take the recommendations very seriously and to prepare regular reports on their implementation. The membership of HAS teams is drawn from the NHS itself and this factor makes it less easy to disregard their reports.

Another body set up under the 1990 NHS and Community Care Act is the Clinical Standards Advisory Group, whose job is to advise ministers and to make investigations into matters of clinical care. It is not yet clear whether this group will promote specific national clinical standards, and to what degree it may be used by ministers to put pressure on the medical profession. At an individual level, the Health Service Commissioner can act on behalf of those who have not been satisfied with a Health Authority's investigation of their complaint, providing it is not of a purely clinical nature (see Chapter 13).

Successive governments have sought new ways of making the NHS more accountable, and this has brought about its own tensions. At times the NHS has been asked to make inappropriate changes inspired by short-term expedients; but often governments have witnessed the thwarting of their plans for change by the capacity of the NHS to maintain the status quo. Some governments are more prescriptive than others: the 1974–79 Labour Government issued a policy document, *Priorities for Health and Personal Social Services in England*, in 1976 [10], whereas the Conservative document, *Care in Action* (1981) [11], was far less specific, allowing health authorities to make their own judgements about priorities. By the late 1980s more detailed schemes were being introduced targeted on such specific problems as breast and cervical cancer screening programmes, waiting-lists and active measures to combat the spread of AIDS. Health authorities are monitored to check that they have implemented the policies, and it has been found, not for the first time, that co-operation in implementing policies can be bought: the NHS is much more likely to accept a change if the directive is accompanied by earmarked funds. The publication of *The Health of the Nation*, in 1991 [12], has further encouraged the NHS to be concerned with promoting health as well as treating sickness (see Chapters 1 and 8).

At the time of each reorganization, the Government has claimed it is delegating more authority down the line. But in 1993 this principle was called into doubt by major scandals in the West Midland and Wessex Regions, where computer procurement had been mismanaged to the extent that many millions of pounds were squandered. Similar scandals in the private sector had led to the setting up of the Cadbury Committee on corporate governance [13]. A Departmental Task Force on this topic culminated in the publication of an

Executive Letter on codes of conduct and accountability [14]. Other guidance was also aimed at improving board performance [15]. Greater delegation also requires more rigorous accountability.

CONCLUSIONS

Throughout the many changes in roles and functions of ministers, the Department, its executive and the intermediate tier of management in the NHS, the key tasks of devising policy, setting and monitoring performance targets and ensuring that an ability exists to influence the organization as a whole have remained, with such control balanced by some process of accountability.

Changes in how and by whom these tasks are performed have arisen for a number of reasons, from straightforward politics to the need to realign functions and roles in the light of other policy changes. The latest set of changes, emerging from the Functions and Manpower Review are the most recent attempts by government to be seen to be readdressing the tendency to promote a top-heavy bureaucracy. But the Review also recognized a real need to re-organize management at the centre so that it is more in tune with the spirit of recent reforms and the actual outcome of these reforms as they have developed.

NOTES

1. DoH (October 1993) *Managing the New NHS*, Department of Health.
2. DoH (January 1989) *Working for Patients*, HMSO, London (Cm. 555).
3. DoH (February 1991) *A Review of the Functions and Organisation of the Management Executive*, NHSME.
4. DoH (1990) *Functions and Structure of the Department of Health* (Gwynn Report).
5. Ministry of Health, Central Health Services Council (1954) *Report of the Committee on the Internal Administration of Hospitals* (Bradbeer Report), HMSO, London.
6. Ministry of Health, Central Health Services Council (1959) *The Welfare of Children in Hospital* (Platt Report), HMSO, London.
7. DHSS and Welsh Office, Central Health Services Council (1969) *The Functions of the District General Hospital* (Bonham-Carter Report), HMSO, London.
8. Ham, C. The latest Reorganisation of the NHS. *British Medical Journal*, **307**, 1089–90.
9. DHSS (1969) *Report of the Committee of Inquiry into Allegations of Ill-treatment and other Irregularities at the Ely Hospital, Cardiff*, HMSO, London (Cmnd. 3975).
10. DHSS (1976) *Priorities for Health and Personal Social Services in England – a Consultative Document*, HMSO, London.
11. DHSS (1981) *Care in Action – A Handbook of Policies and Priorities for the Health and Social Services in England*, HMSO, London.
12. DoH (1991) *The Health of the Nation*, HMSO, London (Cm. 1523).

13. *The Financial Aspects of Corporate Governance* (Cadbury Report), December 1992, Gee & Co., London.
14. DoH (1994) *Code of Conduct and Code of Accountability* (EL(94)90), Department of Health.
15. Wall, A. (1993) *Healthy NHS Boards*, NAHAT, Birmingham.

4

The Purchasers

Working for Patients has instigated changes to the NHS far more profound than any of the previous managerial reforms. As Chapter 2 indicated, one of the key elements of these changes was the separation of the purchasing of health care from its provision. This chapter looks first at the historical functions of Districts, before examining the changes this separation has brought about for the two sets of public sector purchasers: the Districts and GP fundholders. Chapter 5 then turns to the providers.

THE FUNCTIONS OF THE DISTRICTS

There has always been a tier of management at local level in the NHS. Before 1974, the responsibility for providing care and treatment to patients was shared among three bodies, hospital management committees, local health authorities and executive councils. The 1974 reorganization brought the functions of the first two together through District Management Teams, accountable for the operation of hospital and community care. Planning was the responsibility of the newly formed Area Health Authorities, placed below the Regions in the chain of command, most of whom covered several Districts. This division of labour proved controversial for several reasons, but principally because those providing care locally claimed they were in the best position to be able to plan appropriately for the future of their District.

Following years of difficulty, during which these disputes between Areas and Districts were not fundamentally resolved, Areas were abolished in 1982. Districts became responsible for the planning, development and management of their health services in accordance with national and regional strategic guidelines. Their functions were described in circular HC(81)6 [1] issued in May 1981. Specifically, from April 1982, the new District Management Teams, with their own District Health Authorities, had to make integrated plans for the provision and development of primary care, general hospital services, maternity and child health services; for services for people with mental handicaps and mental illness and for the elderly, who have become the largest single group requiring health care.

What principles underlay the concept of the District? On what basis was it considered necessary to divide the country's total population of over 50 million into smaller groups for the purpose of provision of services? Although the size of these groups reflected the geographical distribution of the population, the main determinant was the number of patients who could be cared for in a single district general hospital (DGH), that is, a hospital capable of dealing with all the common types of specialist cases, including emergencies. The function of the DGH was the subject of the Bonham-Carter report [2] published in 1969. For effective deployment of expert staff, it is now assumed that all major specialties should have at least two consultants so that a continuous service of high standard can be assured. The number of beds is generally around 20–40 per consultant, which in turn supports a district population of a certain size, assuming 3.5 acute beds per 1000 resident population. From practical experience it has been found that a DGH will seldom be optimally effective with less than 400 beds. The clinical catchment area of a DGH often reflects local patterns of health care dating back over a century. These traditional determinants of local communities owe little to more modern administrative boundaries.

The District's resident population is the basis for its financial allocation from Region. From a theoretical point of view, the size of the District should ideally enable efficiency and effectiveness to be optimized. Too small an organization would not be able to employ an adequate range of skilled staff or would be unable to provide continuous staff cover; but too large an organization would become cumbersome to run, and good standards of communication might well be a problem. The majority of Districts serve a population of between 250 000 and 350 000. This supports a DGH of over 600 beds, together with associated hospitals for longer stay or more specialized care.

This size of organization nevertheless requires some subdivision. Following the 1974 reorganization, Sectors were set up to look after parts of each District's services. They were based on institutions, on functions or on care groups, and after 1982 were retitled Units. Whichever organizational design is chosen, some services do not always fit well. So, for instance, the elderly are cared for in parts of several hospitals. If the Unit is organized around them it may prove to be impractical to implement an institutional management model that assumes one manager in charge of a hospital. There is no simple solution to this management problem.

DISTRICTS: 1974–1990

Following the reorganization of 1974, the newly created Districts each set up a District Management Team (DMT) which was collectively responsible to the Area Health Authority (but not to the Area's own Management Team who only had monitoring powers) for the proper running of the District. DMT membership comprised four full-time paid senior staff, the Administrator, the

Nursing Officer, the Treasurer and the Community Physician, plus two other doctors nominated by their professional colleagues, a consultant and a GP. In teaching Districts there was also a representative of the medical school. Neither the Area Authority nor the DMT had any direct control over which doctor was to be put forward or how long they would serve. At Area level, and equal in status to the DMT, the four full-time posts were replicated with the addition of a Works Officer. The 1982 changes removed the Area tier and created District Health Authorities. The chief officers remained the same except that the community physician was now retitled the District Medical Officer.

The 1983 Griffiths report [3] on general management, implemented from late 1984, altered all this and removed the concept of consensus or team management in favour of general management, designating one person to take responsibility for the whole organization. Apart from this overall change in managerial style, Griffiths was conspicuously unspecific about how the management of a District's affairs should be organized. It was up to each DHA, once they had appointed their new District General Manager, to decide how the District should be managed in terms of the number and types of Units and the designation of senior staff. This caused considerable resentment from those staff who found their status reduced. Nurses, who had a DMT member to represent their interests before, now found that the chief nurse was accountable to the District General Manager; within the District there was no guarantee that nurses would be represented at a level higher than the ward or department. Similarly Works Officers who had been members of the Area Management Team were made subordinate to the District General Manager.

The chairman of each Area Health Authority and, after 1982, each District Health Authority, was appointed by the Secretary of State. Governments were repeatedly accused of making overtly political appointments, but most health authorities did not act in a narrowly party political way. Members of some inner-city authorities conducted themselves similarly to local government authorities with party caucuses, but, for the majority of health authorities, debate was usually relatively free of explicit party statements, even, surprisingly, on such subjects as private practice, which contain a strong ideological element. As with many public bodies in the United Kingdom, the selection of a candidate for the post of Chairman of a health authority was done via the semi-secret 'old boy' network, whereby those in influential positions were encouraged to suggest names of suitable individuals. During the 1980s there were attempts to attract people with broader experience, particularly from industry and commerce, instead of relying on the traditional source, the voluntary sector.

The Chairman was paid an honorarium and expected to devote about two days per week to health authority business. As an appointee of the Secretary of State, the chairman was assumed to have accepted that some sort of accountability to the Government of the day was expected; this was challenged by those Districts who refused to concur with government priorities. The manner in which chairmen performed their duties varied considerably. Some were present most days and may have felt more closely affiliated with the officers than with the members, while others attended infrequently, content to let the officers run the District virtually unquestioned and acting only as a nominal bridge between the officers and the Authority members.

The members themselves were selected from nominations received from a variety of sources. Circular HC(80)8 [4] specified that each Authority should include one hospital consultant, one nurse or midwife or health visitor, one GP, one nominee from the Region's medical school, one trade union member nominated from the local trades council, four (or more in certain cases) local authority nominees and seven (or more) generalist members. The total could not exceed 19 members plus the chairman. The consultant and the GP were chosen by their peers. The nurse was not to be a member of the staff of the same DHA; this had been allowed previously and created the anomalous position in which a nurse managerially subordinate to the District Nursing Officer was, as a member of the District Health Authority, the District Nursing Officer's employer.

The Labour Government of 1974 had proposed improving staff representation on health authorities in its paper on democracy in the NHS [5], but the Conservatives, when they returned to power in 1979, decided to reduce anything that could be seen as the beginning of worker control. Circular HC(81)6 [6] specified that a trade union member need not be from a trade union affiliated to the TUC. The District's own staff and full-time trade union officers were barred from Authority membership. This bar did not apply to the consultant member of the District Health Authority, on the grounds that his or her contract was held at Region, so, arguably, the consultant was not an employee of the District in which he or she worked.

Local authority membership was, in practice, subject to some negotiation with the Regions. Large Districts may well have covered more than four county and district councils, who had to agree among themselves who their nominees would be. Unlike other members, these were appointed for a four-year term of office. This difference in status was not seen as particularly significant until 1983, when certain DHAs were rebelling against the manpower cuts and financial limits imposed by the government. It was then noted that Regions could dismiss all members of a recalcitrant DHA, except those from local authorities, who had the statutory right to continue even if the Region were to appoint new members to the other seats.

It was, nevertheless, usual for local authority members to be nominated because they had already had some experience in kindred services, such as social services or education. Regions were obliged to do their utmost to appoint members from a wide cross-section, taking into account gender, age, geographical location and professional and political affiliations. In consequence, though health authorities were labelled undemocratic because their members were not directly elected, they were usually more broadly representative of a community than the elected local authorities. All authorities had some difficulties in obtaining younger members or those from ethnic minority and working class backgrounds.

No rules were laid down for the formation of subcommittees of the authority, whereas the finance subcommittee of the AHA had been required by statute. DHAs were free to arrange their affairs as they thought fit, but Circular HC(81)6 warned against three trends: first, a disproportionate increase in administrative workload and expense; second, an erosion of members' corporate responsibility by giving too much authority to small sub-groups of members; third, secrecy by not discussing matters in public. DHAs were reminded that they were governed by the Public Bodies (Admission to Meetings) Act, 1960.

THE NEW PURCHASERS: DISTRICTS AFTER 1990

These arrangements were superseded by the reforms of *Working for Patients* which changed the functions and constitution of Districts. From 1 April 1991, Districts, and trusts as they gradually gained approval, were completely reconstituted on the model of a management board in industry. No longer was a group of people appointed as the local community's advocates. Instead there are five non-executive members (sometimes called independent executives), up to five executive directors and a chairman.

The criteria for selecting the new non-executives are more to do with business acumen and ability to make sense of complex issues than representing local interests. Despite this, many of the new non-executives still feel that they are also there to endeavour to do the best for their local communities. They are therefore obliged to satisfy government intentions by overseeing an efficient organization, but also to honour the wishes of their local communities.

For the executive directors a similarly paradoxical situation also arises, whereby, as members of the corporate board, they are all of equal status, but in their separate functional roles they are subordinates of the chief executive. These tensions may explain why, in the early years, there have been difficulties with the manner in which some boards conducted themselves: the computer acquisition scandals of the Wessex and West Midlands Regions were compounded by insecure board relationships.

The result of these problems was more investment in board development. For instance, National Association of Health Authorities and Trusts (NAHAT) set up their Centre for Board Development in 1994 aimed at helping non-executives to become more expert. The Secretary of State issued codes of conduct in May 1994, designed to remove any ambiguity about how boards should behave if they were to act as appropriate stewards of public money and advocates for the public interest.

New roles

By April 1994 virtually all Units (just over 95%) had become trusts and Districts ceased to be in charge of the operational aspects of health care. Instead, Districts became responsible for purchasing health care. How have Districts approached the organizational implications of this separation between purchasing and providing? The responsibilities of District purchasers were set out in paragraph 2.11 of the White Paper. They were simply stated as being to ensure that the health needs of a given population were met; that there were effective health promotion and disease prevention policies in place; that the provision of health care was comprehensive; and, finally, that by setting targets and monitoring performance providers would be kept up to the mark.

Needs assessment and priority setting

Crucial to the purchasing role is the contribution from the Director of Public Health (DPH). The reform of public health medicine outlined in the Acheson Report [7] has been of the greatest importance in providing districts with the means to fulfil their obligation to establish the needs of their population. Without sound epidemiological research, no District can hope to have more than a subjective and selective view of needs. The special pleading of doctors and other professionals is no substitute for an objective assessment of needs. Public demand, often excited by media coverage, may exaggerate the priority of a particular aspect of health care, forcing other, and greater, needs to struggle for recognition.

Under the new arrangements each Director of Public Health is expected to produce an Annual Report which is an independent assessment of the health of the District. From this, the District can decide what the pattern of health care should be for the ensuing year. Approaching health needs in this way, not blinkered by the constraints of limited resources, is meant to lead to a more proactive approach. It is intended that more confident plans for health promotion and disease prevention will arise because the Districts are less embroiled in the day-to-day business of providing patient care.

Governments have found that too many national initiatives have not proceeded much beyond the status of symbolic statement as long as little or no extra funds have been allocated to back up the policies. In cases where publicity has exposed the heart disease statistics, increasing infection rates from bad hygiene, the causal relationship between life style and particular diseases, for example, governments have found it politically expedient to earmark funds to force Districts to establish particular programmes of health promotion. Government reaction to international calls to take the threat of AIDS seriously has, by funding a major campaign of public education, undoubtedly helped to increase public awareness.

In practice, the impact and influence of the needs assessment process on the priorities and purchasing decisions of Districts has been limited [8] (see Chapter 2). There are a number of reasons for this. First, Districts have been under enormous time pressures to complete their annual contracting rounds and because it takes time to carry out properly informed needs assessments, this has caused many public health departments to lag behind. Secondly, Districts have run into problems concerning the paucity of epidemiological and medical information required to do needs assessments. One response to this by the

Department of Health has been to sponsor research in this area [9]. Thirdly, there is the problem of reconciling the results of needs assessments with budgetary limitations in order to produce a set of actual purchasing priorities. Although a needs assessment may reveal a 'need' for medical care and treatment, it does not (and cannot) reveal anything about whether one particular need should be met in preference to another. Districts have explored concepts such as health gain [10] and the use of outcome measures such as the quality adjusted life year (QALY) [11] as methods for setting priorities, but so far their use is very limited [12].

Purchaser power

A potential danger foreseen by critics of the purchaser/ provider separation was that Districts would be unable to ensure continuity of access to a proper range of health care and treatment for their population. It was feared that providers might be able to insist on dictating what they were able to supply, rather than striving to provide what the purchasers said was wanted. The analogy of a commercial supplier dictating to its customers was cited. Districts should be able to ensure through their purchasing powers that reasonably comprehensive services are still accessible to patients because, in setting the provider targets through contracts, the District has an important strength – it can buy the services from whichever provider is prepared to make them available.

In terms of the market environment, the power of purchasers to influence uncooperative providers rests ultimately on the sanction of moving their contracts elsewhere. In other words, without this choice purchasers would be 'captured' by their providers and their influence would be much reduced. Nevertheless, in practice, except for some urban areas, purchasers have comparatively little choice of providers (and vice versa) [14]. The extent of purchasers' influence has thus been somewhat limited. For over forty years the NHS has planned its services in a way that – for good reasons of non-duplication and efficiency – has minimized this sort of choice. Moreover, one of the main reasons Districts give for choosing the providers they do is proximity to their local populations, because geographical access is important [13].

Professional advice and accountability

Working for Patients emphasized the importance of professional advice other than that provided by the Director of Public Health. Apart from the obvious common sense requirement for expert opinion to be sought, this was the Government's answer to the criticism that the reforms prevented doctors and nurses from being members of their own health authorities. Schedule 1 of the 1990 Act stipulates that they can only be part of the new DHA if they are appointed as one of the executive members, composed of 'the chief officer and the chief finance officer' and up to three others (the rules for FHSAs are slightly different: see Chapter 5). The issue of professional advice (particularly medical advice) is very important for Districts as its absence can again lead to 'provider capture', whereby the District's providers become the purchaser's professional advisers, if not directly, then by default. Although, as ministers and others, such as the Audit Commission, have urged, purchasers and providers need to work together [15], there is also a need to maintain a degree of independence and to have access to independent advice if Districts are to make effective purchasing decisions.

After several hints that the Government, irritated by the attitude of some Community Health Councils (CHCs), would do away with this channel of public representation (see Chapter 13), the CHCs nevertheless continue to be held responsible for voicing the view of the District's public in general. With their wider membership, they may well prove to be more capable than in the past of holding the new DHAs to account. Previously, the authorities were disinclined to acknowledge the influence of CHCs: they preferred to identify themselves rather than the CHCs as the 'true' voice of the public.

The new DHAs have had to examine their internal relationships in order to ensure that there is a sensible separation of roles between the executives, who were previously used to being accountable to the Authority, and the non-executives, who are loosely described as responsible for strategy. The manner in which individual Districts have organized their work varies, and the Department of Health has given little advice apart from such obvious points as the importance of conducting business in public [16]. One difficulty that is a consequence of the small total membership of the new Districts is how to cover all necessary responsibilities without overworking the non-executive members, who are expected to set aside only about 20 days a year for this. The 1990 Act, therefore, allows other people to be given delegated authority, for instance to manage the administration of the Mental Health Act 1983, which requires Authority members to act as 'Hospital Managers' to review seclusion orders of individual patients and other matters. Panels to hear complaints of aggrieved staff who have suffered from some disciplinary action or who are, in their own opinion, undergraded, also need to be set up. There is usually no payment for these tasks, although expenses are reimbursed.

Some Districts have a range of directorates where not all directors have Authority membership, while others have preferred to group all the functions under directors on the Authority. The Act lays down that officers, other than the Chief Executive and Chief Finance Officer, are directors first and DHA executive members second. This means that if they lose their seat on the DHA they can still continue in their job. The tenure for officers is not prescribed, unlike their non-executive colleagues, who may only serve for up to four years at a time but are eligible for re-election.

Contracting

Of all the responsibilities each District has to cover, drawing up service agreements or contracts is crucial. The 1990 Act made it clear that these contracts were not to be seen as legally binding and, for this reason, the term 'service agreement' might have been a better description of what was intended; nevertheless the term 'contract' seems to have stuck. It became clear from early experience that specifying very detailed contracts would strain most Districts' information and financial resources beyond their limits. Initially, therefore, contracts aimed at agreeing with a provider an overall cost for a given volume of work within identified quality and other standards. To prepare such contracts, Districts must possess adequate information and financial expertise. These two major functions are led by directors. Setting the standards and monitoring performance against contract are essential further tasks.

Early evidence from the first two years of the reforms shows that there has been some change in the type of contracts agreed between Districts and their providers, towards more sophisticated forms and greater attention to the analysis of financial and other risks involved [17] (see page 39).

The evolution of the new Districts has taken time. While the strategic aspect of their role is clear, other aspects have been more difficult to disentangle from the previous arrangements. Districts with around 60 staff now have little need for personnel and estate managers. New skills are required in specifying, pricing and negotiating contracts and then ensuring that providers comply with them. Deciding which type of contract will result in the best value has been difficult. Block contracts are crude but simple; cost and volume contracts are more likely to secure specific activity targets; cost per case contracts may be needed for a few high-cost patients [18]. Detailed reports are still required by the Regions, and the maintenance of a sound information base has proved difficult because some trusts are reluctant to produce the data.

A new map of the country

A significant managerial and organizational change for Districts since 1991 (which was referred to in Chapter 2) has been the merging of Districts, creating much larger purchasing organizations. Such mergers were not part of the original reforms, but have since been taken on and actively promoted by the Department of Health. Following the Functions and Manpower Review (see Chapter 3), the Department has encouraged the merger of Districts and Family Health Service Authorities (FHSAs) and is drawing up the necessary enabling legislation. In the mean time, Districts and FHSAs are already realigning their boundaries and appointing single chief executives in charge of the FHSA and associated District(s). By 1996 the number of Districts will have fallen to around 90 in England (matching the number of FHSAs) from a total of 192 before the reforms.

For the Department of Health, one reason for these mergers is the wish to have a single authority at local level with responsibility for implementing national health policy. Moreover, with changes in the types of care that will be required in the future and the need for a more integrated purchasing strategy crossing primary and secondary care boundaries, separate organizations at local level become increasingly redundant. For Districts and FHSAs themselves, mergers may also bring economies of scale, concentrating scarce resources such as in public health services.

THE NEW PURCHASERS: GP FUNDHOLDERS

Apart from reconstructing Districts as purchasers of health care on behalf of their populations, *Working for Patients* also created a completely new breed of public sector purchaser: the GP fundholder. The idea of GP-based purchasing was originally proposed by Alan Maynard, Professor of Economics at the University of York, as a British version of the American health maintenance organization (HMO) [19] – which was Alain Enthoven's preferred model (see Chapter 2). The actual scheme to emerge from the reforms initially invited large GP practices (with over 11 000 patients) to apply to hold and manage a budget designed to buy a limited range of in-patient, day-case, out-patient and diagnostic services for the patients on their lists. GP fundholders' budgets also covered pharmaceuticals prescribed by the practices and the costs of staff employed. Although each of these budgets was calculated separately, they were pooled, and savings in one could be used to spend more in another. Budgets for fundholders are deducted from the local District allocation. In general, budgets were held by FHSAs and calculated to cover non-emergency care only and there was a limit of £5000 on the total amount a practice could spend on any one episode of care for a particular patient. Patients whose care cost more were paid for by the local District Health Authority.

Regions were given the task of screening practices who applied for budgets, and assessed practices in terms of managerial and technical skills and also commitment to the scheme. GP fundholders were restricted in the way they could spend their budgets – in particular, the budget could not be used simply to increase GPs' own incomes nor to benefit the practice generally.

The reasons *Working for Patients* put forward for setting up the scheme included the argument that hospitals and their consultants needed a stronger (financial) incentive to look upon GPs as people whose confidence they must gain if patients were to be referred to them. The White Paper also argued that GPs themselves needed stronger incentives to offer patients a choice of hospital. Finally, the White Paper stated that GPs who referred patients to a hospital not covered by a contract arranged by the GP's local District could cause financial problems for the hospital (Districts may refuse to pay for such an extra contractual referral) or to the local District (if they did agree to pay).

In the first year of the scheme in 1991 (the qualifying list size having been

Table 4.1 The population in GP fundholding practices, by Region, 1993

	% Total
Mersey	35
Oxford	33
Wessex	33
Yorkshire	33
Trent	31
North West Thames	27
West Midlands	26
East Anglian	25
Northern	25
South West Thames	25
South East Thames	22
South Western	19
North Western	17
North East Thames	14

Source: Glennerster, H. *et al.* (1994) *GP Fundholding: Wild Card or Winning Hand?* in Robinson, R. and Le Grand, J. (eds) *Evaluating the NHS Reforms*, King's Fund Institute, London.

reduced to 9000), around 7% of the population was covered. In the second year this doubled, and by the third year (the list size criterion having been reduced again to 7000) over a quarter of the population was covered by fundholders. Table 4.1 shows the geographical spread of fundholding by region in 1993.

Although the coverage of fundholding in population terms has been quite high, even if everyone were registered with a fundholding practice this would only mean that fundholders controlled about 15% of the hospital budget [20]. Moreover, as Table 4.1 shows, the spread of fundholding has been uneven; but it has also been uneven within regions with a definite bias towards well-off suburban areas of the country.

Developments in fundholding

Since the fundholding scheme was first introduced there have been a number of changes, apart from the reduction in qualifying list sizes. From April 1993 the range of services fundholders were allowed to buy was expanded to include community services, district nursing, health visiting and other services such as mental health counselling and services for people with learning difficulties. Terminal care, maternity and emergency treatment remained outside the scheme and the £5000 limit – designed to protect budgets from unexpectedly large claims – also remained.

Other changes and developments also took place. Small practices, with list sizes below the minimum required to join the scheme, had at the outset been allowed to combine with other practices to overcome this. Over recent years there has been a growth in practices joining together in loose alliances for other reasons. Known as multifunds and consisting of up to 70 GPs, a number of these groups have been established around the country and have employed their own management staff (often recruited from Districts). One of the advantages multifunds claim to possess is the extra purchasing leverage they can wield over providers. In the first year of the reforms, many providers did not pay much attention to their fundholder purchasers: providers merely assumed fundholders would fit in with their local District's block contracts. Multifunds also allowed GPs to act separately as individual practices if they wanted. The funds have also potentially given participating practices savings through economies of scale (reducing time spent on contracting for example).

Districts have also been prompted, partly by the fundholding initiative and partly by their dependence on GPs in general as referral agents (who have the potential power to upset Districts' contracting arrangements), to explore new models of purchasing, involving GPs more closely in purchasing decisions. Virtually all Districts now have a much closer partnership with their local GPs, and many have taken this to the point of effective devolution of parts of their allocations to GPs.

In 1994 another development in fundholding took place – the creation of total fundholding. One example of this occurred in Bromsgrove, in the West Midlands. Four GP fundholder practices combined to take on the complete health care budget for the patients on their lists and responsibilities for national policies such as the waiting-times initiative and the *Patient's Charter*. This experiment was a local initiative, although it received enthusiastic backing from the local Region and the Department of Health. It is unlikely that this extension of the scheme will be the way forward for the whole of the country as there were particular circumstances in Bromsgrove which precipitated this move.

There are doubts among fundholders themselves about the original fundholding scheme, which suggests that there will be limits to its implementation. A survey in December 1993 revealed that over half of all GPs who became fundholders in 1992 and 1993 paradoxically did not support the scheme, and among non-fundholders, ethical objections cause over 80% to be against fundholding [21].

Two controversial issues associated with fundholding are as yet unresolved. The first concerns the method (or lack of it) for calculating fundholders' budgets. District allocations (from which fundholders' budgets are deducted) are based on a formula reflecting each District's population and weighted for factors affecting the need for health care services (principally an age-standardized death rate as a proxy for need). However, fundholder budgets were originally based on past referral patterns (often derived from data held by the GPs themselves). There was some evidence that, in their negotiations with Regions, many GPs were successful in securing larger budgets than their referral patterns suggested they needed. There was undoubtedly a political imperative to get the scheme going and so Regions were less likely to argue too much over budgets. However, as budgets were deducted from District allocations, health authorities took a dim view of fundholders receiving more than their share, and argued for an allocation formula similar to their own. As yet no national formula has been devised. One of the main problems is constructing a population and mortality database which ties in with practice populations, in order to use a formula similar to that used for Districts.

The second issue concerns fundholders' ability to secure better services for their patients compared with non-fundholders and Districts in general. Such inequality has always been a feature of the NHS, despite its universal coverage (see Chapter 14). Fundholders were not, in general, against greater inequity for, they argued, the whole point of fundholding was to improve services for patients. Fundholders also argued that, in fact, many of the improvements they secured – speedier laboratory test results, for example – became available to all patients in a District. The fact that many fundholders also secured shorter waiting-times for their patients (against BMA advice) tended to be less well advertised.

Clearly, devolving budgets to GPs has empowered them to do good things for their patients, and there is much evidence to show that fundholders have caused their hospital-based colleagues to take a new interest in the demands of GPs and of their patients. The equity implications associated with fundholding are nevertheless important, although how important depends on a judgement about the value attached to the distribution of health care among local populations compared with the gain in total health care provision (that is, efficiency).

CONCLUSION

The new purchasers in the NHS – Districts and GP fundholders – experience a very steep learning curve as they get to grips with their new roles and responsibilities. Although there has been some competition between these two categories of purchaser, together with unresolved issues concerning, for example, fundholder budget levels, there have also been interesting developments in collaborative purchasing and a new resurgence of the importance of the role played by GPs in general. It is also clear that the reorganization in Districts is not complete and that developments in their functions and their organization, given their merger with FHSAs, are set to continue.

NOTES

1. DHSS (May 1981) Circular HC(81)6 *Membership of Health Authorities.*
2. DHSS and Welsh Office (1969) The Functions of the District General Hospital (Bonham-Carter Report), HMSO, London.
3. DHSS (October 1983) The NHS Management Inquiry (Griffiths Report), HMSO, London.
4. DHSS (July 1980) Circular HC(80)8, *Health Service Development Structure and Management.*
5. DHSS (1974) *Democracy in the National Health Service: Membership of Health Authorities,* HMSO, London.
6. Op. cit., HC(81)6.
7. DoH (January 1988) *Public Health in England* (Acheson Report), HMSO, London (Cm. 289).
8. Appleby, J. *et al.* (1994) *Monitoring Managed Competition* in, Robinson, R. and Le Grand, J. (eds) *Evaluating the NHS Reforms* King's Fund Institute, London.
9. For example, the Department of Health has sponsored the Clearing House on Health Outcomes at the University of Leeds and the production of Effective Health Care Bulletins which draw together medical and economic effectiveness data on specific diseases.
10. 'Health gain' refers to the notion that the job of health services is to add 'years to life and life to years'. In other words, health care is about extending the length of life and the quality of life.
11. 'QALYs' (quality adjusted life years) are one generic measure of the outcome of medical intervention. They combine length of life with quality of life into one index, and have been used as a way of ranking health services on the basis of the cost needed to produce one QALY from different treatments.
12. Robinson, R. and New, B. (1992) Health economics and economists in the NHS. Letter, *British Medical Journal,* **305,** 1361.
13. Empirical evidence of the degree of competition between providers in the NHS is virtually non-existent. However, an index of competition (the Hirschman–Herfindahl index) used in the US to assess whether businesses (including hospitals) are monopolies and thus potentially subject to investigation by the US Department of Justice as part of its anti-trust (monopoly) work, has been applied in the UK (see note 8 for reference).
14. Op. cit., Appleby *et al.*.
15. Audit Commission (1994) *Trusting in the Future: Towards an Audit Agenda for NHS Providers,* HMSO, London.
16. DoH Executive Letter EL(90)155 *Guidance on the Meetings and Proceedings of NHS Authorities, 27 July 1990.* See also Statutory Instrument, SI 1990 No. 1331 for other regulations regarding the new health authorities.
17. Op. cit., Appleby *et al.*.
18. 'Block' contracts define a service to be provided, for example accident and emergency, to a local population for a certain cost; 'cost and volume' contracts tend to be more specific, setting out details of how many patients are to be treated for a certain cost; 'cost per case' contracts, as the term implies, set out an individual price for a specific patient or procedure. In practice, contracts do not always easily fit these definitions and, over recent years, purchasers and providers have refined the

'contract currency' from a whole service or patient group to packages of care which can cut across traditional definitions of specialties.

19. See, for example, Maynard, A. (1986) Performance incentives in general practice, in Teeling-Smith, G. *Health Education and General Practice*, Office of Health Economics, London.
20. Glennerster, H. *et al.* (1994) *GP Fundholding: Wild Card or Winning Hand?* in Robinson, R. and Le Grand, J. (eds) *Evaluating the NHS Reforms*, King's Fund Institute, London.
21. Your concerns: the fund and the future. *Fundholding*, 7 December, 1993.

5

The providers

The new arrangements and organization of the purchaser side of the market introduced by the 1990 NHS and Community Care Act the history of district health authorities and their development up to their merger with Family Health Service Authorities were covered in Chapter 4. This chapter examines the other side of the market, the providers of primary and secondary care and the role and functions of the Family Health Service Authorities.

HOSPITALS

Only in the twentieth century have hospitals have come to be seen as the most important element of health care. Their continuing dominance is less certain as medical advances and economic pressures shift the principal setting of care back to the community. The history of hospital-based care can be traced back centuries – the first recorded general hospital was St Peter's in York, founded by the Saxon king Athelstand. In 1994 St Bartholomew's, London, founded by the monk Rahere in 1123, was under threat of closure. By the beginning of the eighteenth century, apart from Barts, London contained seven general hospitals with 2000 beds in all – as many as the total in the rest of the country and representing one bed per 5000 of the population [1].

An important role of most hospitals in the eighteenth and nineteenth centuries was not only, as Florence Nightingale put it '[that] they should do the sick no harm' [2] but also to provide medical care and treatment to the poor. Many hospitals in the eighteenth century were founded as charities for this purpose, while the rich employed their own private medical advisors. Many of these physicians and surgeons also provided their services to charitable hospitals for little or no remuneration. The origins of many of the duties and roles of doctors in hospitals today are to be found in the way hospitals organized themselves in the eighteenth century. For example, at St Thomas' Hospital in London, in 1760, senior doctors were required to carry out a ward round twice a week, while assistant physicians had to attend wards three times a week, run out-patient clinics and generally fill in when their seniors were absent [3].

By the middle of the nineteenth century the number of beds in England and Wales had grown to over 7500 and advances in scientific medical knowledge were stimulating larger numbers of beds and hospitals.

Over time, hospitals (rather than the universities) also became centres for medical teaching and research, giving doctors a more central role. The medical hierarchy increasingly reflected the higher status of hospital practice. Up to the First World War, existing hospitals expanded with the growth in medical knowledge; 'cottage' hospitals flourished and doctors established new, specialist hospitals. By the Second World War, a great variety of different organizations and agencies were running, funding and maintaining a great diversity of institutions. There were about 3000 hospitals in England and Wales in 1939, with about 500 000 beds. About a third of hospitals were voluntary foundations and the rest were run by local authorities. A number of government and independent reports on the state of the country's health services (particularly the hospital sector) between 1900 and 1946 pointed to the need for improvements. The Nuffield Provincial Hospital Trust report of 1946 revealed that many hospitals were over 50 years old, with quite a number being over a century old. The Nuffield report concluded that hospital services were failing the public in terms of the quality of care that was medically possible [4].

Following the establishment of the NHS in 1948 and the enormous cost pressures that quickly became apparent, the Conservative Government of 1951 appointed Claude Guillebaud, a Cambridge economist, to investigate the costs of the service. It hoped he would recommend ways to cut costs and make the NHS, particularly the hospital sector, more efficient. In fact the Guillebaud report [5] could find little room for efficiency improvements, pointing out that, in terms of its share of national income, spending on the NHS had actually fallen, while the service had, at the same time, made enormous strides in the quality of provision of care. One area selected for some criticism again was the quality of hospital buildings, and Guilleband recommended trebling the capital allocation to the NHS – although this was not accepted by the Government.

It was not until 1962, when the Minister of Health, Enoch Powell, announced the *Hospital Plan for England and Wales* [6], that a concerted attempt was made to improve the physical state of hospitals in the NHS. The Plan was ambitious, hoping to replace around a quarter of the then 2800 hospitals over a 13-year period. The Plan proposed a network of district general hospitals (DGHs) of around 600 to 800 beds serving populations of about 125 000. The services to be provided by DGHs would cover acute care as well as maternity care, with accident and emergency units being located in DGHs on a regional basis. In the event, the Plan was not fully implemented. However, it did establish a new pattern of hospital services which largely survives today. Figures 5.1 and 5.2 show how the numbers of hospitals and beds have changed in recent times.

The creation of the NHS took over the management of all but a few private hospitals. The introduction of the Griffiths general management approach in the mid-1980s created new arrangements within districts. The reforms of the

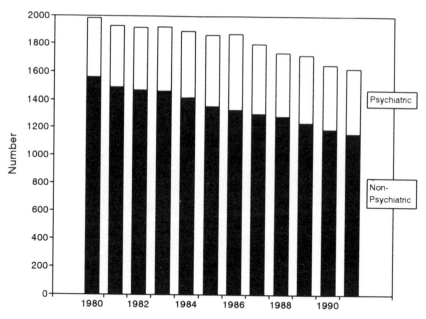

Figure 5.1 Numbers of psychiatric and non-psychiatric hospitals in England: 1980–1991.

Source: NAHAT (1994) *NHS Handbook*, 9th edn, NAHAT, Birmingham.

1990 NHS and Community Care Act introduced further changes to affect the hospital sector in the NHS, disengaging them financially and managerially from their local District Health Authorities. Before the 1990 Act, hospital and community units were clearly subordinate to the district, with unit General Managers (UGMs) accountable to the District General Manager (DGM). After the Act was implemented this arrangement altered, so that districts became purchasers and Units became providers in a more equal relationship. Abolishing directly managed Units and giving trusts their own boards of management has now completed the separation.

TRUSTS

The idea of independent trusts probably prompted more attention than any other element in the White Paper *Working for Patients*. To opponents of the Government, trusts were clear evidence of privatization. Despite the Secretary of State's constant rejection of this claim, opponents of the trusts continued to stress this. In fact, trusts are independent, non-governmental organizations which have taken on assets previously held by the state and for which they must make an annual repayment (although the timing can be varied at the discretion of the Department of Health). Managerially, all trusts are accountable to the Secretary

The providers

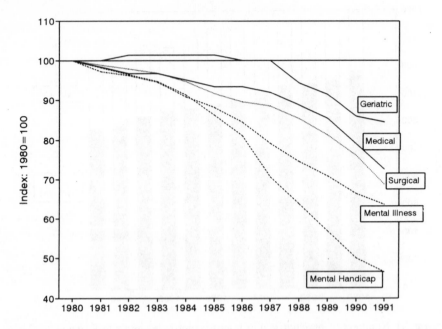

Figure 5.2 Beds in UK hospitals by type: changes in numbers between 1980 and 1991.
Source: NAHAT (1994) *NHS Handbook*, 9th edn, NAHAT, Birmingham.

of State, and the Regional Offices (now incorporating the former Regional
Outposts – see Chapter 3) act as monitoring organizations on behalf of the
Secretary of State. As with the confusion over the exact nomenclature for describing the internal market, to call trusts privatized organizations is not entirely true,
but neither are trusts wholly inside the NHS, as their predecessors, Units, were.

The first wave of trusts (those created in the first year of the reforms, 1991)
excited a great deal of interest, but, in the end, only 57 applications were
approved, mostly from District General Hospitals. By the autumn of 1990 it
was becoming clear that the split between purchaser and provider could only
be achieved by a more obvious separation of duties between Districts and Units.
For this reason the second wave of applications for self-governing status was
substantially larger, and by 1994 around 95% of all Units had become trusts.

Becoming self-governing had other attractions, not least the promise of some
degree of freedom in handling money and developing capital schemes. The
collapse of the property market in 1990 had a devastating effect on the NHS
capital building programme, and led to Regions imposing extreme measures
which were often unfair to individual Districts and Units. Under the rules of
self-governance, each trust is free of this sort of central control, and, although
they cannot escape the disciplines of financial reality – including the rate of
return they must make on their assets (6%), capital spending controls imposed
by the Department through 'external financing limits' [7] and the need to break
even financially – local autonomy is still more attractive.

But, along with autonomy and freedom comes responsibility and, in the context of the new health care market, uncertainty. If a trust does not secure sufficient contracts to maintain its organization, it will fail and have to be annexed to another trust. It is not clear what the most likely route to success is. Very small trusts will be burdened by excessive overheads, but too large an organization might not be able to benefit from the local autonomy which is regarded as their *raison d'être*. The potential for improved efficiency and value for money through competition works only as long as patients choose or agree to be moved from one provider to another and, in theory, as long as it is understood that market failure can lead to closure. Hypothetically, a trust would have to close if it were not competing effectively. A prime example of this – euphemistically dubbed by economists as 'market exit' – has been the changes in London's health services (see Chapter 2). But similar rationalizations have occurred all over the country as purchasers realign their contract portfolios and hospitals are forced to merge or restructure themselves as 'community hospitals'.

To critics, trusts may be no more than an ideologically inspired idea with limited potential for improving performance. Proponents argue that trusts release purchasing managers from day-to-day managerial issues, enabling them to concentrate instead on health care choices for the district's population. In terms of the performance of trusts, direct evidence is poor and confusing. Although first wave trusts appeared to do better than others in terms of increases in the number of patients they treated, in many ways this first group of trusts were special, having been self-selected and having operated in a very tightly controlled market. Some research has suggested that the microeconomic conditions theoretically necessary to make the market in which trusts operate work are generally in place in the NHS market and that therefore at some stage improvements in efficiency should occur although there are concerns about equity [8].

Clinical involvement in management

The 1990 reforms brought about important changes in nurse and medical management. For nurses, the further undermining of their status caused by the introduction of general management in 1984 continued (see Chapter 10). Under the new arrangements each trust must have a nursing organization capable of deploying nurses effectively, in line with the standards laid down locally by purchasers and nationally by the United Kingdom Central Council for Nursing, Midwifery and Health Visiting (UKCC). Within the trust, therefore, nurses are usually grouped in relation to clinical practice so as to maximize their expertise in the various specialities, medicine, surgery, gynaecology, paediatrics and so on. Nurses also have a role in quality assurance, using their knowledge of patient care to raise standards.

The attempts to involve doctors in decision making, which had worked somewhat spasmodically through the 'Cogwheel' system of clinical committees [9] (see Chapter 9) and through membership of management teams and of the health authorities themselves, were brought into focus, with proposals that forced them to behave more consciously as the key managers of health care resources. A consequence of the increased involvement of doctors in management is the risk of threatening the professional status of nurses and therapists with whom they work. *Working for Patients* stressed that it was important to ensure that doctors were properly accountable for the consequences of their clinical decisions. This meant that they should no longer continue to treat patients with little regard for financial and other resource consequences. Two measures were suggested: medical audit, to look more closely at outcomes, and the creation of clinical directors to head teams in each main clinical speciality.

Within one large trust there may be over a dozen such clinical directorates, accountable to the trust Chief Executive for the proper management of patient care within allocated resources [10]. This managerial responsibility also encompasses the task of getting agreement to protocols aimed at increasing the effectiveness of the clinical care of patients. The implications of this way of working may be threatening to those other professions who have long sought to free themselves from being seen as the servants of doctors and have demanded a more equal partnership. Some clinical directors insist upon complete control of the staff within their directorate. This may lead to tight management, but could also decrease the mobility of staff within a hospital, which may be desirable for training and experience purposes or simply in order to make the best use of limited resources. It is unlikely that the clinical directors really have the time to undertake the full managerial function: they need support from a business manager to ensure they do not neglect essential clinical work. However, clinical directors do provide incentives to small teams to bring about change and introduce new ideas, particularly if they release resources for the directorate itself to redeploy.

THE AMBULANCE SERVICE

Before 1974 the ambulance service was run by 142 local health authorities (not every health authority ran its own). In 1974 the service was transferred to the new AHAs, with the exception of London, where the South West Thames Region ran (and continues to run) the service for the whole of the capital, and the six metropolitan counties where the service was run by the appropriate Regional Health Authority. During the 1970s and 1980s, the demand for ambulance transport rose with the ever-increasing numbers of patients, and also partly because of the worsening availability of rural public transport. There has been a continuing debate about whether the emergency service should be separated from other ambulances, particularly as it represents less than 15% of the total number of journeys. A DHSS working party [11] set up in 1980 under the chairmanship of Maurice Naylor, the outgoing administrator of the Trent Region, rejected the idea of a two-tiered service, with the possible exception of metropolitan areas, but suggested more could be done to create community transport for those in need, and that this might be a suitable project for collaboration with local authorities. The Naylor report was critical of the lack of good management and financial information, and recommended that the Steering Group on Health Services Information (the Körner Committee) should examine this. The Körner report on patient transport [12] was published in 1983, recommending a more comprehensive collection of operational statistics.

The Naylor report had also emphasized the need for greater operational efficiency, and, by 1990, the number of separate ambulance services in England had been reduced to 45, with nine in Wales and only one in Scotland. Training of ambulance personnel was gradually improved, and this increase in professional expertise was a major issue in the long and damaging pay dispute which, in 1989, after months of industrial action, had failed to convince the Government that ambulance staff deserved to be treated comparably with other emergency service personnel, firemen and the police. The separation of emergency work from the rest of the ambulance service is seen by some as the way to help improve the pay prospects of at least the more highly trained staff. A National Audit Office Report [13] in 1990 found that there was still room for increased efficiency through greater computerization, leading to a better scheduling of work and revised response times. In some cases a helicopter service could overcome traffic congestion; this in turn could produce cost savings.

The 1990 NHS Act allowed ambulance services to apply for trust status and by 1994 all had become trusts.

THE FAMILY HEALTH SERVICES

General practice in the United Kingdom is a unique phenomenon. In most other countries doctors are specialists who have access to hospitals to investigate and treat their own patients. In this country, most general practice work takes place in the GPs' own surgeries or from health authority owned health centres, although a few general practitioners have direct admitting rights to their own beds in community hospitals, and some may also hold contracts with the local trust to enable them to work as clinical assistants to a hospital consultant.

General practice up to 1990

Doctors initially all worked in the community as generalists until the nineteenth century, when the development of hospitals encouraged increasing specialization. The professional status of general practice suffered from the rise of hospital medicine, although the public's image of the GP as family friend and counsellor remained strong. Older people still recall, accurately or otherwise, the days when the family GP was constantly available and on call, when locums (temporary deputies) were unheard of, when a request for a home visit was not contested by the GP's receptionist but willingly accepted. The GPs claim a less rosy picture of the past and draw attention to the gradual decline in their professional esteem and their diminishing earning power. By the mid-1960s, GPs were so dissatisfied that only a major initiative by the Minister of Health, Kenneth Robinson, saved the NHS from GPs' mass resignations. Since then, they feel general practice has become recognized as a worthwhile alternative to hospital medicine. In terms of earning power, the GP can now reach his or her optimum salary much sooner than a hospital doctor whose training may require up to fifteen years to reach consultant status.

The organization of general practice was haphazard during the first part of the twentieth century. In 1920, the Dawson Report [14], still quoted with approval by today's advocates of state-controlled medical care, proposed that GPs should work from health centres, which would also be centres of primary health care. The 1948 Labour Government continued to support this idea. In some counties, such as Devon, good progress was made in setting up health centres. Elsewhere, GPs showed a reluctance to operate from state-owned premises, fearing that this would compromise their independence. The policy is now so far advanced that health authorities are selling off health centres to the GPs who practise in them. The idea of an integrated primary health care team is as strong as ever, however, and is at the heart of the most recent reforms in general practice.

The 1946 NHS Act missed the opportunity to integrate the management of the three arms of the health services: it established administrative bodies called Executive Councils to look after general practice and the regulation of retail pharmaceutical services, opticians and general dental practitioners. As far as GPs were concerned, this separation from the hospital services was necessary for them to retain their professional autonomy: they were strenuously opposed to being made employees of the health service. The principle of being contracted by, rather than employed by, a health authority has remained central for them. Consultants had accepted employee status in 1948, but until 1990 had successfully resisted local controls.

Executive Councils were renamed Family Practitioner Committees (FPCs) in 1974. They were usually coterminous with Area Health Authorities and thus with the non-metropolitan county or metropolitan district council boundary. With the disbanding of the AHAs in 1982, because the FPCs did not match District boundaries, there was less encouragement for joint working. This became a significant issue in 1990, when Family Health Services Authorities (FHSAs), successors to the FPCs, were given a greater role in planning. In 1974, of the 90 FPCs in England, 60 related to one or two Districts, 17 to three Districts, seven to four Districts and, in six instances, the FPCs had to cope with five or more Districts. This uneven organizational basis emphasized the separate position of FPCs in relation to Districts, and there were few efforts to overcome the administrative obstacles in order to work together to improve primary care.

The membership of FPCs included equal numbers of professional and lay people. Of the 15 lay members, one had to be a nurse, four each from health and local authorities and the rest from the local community. A survey published in 1985 demonstrated that middle-class people, lawyers, accountants, company directors, teachers and personnel experts, predominated over those from other backgrounds. Drawing recruits from a relatively narrow social band is typical of the public services, and illustrates the relative ease with which those individuals can arrange time off work to undertake these duties. There were eight medical members, who could include GPs working in the FPC's own area, three dentists, two pharmacists and two opticians. The professional members of the FPCs probably shared many of the social values of the lay representatives, so criticism that FPCs were dominated by professional interests was difficult to refute. It was evident in the strict procedural rules for a patient making a complaint, for instance; FPCs were repeatedly and justifiably criticized for being insensitive to their consumers. This explains the considerable emphasis on consumers' needs found in the subsequent reforms.

From 1974 to 1982, the FPCs were an administrative division of the Area Health Authorities, although the retention of their own committee enabled them to preserve their much-guarded autonomy. Following the disbanding of the Areas, they were briefly made accountable to a designated District, but from 1 April 1985, under the Health and Social Security Act, 1984, they became wholly independent. The membership categories remained the same until their reconstitution as FHSAs in September 1990.

Over the years, the organization of general practice has changed considerably. GPs have increasingly grouped together, instead of practising alone, not only to reduce the burden of constantly being on call, but also to benefit from the advantages of a larger organization which can command attached staff, better administrative support and more modern premises. In 1967 there were 4406 GPs in single-handed practice, but 20 years later this had diminished to 2875. Correspondingly, practices with six or more doctors had grown from 736 in 1967 to 5002 in 1987. In the same period, the total number of GPs in England and Wales has increased from 20 260 to 27 023. By 1992 the number of GPs had reached 30 020, reducing the number of patients on each doctor's list; the average is now under 2000. In theory, the smaller the list, the more time the doctor can spend with each patient. But this has to be set against the amount of time the GP spends at work; the average length of the GP's working week has shortened substantially, much as it has for most other people in the last 20 years. Indeed, the GPs' contract now stipulates that they only have to be available for patients for 26 hours a week, and this can include travelling time. The increasing number of doctors who choose to work as general practitioners makes it likely that list size will continue to fall as long as the population does not grow significantly.

A typical GP surgery comprises a group of doctors, most of them fully trained and therefore holding principal status, with one or two part-timers or trainees. Attached to this practice will be other professional workers, particularly nurses.

A district nurse, trained for work in the community, is associated with the doctors but not usually under their direct supervision; most nurses still belong in the nursing hierarchy in the local trust. Similarly, the health visitor, a specialist nurse who works with children and mothers and the elderly, will also usually be employed by a trust. More directly under the direction of the GPs is the practice nurse, who provides a nursing service in the surgery. This nurse usually works from a treatment room, undertaking relatively minor procedures such as dressings or testing of specimens that do not need the sophisticated analysis of hospital pathology laboratory.

Some practices do a great deal more to provide comprehensive primary care for their local community. This was one of the main reasons for establishing health centres, but large practices without custom-built premises have also developed the concept of primary care, offering a base for a range of other disciplines such as social work, chiropody and occupational therapy and physiotherapy. Space is sometimes made available for voluntary agencies to provide counselling support for patients with problems related to bereavement and to those who are suffering from the effects of alcohol or drug misuse.

The larger the practice and the more services it offers, the more it needs to be well organized. All but the smallest practices now have a practice manager. This was encouraged by the former FPCs, partly because it allowed GPs to concentrate on clinical rather than administrative matters, and partly because it ensured that the administration was conducted in a manner that allowed FPCs more easily to collect the data they needed to calculate GPs' pay. Many practice managers are people on their second careers, often originally from the armed services, who encountered much less difficulty penetrating GP practices than they did the more closed management hierarchies of hospitals and Districts.

Each practice generates a great deal of administrative work. Most GPs still use the small old-fashioned envelope patient record which was standardized over 70 years ago. They claim that a modern A4-size record would be difficult to handle when doing home visits. But the disadvantages of the small record are obvious if the patient has had more than a minimum number of investigations and the envelope is stuffed full of correspondence and laboratory or X-ray reports, all necessary to ensure a properly documented patient history. At the other extreme, experiments are proceeding using a single credit card format computerized record, which can hold all significant data for the average patient. The patients can then carry the card themselves. In 1984, the DHSS encouraged the introduction of computers into general practice, essentially to make doctors maintain an accurate list of current patients. In the past, most lists were inflated by patients who had died or moved but whose names still appeared. This was revealed, for example, when the lists were used for calling up women for routine cervical smears. Computerization of practice records has advanced considerably over recent years and has provided important information about GPs' prescribing and referral patterns.

Most practices have an appointment system managed by the receptionist. There has been considerable criticism of the way these staff make an initial assessment of the patient's request and decide whether and when the patient should come to the surgery or receive a home visit from the GP. The effectiveness of their gate-keeping, or just the greater mobility of patients generally, is responsible for the number of home visits steadily declining. Patients may also believe that the wider facilities at the surgery allow them to be treated more effectively there than at home. A GP can obviously see far more patients if they come to the surgery than if he or she has to make many home visits.

General practice acts as an important filter, caring for those patients who do not need the more expensive resources of the hospital. There are over 257 million GP consultations a year in the United Kingdom (1992) [15], many of which would probably be dealt with by a specialist in other countries and would result in many more referrals to hospital. Moreover, the GP who is aware of the patient's home and family context is better able to understand their overall health needs, instead of treating the symptoms in isolation. In highly specialist-dominated health care systems, the patient is at greater risk of being misdiagnosed. Though the cost of general practice is large – £6.5 billion in 1994 nationally – a more specialized service, with greater hospital emphasis, would be even more costly. This is one of the reasons other European countries spend more on health services: they provide more hospital beds.

Dentists

Dentists opt to work as general practitioners, or in the community, especially with children and the disabled, or as hospital specialists in oral surgery or orthodontic remedial work. Before the NHS was founded, the general state of dental health was poor, and, although dental benefits were available under the National Health Insurance Scheme to 13 million of the working population, only about 6 million made claims. The division of the profession into three main areas of activity encouraged standards to improve. For instance, the 1944 Education Act provided for free dental inspection for all children in state schools, and enlarged the scope of the School Medical Service which, though it had been founded as long before as 1907, had failed to diagnose and treat sufficient numbers of children needing attention. General dental practitioners have always worked from their own premises. They had no continuing responsibility for their patients until this became a feature of the 1990 contract (see Chapter 11 for details).

Pharmacists

Pharmacists also specialize, working in a variety of settings, retail, hospital or in commercial manufacturing and research. In 1991 there were around 12 300 chemist and appliance contractors in the UK – 8% more than a decade earlier. The FHSAs were only responsible for the regulation of the retail pharmacists who dispense and sell medicines to patients over the counter. Some GPs, particularly in rural areas, also supply the drugs they prescribe. In theory, GPs can only prescribe drugs or appliances (but not foods or toiletries) that will, in their opinion, benefit the health of their patients. The pharmacist, more popularly called the chemist, supplies the prescribed drugs on receipt of the doctor's prescription. The pharmacist purchases drugs from a wholesaler or direct from the manufacturer and is reimbursed by the FHSA. At the end of each month the pharmacist sends the prescription forms to the Prescription Pricing Authority and it calculates the costs of the ingredients according to the Drug Tariff – a list of approved drugs issued by the Department of Health. For each prescription, the Prescription Pricing Authority also calculates the on-cost allowance for the pharmacist's overhead expenses and profits, the dispensing fee and an allowance for containers. The FHSA is then notified of the amount to be paid to the pharmacist for the month's prescriptions.

The Prescription Pricing Authority (PPA) came into existence in 1974 to continue the work that had been carried out since 1948 by the Joint Pricing Committee and, before that, by the Joint Pricing Bureaux under the National Insurance Scheme. Its main offices for England are in Newcastle-upon-Tyne, and there are eight other offices in the north of England, each handling the prescriptions from a particular part of the country. The other parts of the United Kingdom have their own local offices. The PPA has eight members nominated by the FHSAs and the Department of Health nominates one doctor and three pharmacists. In 1991 there were over 467 million NHS prescriptions (8.1 per head of population) costing £3.34 billion. This was a 25% increase in the number of prescriptions over ten years, and a 160% rise in costs (Figure 5.3)[16].

The information prepared by the PPA has become more detailed and prompt with the introduction of PACT (Prescribing Analysis and Cost). This new scheme was started in 1988 and not only makes monthly reports to the FHSAs but also provides the GPs themselves with quarterly and, from 1991, monthly information to help them monitor their own prescribing. PACT provides three types of report: it shows an individual practice's costs against the average in the FHSA and the national average, and it gives the number of items prescribed and the average costs of items in that practice; it allocates the prescribing data into six major therapeutic groups; it can give a breakdown of costs for each GP (this is only done on request, and may be asked for if a practice or a GP is showing persistently higher than average prescribing costs).

A pharmacist wishing to set up as a retail chemist must register his or her premises in accordance with the Medicines Act, 1968, and this is done through the mediation of the Pharmaceutical Society of Great Britain. The chemist then has to apply to the FHSA for a contract, which will specify terms and conditions. These include opening hours and participation in the out-of-hours rota. As businesses, chemists' shops can only succeed if they also sell toiletries and other goods as well as proprietary non-prescribed drugs and preparations.

Opticians

The fourth professional group regulated by the FHSA is the opticians. At the time of the introduction of the NHS, there were several groups testing sight

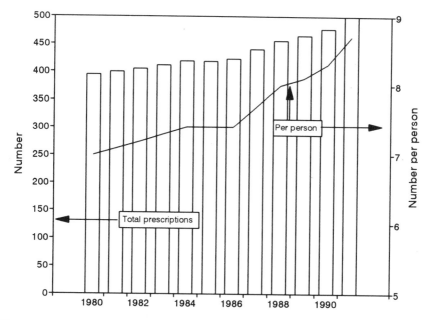

Figure 5.3 Total and per capita prescriptions: United Kingdom: 1980–1991.

Source: OHE (1992) *Compendium of Health Statistics*, 8th edn, OHE, London.

and supplying spectacles, and they possessed varying standards of professional qualification. In order to regularize the situation, it was decided to place all sight-testing in the hospital sector under specialist doctors (called ophthalmologists) while the dispensing of spectacles was allowed outside hospitals. But, because hospitals seemed unlikely to be able to cope, a Supplementary Service was set up by the 1946 National Health Service Act. It allowed ophthalmic opticians to continue testing sight as well as dispensing spectacles. They were placed under NHS contracts, administered through the Executive Councils (later FPCs and then FHSAs). The National Health Service Act, 1968, removed the word 'supplementary' and the name changed to General Ophthalmic Service.

Ophthalmic medical practitioners only test sight and prescribe lenses, ophthalmic opticians test sight and prescribe and dispense lenses, while dispensing opticians only supply spectacles and contact lenses prescribed by either of the other two. Most of the work is done in the community, although orthoptists, who treat squints and other malfunctions of the eye, mainly work in eye departments in hospitals. An optician does not have a list of patients like a medical GP but is paid a separate fee for each item of service under the terms of his or her contract with the FHSA. Since the National Health Service Act, 1984, the NHS no longer pays for spectacle frames and only partially subsidizes the cost of lenses, although children and other high risk groups are exempt from charges. The increase in charges was a prelude to the introduction of charges for sight-testing and dental treatment brought in under the Health and Medicines Act in 1988.

All four professions with FHSA contracts have local representative committees at which they can record their views on the way the FHSA is operating. When new contracts for GPs and Dentists were being negotiated and implemented, this 'safety valve' was particularly valuable (see Chapters 9 and 11).

Major changes after 1990

The improvement in status of general medical practice has been steady since its low point in the early 1960s. Numbers of GPs increased, working hours were reduced, training was improved and practice conditions modernized. Despite this, there remained some public dissatisfaction. There was a strong feeling that GPs were less interested in their patients' needs and less reliable in their attendance. It was a common experience for a patient on one GP's list always to be seen by other doctors, not even partners, but locums or deputies who were sometimes hospital junior doctors earning extra money and certainly not trained in general practice. From the NHS itself, Districts were critical of the GPs' ability to run effective primary care health programmes; they cited the public's use of the Districts' own child health departments and family planning clinics as evidence that general practice was failing to be the single reliable provider of comprehensive family care, which is what the GPs claimed to be.

In response to these criticisms, in April 1986, the Government issued a Green Paper entitled *Primary Health Care – An Agenda for Discussion* [17]. It concentrated on increasing the overall standard of general practice through introducing a payments system that would give incentives to GPs who were more available to their patients, who increased their range of preventive work and who reached certain targets in such services as vaccination and cervical screening. The Government said that patients should have more information about GP services and should be allowed to choose or change their GP more easily. It suggested consumer opinion could be voiced through patient participation groups. The FPCs themselves were asked to spend more time clarifying their role with Districts and to be more cost conscious. These broad recommendations formed the basis of the subsequent reforms and they influenced the new GP contract, published in February 1989 [18], just two weeks after the White Paper, *Working for Patients*. The contract specified, among other conditions of service, compulsory retirement of GPs at 70 and the requirement to publish practice details.

The 1986 Green Paper covered other aspects of primary health care. It said that dental services could be improved to encourage continuity of care and preventive work. The possibility that doctors and dentists should advertise their work was seen as a way of improving public awareness. The removal of the subsidy on spectacles was a proposal of a more overtly political nature, guaranteed to offend those wanting the NHS to be free of all direct charges to patients.

Eighteen months after the Green Paper, the Government issued a more definitive White Paper, *Promoting Better Health* [19]. The proposals built on the responses to the Green Paper and deliberately focused on three main objectives: improving general standards of primary care, giving the consumers greater choice and increasing the emphasis on health promotion. The Government said these objectives could be met by enhancing consumer power, by stimulating some degree of competition between GPs and by offering new financial incentives to GPs to co-operate with these policies (doctors' pay is discussed more fully in Chapter 9).

The White Paper was greeted with enthusiasm because it appeared to place primary care in a more favoured position, demoting acute care from the lime-light it had long monopolized. Nevertheless, the GPs' negotiators soon decided that the White Paper was a threat to their autonomy. The relationship between the doctors union, the British Medical Association (BMA), and the Government, always uneasy, deteriorated rapidly. Despite this, the Government pressed on with both *Working for Patients* and the new GP contract which incorporated many of the ideas in *Promoting Better Health*. These simultaneous initiatives became confused in the minds of the public (and GPs). A poll at the time found that only one in five members of the public had a clear idea about the point or the substance of the reforms.

The White Paper proposed that the FPCs be reformed. Although the mix of lay and professional elements was to be retained, each new authority was only to have 11 members, five lay, one GP, one community nurse, one pharmacist, one dentist and the general manager, all appointed by the Regional Health Authority, plus a chairman appointed by the Secretary of State. The new Family Health Services Authorities, authorized by the National Health Services and Community Care Act, came into being in October 1990. They were account-able to the Regional Health Authority. A significant change was demonstrated when the FHSAs' new general managers were appointed, many of the candid-ates coming from the mainstream of health services management. The status of these appointments ended some years of frustration among FPC chief officers who had been allocated lower rank than their counterparts in the rest of the NHS. Now with additional responsibilities created by the 1990 reforms and the GP contract, the FHSA chief executives can attain similar salaries to colleagues in trusts and Districts. This in turn has helped the spirit of collabor-ation, essential if other aspects of the reforms are to work.

The new FHSAs must reduce drug expenditure in general practice by means of indicative drug budgets. The Regions set an overall drug budget based on assumptions about average prescribing costs. FHSAs allocate this money in turn to each practice, not each GP. The aim is to place drug expenditure under pressure without going so far as to fix a cash limit for it. Patients are not denied the drugs they need (although some dissident GPs said that any control on their prescribing practice would, in fact, do that). The information provided by PACT is clearly important to the FHSAs and the GPs themselves in this context.

Charges for prescriptions were first introduced in 1952, abolished in 1965 and then reintroduced in 1968, since when they have been increased virtually on an annual basis. Charges have raised increasing amounts of money, despite increases in the number of people exempt from paying. In 1992, charges covered nearly 50% of the net ingredient cost of prescribed drugs, compared with 25% in 1979. Although basic economic theory would suggest that charging for a good or service will reduce demand, there is surprisingly little unambiguous evidence that charging for prescriptions has had much impact on demand by those in need. It has been suggested that a more effective way to reduce 'frivolous' prescriptions would be to charge the doctor for writing a script rather than the patient for presenting it. Despite the introduction of, effectively, just such a scheme for GPs, charges still remain, which suggests that governments are keen on the other reason for charges – as an additional source of funding for the NHS (see Chapter 7).

GPs are encouraged to behave competitively. Advertising, long ruled unethical, is allowed. Larger practices (or combinations of smaller practices) with at least 7000 patients were encouraged to become fundholders (see Chapter 4). This initiative was an outcome of the White Paper, *Working for Patients*, as was the importance given to medical audit. GPs, like hospital doctors, are now obliged to undertake a systematic review of their clinical practice and its effect on patients. Each FHSA has a Medical Audit Advisory Group with a membership not exceeding a dozen people, of whom one should be a consultant and one a public health doctor. It must report regularly to the FHSA.

The 1990 GP contract

Promoting Better Health contained proposals through which family practitioner services could be more effectively managed in line with the overhaul of the rest of the NHS following the introduction of general management in 1985. FPCs, and then the FHSAs, were expected to set objectives, allocate resources and monitor and evaluate results in the same way as Districts do for the rest of the NHS. But to achieve this required a much more explicit relationship with general practitioners, and this needed measures such as indicative prescribing budgets, proper GP practice budgets, medical audit and more sophisticated information systems to monitor GPs' prescribing habits and hospital referral rates. This level of scrutiny was greeted with nervousness by many GPs, particularly when it was linked to the specific conditions to be written into their new contract which the BMA negotiated with the Department of Health from March 1988 to May 1989. When the BMA had agreed the terms, the general membership rejected the agreement. Despite this, the Secretary of State, Kenneth Clarke, published the final contract with some minor amendments in August 1989 for implementation from 1 April 1990. As with many of these battles with the doctors in the past, the experience of the new arrangements was not as bad as predicted, although there is undoubtedly now a considerable increase in administration for GPs.

In retrospect it is clear that the open-ended cost of GP services could not be allowed to continue, especially as Districts had always had to work within a cash limit, whatever the needs of patients. Scrutiny of prescribing practice and referral patterns had shown variations which were not clinically necessary but were very wasteful. Medical audit was long overdue. Under their new contract, GPs lost some of their independence and are now much more closely scrutinized by their FHSAs. Examination of their efficiency and effectiveness is also more in the public eye than before. For instance, vaccination rates are published by some FHSAs, showing which practices are not meeting the targets.

The contract's origins go back to the 1986 White Paper, *Promoting Better Health*, which emphasized the importance of health promotion and consumer choice. The contract, therefore, requires GP practices to publish a directory of services so that the patient can be better informed. GPs must give personal details, age, gender, special interests and deputizing arrangements. The contract itself specifies minimum standards of medical care. GPs have to be available for patients 26 hours per week, over five days, and to accept 24-hour responsibility for their patients. This means that deputies are only acting as agents of the GP, who, therefore, has to be confident of the ability of the deputy to look after his or her patients to a proper standard. To facilitate their continuous responsibility, GPs are expected to live reasonably near their patients, even if the practice is in an inner city area. Each practice is expected to publish an annual report describing the facilities and premises and staffing levels, together with detailed statistics on prescribing practice and hospital referral rates. By the autumn of 1990 the new contract was implemented. Initial difficulties with the new payment system were made much of, but it seems likely that it will bring general practice into a better managed state (see Chapter 9 for more details about the 1990 contract).

CONCLUSIONS

In the 1990s there have been significant changes in the provision and organization of a range of NHS services. Many of these changes have resulted from the reforms of the NHS – the creation of semi-autonomous trusts and fundholding GPs. Others have occurred as a result of new contracts between the NHS and GPs and dentists, for example. The reorganizations on the provider side of the market have been a mix of devolution, of empowerment – financially for fundholders, managerially for trusts – with a tightening of the reins by the centre; trusts are scrutinized more closely by the NHSE and the Department of Health, for example. The key theme throughout these changes has been an attempt to promote efficiency and, implicitly at least, to exercise greater control over doctors. One of the trade-offs that governments seem to have been willing to accept as a result is the rise of efficiency at the expense of equity (particularly as far as the fundholding scheme has been concerned).

NOTES

1. Allen, D. (1979) *Hospital Planning*, Pitman Medical, Tunbridge Wells.
2. Nightingale, F. (1863) *Notes on Hospitals* (3rd edition), London.
3. Abel-Smith, B. (1964) *The Hospitals: 1800–1948*, Heinemann, London.
4. Nuffield Provincial Hospitals Trust (1946) *Hospital Surveys*, HMSO, London.
5. Ministry of Health (1956) *Report of the Committee of Enquiry into the Cost of the National Health Service*, Cmnd. 9663, (The Guillebaud Report), HMSO, London.
6. Ministry of Health (1962) *A Hospital Plan for England and Wales*, Cmnd. 1604, HMSO, London.
7. 'External financing limits' (EFLs) are allotted by the Department of Health to every trust each year, following scrutiny of each trust's business plans, and effectively proscribe the amount trusts are able to spend on capital schemes, either from borrowing or from internally generated income. In a sense, EFLs act as a cash limit on capital spending.
8. Bartlett, W. and Le Grand, J. (1994) *The Performance of Trusts* in, Robinson, R. and Le Grand, J. *Evaluating the NHS Reforms*, King's Fund Institute, London.
9. Ministry of Health/DHSS (1967, 1972, 1974), *Joint Report on the Organisation of Medical Work in Hospitals* (Cogwheel Report), HMSO, London.
10. M. Dixon *et al.* (1990). *Models of Clinical Management*, Institute of Health Services Management, London.
11. DHSS (1980) *Report on Patient Transport Services* (Naylor Report), HMSO, London.
12. DHSS (January 1983) *Steering Group on Health Services Information, Working Group G, Interim Report*, HMSO, London.
13. National Audit Office (July 1990) *National Health Service – Patient Transport Services*, London (Cm. 565).
14. Ministry of Health Consultative Council on Medical and Allied Services (1920) *Interim Report on the Future Provision of Medical and Allied Services* (Dawson Report), HMSO, London.
15. Office of Health Economics (1992) *Compendium of Health Statistics*, 8th edn, London.
16. For more statistical information see *Compendium of Health Statistics*, ibid.
17. DHSS (1986) *Primary Health Care: An Agenda for Discussion*, HMSO, London, (Cmnd. 9771).
18. DoH (August 1989) *General Practice in the National Health Service: The 1990 Contract*, HMSO.
19. DHSS (1987) *Promoting Better Health: the Government's Programme for Improving Primary Health Care*, HMSO, London (Cm. 249).

6

The NHS in Scotland, Wales and Northern Ireland

Because the general principles governing the NHS are the same throughout the United Kingdom, and while the principles and issues associated with the most recent reforms of *Working for Patients* have applied throughout the UK (although a year later in Scotland and Northern Ireland), it is easy to assume that the way health services are organized in Wales, Scotland and Northern Ireland is exactly the same as in England. This is not the case. This chapter outlines the more important variations between the four countries.

SCOTLAND

Scotland became part of the United Kingdom 400 years ago but retains many of its own traditions, which are reflected in its constitutional and legal framework. Geographically it comprises two distinct areas: the sparsely populated Highlands and Islands and the densely populated and industrial Lowlands. The policies devised by Parliament in London have to be tailored to fit Scotland's circumstances. The legislation that originally created the Scottish Health Service was the National Health Service (Scotland) Act, 1947, passed on 21 May 1947, which established an organization based on the same tripartite principle as in England and Wales. The hospital and specialist services were administered by five Regional Hospital Boards: Northern, North-Eastern, Eastern, South-Eastern and Western with 65 Boards of Management, analogous to the Hospital Management Committees in England and Wales. Family practitioner services were administered by 25 Executive Councils, and there were 55 local health authorities providing community and environmental health services. The Secretary of State for Scotland was responsible for the whole of the NHS in Scotland, with support from civil servants in the Scottish Home and Health Department.

In December 1968, after extensive consultations with a wide range of interested parties both within and outside the NHS, the Secretary of State for

Scotland published a Green Paper containing suggestions for reorganizing the service, *Administrative Reorganisation of the Scottish Health Services* [1]. It met with a wide measure of support which enabled the Secretary of State to proceed with the publication of a White Paper in July 1971, entitled *Reorganisation of the Scottish Health Services* [2] containing the Government's proposals for legislation to institute the reorganization.

The National Health Service (Scotland) Bill was introduced in Parliament in January 1972 and received Royal Assent on 9 August 1972. The appointed day for the first reorganization of the NHS in Scotland was 1 April 1974, as it was in England and Wales, so there remained just under two years for preparations to implement the new arrangements. No specific study was commissioned to analyse the management arrangements in the new structure, although the Grey Book (published by the DHSS) did not apply to Scotland. However, the Scottish Home and Health Department started a new series of circulars giving guidance to the health authorities (HSR Series – Health Service Reorganisation Scotland), and the Information Office of the Scottish Office was also very active in disseminating information to bodies within and outside the NHS.

Under the National Health Service (Scotland) Act, 1972, amended and consolidated by the National Health Service (Scotland) Act, 1978, health boards were created for each area of Scotland, to act as the single authority for administering the three branches of the former tripartite structure (Figure 6.1). The Scottish National Health Service Staff Commission was consulted on recruiting, transferring and appointing staff before and during the period of reorganization, and reviewing the arrangements so that the interests of the 100 000 affected staff would be safeguarded.

Two new bodies, without precedents in the pre-1974 structure, were created at national level – the Scottish Health Service Planning Council and the Common Services Agency. These are not precisely mirrored in England, their functions being shared by the DHSS and the Regional Health Authorities, although in Wales there is also a Common Services Agency. Provision was made for professional advice to be available both nationally and locally through consultative committees, but no specific bodies were established to pursue collaboration between the local and health authorities in the same way as the Joint Consultative Committees in England and Wales. There were bodies for representing the views of users of the health services in each district or undivided area, called Local Health Councils. The 1972 Act also established the Health Service Commissioner for Scotland, who started work on 1 October 1973.

The reorganization of local government created new local authorities in Scotland which came into being on 15 May 1975 – that is, just over a year after the NHS reorganization and the new local authorities in England and Wales. There were nine Regional authorities divided into 56 districts, and three Island Councils created by the Local Government (Scotland) Act, 1973, whose boundaries closely followed the health board boundaries, the main difference being

Figure 6.1 Scottish Health Boards 1994.

Source: *Hospital and Health Services Yearbook: 1994*, Institute of Health Services Management, London.

that the Strathclyde Region contained four health boards. This Act also provided for local community councils within the districts – a feature absent from the arrangements in England and Wales.

Health boards

The 15 health boards in Scotland were directly responsible to the Secretary of State for Scotland for the planning and provision of integrated health services in their areas; 10 of the 15 areas were divided into districts. Each board had a chairman appointed by the Secretary of State, and between 14 and 22 members appointed from nominations put forward by regional and district local government authorities, trade unions, the health care professions, the universities and a variety of other organizations.

The health boards were mainly concerned with major policy matters and the broad allocation of resources, delegating authority to manage the service to four senior officers of the board – the Chief Administrative Medical Officer, the Chief Area Nursing Officer, the Treasurer and the Secretary – who together constituted the Area Executive Group. These officers had both individual professional and team responsibilities in a similar way to the Area Team of Officers of the AHAs in England and Wales. The Chief Administrative Dental Officer and the Chief Pharmacist joined the Area Executive Group for the discussion of items relevant to their responsibilities. The team had to present advice and information to the board to help it to establish policy and priorities. Health boards were encouraged to set up area programme planning committees, similar to the English district health care planning teams (Chapter 8). Most boards created such committees for the main groups of users.

In each of the districts, there were four officers directly responsible to their counterparts on the Area Executive Group, but they had a considerable degree of independence. The District Administrator, District Nursing Officer, District Medical Officer and the District Finance Officer constituted the District Executive Group, and they were, as such, jointly accountable to the Area Executive group for a number of functions. An important difference between the District organizations in Scotland and in England and Wales was, therefore, that the Scottish District Officers were directly subordinate to their Area Officers, although both were officers of the health board. The relationship in England and Wales was described in terms of monitoring and co-ordinating rather than direct line responsibility, with a view to ensuring that the District organization was not placed in a subordinate position. Another important difference is that in Scotland there were no GP or hospital consultant representatives directly involved in the District management arrangements. This is because there was always a much stronger tradition of medical administration in Scotland. Before 1974, medical superintendents had not dwindled as they had done south of the border. Clinicians were used to working with administrative medical colleagues.

Further reorganization

The criticism regarding too many levels of management was not appropriate to Scotland, where health boards in some respects undertook both the Regional and Area role. *Patients First* applied only to England and Wales, but a similar document was issued for Scotland [3], suggesting that health boards review their administrative structures with the aim of simplifying them. A reduction in functional management and more devolution to Units was also suggested. This review was to be undertaken and changes made by the date of the English reorganization, 1 April 1982. In the event, reorganization in Scotland took much longer. Only ten of the health boards had subordinate districts. Glasgow and Lothian were very large. For instance, the Greater Glasgow Health Board administered 14 500 beds, 32 000 staff and a budget of £330 million (1982 figures) to serve a population of 1.2 million. Lothian's 1982 budget was £250 million. Both these Boards were, therefore, much larger than a District in England. The Highland Board, however, with a relatively small population, covered an enormous area so that some sort of subdivision seemed desirable. Lanarkshire and Tayside also wished to keep a District structure. Late in the day Argyll and Tayside, having first opted in favour of a single District, changed its mind.

Difficulties arose from the inability of the Whitley Councils and others to agree on the appropriate grades for posts in the new structure, particularly those at Unit level where many of the Units were as large as English districts. Somewhat suddenly, and apparently disregarding much preparatory work that some health boards had done, the Secretary of State for Scotland announced on 10 November 1983 that all districts would be scrapped leaving health boards with subordinate Units only. Inspired by the spirit of the Griffiths Report (which had not considered Scotland or Northern Ireland), the Government believed a simpler organization would improve management. The gross disparity in Unit size led to problems, and appointments of Unit General Managers took some time.

The provisions of the National Health Service and Community Care Act, 1990, apply to the whole of the United Kingdom; Part II refers particularly to Scotland. Political support was slight in Scotland for the Conservative Government that introduced this legislation; there was little enthusiasm for trusts. There had been a more marked tradition of involvement by the local community in the NHS in Scotland, and the appointment of the new Boards under the Act was seen as a potential threat to this, because they were less representative. The Local Health Councils set up by the 1974 reorganization arguably had had more influence than Community Health Councils, their English counterparts. In the late 1980s their functions were reviewed and, although they were not abolished, the Secretary of State for Scotland reduced them in size and removed trade union representation, making them more narrowly representative of the consumer interest.

Another difference from the English NHS is that there has never been a separate authority for the family practitioner services. This had not led to difficulties, and there was a growing feeling that the setting up of autonomous FPCs in 1985 and FHSAs in 1990, in England and Wales, was unnecessary and would lead to duplication of planning and purchasing effort. The merger of districts and FHSAs in England and Wales in the near future would seem to confirm this view.

Scottish Home and Health Department

The Secretary of State for Scotland is, through the form of the NHS legislation, personally accountable to Parliament for the Scottish health services in the same way as the Secretary of State for Health and the Secretary of State for Wales are for the NHS in England and Wales. In Scotland, the supreme government department is the Scottish Office. The senior civil servant in the Scottish Office is the Permanent Under-Secretary of State, and he presides over the Management Group which includes the senior civil servants from the other major government departments in Scotland. The department responsible to the Secretary of State for the central administration of the Scottish NHS is the Scottish Home and Health Department (SHHD). This department is also responsible for the central administration relating to the police service, criminal justice, legal aid, the administration of prisons, administration and legislation relating to superannuation of public service employees, the organization of the fire service, home defence and emergency services, legislation relating to shops, theatres and cinemas, licensed premises and land tenure matters.

Following the lead of the Department of Health in England, a Chief Executive has also been appointed. There are also heads of each professional group: doctors, nurses, dentists, pharmacists and scientists. Of the divisions of the SHHD exclusively concerned with health matters, within the Chief Medical Officer's department there are five groups covering primary care with maternal and child health; acute services and medical manpower; mental health and geriatric services; epidemiology and environmental health; and radiation and emergency services.

The 1972 Act created the Scottish Health Service Planning Council, which was partly derived from the former Scottish Health Services Council, an influential body that advised the Secretary of State on shaping policy for health service provision in Scotland. Like the Central Health Services Council, its counterpart in England and Wales, it was made up of representatives from all the major professional groups with an interest in the health services. The new Planning Council was created to ensure that effective strategies could be devised and implemented to improve Scottish health service provision on an integrated basis, in a context of limited resources, with the fullest participation from the health authorities. The membership, therefore, specifically includes representatives from health boards, universities with medical schools, officers from the SHHD and some other members appointed by the Secretary of State, as is the independent chairman of this Planning Council.

Just as the Department of Health has to work closely with the regional health authorities in England and with the Welsh Office to secure effective planning, so the Scottish Planning Council has to ensure comprehensive targets can be established, and that progress towards their achievement is carefully monitored. A number of programme committees have been set up with members of the Council and specialists nominated by the eight national consultative committees of the various health professions. The Council gives advice on the implementation of agreed policies and on evaluation of the success of the policies. A policy group of top Scottish Home and Health Department officials is linked to the Planning Council by the Planning Unit of Officials. The Council prepared a report, published in December 1980 with the Secretary of State's blessing, entitled *Priorities for Health Care in Scotland* [4]. The report allocated services into three categories as follows:

Category A – Expenditure to grow faster than overall expenditure
Prevention
Services for the multiply deprived
Community nursing services
Care of the elderly
Elderly with mental disability
Mental illness
Mental handicap
Physical handicap

Category B – Expenditure to grow but at a slower rate than Category A
Primary dental services
Maternity services
General medical services
General ophthalmic services

Category C – Expenditure to remain static or to decline
Child health services
Acute hospital services
General pharmaceutical services

A further report was published, in November 1988, entitled *Scottish Health Authorities Review of Priorities for the Eighties and Nineties* [5] (SHARPEN), which stressed the needs of people with dementia and encouraged further development of community services, particularly for the elderly. Health indicators show a worse picture in Scotland than elsewhere in the United Kingdom, particularly for heart disease, where the incidence is among the worst in the world. Health education is therefore another priority area. Other aspects of health care have also lagged behind; services for mentally handicapped people are still mainly institutional.

Outside the SHDD there is the Common Services Agency (CSA), whose management committee is responsible for providing a wide range of services to the SHHD and other government departments and also includes representatives from health boards. In 1985 the Scottish Health Management Efficiency Group (SCOTMEG) was set up to undertake a national programme of efficiency reviews and to monitor the progress of the CSA and the health boards in implementing their recommendations. They first studied the hotel services and then began to scrutinize clinical work. In this they are helped by the Clinical Resource Use Group set up in 1987 to disseminate good practice.

Scotland has for centuries maintained a strong tradition of medical education to very high standards, and its four university medical schools (Edinburgh, Glasgow, Aberdeen and Dundee) produce one fifth of all medical graduates in the United Kingdom. The professional bodies have grown up independently of those in England and have achieved notable prominence. The Royal College of Physicians (Edinburgh), the Royal College of Surgeons (Edinburgh) and the Royal College of Physicians and Surgeons (Glasgow) are the oldest; the Scottish Radiological Society, the Scottish Committee for Community Medicine and Scottish members of the Royal Colleges of General Practitioners, Obstetricians and Gynaecologists and Pathologists, the Faculties of Anaesthetists and of Community Medicine join them in being recognized professional groups contributing advice through the National Medical Consultative Committee to the Planning Council. The BMA is also active in Scotland, and its Scottish General Medical Services Committee contributes to the National Medical Consultative Committee. The Scottish Junior Staffs Group Council is a similar body to the Hospital Junior Staffs Group Council for England and Wales, while hospital consultants are represented through the Scottish Committee for Hospital Medical Services.

Collaboration between medical schools and the health boards is formalized through four University Liaison Committees. In the field of postgraduate medicine, the Scottish Council for Postgraduate Medical Education was founded in May 1970 to promote the ongoing development of medical practitioners through extensive programmes of teaching and refresher courses.

Health centres are a more prominent feature of health care in Scotland than in England and Wales. Average list size is lower than in England. Links with the hospital service are strong, many GPs hold hospital specialist appointments, while others have access to beds in community hospitals. Major hospital redevelopment has taken place in Scotland in the last 20 years, starting with Ninewells Hospital, Dundee, and Victoria Hospital, Kirkcaldy.

There are a number of other professional and administrative bodies with important duties in the Scottish National Health Service which are similar in constitution and objectives to those bodies described in the chapters relating to England and Wales. They include the Scottish Hospital Advisory Service, the Scottish Medical Practices Committee, the Scottish Tribunal, the Mental Welfare Commission and the Scottish National Board for Nurses. In addition, the mental health services are governed by the provisions of the Mental Health (Scotland) Act, 1966, and social work, probation and after care services are covered by the Social Work (Scotland) Act, 1968.

Scotland spends more on the NHS per person than England and Wales: £680 in 1990/91 compared to about £580. This is partly accounted for by the higher staffing levels: the average GP list size in 1990 was around 1600 patients per doctor, 250 smaller than in England. There is a higher proportion of hospital medical and dental staff per 1000 population, 94 as compared with 81 in England and Wales. Of the total employees in 1990 half were nurses and midwives, proportionately more than in England and Wales [6].

WALES

The laws of Wales are generally much closer to England's than are those of Scotland or Northern Ireland. Arrangements for health care are similarly more alike, and, although the provisions of the NHS and Community Care Act 1990 applied to Wales, organizationally there are differences. Up to 1974 there existed a Welsh Hospital Board, local health authorities and executive councils as in England. Thereafter, the Welsh Office was allocated both departmental and regional responsibilities with a Health and Social Services Department under the overall responsibility of the Secretary of State for Wales. This minister is responsible to Parliament in Westminster for many functions in addition to health, which has led to periodic criticisms: the Royal Commission noted in 1979 that the Welsh Office was too remote from health authorities and their prob- lems [7]. However, a Regional Authority as well as the Area tier would have been excessive, given that the whole population of Wales is only 2.85 million (similar to that of a small region in England). Communication within Wales has always been difficult, with the industrialized South separated from the rest of the country by mountains and relatively poor road and rail services.

In 1982, the eight area health authorities became nine DHAs (Figure 6.2). Except in Glamorgan, the most populated county, the DHAs were coterminous with county councils, and FPCs (later FHSAs) and Community Health Councils continued as in England. A reduction in the number of commissioning health authorities is likely in 1996. Within the Welsh Office the managerial approach is similar to the English Department of Health (Chapter 3), although the Principality's small population makes the formulation of major initiatives comparatively easier. There is a Health Policy Board and an Executive Committee accountable to it with its own Director. The director is answerable directly to ministers through the Health Policy Board, for the management of the NHS in Wales, but to the Permanent Secretary for Departmental manage- ment matters. With the Permanent Secretary and like the Chief Executive counterpart in England, the Director is an Accounting Officer to Parliament, and chairs the Common Services Agency.

On the Executive are professional heads and directors of planning, infor- mation, management development, personnel, finance and family health services, matched by civil servants in a health professional group, responsible for developing policy for the Health Policy Board. The Welsh Planning Forum

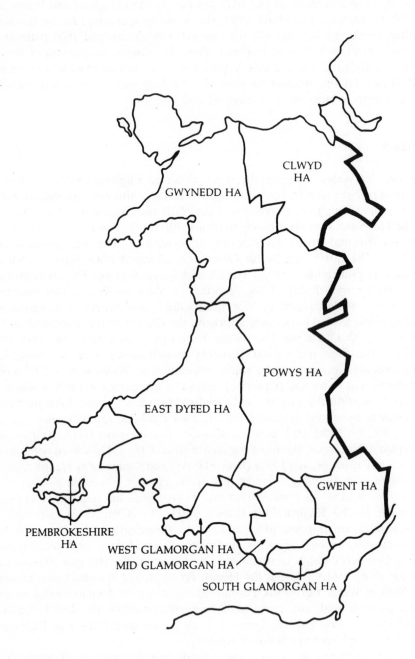

Figure 6.2 Welsh Health District boundaries 1994.

Source: *Hospital and Health Services Yearbook: 1994*, Institute of Health Services Management, London.

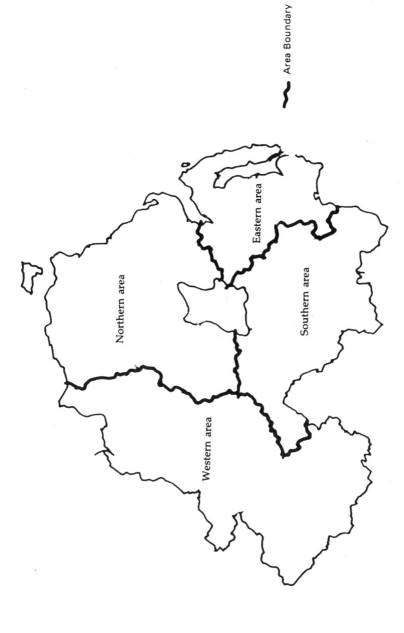

Figure 6.3 Northern Ireland Health and Social Services boundaries 1994.

Source: Northern Ireland Office.

was set up in 1988 as an advisory sub-group of the Executive Committee, chaired by the Welsh Director. In November 1989 it published *Strategic Intent and Direction for the NHS in Wales* [8], which declares three main goals: to improve health, to be more responsive to the consumer and to make more effective use of resources. Towards the first aim, three aspects of health are targeted, maternal and early child health, cardiovascular disease and cancer.

Professional review panels are developing practical advice on how to achieve these aims, and the Welsh Health Promotion Authority, headed by a chairman, executive director and a small management board, initiated what has been described as the largest campaign of its kind in Europe, Heartbeat Wales, started in 1985, aimed at reducing heart disease.

As in Scotland, there is a Common Services Agency, previously called the Welsh Health Technical Services Organization. There are separate divisions for capital and the estate, supplies, manpower, information technology, prescription pricing and for artificial limbs and appliances.

NORTHERN IRELAND

The organization of health services in Northern Ireland is the most different from that in England. This reflects different local traditions and the unstable political structure of the country. During the last half-century, Northern Ireland has at times enjoyed considerable legislative autonomy, with its own parliament at Stormont. Recently it has been subject to direct rule from London.

The first reorganization of the health service took place slightly earlier than in England, with legislation passed in 1972 being implemented in October 1973 [9]. From that day the Province was organized into four Health and Social Services Boards (Figure 6.3), accountable to the Secretary of State for Northern Ireland, who appointed, and still appoints, directly their chairmen and vice chairmen. The Boards had a mixed membership: 30% were district council nominees, 30% were from the health professions and the remainder from voluntary and other lay bodies. The Boards were geographical, as their names suggest; Eastern, Northern, Western and Southern were responsible for 17 districts, covering populations from 43 000 in Omagh to 250 000 in North and West Belfast. The total population of Northern Ireland is 1.65 million. The districts were roughly coterminous with local authority district councils, but these bodies have fewer responsibilities than their counterparts in England. For instance, education and library services are run centrally for the whole of Northern Ireland, and housing, a policy area important for the NHS, is managed by the Northern Ireland Housing Executive operating through its own regional offices.

As health and social services are run by one administration the need for the English style of joint planning and joint financing arrangements is much reduced. Statutory responsibilities are not always held by the same authorities as in England: the education of the learning disabled remains with the Health and Social Services Board in Northern Ireland, whereas in England it was transferred to education authorities in 1972.

Within the Department of Health and Social Services in Northern Ireland there are 11 divisions covering policy, professional advice and such services as audit and works.

As in Scotland and Wales, certain functions are not provided by the Boards directly, but are undertaken centrally through a Central Services Agency. In Northern Ireland this body does work that in England is the responsibility of the Family Health Services Authorities (FHSAs). The Agency is also responsible for prescription pricing, for certain personnel duties concerning hospital doctors down to registrar level, for supplies, support services, advice and legal matters. Consumer interests in Northern Ireland are represented by District Committees, operating in a manner similar to the English CHCs.

Districts are responsible for managing, planning, monitoring and co-ordinating the health and social services together. This way of combining health and social services has long been attractive to observers who see the aims of the NHS in other parts of the United Kingdom continually frustrated by the administrative and legislative separation of the two. But in Northern Ireland enthusiasm is muted; in practice, chief officers still tend to remain loyal to their own discipline's priorities before those of the District as a whole, so that the advantages of integration are modest. Following the publication of *Working for Patients*, the Southern Health Board proposed separating the health and personal social services into three managerial divisions, primary care, secondary provision and personal social services.

Before then, reorganization had encountered more problems than elsewhere in the United Kingdom, because the Eastern Board (Belfast) was so much larger than the other three. In 1980 the Secretary of State requested more consultation on the future organization, while insisting on a scheme of four Boards. Proposals were published the following year, but the Eastern Board, reviewing its organization again in 1989, wanted to reduce the number of Units from fourteen to five hospital-based and four in the community. By 1994, the future structure had still not been agreed.

Northern Ireland spends more per head on health and social services than is spent elsewhere in the United Kingdom. This is not only a response to the consequences for health of its prolonged sectarian and political problems but also simply a result of high numbers of professional staff. In 1987, a report prepared on behalf of the Northern Ireland Industrial Development Board said that the Province spent 25% more on health and social services compared to the rest of the United Kingdom, and had 36% more staff and 46% more beds [10]. These differences still remain.

CONCLUSION

The differences in the organizations of the health service in the four countries comprising the United Kingdom arise from the different legal and political traditions of each country. They also reflect demographic and geographical differences. A fuller analysis, based on detailed comparisons of epidemiological and health services statistics, enables the effectiveness of the four services to be assessed. For example, although Scotland has more doctors per head of population than the rest of the United Kingdom, the population's expectation of life is two or three years less. Such data means little until set against various other health and performance indicators. As will be seen in Chapter 14, comparisons with other countries certainly help to judge how effective a health service is. Comparisons within the NHS also show that, despite its achievements to date, fundamental differences in standards of health care and of patient care still persist in the United Kingdom itself.

NOTES

1. Scottish Home and Health Department (1968) *Administrative Reorganisation of the Scottish Health Services*, HMSO, Edinburgh.
2. Scottish Home and Health Department (1971) *Reorganisation of the Scottish Health Services*, HMSO, Edinburgh, (Cmnd. 4734).
3. Scottish Home and Health Department (1979) *Structure and Management of the NHS in Scotland*, HMSO, Edinburgh.
4. Scottish Home and Health Department *Scottish Planning Council (1980). Priorities for Health Care in Scotland*, HMSO, Edinburgh.
5. Scottish Home and Health Department *Scottish Planning Council (November, 1988). Scottish Health Authorities Review of Priorities for the Eighties and Nineties*, HMSO, Edinburgh.
6. Office of Health Economics (1992) *Compendium of Health Statistics*, 8th edn, OHE, London.
7. *Royal Commission on the National Health Service* (1979), HMSO, London, (Cmnd. 7615), p. 305, para. 19.25.
8. Welsh Office. Welsh Health Planning Forum (November, 1989) *Strategic Intent and Direction for the NHS in Wales*, HMSO, Cardiff.
9. *The Health and Personal Social Services (Northern Ireland) Order*, 1972.
10. *United Medical Enterprises*. Study commissioned by the Northern Ireland Industrial Development Board, 1987.

7

Financing the National Health Service

In its first year of existence, the NHS spent around £440 million. Nearly fifty years later, by the mid-1990s, this had risen to over £38 000 million – a massive increase. Allowing for inflation, the NHS today spends nearly 3.5 times more than it did in 1948, and yet, in comparison with most industrialized countries, the NHS is not only inexpensive (some would argue too cheap) but represents good value for money. This chapter is concerned with three basic questions: Where does the money to pay for the NHS come from? What does it cost to run the service? What are the implications of this system?

SOURCES OF FUNDING

Money for the NHS is derived from three sources (Figure 7.1): central government tax revenues, national insurance contributions and charges to patients. Before 1974, community health services were funded from local authority rates and the rate support grant from central government; thereafter, these came within the health authorities' budgets.

There is a popular misconception that the national insurance contribution is the main source of NHS funds, but, as can be seen, national taxation provides most of the money. Most national insurance contributions are paid by employers and employees within the Pay As You Earn (PAYE) system. Direct payments by patients themselves were not part of the original plan for the NHS but were started in 1951. There has always been opposition to them, and the introduction of charges for sight tests and dental examinations (in 1989) markedly decreased the number of people presenting themselves, with consequences for their health. Charging for doctors' prescription medicines began in 1951, was abolished in 1965, and then reintroduced in 1968 – although pregnant women, mothers, children, some elderly people and patients with some chronic conditions have always been exempt. By 1994, 85% of all prescriptions were exempted [1], which

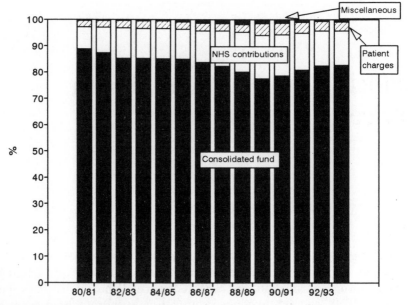

Figure 7.1 Sources of NHS Finance.

Source: *The Government's Expenditure Plans 1994/5 to 1996/7: Departmental Report*, HMSO, London (Cm. 2512).

may partly explain the successive increases in prescription charges well above the rate of inflation (see Chapter 5). Patients also pay for private beds in NHS trust hospitals, and this money is simply counted as income for the trust; until 1991 individual hospitals were not allowed to make a profit on these services, which were subject to fixed pricing by the Department of Health.

Because the main source of funding for the NHS is general taxation, and because the tax structure – at least for direct taxes – is mildly progressive, this means that the financing of the NHS is also mildly progressive, that is, it is inequitable – in favour of the poor (see Chapter 14 for more details).

HOW THE GOVERNMENT PAYS

The major source of money for the NHS, the Consolidated Fund, is not automatically administered year by year, but only made available after an intricate process of negotiation within central government departments. Discussions between senior officials in the Department of Health and the Treasury on the development of policies lie at the heart of the way money for the health service is obtained. The public services divisions of the Treasury are key elements in this: they supervise all national government expenditure through a series of consultations during the year with the spending departments, Treasury Ministers and the Cabinet.

Each spring, all the spending departments (e.g. the Department of Health, the Department of the Environment, the Department of Trade and Industry, the Ministry of Defence) submit preliminary returns to the Treasury. These are prepared in accordance with guidelines agreed by the Cabinet. They outline the revalued figures for the four years covered by the previous plan, with proposals for any new expenditure and for possible savings, together with figures for the new fifth year and plans for a further two years. They take account of a Cabinet discussion of the medium-term economic outlook and of their priorities, as well as of detailed economic assumptions provided by the Treasury. In preparing them, the departmental officials confer with their ministers in order to work out their proposals for the continuation of existing policies and the development of new ones. This process is not always straightforward since there may well be disagreement about what current policy actually is. Then, from March to May, the departmental officials have very detailed discussions with officials from the public services division in order to agree on statistical assumptions and their effect on the projected future cost of existing policies. In May, the Principal Finance Officers from each spending department meet officials from the General Expenditure Division of the Treasury and write a report, which projects the future cost of all the national policies as they stand and defines the areas where agreement has yet to be reached.

Their report is called the Public Expenditure Survey Committee (PESC) Report, and it is a key document on which the Government's subsequent deliberations are based. The Principal Finance Officers, although officials of their own departments, need to foster the closest confidential relations with the Treasury, in order that they may give their own department an accurate picture of the proposals that are likely to be successful with the Treasury, and those that will need persuasion to be acceptable. When they meet their opposite numbers to draw up the PESC report, they are in a position to assess the likely balance of demands for new spending between competing departments, and they attempt to get as much as they reasonably can for their own departments, without antagonizing the Treasury officials. The process very much depends, at this stage, on the trusting and co-operative nature of the relationships between these officials.

The next stage of the process involves the Treasury Ministers. They receive the PESC report (as does each of the departments) and, together with Treasury officials, study the implications of its expenditure proposals in the light of their assessment of the economic climate and the Government's strategy. They have to decide whether the proposals could actually be paid for within the overall spending limit set by the Treasury. The Chancellor of the Exchequer's view is presented to the Cabinet and, exceptionally, it may be that increased spending will be possible in some areas, but more often it is suggested that some cuts in the projections of individual departments will have to be made, or that increases in one department have to be matched by decreases in another. The Cabinet discusses these points, and individual Ministers have to try to persuade their colleagues of the precedence of their claims for resources. Much may depend on whether the Prime Minister (who chairs Cabinet meetings) is in favour of certain policies rather than others. He or she will have already had confidential meetings with the Chancellor and the Secretary of the Cabinet and made a decision before the Cabinet meets.

Nevertheless, the discussions continue from June to November, after which the Cabinet's decisions are revealed in the Chancellor's Autumn Statement. Since 1993, the Autumn Statement has been combined with the Chancellor's Budget (bringing together the Government's plans for raising money with its plans for spending it). Subsequently, spending plans are embodied in the White Paper on Public Expenditure, which is published early the following year as a series of Departmental Reports. It is also debated for two days in the House of Commons, but this is now usually a formality and few if any amendments are made to it. The House's Select Committee on Expenditure chooses topics in the White Paper for study by each of its six subcommittees and reports on its findings to the House of Commons. Although this represents a more critical look at policy decisions than the debate on the White Paper achieves, its influence on the proposals, which are, after all, largely constructed by departmental officials, is relatively small, because MPs do not always have a grasp of the broad issues and forward implications of decisions that the full-time officials can develop. This is, however, an area where MPs could exert more influence over future government policy, if they chose to play a more active part. The PESC plans are given up-to-date prices and set out in the form in which Parliament actually votes the money for the year ahead. At the same time, a cash limit is calculated, incorporating projections of future inflation and representing the limit on the amount of extra money which the departments can expect on grounds of price increases.

Once Parliament has agreed to the allocations for each department through the annual 'Votes', its involvement is temporarily ended. Later in the financial year covered by the vote, departments may, through their Ministers, come back for more money (subject to the overall cash limits); the Treasury puts forward requests for supplementary allocations after discussion with the departments, and Parliament agrees to allow the additional money. Since the beginning of the 1990s supplementary additions to the NHS budget have been very rare, as the Government has maintained a tighter grip on public spending as part of its overall macroeconomic policy. Parliament is subsequently involved in the scrutiny of departmental spending through the work of the Comptroller and Auditor General and the investigations of the Public Accounts Committee.

The public expenditure system as described is not only an administrative process essential for the everyday conduct of the nation's major public services, but also a means of putting into effect the political choices of the Government of the day.

DISTRIBUTING THE FUNDS

When the Department of Health finally receives notification (usually in late December) of its allocation for the following financial year, beginning in April, it is able to pass money on to the Regions (and then on to purchasers) in accordance with their budgets, previously agreed on a population-based formula. The distribution formula is not applied rigidly, however, ministers have the discretion to change Regional allocations. This has happened most notably for the Regions covering London and south-east England which have received larger shares of the total NHS budget than indicated by the distribution formula in order to protect London's health services.

From 1975 to 1991, historical imbalances began to be corrected through RAWP, named after the report of the Resource Allocation Working Party [2], which suggested that each Region should have a target allocation based on a formula that took into account the age structure of its population and factors which affected the need for health care – chiefly (as a proxy for morbidity) death rates standardized for age. A similar formula was also applied to the distribution of capital money (see below). This has enabled health authorities to anticipate their likely future financial allocations and thereby enhanced their ability to plan strategically. But no Region can claim to have eliminated inequities yet. It takes a long time for significant funds to be made available for deprived areas and for that extra spending power to show up as improved health care. Regions have relied on the growth element in their annual allocations from the Department when trying to obey the RAWP criteria for distributing money to their Districts according to relative need. They had difficulties in those years when the money had first to be used to meet shortfalls in mainstream revenue budgets, arising from the Department's failure to compensate fully for the effects of inflation.

Under the 1990 Act RAWP was scrapped, but replaced with a very similar formula, under which districts are expected to work on the basis of budgets calculated from the size of their resident populations, weighted to reflect relative need for health care. The progress of Regions towards their RAWP targets between 1975 and 1991 was generally consistent but slow. By 1991, however, most Regions were within 1% or 2% of their target allocations. It is important to point out that over this period (and, indeed, after 1991) the formula for distributing funds to Regions was not consistently applied: every year ministers and the Department exercised considerable discretion over the actual allocations each Region received, and hence the speed with which each Region moved towards its target. The most notable example of this has been the protection received by the Thames Regions covering London, which have consistently received a greater share of funds than the formula strictly would allow. Traditionally London has been over-provided with health services in comparison with the rest of the country, and also compared with the need for services suggested by the distribution formula. However, ministers and the Department felt that moving money out of London as quickly as the distribution formula suggested would disrupt services too much. Therefore the pace of change was deliberately slowed down.

Once Regions have received their share of national funds, they then implement their own formulae (largely based on the national formula) to distribute funds to their district purchasers. At this point, some money is retained to fund the Region itself, plus any services purchased by Regions on behalf of districts. Many Regions adapted the national formula, introducing refinements to the factors affecting the need for health care such as socio-economic deprivation variables. Regions, along with FHSAs, are also responsible for calculating GP fundholder budgets. By 1994 there was still no nationally agreed formula equivalent to that used for districts to distribute funds to fundholders (see Chapter 4). A review of the weighted capitation formula for districts and GP fundholders was instigated in 1993, and it is likely that the Department of Health will distribute allocations directly to districts and GP fundholders on the basis of a modified national weighted capitation formula which will take account of socio-economic factors.

Although most Districts' revenue money comes from the Exchequer via the Department of Health, they do have other sources of income, one of the most important being joint finance. The local authorities' shortage of resources had meant that patients no longer requiring NHS hospital care remained in hospital because social services departments were unable to pay to accommode them in the community. Until 1976 Health Authorities were not authorized to transfer money to the local authorities, but, in that year, the rules changed, in return for a commitment to set up specifically agreed new services that would benefit both sets of authorities [3]. However, with continuing pressure on budgets in the 1980s, authorities became unwilling to commit future funds in this way, and joint finance ceased to be a useful vehicle for achieving flexible improvements in community care. A DHSS working party [4] in 1985 and the Audit Commission [5] in 1986 underlined the difficulties, and the second Griffiths report [6] in 1988 advocated a simpler system by assigning to one or other authority the lead responsibility for a care group. *Caring for People* [7] accepted this principle, but the administration of joint finance became further complicated by the new system under the 1990 Act; in this system, social services departments have to construct 'care packages' for individual clients, and may ask the health authorities to contribute financially.

Another special source of funds for Health Authorities is the earmarked sums governments provide as incentives to encourage prompt local implementation of national policies. These are taken from the national NHS budget and are not distributed within the weighted capitation formula. Districts have received these payments for such initiatives as the public education campaign about AIDS, but also to underpin managerial action, for example to speed the introduction of the 1990 Act. In due course, these allowances have to be integrated into the ordinary budget in order not to distort the general process of sharing out funds, but this obviously restricts the impact of the special allocations.

Local sources provide Districts with some funds too. Trusts or 'free monies' are accrued from public donations in support of special local projects, such as the purchase of a scanner or amenities for patients and staff. With the creation of trust hospitals, these funds have now been transferred from districts to the hospitals and community units.

Providers

The providers of health care – NHS trusts and others in the voluntary and private sectors – are at the end of this distribution chain. Public sector purchasers (the Districts, GP fundholders and, for certain services, the Department itself and the Regions) are responsible under the 1990 Act for buying health care for their local populations or patients on their lists. They have the freedom to buy care from whomsoever they please and are not restricted to public sector providers. However, almost all the money voted by Parliament to the NHS does, in fact, find its way to trusts via the contracting system described in Chapter 2. A typical NHS trust receives most of its income from its local district, with the remainder made up from contracts with neigh-bouring districts, GP fundholders and other sources, such as private patients and non-health care related income, like car-park charges, in-hospital cafés, etc. (Figure 7.2).

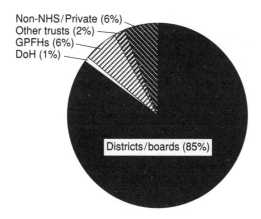

Non-NHS/Private (6%)
Other trusts (2%)
GPFHs (6%)
DoH (1%)
Districts/boards (85%)

Figure 7.2 Sources of income for a typical NHS trust (1994/5).

Source: *Developing Contracting: A National Survey of District Health Authorities, Boards and NHS Trusts* (Research Paper No. 15), NAHAT, Birmingham.

CAPITAL

Traditionally, NHS expenditure is divided into two categories – capital and revenue. Capital expenditure purchases assets which generate benefits over more than one year. Examples of such assets in the NHS include land purchased for building, the erection of new buildings, the extension of old buildings and the adaptation of existing buildings for health purposes, and the cost of initial equipment, furniture and stores for these buildings. These costs are incurred in relation to hospitals, clinics, health centres and offices of administrative bodies such as the health authorities themselves. Revenue expenditure, on the other hand, covers the costs of services in the current year. These include the remuneration of medical, nursing, paramedical and other professional staff; the remuneration of managers, accountants, storekeepers, cooks, domestics, porters, engineers and maintenance staff; the cost of goods and services needed to provide residential care for patients and accommodation for staff; the cost of drugs, appliances, fuel and the repair of equipment and maintenance of buildings. These lists of items are not exhaustive but simply indicate how health service costs have been classified.

The reason for making a distinction between capital and revenue expenditure may not immediately be clear: in private sector organizations it is essential for the calculation of the annual profit margin, where profit is the income derived from a given level of expenditure. This calculation is obviously difficult to transfer to the accounts of the NHS, where the 'income' is not obtained in monetary terms. There are, however, four reasons why the capital/revenue distinction is made in the financing of the NHS.

First, a decision on spending priorities must involve some analysis of whether the expenditure is part of a commitment made in the past (e.g. staffing a hospital built many years ago) or expenditure which will require funding over future periods (e.g. the maintenance of a new operating theatre installed during the current year).

Second, in order to analyse trends of expenditure over several years, it is wise to separate out those items which represent the cost of maintaining existing services from items for new services for which large sums of money are required at the very start. If this distinction is not made, there is a danger that total expenditure patterns over a period of several years will not reflect the fact that expensive projects were started in some years and not in others. Taking an example over ten years, it can be seen from Figure 7.3 that a project was started in year 3 and another in year 7. Assuming for simplicity's sake that these two projects were new wings of an existing hospital and that the building work was completed in one year, it can be seen that each new wing requires revenue expenditure for running costs in all subsequent years. If only the bottom line (total expenditure) were taken, this would give a distorted picture for analysis of the increased costs over that period.

Third, it is necessary to make the capital/revenue distinction in order to compare NHS Regions, and also to compare expenditure on the NHS and other

YEARS	1	£ million – excluding inflation								
		2	3	4	5	6	7	8	9	10
Current expenditure: original hospital premises	5	5	5	5	5	5	5	5	5	5
Current expenditure: first new wing			1	1	1	1	1	1	1	1
Current expenditure: second new wing							1	1	1	1
TOTAL CURRENT EXPENDITURE	5	5	6	6	6	6	7	7	7	7
Capital expenditure: first new wing		5								
Capital expenditure: second new wing						5				
TOTAL CAPITAL EXPENDITURE		5				5				
TOTAL (CAPITAL & CURRENT EXPENDITURE)	5	10	6	6	6	11	7	7	7	7

Figure 7.3 Capital and current expenditure.

government departments. Capital expenditure almost always involves large sums of money and, if the distinction is not made, public expenditure is difficult to plan. Capital projects which were necessary for the adequate maintenance of existing assets (e.g. replacing worn-out equipment) might otherwise not obtain sufficient priority, bearing in mind the scarce resources available to the public sector.

Fourth, in judging the timing of expenditure, current items represent a continuing financial commitment which cannot normally be significantly reduced. Capital commitments on the other hand can be brought forward or postponed depending on a government's overall economic strategy. In practical terms, this means that there is normally no possibility of deciding that hospital sheets should not be laundered or that nurses should not be paid, whereas building a new hospital can be delayed for one or two years if the government wishes to save that money in the current year.

The rigid application of the distinction between capital and revenue expenditure has, in the past, been criticized for discouraging local managers from using their discretion to finance services in a flexible and economic way. It also used to be the rule that all unspent money had to be returned at the end of the financial year, thus penalizing those authorities who, through wise financial management, had been able to achieve economies. They found that their under-spending could result in a reduced financial allocation for the following year. However, these anomalies have been recognized, and health authorities are now permitted to carry over underspendings of up to 1% of their budgets into the following year, and to transfer up to 1% of revenue allocation for capital spending and up to 10% of capital allocation for revenue.

Capital charges

Following *Working for Patients*, capital was redefined as an asset which would cost £1000 or more to replace [8]. Before 1991, capital expenditure in the NHS had always been considered as buying fully depreciated assets, so that once a new building was acquired, it was treated as having no financial value. The value of equipment was not amortized over a period, with the result that when it came to be renewed there was no existing money ready to pay for it.

In a service funded annually by taxation there are arguments for treating capital money in this way, on the grounds that if each health authority had to set aside all the funds it expected to need for its future capital purchases, a considerable sum of money would have to be held in reserve and could not be used meanwhile for legitimate recurring expenditure. The effect of this nationally would be to freeze large sums of public money, which could otherwise be put to immediate use. *Working for Patients* challenged the old assumptions. It encouraged trusts to value their capital stock at current prices and to make efficient use of all their capital assets. For instance, land should no longer be left unused if its sale could benefit the trust. Trusts are now required to maintain asset registers which include all equipment with a value of over £1000. Depreciation is calculated on ordinary accounting principles but based on the current value of the capital assets. Interest charges are calculated on the current value of those capital assets. Land and property values are calculated with the assistance of the District Valuer. For depreciation purposes the Government expects that the life of a building will not exceed 100 years, an interesting judgement given the number of hospitals that still occupy buildings considerably older than this.

Distributing capital

Under the RAWP scheme, capital money was distributed to Regions on a similar basis as revenue. However, the need for, say, new hospitals or maintenance or, to a lesser extent, equipment in hospitals, does not follow the exact pattern of the need for services provided from the revenue budget. Capital is required more sporadically: an area may need considerable capital investment over a short period of time, after which its need for capital will be low for some years. Therefore, the distribution of capital below the level of Regions has been much less based on rigid formulae and more on bids and negotiations reflecting long-term plans to renew or replace buildings and equipment. In the past, every Region has received a long list of capital schemes put up by its Districts. Most major building works took years to be realized, as they were fought for through the evaluations and option appraisal process. Depending on the scale of the scheme, approval was given either by Regions, or the Department of Health or, for very large projects, the Treasury.

Since the 1990 reforms several changes have occurred in the way capital is distributed in the NHS, but a number of issues remain unresolved. Relatively small-scale capital investment (new equipment, upgrading the estate and build-ings, etc.) is the responsibility of trusts and has to be funded from their own internally generated income (received largely from Districts) and/or external borrowing (mainly from the Department which offers loans at low interest rates). Trusts need to plan their capital investments and make sure that they will have sufficient income over the years to pay associated capital charges (see above). There is some evidence to suggest that the introduction of capital charges has significantly reduced the number of potential capital works, because trusts have had difficulty guaranteeing that future streams of income will cover the charges. The Department set a limit on the amount of internally generated income and borrowings each trust can devote to capital investment by estab-lishing an external financing limit each year (see Chapter 5, note 7). To the extent that trusts use internally generated income for capital projects, the old distinction between capital and revenue no longer applies. However, large schemes such as a new hospital are still effectively subject to a system of bidding and evaluation if trusts are to secure capital money held by their Regions. Regions themselves, in consultation with local purchasers and providers, can also initiate new schemes.

THE COST OF THE NHS

Over the years the amount of money spent on the NHS has risen substantially. There are three ways of looking at the increase (Figure 7.4 shows changes since 1971). First, the rise in the actual cash totals, from £0.5 billion in 1949 to over £36 billion in 1994; but these amounts are misleading because inflation has reduced the value of money over that period. Recalculating the figures at a constant value shows the true size of the increase. This is also illustrated by the third measure: the NHS's share of the Gross National Product (GNP), which has risen from under 4% in 1949 to about 6% in 1994. These trends make more sense when compared with others, such as the proportion of GNP that different countries devote to their health services (Figure 7.5). Of course, spending more money does not necessarily buy better health care. For example, costs reflect to some extent how much doctors are paid (one of the reasons for the UK's lower expenditure). Within the UK the resources allocated to the NHS can also be compared with the allocations to other public services (Figure 7.6). Whether the

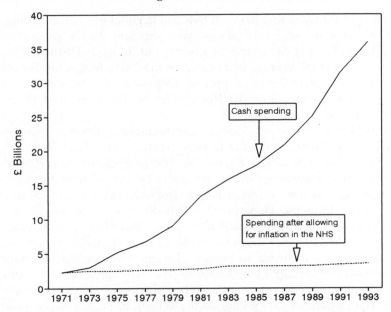

Figure 7.4 The cost of the National Health Service.

Source: OHE (1992) *Compendium of Health Statistics*, 8th edn, OHE, London.

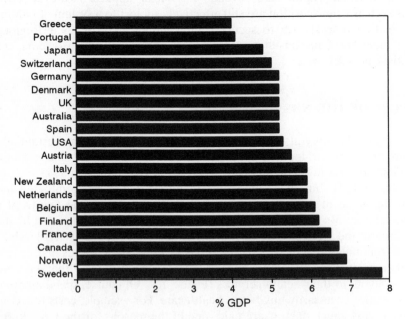

Figure 7.5 International comparisons of public health care spending: 1990.

Source: OHE (1992) *Compendium of Health Statistics*, 8th edn, OHE, London.

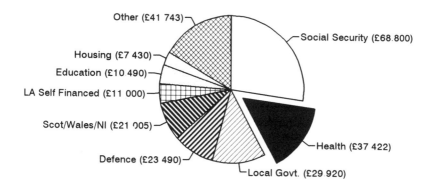

Total spending = £251 300m

NB: All figures in £millions

Figure 7.6 NHS share of public spending: 1994/5.
Source: *NAHAT (1993)* Budget Briefing: 1993, NAHAT, Birmingham.

UK obtains value for money for its investment in the NHS is not a simple question to answer. Some measures to promote efficiency are discussed below.

Health services throughout the world display a continuing rise in their costs. Ironically, in 1944 Sir William Beveridge's proposals for a comprehensive health service, assumed that improving the health of the nation would reduce demand for health services, whereas it is now understood that demand for health care is virtually infinite and there is thus no escape from the permanent need to set priorities and, ultimately, to ration access.

The analysis of total NHS spending (Figure 7.7) shows that hospitals' share started at about 55% and has risen to over 65%. This is meant to fall, following the government's intention to give greater priority to community care and family health services. The number of NHS hospitals has declined from 2441 (1959) to around 1600 (1994), and beds have similarly been cut back from 455 100 to 216 000 over that period. Yet, since 1975, the proportion of the budget spent on direct care and treatment as opposed to preventive and supporting services, has climbed to 67% of the total hospital spending.

CONTROLLING EXPENDITURE

Critical to the good management of public money is a sound financial system. In the NHS, each level of authority monitors the planned and actual spending of the one below it. The Department sets guidelines for the Regions and they in turn watch how Districts keep within the limits they have set them. Each

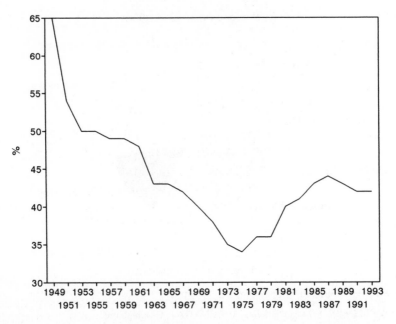

Figure 7.7 Spending on the NHS: family health services as a percentage of spending on hospitals.

Source: OHE (1992) *Compendium of Health Statistics*, 8th edn, OHE, London.

District then monitors its providers through the contracting process. The more detail each level builds into its guidelines for the one below, the less freedom it allows for local discretion. This system of global budgets has acted as an extremely effective constraint on total expenditure, to the extent that, while the chief concern in most other countries is cost containment, in the UK there has been a concern that too little is spent.

Budgets serve three main functions in commercial organizations: planning, control and costing. In the NHS these functions traditionally had a low priority, but, since 1974, the parallels with business have become stronger. Business planning and the systematic approach to controlling expenditure that it implies are now accepted. The discipline of cash limits, too, has been imposed rigorously in the NHS and other public services. Health authorities are notified of their revenue allocations for a year and have to manage within these whatever happens. This has sometimes forced them to cut services to make their books balance at the end of the financial year each March.

In the USA there have been sophisticated attempts to help clinicians to understand the cost of what they do to patients. Diagnostic Related Groups (DRGs) have been developed there over the last decade. DRGs classify patients according to a predetermined list of around 500 separate conditions which have been costed to enable a doctor to check the actual cost of his or her treatment of that condition with an average. Given the concern of medical insurers about spiralling costs, DRGs provide an important check on excessive care given to patients. The disadvantage of the system is its own high administrative cost; every procedure in the USA needs to be priced for billing purposes, thus requiring the inclusion of an administrative overhead. Moreover, a problem known as 'DRG creep' has reportedly occurred, whereby doctors have classified patients in DRG categories attracting higher payments from insurers than are warranted by a patient's actual condition, age, etc. The National Casemix Office in the UK [9] has been actively working on a British version of DRGs – Health Related Groupings (HRGs). So far (1994) there is no national system, although trusts have in some cases used a DRG/HRG type of classification for some of their services [10].

Since the NHS reforms of 1990, the system of global budgets at national level as a way of controlling expenditure still remains. At a local level, purchasers exert some financial control pressure on providers through their contracts which can, in effect, specify budgets and activity levels. For GP fundholders, control has been extended through the creation of budgets (in effect a transfer from districts' budgets). Expenditure control within trusts is derived partly from market imperatives (if costs and hence prices are not controlled then there is the risk of losing business) and partly through external controls, such as accounts audited by the Audit Commission (which also carries out value for money investigations – see below) and Departmental controls, such as external financing limits.

VALUE FOR MONEY

As well as controlling cash, purchasers and providers must be sure the cash has been well used. One incentive for doing so was 'cost improvement programmes' (CIPs), introduced in 1984, which were part of the yearly financial calculations. Districts were expected to release money from their main budgets by running services with greater efficiency, not by cutting services. The target was usually set at about 1% of the total budget. Whereas, initially, such efficiencies were readily identifiable, for example more careful spending on ancillary services, it became progressively harder to find candidates for improvement and, therefore, to reach the target without reductions in service levels.

'Easy' savings having been exhausted, it was then necessary to look at the core of the expenditure, the cost of patient care itself. In the past, doctors were given a relatively free hand to treat their patients as they wished, with little consideration of the financial consequences. This changed as attempts were made to raise the awareness of costs generally in the NHS. 'Clinical budgeting' as it was first called was redubbed 'Resource Management', which aimed to help those who make decisions about patient care to do so with an idea of the actual costs of their decisions.

As a system for looking ahead at intended decisions, it requires doctors to conduct regular reviews of expenditure against the speciality budgets they create. Incentives can be built in to permit one speciality's savings to be returned to it for its own development schemes. What should these budgets include? Should nurses be counted in or are they part of the hospital's overall responsibility? If nursing costs fall on a speciality budget, the doctors might wish to reduce the number or seniority of the hospital's nurses in order to make savings; but this might be unacceptable to the hospital's chief nurse, if it would reduce nursing standards or hinder his or her authority to deploy nurses throughout the hospital. The only sanction a doctor who overspends experiences is pressure from his peers.

Somewhat paradoxically, given that the main benefit of a market is to drive out inefficiencies through the process of competition, a version of CIPs still remains following the introduction of the NHS market. Each year, districts have been set an efficiency target – the 'efficiency index' – which they are expected to build in to their contractual arrangements with their providers. Unlike CIPs, this is not just concerned with realizing cash (and to an extent non-cash) savings for redeployment, but with improvements in 'technical efficiency' – or achieving more activity for every pound spent. In general, the target has been set at around 2% to 3% each year. However, the index has been heavily criticized (see Chapter 2, note 14), and the Department of Health has attempted to modify it. The index is similar to an overall measure of technical efficiency known as the 'cost weighted activity index'. Figure 7.8 shows how the English NHS has increased its technical efficiency between 1981 and 1991. The figure shows that while spending on the NHS has increased in real terms, the number

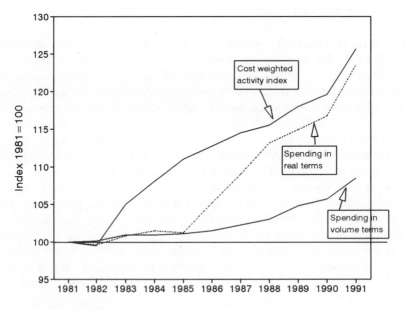

Figure 7.8 Cost weighted activity index: England.

Source: *The Government's Expenditure Plans 1993–94 to 1995–6: Departmental Report*, HMSO, London (Cm. 2212).

of patients the NHS has treated has increased even more, hence the cost weighted activity index has increased (since 1981, by over 25%).

All Health Authorities are accountable for the proper spending of public money. The Permanent Secretary and the Chief Executive at the Department are the designated Accounting Officers who must answer any expenditure questions put to them by the Public Accounts Committee. The Department recently considered extending the Accounting Officer status downwards to lower managerial grades as well (as part of the 1994 changes affecting Regions: see Chapter 3). Health Authorities' accounts are externally audited to satisfy the Government that public funds have been properly used, and each health authority has its own audit staff. The 1990 Act transferred responsibility for the Government's audit, previously undertaken by the Department's own audit staff, to the Audit Commission which must report to the Secretary of State any unlawful expenditure or financial loss. But their remit is much wider than this, and they undertake various surveys to assess value for money. The National Audit Office, responsible to the Government for scrutinizing all public authorities, also conducts reviews of services from a financial perspective. For example, a study into the use of operating theatres [11] demonstrated poor use of this expensive facility.

Detailed control of expenditure requires more than this periodic and retrospective scrutiny. Only by understanding the cost of the main components of each health service activity can real control be achieved. One of the obligations of the NHS is to obtain the maximum benefit from the resources that it uses, in order to maximize the health of the community. Measuring both health and benefit is difficult.

One method is to measure outputs, using statistics that have been recorded since 1948. From the accounts, department spending is costed in relation to in-patients and day patients for each hospital. This provides figures for per patient costs of departments and for average costs per in-patient week, and the average cost per 100 out-patient attendances. In-patients and out-patients are divided according to clinical specialty, and total out-patients and in-patients are counted under these headings. The data that result from these analyses, although useful to the hospitals concerned, do not give more than a superficial picture of clinical activity; they do not establish relative efficiency.

In 1965, a new system called Hospital Activity Analysis (HAA) was introduced: for each in-patient, date of birth, sex, marital status, area of residence, length of stay, hospital consultant and specialty are recorded. This gave information about rates of discharge and differential lengths of stay between specialties and hospitals and Regions. Its limitations – for instance, it did not differentiate deaths from discharges – led to the setting up of the Steering Group on Information Systems [12], chaired by Edith Körner, to recommend reforms. Under the so-called Körner system, a better selection of data is being collected, which presents more relevant information about patients. This includes, for example, 'finished consultant episodes' (FCEs) instead of deaths and discharges and the post code of the patient's residence, a small but relevant factor in the new charging arrangements between purchasers and providers in 1991. As the new health care market has developed, defining 'contract currencies' in terms of FCEs has begun to appear more and more inappropriate. Purchasers have started to buy packages of care – such as stroke treatment – which, for a single patient, may include a number of FCEs as they progress from one consultant to another within a hospital.

Since the 1980s, the Department has developed a package of statistical measures – performance indicators, now known as health service indicators (HSIs) – which draws together a whole range of financial and other perform- ance measures for providers and purchasers. These have provided a useful source of performance comparisons. More recently, the requirement for providers to publish prices for the procedures that GP fundholders are allowed to buy, and also the prices for extra-contractual referral procedures, has provided another source of information for purchasers to use to compare providers. The accuracy of these prices is doubtful, however, given current accounting systems. Without national collation of ECR and fundholder prices comparisons are somewhat limited. A further factor reducing their usefulness is the extent to which purchasers base their purchasing decisions on price. Chapter 4 noted that there was some evidence that in the first few years of reforms purchasers rated other criteria (e.g. proximity of services, the wishes of GPs) more highly than prices as far as their purchasing decisions were concerned. So far, therefore, some market mechanisims appear to have had little impact on value for money. Whether this will be true in the future remains to be seen.

General practice has had even less information by which to judge its effic- iency. Prescribing habits have been monitored by the Prescription Pricing Authority which now has a more sophisticated system through PACT (described in Chapter 5). Further information on GP patients and their treatment depends on the success of plans to standardize GP records.

Monitoring expenditure and making comparisons is one important way of calculating efficiency, but, in terms of health itself, effectiveness is a better index of value for money than efficiency. How does the NHS make sure that what is being done is worth doing? Only by auditing outcomes. One economic technique that was regarded in the 1960s as a breakthrough in evaluating alternative choices was cost–benefit analysis. It aims to evaluate both the costs and benefits of any course of action in a way which allows direct comparison between the costs and benefits. The simple decision rule that follows such an evaluation is that a project, treatment or service is worth doing if the benefits exceed the costs.

However, economic evaluation is not the only criteria that should be, or is, used to make such decisions. For example, the Government's policy for introducing cervical screening for all women aged between 20 and 65 years illustrates how political choices can obtrude into strictly economic or medical decision making. Health economists have argued that total population screening is expensive, and, where the number of positives detected is low, this cost may be unjustified. The concept of opportunity cost states that every decision in favour of one course of action prevents another course of action being pursued. So the £300 000 spent to find one positive cervical smear is not available to help other patients who may have more serious clinical conditions. This raises ethical as well as economic considerations, and clinicians and managers are aware that effectiveness in health care is often difficult to agree upon and certainly cannot be assessed without a rigorous look at outcomes.

PRIVATE HEALTH CARE

In August 1975 the DHSS published a consultative document called *The Separation of Private Practice from the National Health Service* [13], which set out proposals to reduce the number of pay beds in NHS hospitals and to control developments in private practice, in line with the Labour party's stated commitment to the electorate. The proposals met with fierce opposition, particularly from hospital doctors who had already been in dispute with the Government in 1974/75. Nevertheless the Health Services Act, 1976, enabled the Secretary of State to promote the separation of facilities available for private practice from NHS premises, and a quarter of the 4000 beds available in the NHS were withdrawn. A new Health Services Board monitored and authorized private hospitals and nursing homes to ensure that the interests of the NHS and its patients were not disadvantaged. With the change of government the Board and the other provisions were repealed by the Health Services Act, 1980. It has since become easier for a patient to change from NHS to private status even during the course of one particular treatment, and managers cannot ensure that there is no manipulation of the system to benefit private patients.

From the patients' point of view, however, private health care ensures that treatment will be obtained from a chosen consultant, in accommodation that will probably be private, and that little or no waiting will be required. By 1994, around 12% of the population had insurance cover to allow them access to private care if they should wish it [14]. However, in terms of the proportion of operations, up to 30% of all treatments (such as hip replacement operations) in certain areas (such as London) are carried out privately. Clearly this raises implications for NHS financing, and also for the controls currently in place to enforce consultants' NHS contracts [15].

Although there is not much evidence at the moment, private medicine may expand even further, as a result of the 1990 Act, if purchasing authorities find that they can get better value from the private sector than from their traditional providers, the NHS hospitals. A pluralist approach may result in a two-tier system, in which more disadvantaged people lose out. It is for this reason that the issue of private care and funding is a persistent feature on the political agenda of the NHS.

CONCLUSIONS

How societies pay for their health care is not simply an accounting matter but is bound up intricately with the way societies view health, health care, the rights of the individual and the role of governments. In the UK, political decisions taken at the inception of the NHS have meant that health care is funded largely on a community-wide basis out of general taxation. Over the years, there have been some fluctuations in sources of finance, but these have been minor. Even with the radical reforms of the 1990 Act, the method of funding the NHS was left unchanged, reflecting recognition of the broadly held view that health care is a special service which, for ethical, social and political reasons, should not be treated purely as a commodity to be traded in an un-regulated market.

The internal financing arrangements within health care systems – how purchasers receive their allocations, how hospitals are reimbursed and so on – is also more than a straightforward question of accounting. Allocation methods and payment systems can be powerful forces for change – whether by ensuring a degree of equity in provision or promoting changes in the way providers operate, the level of services they produce or whom they serve. And it is at this level that the 1990 reforms of the NHS have had their biggest impact. The way the NHS does its budgeting has been the most import-ant factor in containing costs – an issue many other countries have struggled to deal with.

NOTES

1. Office of Health Economics (1995) *Compendium of Health Statistics*, 9th edn, OHE, London.
2. DHSS Resource Allocation Working Party (1976) *Sharing Resources for Health in England* (RAWP Report), HMSO, London.
3. DHSS Circular HC(76)16 *Joint Care Planning: Health and Local Authorities*.
4. DHSS (July, 1975) *Progress in Partnership*, HMSO, London.
5. Audit Commission (December, 1986) *Making a Reality of Community Care*, London.
6. Griffiths, R. (March 1988) *Community Care: Agenda for Action*, HMSO, London.
7. Department of Health (1989) *Caring for People*, HMSO, London (Cm. 849).
8. Department of Health (1989) *Working for Patients. Working Paper 5. Capital Charges*, HMSO, London, para. 2.2.
9. The National Casemix Office was set up as part of the Department of Health Resource Management Initiative. It acts as an information source on Casemix measures and as a centre for the development of Casemix measures, such as DRGs and HRGs.
10. NAHAT (1994) *Developments in Contracting: A National Survey of Purchasers and Providers*, NAHAT, Birmingham.
11. National Audit Office (November, 1987) *Use of Operating Theatres in the NHS*, HMSO, London.

12. DHSS *Steering Group on Health Services Information* (chaired by Mrs Edith Körner), reports from 1982 onwards.
13. DHSS (1975) *The Separation of Private Practice from the National Health Service*, HMSO, London.
14. Office of Population Censuses and Surveys (OPCS). General Household Survey. Within this figure there are marked differences. Wales and Scotland have only 4% insurance holders compared to England's 10%.
15. Full time consultants in the NHS work to a contract, held by their trust, of 10/11ths of a full working week. The remaining 1/11th allows them to work privately if they wish – a hangover from the inception of the NHS when the then Minister of Health, Aneurin Bevan, negotiated this deal with the BMA to persuade consultants to join the service. However, if private work increases, this will start to raise conflicts (if they do not exist already in some areas) between the consultants and their NHS employers who may well be in direct competition with the private hospitals for whom their consultants also work. (See, for example, Yates, J. (1995) *Serving Two Masters*, Channel 4, London.)

8
Planning services for patients

The opening statement of the National Health Service Act 1946 made it clear that the new health service would be for everyone; it was not just a service for the sick. Has this grand intention been satisfied? This chapter looks at how services for various groups of patients and clients have developed. First, there is a historical account of the rise of service planning within the NHS and a description of the planning process since 1974, culminating in the 1989 White Paper *Caring for People* [1], and subsequent developments following *Working for Patients*.

PLANNING IN THE NHS

Chapter 1 showed that an unanswerable case for a national health service emerged from the recognition that health care was ill-co-ordinated and insufficient. Substantial demands arising from the Second World War, and long before, were not being adequately met. The creation of the NHS in 1948 was expected to pave the way for better planned services in the future. Any party forming a government then would have had to construct new proposals to deal with health care needs, but, for the 1945 Labour Government, the NHS was the principal foundation of its overall concept of the new welfare state. Early on, however, rising expenditure became a major problem, and in 1953 the Guillebaud Committee was set up to examine the financing of the service. Its report, in 1956 [2], exonerated the NHS from the accusation of wasteful use of resources. So the Conservative Government was forced to introduce plans for the more systematic use of NHS resources.

The 1962 Hospital Plan

One result was the publication, in 1962, of *A Hospital Plan for England and Wales* (the 1962 Plan) [3], which might be said to be the first major demonstration of a concern for planning in the NHS, a concern that has become an unavoidable discipline, and which underlies the reorganizations of 1974 and subsequently.

The 1962 Plan recorded that capital expenditure had risen from £8.7 million in 1949/50 to over £31 million in 1962/63. But a sense of overall national purpose was lacking; the capital schemes were largely *ad hoc* solutions to local problems. 'The moment has therefore come to take a comprehensive view of the hospital service as it is today and to draw the outlines of the service which we mean to create' [4].

The 1962 Plan reviewed the existing provision of beds, suggesting norms for each major care group, and integrated these in terms of specific proposals for each Region and within each Region for each hospital management committee. It needs to be emphasized that the 1962 Plan was only about hospitals and about beds. It briefly acknowledged care in the community and accepted that the development of hospital services must be complementary to developments in preventive and domiciliary care. Local health authorities were asked to review their services in conjunction with hospital authorities, but no consultative machinery was suggested, and the overriding impression given by the 1962 Plan was that only hospital development really mattered.

Not that this concern was ill-directed. It has already been said that the state of many hospitals was shameful. Over 45% of them were built before 1891 and some 21% before 1861; many were old workhouses, now often used for geriatric patients. These buildings had mostly been constructed following the 1834 Poor Law Amendment Act. Emergency medical service (EMS) hospitals, in comparison, built at the beginning of the Second World War, had a more flexible, single-storey design. With changes in illness patterns, the time had come to convert some of the special hospitals to more appropriate uses. Infectious diseases hospitals and sanitoria could quite easily be adapted for most uses, although they were often remotely situated. The 1962 Plan envisaged a gradual reorganization, in order to build up a central district general hospital and reduce the number of small and outlying hospitals. A yearly review of progress was intended to assess changes of circumstance and the availability of capital resources.

The 1962 Plan was relatively well received at the time. The process of centralization and the 'bigger-is-better' movement was in tune with the 1960s spirit of optimism and expansion, and in this respect the reception of the 1962 Plan was assisted.

Subsequent hospital plans

The term 'district general hospital' was first used by the Ministry of Health Building Note No. 3, in 1961, to describe a large hospital with between 400 and 800 beds, capable of providing a full range of diagnostic and treatment facilities in all the major specialities and some, at least, of the sub-specialities.

In 1966, the review of the 1962 Plan [5] curbed some of the initial optimism and modified the original plans, but the basic philosophy was endorsed by the Bonham-Carter Report published in 1969 [6], which was devoted to describing the functions of the district general hospital. The logic of its conclusions would have resulted in some district general hospitals becoming very large indeed, with possibly up to 1500 beds. As the number of hospitals with over 1000 beds in England and Wales was small, the idea did not find much support. Opposition to very large hospitals has perpetuated the situation whereby many towns still have two district general hospitals; this both duplicates and fragments facilities.

The 1962 Plan had concentrated on building up the district general hospital at the expense of smaller local hospitals. This proved to be controversial, not only because it provoked powerful local opposition to the closures but also because there was alarm at the high cost of building the new district general hospitals and the increased revenue needed to run them. This led to a change of direction in 1975, with the publication of the DHSS paper on the development of community hospitals [7].

The DHSS's criteria for admitting patients to community hospitals were that such patients needed medical and nursing care which could not normally be provided at home, but which did not need the full range of district general hospital facilities. It was seen as more humane to keep people as near to their own homes as possible, and, in this respect, the community hospital was particularly suitable for elderly patients whose visitors might also be elderly and less able to travel to a district general hospital many miles away. The community hospital idea was not made a sufficiently high priority to be developed systematically during the 1970s or thereafter. Nevertheless, the idea that there should be a balanced relationship between the district general hospital and smaller local hospitals, staffed by GPs, has remained current in the light of continuing concern with the escalating costs of district general hospitals and the determination of local people to keep facilities local.

Planning procedures, policies and priorities

The 1962 Plan and subsequent developments embodied a growing awareness that the NHS had to plan in a systematic manner. Throughout the 1960s it was becoming apparent that such planning could not take place in a vacuum. Attention needed to be given not only to improving hospital facilities but also to reviewing the needs of groups of patients on a wider basis, and to do this required co-operation with other branches of the NHS, particularly local health authorities. The original compromises made in 1946 had resulted in an NHS with three separately administered segments – the hospital service, family doctors and local health authorities – and this three-way split was insuperable, proving an impediment to effective planning.

The Ministry of Health had published a local authority planning document in 1963 entitled *Health and Welfare – the Development of Community Care* [8], but it was much less directive than the 1962 Plan, because local authorities were more autonomous than Regional Hospital Boards. The 1974 reorganization of the NHS was, therefore, not founded on much experience of systematic planning. Hospital management committees were content to run hospitals on a day-to-day basis; they had a poor sense of what was needed in the future.

For most administrators, plans still meant bricks and mortar only. The 1974 reorganization tried to change this by differentiating between two types of administration: one concerned with operational management (mostly in the Districts) and another concerned with planning (mostly at the Areas). Because this broad classification was too crude and simplistic, it never worked in practice, and was a key reason for the abolition of Areas in 1982.

However, after the NHS was restructured in 1974 to make planning a crucial task, the DHSS made determined efforts to provide advice on procedures and policies. First the policies. *Priorities for Health and Personal Social Services in England* (known as the Priorities document) was published in 1976 [9]. Its aim was to make the priorities of the Government more explicit while acknowledging the ever-present constraints, and to state that planning was a 'co-operative enterprise', involving the various tiers of the DHSS and NHS as well as local authorities and voluntary bodies. Only through this form of extended discussion could choices be made. Barbara Castle, the Secretary of State, emphasized that 'choice is never easy, but choose we must' [10]. The document was anchored on the assumption that, if authorities were given more of the facts, they would decide upon priorities more effectively. Studies of policy implementation suggest that so simple a model of rational planning was out of touch with reality. *The Way Forward*, in 1977 [11], was less specific about rates of increase in services and more vague about time-scales, while encouraging a continuing debate on priorities. Nevertheless, the general focus on planning remained, and Areas got down to the process of providing guidelines for their Districts, collating District Plans and developing fruitful relationships with local authorities, particularly social services departments.

One intended encouragement to the authorities to plan was the DHSS's changes to the rules for allocating resources to them. The adoption of the recommendations of the Resource Allocation Working Party report (RAWP) [12] (see Chapter 7), in 1976, required Regions to think much more carefully about how they were spending their money. Those Regions expecting to gain under RAWP clearly were encouraged, but the losers, particularly the London Regions, had to examine their services with even greater rigour if the planned cuts were not to have a devastating effect.

Joint financing was first introduced in 1976 [13]; it provided earmarked money for schemes jointly agreed between Health Authorities and Social Services Departments. In May of the next year a further DHSS circular outlined in some detail the arrangements for joint financing of both capital and revenue schemes [14]. This initiative made a substantial difference to relationships between health authorities and local government. No longer did co-operation rely almost entirely on good faith as there was now extra money, destined for agreed particular uses (the detailed arrangements were described in Chapter 7). Initial caution on the part of the authorities meant that not all of them made use of the joint finance funds they were offered. In 1979 and 1983 further amendments were made to overcome the problems, particularly by extending the period over which schemes could be financed from this special allocation.

Another policy initiative of the 1970s was *Prevention and Health: Everybody's Business*, in 1976 [15]. Health promotion had never had explicit priority in plans, thus ignoring a key goal of the 1946 NHS Act. This was despite considerable success in improving the health of the nation. As the document pointed out, the death rate from tuberculosis and the other main infectious diseases had been substantially reduced. But these successes unmasked other health problems which needed to be tackled, and the document called for discussion on the remaining and emerging problem areas. Although promoting good health is cost-effective, health authorities were slow to produce specific plans aimed at health promotion.

The recent history of health service planning is a story of optimistic intentions then altered by caution. The Priorities document – remarkable for its detailed plans – was trimmed a year later by *The Way Forward*. Similarly, a note of caution was struck by the consultation paper issued in May 1980 by the Minister for Health, Gerard Vaughan, entitled *The Future Pattern of Hospital Provision in England* [16]. The paper put the brake on building district general hospitals. The Minister said this was necessary because of their escalating cost. During the 1970s, attempts had been made to standardize the designs using three different systems entitled Best Buy, Harness and Nucleus, which were intended to cut the design cost and, in the case of Harness and Nucleus, to permit phased construction. Costly monoliths such as the Royal Liverpool Hospital had frightened the DHSS and health authorities alike. The paper proposed that district general hospitals should not normally exceed 600 beds and that smaller hospitals should be retained wherever 'sensible and practicable'. Two other important contributions to priority-setting were *Care in Action* [17] and *Care in the Community* [18], both published in 1981.

Although *Care in Action* was released before the 1982 reorganization, it was addressed to the chairmen and members of the new District Health Authorities. The pamphlet, described as a handbook of policies and priorities, aimed to help the new Districts to take local initiatives, make local decisions and shoulder local responsibility. Local decision making was the general theme of the 1982 reorganization, a reaction against the results of the top-heavy 1974 formula. A separate (and shorter) preface was addressed to chairmen and members of social services committees, emphasizing the responsibility of Health Authorities to collaborate with Social Services committees and Departments. *Care in Action* differed from the 1976 Priorities document in its focus on the range of options for health provision. The importance of the potential contribution from the voluntary and private sectors was underlined. This theme of partnership was to be developed more strongly in later documents. *Care in Action* also stressed the need for greater efficiency so that more patients could be seen for the same financial outlay.

Community care was not only an alternative to but seen as a cheaper option than institutional care (this belief was unsubstantiated). *Care in the Community* stated strongly that most people needing long-term care would prefer to remain at home as long as possible, a view well supported by current opinion, but also fuelled by the less altruistic view that it would be cheaper to reduce the capital costs and a substantial proportion of the revenue costs of running these buildings. Voluntary organizations were seen as being able to play an important part in contributing services to support the community. In 1983, the circular confirming the principles of *Care in the Community* allowed Health Authorities to extend the joint financing arrangements to voluntary bodies as well as social services departments. The circular went further by recommending that control of long stay hospitals could be transferred to local authorities in order to accelerate the discharge of people from health authority administered institutional care. These two DHSS initiatives, however, neglected the crucial message of the Working Group on Inequalities in Health, in 1980 (Black Report) [19], which called for a frank recognition of the links between standards of health and social class. It declared the pressing need for significant targeted funds, over many years, to reverse fundamentally some of the greatest deprivation.

Following the 1982 reorganization, planning took a new direction. The comprehensive overview of the service, relying on national norms for each care group, had proved inflationary, encouraging an over-provision of facilities and manpower which had become increasingly embarrassing to the Government. Looking back over the Priorities document, *Care in Action* and other advice of the middle and late 1970s, it was plain that everything had become a priority. Realism now demanded less idealistic plans, particularly as the national economy had not improved as expected. There was increasing emphasis on efficiency, doing the same for less or doing more for the same; on partnership, getting voluntary bodies and the private sector to contribute to health care; on outcomes rather than on process: *The Health of the Nation* White Paper set health targets to be achieved by the NHS; and, with the report of the NHS Management Inquiry (Griffiths report) [20], on making decisions more quickly and ensuring that they were implemented. This was easier said than done, because the elaborate planning process that had been fostered since 1974 was, by the mid-1980s, proving counterproductive.

THE PLANNING PROCESS

The 1974 reorganization created the first serious attempt to plan the health services in a systematic and comprehensive manner on a multi-disciplinary basis. Prior to this, most disciplines did not bother to plan rationally or, if they did, failed to take all interests into account. Health Care Planning Teams (HCPTs) were set up in 1974 to draw together professionals concerned with particular groups of clients or patients. The idea was that each team should examine the existing level of service and make recommendations to the DMT for improvements. The teams were formally approved by the AHA, but, in practice, membership and scope were decided and arranged by DMTs to whom HCPTs reported. In 1977, HCPTs changed their title to District Planning Teams (DPTs) but their function remained the same.

The 1974 reorganization also created Joint Consultative Committees (JCCs) within each Area, made up of members of county or metropolitan district councils and health authorities. These committees were serviced by the Area Team of Officers. Due to the workload of implementing the reorganization, these planning teams were slow to get under way. In March 1975, the DHSS published a comprehensive handbook called *Guide to Planning in the National Health Service* [21], which set out the detailed tasks to be performed at each level in the structure and explained the concepts of annual and strategic planning. The Guide was implemented in 1976 by a publication called the *NHS Planning System* [22].

Thus, from a situation where little systematic planning had been undertaken, especially at local level, an elaborate infrastructure was established. The NHS Planning System endorsed the original 1972 proposals for an annual planning cycle which, modelled on the PESC system, prepared and processed plans at certain times of the year, allowing District plans, for instance, to arrive at the Region in time (it was thought) to influence budget allocations for the following financial year, and also to give an indication of other developments requiring Regional involvement. The advent of RAWP made the system of bidding for funds less significant because it proposed a formula for the allocation of resources. In the event, RAWP proved slow to implement at District level. As a result of the 1990 Act, it was abandoned before equity of allocation had been achieved (see Chapter 7).

A vital element of the planning process was collaboration with local authorities. Accordingly, in circular HC(77)17 issued in May 1977 (see note 14), the DHSS required health and local authorities, with the advice of the JCC, to set up Joint Care Planning Teams (JCPTs). Unlike the JCC these teams were to be made up of officers of the respective authorities and were to include, wherever appropriate, officers from housing, social and health services. The JCPTs could also include nominees from voluntary organizations and consumer groups. These teams were purely advisory, not executive. Each JCPT advised its JCC, who in turn would make proposals to its respective authorities. Because the Area Health Authority or social services committees might reject the proposals, in some cases joint financing, conducted under the auspices of this system, were very slow. Both JCPTs and DPTs needed information to do their work effectively, but found it was not always available in a useful form. This problem led, in due course, to calls for better information systems and one result was the establishing of the Körner Committee [23].

The work of this group continued for several years and its recommendations were only fully implemented in the late 1980s. Despite the advice in Circular HC(77)17 that membership should be kept within reasonable bounds, planning teams became and remain unwieldy bodies, a point criticized by the Griffiths report. But it has been difficult to find a more streamlined manner of working. Significantly, even after the publication of *Caring for People*, the Secretary of State admitted that he had no clear idea about how to make joint planning of services more effective.

As early as 1979, *Patients First* had acknowledged that the new planning system was not fulfilling its role. Its introduction had varied between Regions, some of them enthusiastically producing their own versions of the system. By 1982 there was serious anxiety. The system seemed to encourage self-perpetuating talking shops, and not all Districts and Regions were committed to making it work properly. Accordingly, the Department of Health introduced a revised planning system. This was necessary in any case, following the abolition of Areas. The revised system designated the District Health Authority as the basic planning unit for health care and asked them to supply five-year strategic plans, with annual operational plans derived from them. The advice also suggested annual reviews, but argued for less consultation because this was now deemed too time consuming. District members succeeded to the AHA places on JCCs. District Joint Care Planning Teams were set up to process the work of the District Planning Teams, which continued. Where there were overlapping boundaries, the District JCPT provided a forum for co-ordinating policies and practices between different social services departments.

The five-year strategic plan was meant to give a concise summary of 'perceived needs, policies and goals' and to include references to capital and manpower costs. In practice, the traditional split between strategic plans and operational plans continued to cause difficulties. In so far as planning is deciding how tomorrow should be different from today (strategy), the chosen means of achieving that difference (operation) determines what to do. Strategies tended to become compromised by events, and some Regions amalgamated the strategic and operational elements of each year's plan. This did not remove the need for Districts to make clear in their annual plans their overall direction, which had to be in line with national and regional policies. In order to make sure that Districts were conforming, the system of annual reviews was introduced in 1982 (see Chapter 2). First, the Secretary of State reviewed each Region, and then, in turn, the Regions reviewed the Districts. The Griffiths report suggested that each District should conduct similar reviews with Unit teams.

Planning for purchasing and providing

The introduction of market competition following the 1990 Act did not do away with the need for planning – either at national or local level. As shown in Chapters 1 and 3, strategic direction from the centre has certainly not withered as the market has evolved. The publication of *The Health of the Nation* White Paper (described in Chapter 1) refocused attention on the final target of the NHS – better health – rather than excessive involvement with 'process' or managerial and organizational reform. At a local level, planning, that is, describing the present, having a view of the future and articulating a route to achieve desired ends, continues in its essentials. Trusts, for example, are required to produce annual business plans which detail their financial futures, articulate their mission in life and set out their schemes for service provision and capital investment. Together with projected income streams, this provides the NHS Executive with the core information on which to base decisions about each trust's external financing limit (EFL – see Chapter 7). These plans cannot be produced in isolation from the purchasers' plans and intentions.

Districts are also required to produce an Annual Report prepared by their Director of Public Health. Although an independent report, it highlights where the health of the District is giving cause for concern. For instance, heart disease rates or death rates from a particular form of cancer may be higher than average, or infectious disease incidence may be related to a lower than normal rate of immunization. From a study of this report, the District can begin to formulate the priorities their purchasing plans should reflect. This health investment plan succeeds the annual plan and is a key input into the district's purchasing plan for the year, showing how resources are to be allocated to providers to meet the health objectives the District has decided upon.

FHSAs are in an ambiguous position, as they are also deemed to have a purchasing role concerning the primary health care needs of the local population. The two authorities, therefore, have to ensure that their plans do not conflict or duplicate. The Department's decision, in 1993, to endorse the merger of Districts and FHSAs into a single local body concerned with purchasing (as well as GP fundholders) will overcome demarcation problems.

Although planning has become much more conscious, rational and, following the reforms of the NHS, to a degree more devolved since the 1974 reorganization, serious practical problems still persist, especially for Districts which are grappling with their new roles and having to develop new skills to tackle the task of planning in a market environment, and for providers who must wrestle with greater uncertainty concerning their income (and hence their very livelihood).

Increased emphasis on accountability implies increased monitoring, and this may be undertaken in a bureaucratic manner. A well-articulated planning system does not guarantee results; the gap between intention and achievement can be difficult to bridge in any large organization [24]. One crucial element for success is compatible plans between health care and social care; in organizational terms, between the NHS and social services. The White Paper, *Caring for People*, addresses this in detail, and was meant to complement the managerial reforms presented in *Working for Patients*, which preceded it.

CARING FOR PEOPLE

Some hospital patients could be better cared for in the community, while others in residential care require nursing support only available in hospital. The elderly mentally confused, for example, are seen as too disruptive for social services homes but are regarded as chronic potential bed blockers in hospitals, yet the availability of local hospital beds has permitted too institutionalized a form of care.

The first attempt to make sense of the planning muddle was a joint working party set up by the DHSS; its report, *Planning in Partnership* [25], was published in 1982. Representatives from health and social services endeavoured to clarify their respective responsibilities. This report made little impact. More outspoken was the Audit Commission's report *Making a Reality of Community Care* [26] in 1986. It castigated all the authorities in detail for their poor performance. For instance, there had been little overall increase in the support given to elderly people requiring home helps or meals on wheels. These simple services are widely recognized as effective in enabling elderly people to live at home rather than needing hospital or residential care.

A more fundamental issue was the rundown of hospitals for the mentally ill and those with learning disabilities. Patients were too often discharged without adequate community support and left dependent and vulnerable. This short-sightedness and inhumanity fuelled regrets that the closure of the larger institutions had been encouraged. They clearly had provided a relatively better quality of life, despite their size and dilapidation, than the isolated existence that many discharged patients were now forced into. The costs of making community provision for them fell, in particular, on the social security system, an important factor persuading the Government that the problem would need to be addressed. The money released by closing down large institutions was meant to be used to better effect in the community, but this needed special allocations to bridge the period of transition and then better control of community support. Because the social security payments had no upper limits for individuals in private accommodation, landlords abused the system by charging excessive rents. Payments were subsequently fixed according to the individual's degree of physical dependency and their personal financial position.

The Audit Commission drew attention to confusion about which agency should be in charge of what services, and strongly urged that lead responsibility should be unambiguously assigned, in order to stop the 'passing the buck' it believed to be rife. The Government's response was to turn to Sir Roy Griffiths again, whose first report on the organization of the management of the NHS it regarded as such a success.

Griffiths's second report, *Community Care; Agenda for Action* [27], appeared in March 1988 and was far less radical than his first. He did not really offer solutions to the problems but rearranged them by introducing arbitrary new definitions of health care and social care. He said more attention should be paid to the individual and less to the organization, and to making voluntary or private care equally available alongside statutory provision. The state was not to interfere as much as it had done, rather it should adopt an enabling role, fully in line with the Government's overall philosophy. However, clear direction was needed, from a minister with particular responsibility for formulating objectives and monitoring results. Griffiths favoured transferring the management of community care to local authority social services departments, and it may have been this, as well as his rather vague financial proposals, which delayed the Government's response.

Eventually, the White Paper, *Caring for People: Community Care in the Next Decade and Beyond* [28] was published in November 1989. It presented a new concept of case management, whereby each person requiring care is assessed, often by a multi-disciplinary process, prior to the preparation of their individual care package. Clients' own views were to be taken into account, but they would no longer receive payments from the social security office; instead, the money was to be administered by social services departments, who were to use means tests to establish client eligibility and provide a more sensitive and economical use of funds. One of the Government's concerns had been the huge growth in payments from the Exchequer via the social security system into private and voluntary nursing and residential care over the previous decade – a subsidy estimated at over £1 billion [29].

The doctrine of separating purchasing and providing, central to *Working for Patients*, was also prominent here: social services departments were encouraged to give up their direct management of residential accommodation and to buy what they needed from the independent sector. To ensure standards were maintained in this 'arm's length' arrangement, they were required to set up inspection and regulation systems along the lines of those used by health authorities in relation to private nursing homes.

The White Paper allocated lead responsibility, as the Audit Commission recommended, to social services departments, who took on the prime responsibility for people with learning disability, while using health service staff in a specialist role. The problems of patients discharged from long-stay mental illness hospitals was acknowledged, and a new grant was introduced to enable social services departments to improve community services in advance of patients being discharged.

The main criticism of the White Paper was the lack of convincing financial detail. Some feared that social services departments might run out of money before the end of the year and, to avoid this, would accept lower standards. The 1990 Act, which implements the new arrangements, did not clarify this. Subsequent statements by ministers and the Department of Health implied that in assessing clients' needs, social services departments should be aware of the limits to their budgets. Finance, not need, was the ultimate constraint on care. Whether the seemingly intractable difficulties of providing effective care in the community have at last been mastered is still unclear. The Government chose to slow down the timetable of change, retaining the original deadline of 1 April 1991 only for such elements as inspection procedures and complaints systems. *Caring for Patients* was finally implemented in 1992, with the means testing element only being felt by patients and their carers in 1994 when local authorities started to charge for services previously provided at no cost.

The remainder of this chapter discusses each care group in more detail, examining policy intentions and what has been achieved through the implementation of these policies.

PRIMARY CARE

This term covers both clients and patients. It refers to the work undertaken by general practitioners and other community staff in maintaining health and supporting the ill when out of hospital.

First, the maintenance of health. This is supported in a national way through such public health measures as clean air regulations, proper sewerage systems, environmental health inspection and through occupational health services and systematic surveillance of babies and children. All children can be immunized against infectious diseases, although this is not obligatory. The environmental health services, rather surprisingly, have never been formally integrated with the NHS, except that the Director of Public Health often acts as the named officer responsible to local authorities for giving medical advice. He or she will sometimes also act as the local authority's agent in implementing such regulations as those governing the transfer of someone with an infectious disease to a hospital for treatment.

It is difficult to define the proper limits on the extent of the functions of the health service. No one would suggest that the NHS should try to tackle bad housing or unemployment, even though both are proven causes of ill-health. The public health programme of the last 100 years is a success story. In the United Kingdom, clean water is now universally available and cholera totally eliminated. Similarly, enteric fevers such as typhoid are rare. The steady control of air pollution following the Clean Air Act, 1958, despite a recent increase in childhood asthma has reduced the incidence of chronic chest diseases. A century ago four babies in every ten did not survive childhood and maternal mortality was common. Now there are fewer than 50 maternal deaths per year. The infant mortality rate (deaths per thousand live births) is 7.3 (1991) – half the 1976 rate and less than a third of the rate in 1960.

Immunization programmes have controlled many infectious diseases, and smallpox has been eradicated world-wide. In the United Kingdom, diphtheria, polio and scarlet fever are relatively rare, and tuberculosis, measles and whooping cough much diminished. During the last 30 years, primary care services have made a concerted effort to improve health. Health visitors have had a particular responsibility for raising the general level of health, and increasing attention has been given to health promotion by health education officers.

Preventing illness is not the only responsibility of those working in primary care. Their other work relates to the care and treatment of those who are ill. The emphasis on the desirability of looking after patients in their own homes arises not only because of the high cost of hospitalization but because removing the patient, particularly the very old and very young, from home may create serious social and psychological difficulties. Young children can become badly distressed unless their parents are able to accompany them to the hospital and remain with them. Some elderly people admitted to hospital become observably more confused and dependent there. Attempts have been made to look after severely ill patients at home through 'Hospital at Home' schemes [30] but it is debatable whether this is more cost effective than hospitalization; making the most economic use of professional time is difficult in such circumstances.

For every 100 patients attending a general practitioner, 12 will attend hospital as out-patients and two will become in-patients. The rest are looked after by the primary care team, which is headed by a general practitioner and includes a district nurse and perhaps a health visitor and social worker. The team also calls in other professionals such as chiropodists and physiotherapists. Chapter 5 described the organization of family health services and how the new GP contract and the 1990 Act attempt to place more responsibility for primary care with GPs.

The district nurse works in the community and is usually attached to a particular surgery. The Cumberlege Report on *Neighbourhood Nursing* (1986) [31] envisaged a more autonomous professional role for such nurses than at present. He or she works closely with the GP, visiting patients in their own homes or seeing them for treatment in the surgery or health centre. The work covers such aspects as wound dressing and giving medication, together with psychological support and advice to patients or to relatives who may be worried by the patient's illness.

The health visitor is highly trained, a State Registered Nurse as well as a midwife. The work of the health visitor is less illness-centred than that of the district nurse, and has particular responsibilities for the promotion of health. Traditionally, health visitors spent most time with children, but increasingly they undertake more work with women and the elderly. They are well placed to observe difficulties in the home and to alert other professionals to avoid crises [32].

The chiropodist is responsible for looking after people's feet – a particularly valuable service for old people. A chiropodist can either work independently or be part of a community trust, sometimes based at a clinic and sometimes visiting patients at home. The dental officer provides regular dental care for children and is closely involved with the school health service. Dental care for the elderly is available at clinics. General dental practitioners work from their own surgeries. Their services were described in Chapter 5.

The physiotherapist is attached to a hospital department or GP surgery, but also does domiciliary work. Most physiotherapy departments now accept referrals direct from general practitioners. Hospital-based occupational therapists may do domiciliary work, although others are exclusively employed by social services departments. Speech therapists are independent professionals who take referrals from doctors. They diagnose speech defects in children and help a wide range of other patients, including those with strokes or who have had a head injury and have lost speech. Since the introduction of GP fundholding, some GPs are now responding to patients' demands for better access to services offered by chiropodists and physiotherapists by employing such practitioners to hold sessions in their surgeries.

In addition to GP surgeries and health centres, community trusts run clinics in the community, either in their own premises or in rented accommodation such as church or school halls. Child care starts by making sure that a baby's health is supervised from birth and that he or she is developing satisfactorily. Routine examinations detect hearing, speech or sight abnormalities, and the child can then be referred for suitable specialist treatment. Once at school, the child is examined by the school doctor at least twice during his or her school career, and has more regular supervision from nurses attached to the schools. Continuous scrutiny by teachers also helps identify health or developmental problems. Health problems among adolescents, such as precocious sexual activity or addiction to smoking, drugs or solvent abuse make particularly difficult demands that the school health service is not really equipped to handle.

Family planning services are obtainable either from the GP at the surgery or, in the past, from health authority-run clinics staffed by doctors and nurses specializing in family planning work. These latter clinics have reduced substantially in number in the 1990s. Apart from the GP service, independent clinics have also supplied advice and contraceptives, and independent agencies also provide abortion facilities for those women having difficulty because of the consultant's opposition or because the NHS is unable to provide an adequate service. Male and female sterilization does not require hospital admission. Some health authorities fund Well Women Clinics. These provide a screening service including smear tests to check whether cancer is present in the cervix, routine breast screening and advice about regular personal health checks. A similar service for men is usually only available in the private sector.

Since the 1990 GP contract was introduced (and the advent of the fundholding scheme), an extended range of services is becoming available to patients at GPs' surgeries, including minor surgery and consultant clinics.

PREVENTION OF ILL-HEALTH

Although the maintenance of health was a fundamental principle of the 1946 NHS Act, for the first 20 years it was left to members of the primary care team and those responsible for clean water, good sewerage and clean air. In 1968, the Health Education Council was established as a government-funded body and, until 1973, its medical research division conducted studies on such issues as the incidence of gonorrhoea, participation in measles immunization programmes and the causes of accidents at home. The Council's successor, the Health Education Authority, was criticized for failing to be effective.

How is effectiveness to be judged in this area? *Prevention and Health: Everybody's Business* [33] gave examples of successes, many of which resulted from public health measures initiated in the nineteenth century. In the twentieth century, immunization programmes and new drugs have helped to bring about further changes in the incidence of disease. Disconcertingly, as one

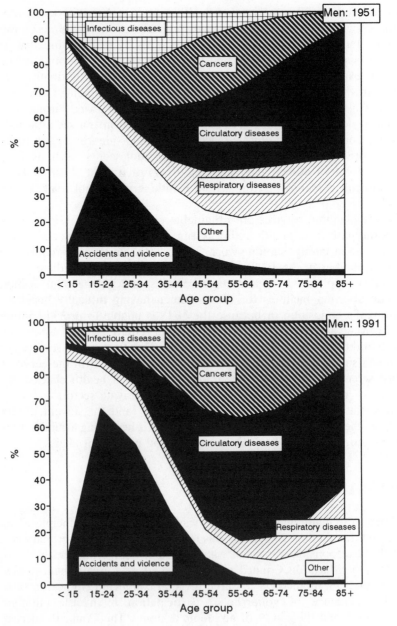

Figure 8.1 Main causes of death: women and men: 1951 and 1991.

Source: Office of Population Censuses and Surveys (OPCS).

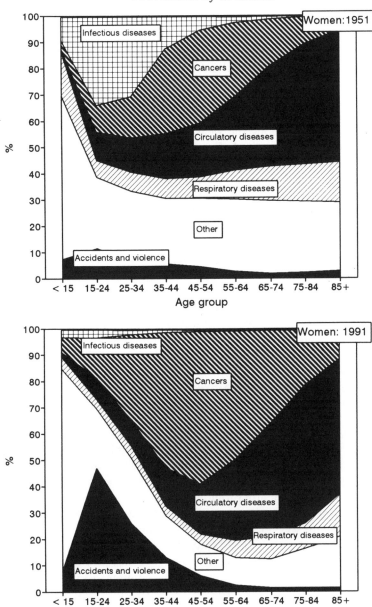

Figure 8.1 continued.

problem has been tackled another has arisen: TB is now a small problem, but venereal disease is increasing; young children survive to become part of an increasingly elderly population which makes new and greater demands on services; and, over time, the general pattern of illness and disease changes – as illustrated by Figure 8.1.

Governments have been unwilling to face the short-term political costs that some health-promoting measures incur. For example, the protracted campaign to introduce legislation making the wearing of car seat belts compulsory could have been significantly shortened if support from health ministers had been unequivocal. Clear evidence from other countries was disputed by many MPs who preferred to discuss the issue as a question of infringement of personal liberty. The substantial reduction in serious and costly accidents since the law was implemented shows the price of that extended discussion. Similar equivocation concerning banning tobacco advertising should also be costed in terms of avoidable illness and premature deaths [34].

On the whole, it is left to pressure groups to remind the community of the risks associated with various lifestyles and the alternatives available. As in other industrialized nations, notably the USA, promoting good health has become more fashionable. Interest in physical fitness programmes, better diet and reducing smoking and excessive consumption of alcohol is growing. Health authorities were encouraged to set up health education departments in Circular HRC(74)27. 'Health Promotion' and 'Positive Health' initiatives in the style of commercial advertising campaigns are needed if the fatalistic attitude of the public and other health service staff is to be overcome. Student nurses still smoke more than their peer age group, despite the dangers of smoking.

The Prevention and Health document, although a useful review, ended lamely by encouraging further discussion on ways in which people might help themselves to become fitter. It suggested that authorities should take action 'with whatever resources can be made available'. That remains the heart of the problem; too many within the NHS see health promotion as an 'extra', which can be curtailed in times of financial difficulty. Governments also react in this way, which explains why the Black Report was rejected by the Government in 1980. Its cost implications were allowed to be made the obstacle to implementation.

Rather more positive Government advice was also contained in *Care in Action* (1981) [35], which specifically set out the components of a local strategy for health authorities to pursue. The issues to be addressed by this strategy included a policy on smoking, the development of genetic counselling and family planning, improvement in school health services, the extension of immunization, a programme for reducing heart disease, better health education in schools (particularly covering smoking and alcohol use); nutrition and preparation for parenthood; the reduction of accidents on the road and in the home; a renewed attempt to fluoridate water supplies; and further encouragement to maximize the contribution from voluntary, community and commercial organizations to improve health care. With the publication of *The Health of the Nation*

[36] in 1991, the Government demonstrated a greater commitment to health promotion and disease prevention (although, as mentioned earlier, this does not extend to banning tobacco advertising).

Apart from support for fluoridation, successive governments have neglected prevention of dental ill-health. The British Dental Association, in a submission to the Secretary of State in 1983 [37], pointed out that the escalation of dental charges amounted to dental practitioners becoming 'tax collectors for the NHS'. This was acting as a deterrent to effective dental care, particularly among those most at risk. As a result, it was increasingly difficult to fulfil the 1981 DHSS Dental Strategy Review Group's aim of 'providing the opportunity for everyone to retain healthy functional dentition for life, by preventing what is preventable and by containing the remaining disease or deformity by the efficient use and distribution of treatment resources'. The new dentists' contract (see Chapter 11) attempted to move dental practice towards a preventive approach (rather than 'drill and fill') through financial incentives. One result, as Chapter 11 notes, was significant withdrawal of dentists from NHS work (although this was also attributed to poor rates of remuneration).

Internationally, the World Health Organization (WHO) tries to encourage governments to do more. In 1985 it published *Health for All 2000* [38], an initiative to reduce the level of sickness world-wide by the complete elimination of some diseases. WHO is also concerned to reduce inequalities and to reorientate health services towards primary care. It launched the *Healthy Cities Project* [39] in 1984. Compared with others, the UK has no excuse to be complacent as long as it continues to rate badly for heart disease and in relation to low standards of environmental health, to give but two examples. A more targeted approach has been forced on the Government by the emergence of AIDS and by the increasing incidence of food-chain and other infections. Salmonella caused the deaths of 29 patients in a mental hospital in Wakefield in 1983 [40], and legionella was, in one case, found in the air-conditioning plant of a new hospital in Stafford, where it was responsible for some patient deaths.

Not all these problems can be dealt with by health promotion initiatives. Altering personal behaviour to reduce avoidable disease is notoriously difficult. The Comptroller and Auditor General calculated, in 1989, that the 180 000 deaths per annum from heart disease (27% of the total) cost the UK £500 million. Heart disease is heavily influenced by smoking and bad diet. The campaign to reduce smoking has been quite successful; less than a third of the population now smokes. Improving diet has proved to be the more difficult aspect, although other Western countries have shown impressive reductions in heart disease where governments have been determined to change eating patterns away from highly saturated fat products. In the UK, the official approach to alcohol consumption has also not been unambiguous even though the health cost to the nation of alcohol-related illness is large. A Royal College of Physicians report, in 1987 [41], reckoned that over 20% of all hospital admissions were alcohol related.

Conflicts of interest account for some of the Government's weakness. It does not wish to offend those commercial concerns who contribute to the country's wealth or to forego the tax revenues from the sale of admittedly harmful products. The role of the Health Education Authority reflects this dilemma. The HEA, formerly the Health Education Council and semi-independent of government, was, in 1987, renamed and given special Health Authority status, bringing it more closely under Departmental control. It has been accused of being unduly compliant to the Government's wish not to make enemies in the business world. Nevertheless it has developed several major campaigns, such as 'Look After Your Heart', which have helped to raise the public's consciousness of avoidable ill-health.

OCCUPATIONAL HEALTH SERVICES

A separate but linked aspect of health promotion exists in the occupational health services. Until recently there were enormous gaps in checks on the provision of safe and healthy working environments; responsibility rested outside the NHS, shared between several government departments which organized inspectorates (alkali, clean air, explosives, factories, mines and quarries and nuclear installations). These were not uniformly effective, and the legislation did not require employers to inform their employees of the risks entailed in working under exposure to various dusts, fumes and chemical substances, nor to inform those who were not their employees of the risks entailed in entering such working environments. Occupational health services were set up independently by a number of firms and industries, but it was estimated that only 65% of factories with 100 or fewer employees had the service of a full-time or part-time doctor. Yet, for every working day lost by strikes, about ten days are lost by industrial injury or disease; most occupational accidents and diseases are preventable.

In 1948 occupational health services were not included in the remit of the NHS, and many feel this has led to their neglect and a poor understanding of their relevance to patterns of illness and health. An appointed factory doctor service was run by the Ministry of Labour, but it was only in 1973 that the Employment Medical Advisory Service came into being. This was designed to work through the Department of Employment to provide advice to ministers, employers, trade unions and other interested parties on occupational health and hygiene, and medical aspects of training and rehabilitation. Only about 120 doctors were involved in this service all over the country, the Department of Employment taking the view that engineers, chemists and other specialists, rather than doctors, had the expertise to assess and change the working environment.

In 1972 the Robens Committee published its report, *Safety and Health at Work* [42], and, three years later, its full proposals were embodied in the Health and Safety at Work Act, 1974, which unified responsibility for co-ordinating services with the Health and Safety Commission – an independent body with representatives from employer and employee organizations and the local authorities. The Commission took over the work of the Employment Medical Advisory Service and the former inspectorates, and operates through the Health and Safety Executive, which employs inspectors, engineers and doctors to enforce the application of the Act's provisions. Under these, all employers, employees and self-employed people (except domestic workers in private employment) are protected in the work situation, and risks to the health and safety of the general public arising from work situations must be prevented. This includes control of noise, the emission of fumes, the handling of toxic materials and the risks of specific working environments.

The Act operates through a series of codes of practice and requires employers to maintain safe plant and equipment, safe systems of work and premises, to arrange for adequate training, instruction and supervision, to provide facilities and arrangements for employees' welfare at work, to lay down a health and safety policy in writing and to inform employees about it. The legislation covers all staff and practitioners in the NHS for the first time, and the Department of Health issues guidance from time to time relating to the particular hazards of work in the NHS.

Obviously, occupational health services vary: the requirements of heavy manufacturing industries will differ from those of non-mechanized service enterprises. Some firms have provided services far beyond the pre-1975 legal requirements, and have delegated responsibilities to special fire and safety officers and appointed medical advisers. In October 1978, regulations came into force enabling safety representatives and committees to be appointed by employees. These have the power to make regular inspections and reports on conditions in the workplace, to take the advice of health and safety inspectors and make representations to the management. The health and safety legislation will improve conditions overall, in time, and create a better awareness of avoidable hazards.

The NHS used to be largely exempt from health and safety legislation by virtue of Crown immunity which was based on the idea that it is impractical, in legal terms, for the Crown, the legislature, to prosecute a state-run organization for non-compliance: the Crown could not prosecute itself. The National Health Service (Amendment) Act, 1986, started the process of removing this exemption. First came the right of the Health and Safety Executive's inspectors, working closely with local authority environmental health officers, to check on food hygiene in hospital kitchens. By 1991, health authorities and trusts could no longer claim exemption from the recommendations of fire inspectors; this has proved expensive as they are obliged to improve fire escapes in old hospitals. Another important piece of legislation affecting hospitals is the Control of Substances Hazardous to Health Regulations [43] which imposes a duty on all employers to protect their staff from exposure to contamination of various kinds. The full cost of removing Crown immunity for the health service is likely to be considerable, but it brings the NHS up to the standards required of other employers and service providers.

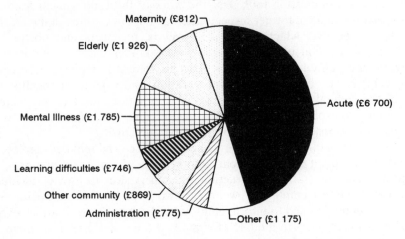

Total spending: £14 788 million

Maternity (£812)

Elderly (£1 926)

Mental Illness (£1 785)

Learning difficulties (£746)

Other community (£869)

Administration (£775)

Acute (£6 700)

Other (£1 175)

Figures in £ millions

Figure 8.2 NHS spending by service group: England: 1990/1.

Source: *The Government's Expenditure Plans 1994/5 to 1996/7: Departmental Report*, HMSO, London (Cm. 2512).

ACUTE HOSPITAL SERVICES

Although it is the stated objective of the NHS to promote health, the fact remains that most of its resources are devoted to the care and treatment of those who are sick and who are treated in hospital. Acute services alone absorb some 45% of the total health budget (Figure 8.2). They include treatment for all urgent or serious episodes of ill-health. This definition generally excludes routine services for children and the elderly (although children and old people may become acutely ill), women having babies, the mentally ill, the physically handicapped and those with learning disabilities.

How is acute care provided? In cases that are not emergencies, the GP refers the patient to a hospital consultant for advice about symptoms or for treatment that requires the consultant's special skills. The consultant has undertaken extensive training in his own speciality and has expert knowledge, access to sophisticated equipment and facilities and, in the case of the surgeon, particular technical skills. For those patients involved in accidents or sudden collapse, referral from a GP is not necessary and they can be taken directly to the accident and emergency department of the district general hospital or to the casualty department of the local GP hospital.

Non-emergency, but not necessarily non-urgent, patients are referred by a GP to a specific consultant or group of consultants working in the appropriate speciality. The patient is given an appointment in the out-patient department which is usually held at the district general hospital. In some Districts, it may be at the GP hospital or health centre. The consultant, or another doctor in their medical team, examines the patient and makes a diagnosis, with the help of various tests and procedures such as blood, urine or tissue analysis, X-ray and other methods of body and organ scanning. This may require several hospital visits as an out-patient and sometimes in-patient treatment will then be prescribed. In 1992/3 there were over 8.4 million new acute out-patient attendances in England; over 32.5 million acute out-patient attendances in total and around 7.8 million in-patient and day case episodes of care. Treatment may involve surgery, drugs, radiotherapy and physiotherapy or a combination of these. Once the patient's condition has improved sufficiently, the consultant will discharge him or her back to the general practitioner. Florence Nightingale defined discharge from hospital as 'dead', 'well' or 'relieved', and the outcome must still be one of these.

The cost-effectiveness of acute care is a controversial question. Patients are submitted to an ever increasing array of sophisticated treatments at great expense to the NHS and yet the outcome may well be inconclusive. Nevertheless, patients' support for what doctors want is demonstrated by the enthusiasm for raising money for high technology medical equipment. New procedures may well be less troublesome for the patient and may greatly improve accuracy of diagnosis and treatment. For instance, patients found air encephalograms (in which air was introduced into the cavities of the brain to demonstrate the presence or otherwise of a tumour) acutely uncomfortable, leaving them with a headache for several days. This has been replaced by computerized tomography (CT) using a scanner, which gives the doctor more information and subjects the patient to no more discomfort than he or she would have from a routine X-ray.

The introduction of fibre optics has allowed surgeons to perform operations on organs inside the body, for example in the bladder, uterus and stomach, without having to open the patient's abdomen. One of the most notable successes of the last 25 years has been joint replacement, particularly the hip. This has been achieved by the anaesthetist and orthopaedic surgeon working together with the instrument and prosthesis maker. With improved control over drugs and gases, the anaesthetist can now anaesthetize patients of any age without undue risk. Orthopaedic surgeons have perfected the technique of joint replacement with the result that many elderly people, previously disabled and immobilised by degenerating joints, can continue to be active and independent.

Such success stimulates its own demand, and the NHS has failed lamentably to keep pace, so that the national waiting-list for surgical operations in 1994 stood at over 1 million (although average waiting-times have fallen [44]). New drugs have also had remarkable effects, but there have, at the same time, been a few controversial failures. There is also disturbing evidence of drug-induced illness due to side-effects or the prescribing of unsuitable combinations of drugs. Compared to pre-NHS days, acutely ill or injured patients now usually have every chance of receiving a high standard of care and treatment wherever they are in the UK.

The 1976 Priorities document was the first realistic attempt to set targets for acute care in terms other than the number of beds in a hospital. It argued that there should be slower growth of resources for this service so that more could be done for the less advantaged services. The document endorsed the idea that the district general hospital should provide for the usual range of medical and surgical patients, as well as having a maternity unit, a psychiatric unit, a geriatric unit and children's department. Most DGHs have full-scale accident and emergency departments, and some also have ear, nose and throat and eye units. A few centres have more specialized departments, such as radiotherapy and neurosurgery.

The Priorities document drew attention to recent trends. First, in-patients' length of stay had been reduced quite remarkably – the average length of stay in 1957 was 21 days, but in 1976 was around 10 days and in 1994 is around 5 days. This is due to changes in medical practice, such as the earlier mobilization of surgical patients, new surgical techniques such as laser treatment for certain ophthalmic problems, which allow patients to be seen as day cases, and possibly also to general improvements in the home environment. Secondly, medical technology was developing too fast for the NHS to be able to cope sensibly. The Priorities document said that the pressure to adopt new techniques and equipment had to be controlled, otherwise it would push up costs per case, even though patients might have to stay in hospital for fewer days.

No policies exist for controlling the cost of developing medical technology. Health Authorities and hospitals have been left to work out their own solutions, so that the distribution of advanced diagnostic equipment is unequal and reflects voluntary fund-raising efforts. Policies could be developed to encourage a more controlled expansion of medical technology and sophisticated techniques by relying more heavily on properly regulated trials and on some form of medical audit. Neither approach has yet found sufficient support from the Government, and it seems likely that health authorities, through their purchasing decisions, will have to continue to balance, as they think fit, the seemingly insatiable demands of the acute sector with the need for improvements in services for other care groups.

The Priorities document listed the main areas of concern as reducing waiting-times; continuing with efforts to reduce the unequal distribution of services; facilitating medical advances; improving services for the elderly and for reha-bilitation. How far have these aims been pursued? Waiting-lists represent the quantity of demand that it would ideally be reasonable to meet, whereas waiting times are ultimately within management's control. However many patients there are on a waiting list, those there for the longest time should be certain to get to the head of the queue and, when they come to hospital for consultation, be seen promptly. Actual progress towards these aims has been abysmal and has stimulated increased use of private medical facilities.

Industrial unrest in 1979, and again two years later, reduced the output of some hospitals and lengthened the waiting-lists considerably. Despite the Priorities document's recommendation that all urgent cases should be admitted within a month and all others within a year, many health authorities had come to accept the waiting problem as inevitable. This fatalistic approach was challenged in 1990, when the Chief Executive of the NHSME suggested that if managers failed to reduce waiting-lists, then performance-related pay would suffer. Other policies, such as the waiting-times initiative and the *Patient's Charter*, have recently tackled the problem head on through targeted funding and research, as well as reinforcing with managers the political message to reduce waiting times. Although the number of people awaiting admission reached over 1 million in 1994, waiting-times fell, with no one waiting more than two years and only 6% waiting more than a year, compared with over 26% in 1987 (Figures 8.3 and 8.4).

CHILDREN

One indication of health service effectiveness is the health of children. To oversimplify: a healthy child means a healthy adult. Apart from the care and surveillance provided by the child health services some children suffer sudden illness and accidents. Over 44% of home accidents happen to children under 15; children are involved in 13% of road accidents [45].

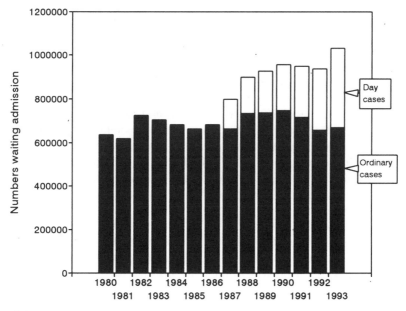

Figure 8.3 Total waiting lists: England: 1980–1993.

Source: Department of Health *Statistical Bulletin*.

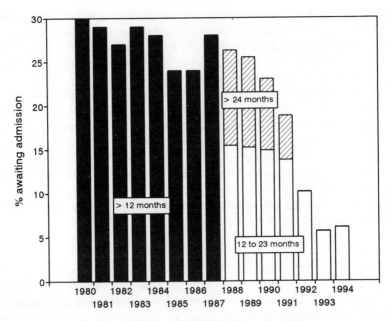

Figure 8.4 Percentage of ordinary cases waiting over one and two years for admission.

Source: Department of Health *Statistical Bulletin*.

The hospital regime for the acutely ill or injured child has changed for the better in the last 30 years. Much of this has resulted from pressure applied by the parents themselves and the National Association for the Welfare of Children in Hospitals (NAWCH). Official reports, including the 1959 Platt Report on the *Welfare of Children in Hospital* [46] and the Court report (1976) entitled *Fit for the Future* [47], have also been influential. In turn, such reports were influenced by the work of enlightened paediatricians such as McCarthy and Jolly [48], who did much to make the child's stay in hospital less of an ordeal. Most hospitals now have some facilities for parents wishing to stay with their children in hospital. This sharing in the care of the child is not always welcomed by nursing staff, and surveys by NAWCH show that completely unrestricted visiting and reasonable facilities for parents on children's wards are still not yet universal.

Surgical treatment of children is less in evidence: routine tonsil and adenoid operations are no longer done and, as a result of more widespread dissemination of evidence of the relatively poor medical- and cost-effectiveness of grommet treatment for persistent glue ear, this operation is also declining [49]. With the increasing coverage of immunization, long term in-patient care for children is now unusual, and the demand for specialist children's hospitals has decreased. Self-contained children's departments have largely superseded previous arrangements, whereby children needing surgery were usually treated in the adult part of the hospital. Concern is therefore switching to children in the community. The Priorities document said, '1976 seems likely to be a critical year for the children's services'. It and the Court report attacked the complacency that characterized government thinking and urged renewed efforts to be made, not least to keep up with the improvements in children's health achieved in many other countries.

Between 1971 and 1988, there was a fall in birth rate in the UK, so that the under 15s were 18% of the population in 1988 compared with 24% in 1971. While the Priorities document concentrated on specifying actions to be taken, the Court report, a very detailed study, focused more on the integration of services. The Priorities document emphasized the need for further improvement in special care facilities for new-born babies. With the large-scale redevelopment programme of maternity hospitals, many units have now been provided. They are run by consultant paediatricians and nurses with special training. The survival rate of low birth weight and handicapped children has increased, and this has increased the survival rates of vulnerable individuals who may need further care later in life. More health visitors have been needed, yet not all authorities have been able to redistribute funds to do this. The Priorities document and *The Way Forward* [50] emphasized the need for better secure accommodation to ensure that adolescents were not remanded in prison. This policy has largely been achieved, although the way borstals and other severe accommodation for children are run has been subject to criticism at times [51].

At the end of the 1980s concern about child abuse of both a physical and sexual nature was high. Health Authorities reviewed their procedures for dealing with such children, who may first appear in casualty departments with unexplained injuries. Diagnosis of child abuse is controversial, and a much publicized case in Cleveland led to an official inquiry into the manner in which two paediatricians had examined children for abuse and the conclusions they had reached.

This affair was one of the factors influencing revision of the statutory protection for children contained in the Children Act, 1989. This Act gave social services departments specific new instructions and duties, with a view to improving confidence that safeguards were sound. The Court report had also influenced the new legislation, and certainly has encouraged health and social services departments to give more thought to the special needs of children.

MATERNITY SERVICES

More pregnant women than ever before are now likely to have a satisfactory outcome to their pregnancy. The infant mortality rate (babies dying within the first year of life) has steadily declined and now rests at 6.6 per 1000 live births (1992). However, this is still not as good a figure as achieved by other

Western countries, notably Sweden. Care of the pregnant woman is one of the areas most susceptible to benefit from efforts made by professional health staff. Examination early in pregnancy by the GP and consultant obstetrician, regular supervision by the midwife and attendance at ante-natal clinics, together with routine scanning and, in cases of risk, amniocentesis (testing the amniotic fluid surrounding the foetus for genetic abnormalities such as Down's syndrome and spina bifida) have all improved the chances of a successful birth and a healthy baby. The reduction of the number of unsatisfactory births (those with a suspect physical prognosis or just unwanted births) has been brought about by regularization of abortion facilities following the 1967 Abortion Act. Women are now able to obtain abortions fairly easily and it is estimated that up to a fifth of all pregnancies are now terminated within the first few months [52].

Some would argue that not all the changes are good for the mother. For instance, hospitalization of almost all births may not be the only or best way to improve the chances of the baby and its mother, given the good results found in the Netherlands where, alone in Europe, there is still a relatively high domiciliary delivery rate. Nevertheless, the recommendations of the Cranbrook report [53] in 1959, which advocated the greater hospitalization of mothers in labour, and of the Peel report [54] in 1970, which emphasized the need for an integrated approach to maternity care, have resulted directly and indirectly in hospital delivery rates of around 98%.

The Cranbrook report was critical of the existing standards which put mothers and their babies unnecessarily at risk. It proposed that at least 70% of mothers should be delivered in hospital. The length of stay was assumed to be ten days, requiring 0.58 beds per 1000 population on the projected population figures for 1975. The 1962 Plan accepted this recommendation unequivocally, and for the next 20 years maternity hospital buildings were gradually renewed throughout the country. With the decline in the birth rate and reduction in length of stay to around six days, some areas then found they had too many beds. Other contributory factors were changes in obstetric and midwifery practice and pressure to reduce the institutional regime of maternal confinement. New – and possibly very old – theories about how best to be delivered in more homely settings with the attendance of the father at the birth, have helped to reduce the institutional atmosphere [55]. Although it seems unlikely that there will be a large-scale return to home confinements, a 1993 Select Committee report (*Changing Childbirth*) [56] moved policy towards a more sensitive service. In some places midwives now take full charge of normal births.

Despite the improvement in facilities for pregnant women, comparative statistics show that the UK has been trailing behind other countries in such matters as perinatal mortality. The Short report of 1980 (a Select Committee report) [57] examined this further and encouraged the Government not to reduce its concern with the improvement of maternity services. Since the 1950s, doctors themselves have undertaken reviews of their practice through triennial confidential enquiries into maternal deaths. These reviews have shown that around half of all maternal deaths need not have happened. Social factors contribute to risk in pregnancy, and the Black report on inequalities [58] demonstrated that a deprived mother was less likely to seek care, and was consequently more likely to put her own health and that of her baby in jeopardy. Maternal deaths in the 1960s among occupational class V mothers were double that of class I and II. Such inequalities still persist.

PEOPLE WITH LEARNING DISABILITIES

Despite improved care of mothers and babies during pregnancy and birth, some babies are born with a learning disability or subsequently develop this impairment. Classification of the numbers is fraught with problems of description. It has been customary to rely heavily on intelligence quotient (IQ): those who score under 50 are reckoned to have severe disability and those between 50 and 70 mild disability. The IQ measure is controversial and not necessarily a good indicator of the needs of a person with learning disability. Accordingly, this has led to attempts to define people in terms of the level of their dependency on others, but this too has proved to be inexact. It is repeatedly found that highly dependent people with learning disability who were institutionalized can make radical progress in a different environment, becoming much more capable than the most optimistic professional staff would have predicted.

There are three or four severely disabled people per 1000 in the 15–19 age group. Learning disability is not an identifiable disease; it is the result of malfunction during pregnancy, injury at birth or subsequently by accident, infection, drugs or a developing degenerative condition. The care of such people has to take account of this variety of causes. Interestingly, the name of the condition has troubled every generation and reflects the changing attitude of society to the problem. From the 'idiots' of the late nineteenth century, the descriptive and legal terms have included 'deficiency, 'subnormality' 'mental handicap', and now 'people with learning disabilities' or 'learning difficulties'. In other countries the preferred term is 'mental retardation'.

With the changes of label have come changed attitudes, and, in the last 15 years, there has been significantly more discussion on how best to look after people with learning disabilities. Some progress is being made, and a few hospitals and social services departments are pursuing increasingly radical policies, particularly those aimed at deinstitutionalizing the service. There were, however, still around 30 000 people with learning disabilities permanently in hospital in 1994.

Government attention has focused on the discharge of children with learning disabilities from long-term hospital care [59], the easiest problem to solve, given the considerable support available to the children's families. As well as health visitors and other specialist staff, there is an increasing number of pre-school groups for the disabled. Attempts to integrate disabled children in ordinary schools have limited success, so special schools continue to fulfil most of this need. Disabled children are entitled to education up to the age of 19, although not all education authorities discharge their obligations in this respect. After 19, adult training centres and sheltered workshops may give people with learning disabilities a place to go during the day. Within some large hospitals similar opportunities for work exist, but many people with learning disabilities spend their days there with little occupation or diversion.

The status of this speciality has gradually risen among professional health services staff, and administrators no longer see it as such a low-prestige area of work. The change was first stimulated by the recurring scandals arising from lack of appropriate care, starting with the Ely Hospital affair of 1969 [60] and Pauline Morris's study *Put Away* [61] the same year.

The most significant policy document was *Better Services for the Mentally Handicapped* (1971) [62], which presents a charter for people with learning disabilities. The long-term aim is to provide a more satisfactory environment for them, whether at home, in a hospital or in a residential home. The traditional segregation from society is deplored; health, social services and educational authorities are encouraged to work together to provide an integrated, readily accessible service. Every effort should be made to support families of such people. The Priorities document endorsed these aims and proposed considerable growth in the number of local authority training centres and residential homes. Staffing ratios in hospitals were to be increased and would help improve the standards.

In 1975, the National Development Group was set up to lead the way to these better standards. Its regular reports were important in maintaining government commitment. Despite this, the Group was disbanded in 1980, after the Government published a review of progress since the Better Services document. In fact, progress had been disappointing. One of the reasons for this was the conflict between professionals about the best way of providing care. Some staff were convinced that the increasing emphasis on community care was wrong, both for the community, who may feel threatened by people with learning disabilities in their midst, and for the people themselves, who may be discriminated against and might lose access to those facilities provided as a matter of course in specialist hospitals. The Jay report [63], published in 1979, fanned the flames of disagreement by suggesting that training nurses in mental handicap was inappropriate and that a less clinically based training would be better. In the event, faced with this professional controversy and because the financial implications were considerable, the Government did not support the Jay recommendations.

After a slow start, the Government's policy of discharging people from hospital has accelerated. By the year 2000 nearly all the so-called 'water tower' hospitals will have closed and former patients will have been relocated into the community. Nevertheless, the majority of these people have no overriding medical condition that requires hospital services; *Caring for People* stressed the importance of individual assessments leading to more appropriate placements. Learning disability is now no longer a health care issue unless gross behaviour disorder or other physical or mental illness requires active treatment.

THE PHYSICALLY DISABLED

Another numerically small group of people requiring considerable support is the physically disabled. This broad label covers people with a variety of conditions. Disablement may be due to injury, particularly the results of a road accident, infectious or degenerative disease, sudden medical emergencies such as a stroke or congenital abnormalities.

The requirements of a disabled person will naturally vary according to his or her problem. At the most severe level the disabled person will need complete medical and nursing care in a hospital. All too often this care is provided in unsuitable accommodation: an acute ward where the arrangements are geared to a high turnover is not suitable for someone having to live there for a long period. Worse still, for a younger disabled person, is a ward of elderly patients, some of whom may be confused. Unfortunately, many health professionals tend to underestimate the potential for improvement in profoundly disabled people, particularly those with head injuries, those with multiple sclerosis and stroke victims. Without an early and co-ordinated attempt to estimate the rehabilitative potential or the appropriate level of alleviation, the patient will not only fail to improve, but may well develop further problems and deteriorate.

Following the passing of the Chronically Sick and Disabled Persons Act, 1970 [65], health authorities started to develop special units for the younger disabled. However, implementation of the policy lost momentum and there are no more than 2000 places in purpose-built hospital units. Since then, there has been much more emphasis on community care or the use of homes run by charitable organizations such as the Cheshire Homes. The Priorities document gave muted support to the provision of such hospital units, although it pressed strongly for a special spinal injuries unit for the south of England to relieve pressure on the unit at Stoke Mandeville Hospital in Aylesbury. A new spinal injuries unit opened at Odstock Hospital, Salisbury, in 1984. Apart from this, emphasis has been on maintaining the physically handicapped in the community or in homes provided by the voluntary sector.

Disabled people who can continue living outside hospital may be usefully supported by cash benefits and visits from NHS staff. State allowances subsidize the cost of someone giving long-term physical assistance. Social services and health authorities are empowered to lend or give the disabled person an extensive array of physical aids to daily living. House adaptations can also be provided free of charge. Nevertheless, the disabled person may still find getting around away from home difficult; public buildings have not yet been adapted as thoroughly as the 1970 Act laid down. Work can be difficult to find for disabled people, particularly in a time of high unemployment. Sheltered working conditions are relatively limited and often provide very tedious work for the physically handicapped person of normal intelligence. Physically handicapped people, unlike those with learning disability, are well able to speak for themselves, and pressure groups such as the Disablement Income Group and the Disabled Drivers' Association continue to put pressure on government and social services and health authorities. Voluntary bodies also provide considerable support, both in the provision of residential accommodation and in advocacy for disabled people's needs.

MENTALLY ILL PEOPLE

It could be said that the physically disabled do better than the mentally ill because their condition does not attract the same amount of stigma. Mental disorders still frighten many people and primitive reactions to madness underlie their responses.

Large mental illness hospitals isolated from the community have now all but disappeared in most districts. The 1962 Plan envisaged the gradual closure of these hospitals, most of which were built following the asylum legislation of the second half of the nineteenth century.

Mental disorder, unlike learning disability, is an illness. Do patients fare better left at home supported by visiting specialist staff, or do they recover more quickly if admitted to a hospital away from the environment that may have contributed to their illness? If the latter, should this be a small local unit close to its own community or is it better to use the larger hospital which, because of its size, can provide a wider range of therapeutic regimes? Such questions remain largely unresolved, and arguments are likely to continue concerning the most appropriate forms of treatment and care. Nevertheless, day care continues to develop, and can be particularly valuable in the support of those chronically ill people whose symptoms are an irritant to their families rather than a cause of profound family disruption. Day care is also more useful in looking after the elderly mentally ill. Whether senile dementia is really a classifiable condition or merely a useful generalization for a range of behaviour problems found in old people is not clear. Admitting a patient to hospital because of episodes of confusion often increases their disorientation, but, although support in their own homes surrounded by their own family and possessions is more humane, the strain on families should not be underestimated.

As with learning disability, the problem of definition is considerable. Leaving aside those radical views which hold that it is not individuals who are ill but society [66], opinions still differ about the nature of mental illness. Traditionally, patients are categorized into two main groups: the psychotic and the neurotic. Neurotic is used as a technical term. Those suffering from psychosis seem to others to have a poor perception of reality; they may be convinced that they are right and everyone else is wrong, and their delusions may be consequently bizarre. The person with neurosis characteristically has a view of reality which most other people would share, but has problems coping and is subject to anxiety and distress that can be sufficiently disabling to require professional support, in or out of hospital. Psychosis is found in all populations and cultures and does not appear to be related to class. Neurosis, however, is more specifically correlated with social conditions and class.

Treatment for the mentally ill varies even for the same conditions. Some psychiatrists, psychologists and nurses feel that the encouragement of self-help through group therapy is both humane and effective [67], while others rely more on helping the patient to cope through drugs and, in some cases, electroconvulsive therapy (ECT). Psychotherapy demands a long and time-consuming interaction with the patient. It is not widely provided within the NHS because of a shortage of resources as well as professional doubts in some quarters about its efficacy. The treatment of mentally ill people depends on satisfactory team working. The doctor, the clinical psychologist, the nurse, the social worker, the occupational therapist and others need to agree a treatment plan to obtain the best results. For many patients, their illness will be a recurring event. In order to take the stigma out of these episodes of ill-health, the Department of Health's policy has been to encourage the development of community support, thus avoiding hospital admission. But, where this is necessary, stigma may be reduced if admission is to a mental illness unit in a district general hospital.

Despite the uncertainty about effective therapies there have been some considerable improvements. In the mid-1950s there were over 150 000 people in mental illness hospitals. The consequent overcrowding meant that standards were very low and wards with over 60 patients were commonplace. The 1959 Mental Health Act did a great deal to reduce the numbers compulsorily admitted to hospital, and this, together with developments in drug therapy, started a gradual reduction in hospital numbers. The 1962 Plan predicted the closure of a substantial number of the older, isolated mental illness hospitals, to be replaced by smaller units attached to DGHs.

In 1975 a White Paper, entitled *Better Services for the Mentally Ill* [68], set out the Government's long-term policies: more facilities would be provided within the community to keep the mentally ill out of hospital, and, consequently, day hospitals, sheltered work and adequate home support all needed to be expanded: if people became ill enough for hospital, they should be admitted wherever possible to either the local DGH or, if old and mentally infirm, to the local community hospital: staffing ratios were to be improved, particularly medical, nursing and social work staff: where older hospitals remained, renewed attempts should be made to improve standards. The Priorities document supported these aspirations, but the Royal Commission, in 1979, found the policies were ambiguous, particularly regarding the closure of old mental illness hospitals. It said that, realistically, any government would have to accept that most mental illness hospitals would remain open for the rest of the century at least. Policy, therefore, should centre on providing a balanced service within which these hospitals could play a part. Financial stringency at the beginning of the 1980s forced many Health Authorities to review their strategies for the mentally ill.

Increasingly, agency agreements between authorities whereby one provided services for another, were causing difficulties. As well as the allocation of resources, the internal organization of the psychiatric services has worried successive governments. The Nodder report (1980) [69] supported the consensus team approach, but was critical of the lack of direction shown by many of these teams. A more structured approach, with annual objectives and routine monitoring of achievement, was advocated. The discussion leading to the 1982 reorganization submerged most of these recommendations, but, in some cases, unit management teams set up after 1982 operated along the lines suggested by Nodder.

Poor results may arise because objectives are poorly formulated, but this is not the case with secure units. The Priorities document proposed a secure unit for each Region and capital monies were allocated immediately. Most of these have still not been built, either because of staff opposition or because of failure to agree on the type of patient who should be accommodated there. Although the Mental Health Act, 1983, gave Health Authorities greater responsibilities for safeguarding the rights of their patients, progress in the care of the mentally ill remains much too slow: many of the principles set out in the 1975 *Better Services* document have still not been implemented. This may be because the range of problems has hampered formulation of a clear sense of direction. Increasing alcohol and drug abuse are causing illness, but more pressing than this are the demands being made by the elderly mentally ill, whose numbers will continue to rise with their proportionate increase in the population during the next decade.

ELDERLY PEOPLE

The largest single category of patients is the elderly: at any one time, over half the beds in the NHS are occupied by people aged over 65, and around 45% of all expenditure in the hospital and community health services sector funds care and treatment for this age group (Figure 8.5). The proportion of elderly people in the population (currently around 15%) is expected to increase to around 17% over the next decade, although the rise in the number of the very old (those over 75) is predicted to be much higher. These statistics reflect steady improvements in child health since the beginning of the century, rather than an increasing life expectancy in the elderly themselves. Broadly speaking, the longer you live, the longer you live. However, the physical quality of life diminishes and those over 75 are ten times more likely to see their general practitioner during a year than the rest of the adult population. Old age brings many symptoms, some due to physical degeneration such as deafness, blindness and arthritis, some because of mental incapacity. Ironically the mental confusion

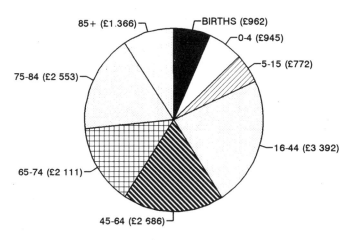

Total spending: £14 788 million

Figures in £ millions

Figure 8.5 Hospital and community health services spending by age group: England: 1990/1.

Source: *The Government's Expenditure Plans 1994/5 to 1996/7: Departmental Report*, HMSO, London (Cm. 2512).

can be increased by the intervention of professional staff, so that an elderly person admitted to a geriatric assessment unit may at first be more disorientated than before admission.

Opinion is divided as to how much treatment, as opposed to care, should be given to the very old. Geriatricians, anxious to attain the status accorded to their general physician colleagues, may be tempted to submit their patients to a battery of pointless clinical investigations. On the other hand, before geriatricians were appointed, the passiveness of care and lack of treatment given in many hospitals for the elderly resembled workhouse conditions. A balance between active intervention and letting life take its course has to be found.

Specialist care of old people is a phenomenon of the post-war era. Geriatricians attempt to see the patient as a whole person, concentrating on their environment as well as their health. Problems often arise after the discharge of an elderly person because insufficient account is taken of their home circumstances. Most elderly people in hospital are not in the care of the geriatrician, but have been referred to other specialists. Nevertheless, most district general hospitals now have specialist geriatric assessment units.

The proportion of old people in hospital or residential accommodation is still small. Remaining at home, old people require increasing support from health and social services and in times of financial stringency, it is often these support services which are cut first. However incapacitated they may be, many elderly people wish to remain at home and may endure considerable physical and financial hardship to do so. Professional staff in the NHS know that more could be done and the elderly have become an increasingly important priority group. The diffuseness of the problem, however, makes coherent planning difficult.

The need for specific plans for the elderly was recognized in the 1962 Plan, which said that every DGH should have an active geriatric unit where elderly patients could be assessed, even those who would subsequently need long term care. The Priorities document reported that it had been DHSS policy for some time to have 50% of geriatric beds provided in a DGH. This has never been achieved and, by 1980, 30% was the interim target. Even these numbers have failed to materialize in many Districts. The Priorities document stated ten beds per 1000 population over 65 was a reasonable guideline. Some Regions have suggested a lower figure. In 1978, the Government brought out a consultative document called *A Happier Old Age* [70], which stressed the need to keep elderly people in the community for as long as possible, giving them support through home helps, district nurses, day centres and meals on wheels. It said that voluntary bodies should be encouraged to help in these tasks. The Royal Commission, a year later, supported this general view, but noted that geriatrics should remain part of the mainstream of medicine if a fully integrated service was to be provided. More active research into the problems of the elderly was encouraged.

In a consultation paper, issued in 1980, called *The Future Pattern of Hospital Provision in England* [71], the idea of an NHS elderly nursing home as an alternative to hospital was discussed and, in 1984, one was set up [72]. The advantages were seen as a less institutional atmosphere and lower running costs. As part of the encouragement of partnership between the public and private sectors, the 1982 Conservative Government increased social security benefits to encourage elderly people to remain in such homes, rather than be admitted to NHS beds. The 1981 White Paper, *Growing Older* [73] did little more than support the general direction that policies had been taking for over a decade. Put simply, these policies supported the maintenance of elderly people in the community as long as possible. When illness necessitated hospital admission, this should be to an acute assessment unit, which had been shown to reduce the overall length of stay. Only for the most dependent should longer term hospital care be contemplated.

Caring for People (1989) [74] stated that there were over 6 million people with some sort of disability. Others have put the figure even higher. Many disabled people are elderly and have multifaceted problems. The process of individual assessment is therefore crucial to deciding what best to do in matching the needs and wishes of the elderly person to the available resources. Despite some criticism, the *Health of the Nation* White Paper [75] was widely welcomed for focusing attention on the outcomes of care. There is evidence that health authorities have yet to appreciate the significance of the growing numbers of elderly, and the Government has been repeatedly criticized for not allocating sufficient resources to keep up with the increase in the demands from the elderly.

CONCLUSION

This chapter has endeavoured to show how plans and policies for patients have been developed over the last 25 years. It is evident that many of the policies have been little more than statements of good intent. Only the 1976 Priorities document made a real attempt to match policies with resources, and this was quickly stifled by the worsening economic climate of the late 1970s. Policies since then have tended to concentrate on alternatives to direct provision by the NHS, in the hope that this will raise standards and redistribute the financial burden of care.

NOTES

1. DHSS (November 1989) *Caring for People*, HMSO, London (Cm. 849).
2. Ministry of Health (London, 1956) *Report of the Committee of Enquiry into the Cost of the National Health Service* (Guillebaud Report), HMSO, (Cmnd. 9663).
3. Ministry of Health (1962) *A Hospital Plan for England and Wales*, HMSO, London (Cmnd. 1604).
4. Ibid., p. iii, para. 1.
5. Ministry of Health (1966) *The Hospital Building Programme. A Revision of the Hospital Plan for England and Wales*, HMSO, London.
6. Central Health Services Council (1969) *The Functions of the District General Hospital* (Bonham-Carter Report), HMSO, London.
7. DHSS Circular HSC(15)75 *Community Hospitals.*
8. Ministry of Health (1963) *Health and Welfare – the Development of Community Care*, London.
9. DHSS (1976) *Priorities for Health and Personal Social Services in England. A Consultative Document*, HMSO, London.
10. Ibid., p. iii, para. 4.
11. DHSS (1977) *The Way Forward*, HMSO, London.
12. DHSS (1976) *Sharing Resources for Health in England. Report of the Resource Allocation Working Party* (RAWP), HMSO, London.
13. DHSS Circular HC(76)18/LAC(76)6 *Joint Care Planning: Health and Local Authorities.*
14. DHSS Circular HC(77)17/LAC(77)10 *Joint Care Planning: Health and Local Authorities.*
15. DHSS (1976) *Prevention and Health: Everybody's Business. A Consultative Document*, HMSO, London.
16. DHSS (1980) *Hospital Services. The Future Pattern of Hospital Provision in England. A Consultative Document*, HMSO, London.
17. DHSS (1981) *Care in Action – A Handbook of Policies and Priorities for the Health and Personal Social Services in England*, HMSO, London.
18. DHSS (1981) *Care in the Community*, HMSO, London. But see also Circular HC(83)6/LAC(83)5 on *Care in the Community and Joint Finance.*
19. DHSS (1980) *Report of the Working Group on Inequalities in Health* (Black Report), HMSO, London.

20. DHSS (1983) *The NHS Management Inquiry* (Griffiths Report), see Chapter 1.
21. DHSS (1975) *Guide to Planning in the National Health Service*, HMSO, London.
22. DHSS (1976) *NHS Planning System*, HMSO, London, 187–197.
23. DHSS *Steering Group on Health Services Information* (Chair, Edith Körner). Various reports from 1982 onwards.
24. Klein, R. and Redmayne, S (1992) *Patterns of Priorities: A Study of Purchasing and Rationing Policies of Health Authorities*, Research Paper No. 7, NAHAT, Birmingham.
25. DHSS (1982) *Planning in Partnership*, HMSO, London.
26. Audit Commission (1986) *Making a Reality of Community Care*, London.
27. Roy Griffiths (1988) *Community Care: Agenda for Action*, HMSO, London.
28. Op. cit., *Caring for People.*
29. Bosanquet N. and Gray A. (1989) *Will You Still Love Me?: New Opportunities for Elderly People in the 1990s and Beyond*, Research Paper No. 2, NAHAT, Birmingham.
30. Hospital at Home was developed in France and has been applied successfully in Peterborough. See F. Clarke (1984) *Hospital at Home: The Alternative to General Hospital Admission*, Macmillan, London.
31. DHSS (1986) *Neighbourhood Nursing: A Focus for Care* (Cumberlege Report), HMSO, London.
32. For a more detailed account of these two branches of nursing see Allan and Jolley (eds) (1982) *Nursing, Midwifery and Health Visiting since 1900*, Faber & Faber, London.
33. Op. cit., *Prevention and Health.*
34. The Chief Economic Adviser to the Department of Health provided statistical and international evidence to ministers that banning tobacco advertising would reduce smoking.
35. Op. cit., *Care in Action.*
36. Op. cit., Chapter 1, *Health of the Nation.*
37. British Dental Association (1983) *NHS Dental Treatment: What it Costs and How the Cost has Risen*, BDA, London.
38. World Health Organisation (1985) *Health for All 2000*, WHO, Copenhagen.
39. World Health Organisation and Liverpool University (1985) *Healthy Cities Project.*
40. DHSS (January 1986) *Report of the Committee of Inquiry into an Outbreak of Food Poisoning at Stanley Royd Hospital*, HMSO, London.
41. Royal College of Physicians (April 1987) *A Great and Growing Evil*, RCP, London.
42. *Safety and Health at Work* (Robens Report), HMSO, London, 1972 (Cmnd. 5034).
43. Statutory Instrument *Control of Substances Hazardous to Health Regulations, 1988*, S.I. 1657; came into force 1 October 1989.
44. Between March 1988 and March 1993, the number of patients waiting over two years fell from nearly 90 000 to zero, and the number waiting between one and two years fell from 120 000 to 60 000. Around half of all patients on waiting-lists are treated within five weeks and 75% within three months.
45. These figures need treating with caution. The home accidents represent hospital-treated non-fatal accidents calculated from a sample of 20 hospitals. The road accidents are calculated from police-reported road accidents.
46. Ministry of Health (1959) Central Health Services Council *The Welfare of Children in Hospital* (Platt Report), HMSO, London.
47. DHSS (1976) Committee on Child Health Services *Fit for the Future* (Court Report), HMSO, London (Cmnd. 6684).

48. McCarthy developed a mother and child unit at Amersham General Hospital in the 1950s. Jolly, first at Plymouth and then at the Charing Cross Hospital, London, was a leading paediatrician.
49. Health authorities have begun to question the medical-and cost-effectiveness of grommet treatment for glue ear – partly as a result of information produced in the *Effective Health Care Bulletin* (see Chapter 2).
50. Op. cit., *The Way Forward*.
51. The Maria Colwell case in the mid-1970s emphasized the dilemma of the health and social services in making decisions about where a child should be maintained. In this case the child died from ill-treatment and the authorities were much criticized for not having taken her into care.
52. There were 165 600 legal abortions in 1991 compared with total live births of 660 800 (OPCS statistics). Miscarriages are not recorded.
53. Ministry of Health (1959) *Report of the Maternity Services Committee* (Cranbrook Report), HMSO, London.
54. DHSS (1970) Central Health Services Council *Domiciliary Midwifery and Maternity Bed Needs* (Peel Report), HMSO, London.
55. Notably F. LeBoyer (1976) *Birth without Violence*, Wildwood House, London, and M. Odent (1983) *Entering the World: the demedicalization of childbirth*, Marion Boyars, London.
56. Department of Health Expert Maternity Group (1993) *Changing Childbirth: Part 1: Report of the Expert Maternity Group*, HMSO, London.
57. Reply to the Second Report from the Social Services Committee (1980) *Report on Perinatal and Neonatal Mortality* (Short Report), HMSO, London (Cmnd. 8084).
58. Op. cit., Black Report, as published by Penguin Books 1982, see p. 82, Table 16.
59. DHSS (1983) Circular HC(83)21/LAC(83)15 *Helping to Get Mentally Handicapped Children Out of Mental Handicap Hospitals*.
60. DHSS (1969) *Report of the Committee of Enquiry into Allegations of Ill-Treatment of Patients and Other Irregularities at Ely Hospital, Cardiff* (Howe Report), HMSO, London (Cmnd. 3795).
61. Pauline Morris (1969) *Put Away*, Routledge & Kegan Paul, London.
62. DHSS and Welsh Office (1971) *Better Services for the Mentally Handicapped*, HMSO, London (Cmnd. 4683).
63. DHSS (1979) *Committee of Enquiry into Mental Handicap Nursing and Care* (Jay Report), HMSO, London (Cmnd. 7468).
64. Op. cit., *Caring for People*.
65. *Chronically Sick and Disabled Persons Act 1970*, HMSO, London. See also Circular HM(70)52.
66. Notably Szasz, T. (1976) *The Myth of Mental Illness*, Harper and Row, New York. See also Illich (1977) *The Limits to Medicine*, Penguin Books, Harmondsworth.
67. Notably at Dingleton Hospital, Melrose, Scotland, described in Jones, M. (1982) *The Process of Change*, Routledge & Kegan Paul, London.
68. HSS (1975) *Better Services for the Mentally Ill*, HMSO, London (Cmnd. 6233).
69. DHSS (1980) Organizational and Management Problems of Mental Illness Hospitals. (Nodder Report), HMSO, London.
70. DHSS (1978) *A Happier Old Age*, HMSO, London.
71. DHSS (May 1980) *Hospital Services: The Future Pattern of Hospital Provision in England*, a consultation paper.

72. In Portsmouth Health District. See description in *Health and Social Services Journal*, 21 July 1983.
73. DHSS (1981) *Growing Older*, HMSO, London (Cmnd. 8173).
74. Op. cit., *Caring for People*.
75. Op. cit., Chapter 1, *Health of the Nation*.

9

Doctors

The development of medicine as a scientifically based understanding of health and disease has depended on the pace of discoveries in the natural sciences. The last 100 years have seen the most rapid changes, although important landmarks date earlier than that. This chapter is concerned with the professional organization of doctors, their education and training, their distribution, their working arrangements in the NHS and their remuneration.

WHO ARE THE DOCTORS?

Broadly speaking, doctors belong in three groups; those working primarily in hospitals, those in general practice, and public health doctors in community medicine, a much smaller group than the other two. All doctors undergo the same training leading to qualification after five years followed by a pre-registration year working in a hospital in general medicine and general surgery. Once registered by the General Medical Council, they can select the branch of medicine they wish to pursue. In hospital medicine, certain choices tend to be much more popular than others. It is not unusual for a registrar to have to change career direction because progress in his or her first choice is blocked or limited. Equally, some specialities are so short of applicants that attaining a consultant post can be rapid, after obtaining the required postgraduate qualifications and working in recognized junior jobs. A trainee is not assured of a career post in such specialities as nephrology, cardiology, infectious diseases, general surgery, obstetrics and gynaecology, ophthalmology, neurosurgery or paediatric surgery. On the other hand, registrars specializing in geriatrics, venereology, chemical pathology and anaesthetics can be sure of obtaining senior registrar posts; and all senior registrars in these last four specialities, plus child psychiatry and radiology, can expect to obtain a consultant post on completion of their training.

The normal time-scale for a newly graduated hospital doctor's promotion is one year as a house officer, two to three years as a senior house officer, three to four as a registrar and up to four more as a senior registrar. A few who are then unable to obtain a consultant's appointment are considered 'time expired' and may find it impossible to secure such a post. Most succeed, although not necessarily in the location where they might have wished to settle. Care is taken by the medical profession to ensure that the number of senior registrars nationally does not exceed the likely number of consultant vacancies.

The clinical work is organized around a basic unit called a 'firm', composed of one consultant and a varying number from the junior grades. Patients referred to hospital by a GP for in-patient or out-patient treatment become the responsibility of the consultant, who has to make decisions about their diagnosis, treatment, referral and discharge. The consultant is helped by junior doctors and by a variety of nursing and paramedical staff, and delegates some of the work to them, while retaining full personal responsibility. In practice, the senior registrars and registrars have some autonomy, although they are responsible to their consultant, and they supervise the work of the house officers. The discretion given to each grade of junior doctor varies considerably from firm to firm, and depends on the nature of the clinical work, the number of staff involved and the inevitable personality influences. Teaching of junior medical staff, medical students and other hospital staff may also play a part in the work of the firm.

For general practitioners the path is simpler. A three-year post-qualifying vocational course is obligatory and includes experience in such relevant hospital specialities as general medicine, paediatrics and obstetrics, together with a period as a supervised trainee in a general practice and an elective period of the trainee's choice. At the end of this, the new GP finds his or her own appointment in a practice. The competition is unequal across the country, with inner-city areas the much less popular choice.

Public health medicine, traditionally considered the least prestigious choice, has recently started to attract more interest from those wanting to take a wider perspective on health. Their specialization starts at registrar level. The most senior appointments are as Directors of Public Health in Districts and Regions, and there are a few other consultant-grade posts.

Most doctors are men, even though over 50% of medical school graduates are female. Attempts have been made through the Women Doctors Retainer Scheme, introduced in 1972 [1], to enable previously unemployed women doctors to undertake part-time work to keep in touch with their profession. The retraining scheme [2], inaugurated in 1969, makes special arrangements for women to work part-time at registrar and senior registrar level. Inevitably, women do better in shortage specialities and community medicine, and in those specialities where there are permanent sub-consultant-grade posts. The proportion who become consultants is remarkably low. In general surgery they are less than 1% of the total. The number of female principals in general practice is also very low, but rising: they now represent about 25% of the total.

Doctors work long hours, particularly junior doctors. The problem is partly a consequence of attempting to provide continuity of care, although the quality of that care is undermined by tiredness and errors if they have had to spend

Table 9.1 Hospital medical and dental staff in England and Wales, analysis by specialty and grade: 1992

Specialty Area	Consultants	Senior Registrars	Registrars	Senior House Officers
All specialties	17198	3958	6651	12380
General Medicine	4115	1011	1937	4294
Accident and Emergency	248	64	70	1426
Surgical	3485	687	1624	2777
Obstetrics and Gynaecology	880	176	622	1440
Anaesthetics	2342	441	877	1102
Radiology	1317	289	252	3
Clinical Oncology	231	55	83	108
Pathology	1685	507	344	164
Psychiatry	2145	701	771	977
Other	164	27	71	88
Dental	586	126	187	294

Source: *Health Trends*, Vol. 25, No. 4, 1993.

too many hours on duty. A report published in 1990 [3] found that for a sample of over 400 doctors, the house officers spent an average of more than 90 hours per week on duty, including the time actually spent with patients and at the hospital on call for emergencies. They had an average of 6 hours sleep in 24, and that was sometimes interrupted. The time on duty decreased with seniority, consultants doing 50 hours per week on average for their NHS work. Those with private practices would work further hours outside the NHS.

In 1991 the Department of Health promised action to reduce junior doctors' hours [4]. Although average contracted hours for junior doctors fell from 92 hours per week in 1978 to 82 hours in 1989, concern about the ability of junior doctors to function properly over such long periods of being on call eventually

Table 9.2 General medical practitioners in England and Wales: 1981–92

Year	All Practitioners	Unrestricted Principals	Restricted Principals	Assistants	Trainees
1981	25906	23701	217	286	1702
1982	26414	24217	208	269	1720
1983	26962	24719	188	286	1769
1984	27449	25132	180	275	1862
1985	27889	25558	171	236	1924
1986	28248	26009	163	262	1814
1987	28793	26509	162	246	1876
1988	29196	26921	161	264	1850
1989	29556	27239	166	251	1900
1990	29323	27257	151	205	1710
1991	29696	27333	139	247	1777
1992	30020	27644	140	490	1746

Source: *Health Trends*, Vol. 25, No. 4, 1993.

Doctors

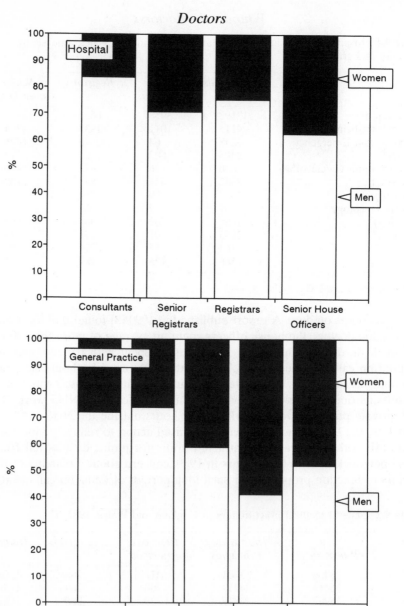

Figure 9.1 Proportion of hospital and general pratitioner posts held by women: England and Wales: 1992.

Source: *Health Trends*, Vol. 25, No. 4, 1993.

led to the Department setting targets for reducing hours. In the short term, junior doctors' hours of work were to fall from 82 to 63 per week, and to 56 by the end of 1994. By 1994, hours had been reduced, but the target had not been attained [5].

Maintaining the optimum number of doctors on duty is not easily achieved. Because all junior doctors are regarded as trainees, periods of study absence have to be allowed. This may oblige general practices and hospitals to employ locums for short-term cover; in 1988 this cost £43 million. Governments have discouraged the use of locums on the grounds of expense and because, as temporary staff, they tend to offer a less informed service.

Despite long hours, lengthy training, the need for continuing study and the competition for promotion, medicine remains a popular profession. It commands social prestige, considerable respect and its members exercise extensive power in the NHS at all levels. Within their ranks, however, there is still no real abatement of the discord and rivalry between the three main groups.

PROFESSIONAL ORGANIZATIONS

Before 1700 the medical profession was firmly divided into three groups: physicians, surgeons and apothecaries, of whom physicians had the highest status. The Royal College of Physicians of London was founded in 1518; members were graduates of Oxford and Cambridge Universities who had received religious and classical education and, subsequently, often studied medical subjects in European universities. Surgeons, on the other hand, were not scholars but craftsmen organized in a guild that was associated with the barbers, and they were licensed to perform the small range of procedures that could be carried out on unanaesthetized patients. The third group, apothecaries, were tradesmen who, from 1617 were licensed by the Society of Apothecaries to sell drugs prescribed by physicians. Until 1700, treatment was essentially carried out in patients' homes. However, the position changed between 1700 and about 1850, partly because that period saw the rise of the great voluntary hospitals which provided the setting for developments in surgery; in comparison, the techniques and abilities of physicians hardly advanced. The prestige of surgeons rose and, in 1745, the Company of Surgeons was founded, cementing their independence from the barbers and enabling educational standards to improve; by 1800 the Company had become the Royal College of Surgeons of England.

Apothecaries also advanced, and by 1703 they were entitled to see patients and prescribe medicines themselves. The result was that they became the 'general practitioners' for the middle classes and the poor. The Apothecaries Act of 1815 gave the Society of Apothecaries the right to license those who had served a five year apprenticeship and passed examinations, and some physicians took this qualification as well. As the voluntary hospitals were closed to these practitioners and only employed the services of those recognized by the Royal Colleges, the distinction between consultants and general practitioners became established. The Society of Apothecaries pioneered improvements in the standard of education and in raising the status of practitioners far more than the universities or Royal Colleges did – from 1842 to 1844, 16 practitioners were licensed by the universities of Oxford and Cambridge, 37 by the Royal College of Physicians and 953 by the Society of Apothecaries.

Despite this success, unqualified practitioners flourished (the 1841 census showed over 30 000 doctors, while the first Medical Directory, published in 1845, listed only 11 000 qualified practitioners), and demand arose for a single licensing authority and a single professional qualification permitting practice in any branch of the profession. The strongest pressure for such a licence came from the Provincial Medical and Surgical Association. This body was founded in Worcester in 1832, and drew so much support that, by 1855, it had changed its name to the British Medical Association. The campaign resulted in the passing of the Medical Act, in 1858, which created the General Council of Medical Education and Registration [6]. It is now called the General Medical Council (GMC) and has 50 members representing the Royal Colleges, the universities, the Crown and the profession at large. Its duty is to maintain a register of practitioners, licensed by recognized authorities, and to supervise the educational standards of training institutions. In practice, the GMC relies on medical schools to maintain standards in undergraduate training, and on the Royal Colleges for postgraduate and specialist training. Hospitals are constantly reminded of the power of the Royal Colleges to remove training approval from hospital posts, and this threatened sanction has done much to improve standards of training and also to promote such facilities as medical libraries.

Following the Merrison Report in 1975 [7], the GMC constitution was changed, and greater attention has since been paid to registration matters, particularly of overseas doctors, who make up over 25% of hospital medical staff. These doctors are given limited registration for up to five years and their admission to full registration relies on satisfactory reports of their work. The GMC is also concerned with disciplinary matters and has the power to remove a doctor from the Medical Register in cases of serious professional misconduct, such as criminal convictions which would make it undesirable for that person to continue in practice.

Other medical corporations have been established, including the Royal College of Obstetricians and Gynaecologists (1929), the Royal College of General Practitioners (1952), the Royal College of Pathologists (1962) and the Royal College of Psychiatrists (1971).

The Royal Colleges and other medical corporations are not trade unions for doctors, but bodies mainly concerned with post-registration training and development, and, until comparatively recently, they only represented the élite specialities of the profession. The British Medical Association (BMA) emerged as the spokesman for the 'underdog' general practitioners. It threatened Lloyd George's government with destruction of the National Health Insurance Scheme, through GPs' refusal to co-operate just as the scheme was about to be implemented. The opposition was dropped in 1912 when the Government agreed to the demand for a higher rate of remuneration for GPs. Before that time, the out-patient departments and dispensaries of the voluntary hospitals provided treatment, subsidized by the charitable organizations, and thus represented an alternative source of treatment for people, instead of going to a general practitioner who contracted to work for a friendly society, if private treatment could not be afforded.

The 1911 Act had the effect of greatly increasing the numbers of people entitled to medical benefit through membership of the approved societies, and hence safeguarded the level of GPs' incomes under the National Health Insurance Scheme. Rivalry between GPs and hospital doctors was considerable, and the BMA set out the terms of their relationship in a code of ethics which made the GP responsible for his patients while the specialists could be consulted for opinion and advice on diagnosis and treatment. This enabled GPs to maintain lists of patients without the fear that, if any of them were referred to a hospital doctor, they would be taken over; to the present day, hospital doctors do not have a list of registered patients for whom they assume continuing responsibility, whereas GPs do.

Other bodies have emerged to protect doctors' interests, including the Hospital Doctors' Association, the Hospital Consultants' and Specialists' Association and the Medical Practitioners' Union, but the BMA is still regarded as the foremost and legitimate voice for all doctors, whether or not they are members. Its role in the setting up of the NHS in the 1940s has been described in Chapter 1, and, since that time, its internal organization has been modified, such that it mirrors the structure of the NHS – hospital doctors are represented in the BMA by its Central Committee for Hospital Medical Services, while GPs are separately represented by its General Medical Services Committee. The constituents of these two committees are, respectively, the Regional Committees for Hospital Medical Staffs and Local Medical Committees, on which doctors working in the NHS are represented. The BMA's leadership has not always been regarded by individual doctors as being in touch with their interests; on a number of occasions the BMA has been publicly unable to present a convincing view of the profession's position. One factor which may contribute to this impression is that there are three separate bodies (or sets of bodies) acting for the profession – the medical corporations for professional representation, the GMC for discipline and self-regulation, and the BMA for pay negotiations.

MEDICAL EDUCATION

The training of doctors involves a large element of practical experience, and, in the past, students were apprenticed to physicians, surgeons and apothecaries, the university part of their training representing a relatively small element. The balance has now altered, although this tradition has had a substantial influence on the style of undergraduate curricula, and postgraduate education is still mainly in the hands of the professional organizations rather than the universities. By 1858 there were 11 medical schools in London and at least 10 in the provinces apart from the universities of Oxford and Cambridge. By 1914, all except four of the present provincial university medical schools were open.

Before the First World War, the teaching of clinical subjects was provided by physicians and surgeons who, although in private practice, gave their services to the hospitals where students were apprenticed as clerks and dressers for short periods. Preclinical subjects were taught by doctors engaged in clinical work who often did not specialize in these subjects. The Haldane Report, published in 1918, strongly criticized these features and recommended there should be full-time clinical teachers of university status, and that units of medicine and surgery, under clinicians with professorial status, should organize and provide the clinical teaching [8]. It was not until the 1920s, however, that things began to change, and this was partly due to the establishment of the University Grants Committee which was given responsibility for the financing of the universities (it was reconstituted in 1989 as the University Funding Council).

The medical schools were becoming steadily more dependent on the universities for funds. Research and specialization extended as a result, but, by 1944, the idea of full-time specialist units had not really been implemented, and there were only seven full-time chairs in medicine, four in surgery and two in obstetrics. In that year, the Interdepartmental Committee on Medical Schools published its report (the Goodenough Report) [9]. It reaffirmed the main points of the Haldane Report and proposed full-time professorial units in obstetrics and gynaecology as well as in medicine and surgery. It suggested premedical studies should be started by potential medical students at secondary school and continued at medical school, and that, after qualification, one year of pre-registration hospital work under supervision should provide the necessary practical experience before a newly qualified doctor could work alone.

The pattern of undergraduate education was further investigated by a Royal Commission chaired by Lord Todd, from 1965 to 1968 [10]. At that time, students with high passes in biology, chemistry and physics 'A' level examinations were admitted to medical schools for five terms of preclinical instruction in anatomy, physiology and biochemistry. After examination, the students then studied for three more years, partly in the hospital wards and partly in formal lectures. The subjects included medicine, surgery and sometimes psychiatry. They took examinations in these subjects, too, before obtaining their qualifying degree (MB, BS or MB, ChB or MB, BChir) [11], and then had to spend one further year in approved training posts as house officers before being registered. There was no compulsory further education, although a junior doctor wanting to advance his or her career in certain specialities would have to take further instruction and examination, leading to Membership of the Royal College of Physicians (MRCP) or Fellowship of the Royal College of Surgeons (FRCS), for example.

The Todd Report is a comprehensive document that questioned the assumptions on which medical education had been based and made several radical recommendations about its future organization. It suggested that the undergraduate curriculum should be broad and flexible, to include sociological subjects and to cover the whole concept of human biology in the preclinical stage, possibly leading to a medical science degree after three years. Four broad modules covering (1) medicine and surgery, (2) psychiatry, (3) obstetrics, gynaecology and paediatrics and (4) community medicine and general practice should constitute the clinical stage, but the qualifying doctor should not be expected to be fully trained. Subsequently, the programme for postgraduate training should be systematically planned to give wide-ranging experience in carefully approved posts, for both hospital specialists and general practitioners, through the development of postgraduate training centres in the district general hospitals. The report also suggested that the number of places in medical schools should be doubled by 1990, that the twelve London schools be merged into six expanded schools and the postgraduate schools consolidated with them, closer links being forged all over the country between the medical schools and multi-faculty universities.

Following the Todd recommendations, three new provincial medical schools – Southampton (Wessex Medical School), Nottingham and Leicester – were set up. The suggestion regarding medical school numbers has been challenged following concern that there might be too many doctors to allow satisfactory career progression. By 1983, the BMA argued that medical school intake should be held at the 1979 level and even that assumed a considerable increase in the number of GPs consequent on a reduction of list sizes to an average of 1700.

The philosophy of the Todd Report has had an influence throughout medical education, and undergraduate curricula are changing quite substantially [12]. Central Councils for Postgraduate Medical Education exist for England and Wales, Scotland and Northern Ireland, with responsibility for monitoring standards and advising the Regional Postgraduate Committees. Joint Higher Training Committees have been set up for a number of specialities, to define the scope of special education within the specialities, to establish criteria for posts and inspect them, to recommend patterns of appointments and to provide accreditation. There is, similarly, a Postgraduate Training Committee for General Practice. In 1976, the National Health Service (Vocational Training) Act was passed, creating a legal framework for the future regulation of training for doctors wishing to become general practitioners.

During the 1980s the future of the London medical schools and teaching hospitals came into question. They had presented an incomparable wealth of clinical material for students and junior doctors, but their geographical concentration had led to the over-provision of beds. Because the London Districts were finding it financially impossible to support this and wanted to cut the bed allocations, the medical schools feared that the quality of medical training would suffer, even though other nearby district general hospitals could offer some of the necessary training material. This arrangement had for some time been able to attract special Department of Health payments to the Districts, payments called the Service Increment for Training (SIFT). Medical schools argued that if the teaching hospitals had fewer beds they would be unable to sustain sufficient academic departments to provide a sound training.

The universities themselves had come under financial pressure, prompting the GMC's Education Committee, which oversees educational standards in the medical schools, to warn that medical educational objectives were at risk. A steering group, under the Permanent Secretary at the Department of Health, was set up and made its first report in 1979 [13]. The need to plan ahead was its principal advice, in particular that each medical school should keep in touch with the needs of the NHS itself so that educational objectives remained relevant to patients' needs. This did nothing to help resolve the immediate problem of the universities, who spent £300 million on medical education in 1988. The Middlesex and University College Hospital medical schools merged in 1988, as did Westminster's with Charing Cross. The sense of crisis in teaching hospitals deepened with the introduction of real cost charging: under the 1990 Act, Districts providing training experience for medical students have to be reimbursed the true costs of this, rather than the notional sums paid through SIFT.

THE DISTRIBUTION OF HOSPITAL DOCTORS

Career progression in hospitals is still a problem. As the DHSS *Medical Manpower* [14] paper pointed out in 1978, hospital medical staffing structure is an 'uneasy pyramidal shape', maintained largely by the employment of overseas doctors and by using junior doctors as 'pairs of hands' rather than as trainees.

The organization of hospital doctors in the NHS was first set out by the Spens Committee on the remuneration of consultants and specialists, in 1948 [15], but there have been a number of modifications since that time, first, as a result of the recommendations of the Joint Working Party on Medical Staffing Structure in the Hospital Service (the Platt Report) [16] in 1961, then the Todd Report [17] had suggested an increase in training posts between the registrar and consultant grades. This was rejected by the Royal Commission, in 1979 [18], which proposed three grades after registration: assistant physician (or surgeon), a grade with a tenure of about four years, and physician which could be either a final post or act as a training post for the consultant grade. This proposal was not accepted and neither was the suggestion in the King's Fund study *The Organisation of Hospital Clinical Work* [19], a year later, that there should be two grades of consultant which, it claimed, would encourage mobility and allow consultants to change and develop their interests within their speciality. At present they may hold the same contract for thirty years.

But before discussing the problem of hospital doctors' careers further and, in particular, the recommendations of the House of Commons Social Services

Committee made in July 1981, it is worth being reminded of the present system.

The House of Commons Social Services Committee (the Short Report) [20] endeavoured to deal with the problems which had been troubling the NHS for some years. It recommended increasing the number of consultants and improving the training of hospital doctors aspiring to be consultants. The report recognized that despite the relatively large number of junior doctors, it was not always easy to find good candidates for certain consultant posts. However, it did not accept that more junior posts were the answer to this problem, despite the over-long hours that many junior doctors worked. The Committee's solution was a substantial increase in the number of consultants, to ensure a consultant-based service which would increase the benefits to patients, many of whom at present only saw a consultant very briefly. To encourage an increase in consultants, the number of senior house officer posts should be frozen at the 1981 level.

These proposals were not received well by consultants, although they were welcomed by the junior staff. The consultants were offended at the implication that many of them had little knowledge of their patients, and they were doubtful whether the career progression could be so finely tuned; in other words, some wastage during training was not only inevitable but possibly desirable to ensure that only the most suitable doctors became consultants. In any case, they argued, it takes time and experience for doctors to decide on a speciality. A study showed that, on qualifying, only a quarter of doctors had made up their minds about career preference [21]. In subsequent discussions, it became clear that a reduction in juniors' working hours in smaller specialities would mean the consultants themselves being first on-call on some occasions – and they felt this was unacceptable.

Previous reports on medical matters have been criticized initially, only to be implemented later on. Presumably working on this premise, the DHSS issued a circular early in 1982, HC(82)4 [22], which accompanied the Government's response to the Short report and welcomed and supported most of the report's recommendations. In particular, Regions were asked to prevent further expansion of senior house officer posts and to draw up plans aimed at achieving, by 1988, a ratio of 1:1 of consultants to training-grade posts and to evaluate the cost of this. Progress has been slow. The freeze on senior house officers has been implemented but its effects have been arbitrary, creating inappropriate imbalances in the number of these posts between specialities. The Short Report had suggested that junior medical staff contracts should be held at the Region, to facilitate the redeployment of posts. This change has not been made, but a corresponding proposal from *Patients First* [23], that consultants' contracts should be held at District level, was adopted in spirit, in so far as the details of a consultant's work plan are agreed with individual Districts and units, although the actual contract is still held at the Region. Since the creation of trusts, hospitals have the power to employ their own consultants on whatever terms they wish, provided an existing incumbent agrees.

The call to increase consultant numbers was echoed in the report *Achieving a Balance* issued by the Department of Health, the Joint Consultants' Committee of the BMA and the Regional chairmen in July 1987 [24]. It said that, to ensure doctors did not get blocked from promotion through the training grades, entry to registrar and senior registrar posts needed to be better planned. In due course, these grades should be merged to shorten the total duration of training. To promote greater flexibility in the system, early retirement without financial loss should be available for consultants. The report also acknowledged that doctors who could not obtain consultant posts might, none the less, make an important contribution to hospital services. Two new grades, Associate Specialist and Staff, akin to Clinical Assistant, were suggested.

The implementation of these proposals was assisted by the Joint Planning Advisory Committee (JPAC), which had been set up in 1985 to advise the Department and Welsh Office on the number of posts in the medical and dental training grades needed to meet expected demand in service specialities and research. JPAC continues to be responsible for the gradual adjustment of numbers of junior posts allocated across the country, in order to reduce the disparities arising from the traditionally generous share of registrars and senior registrars allowed to the teaching hospitals.

Overseas doctors tend to have an unpredictable effect on manpower plans. The GMC's introduction of more stringent language and accreditation procedures has reduced their numbers, as a significant proportion fail these tests.

GENERAL PRACTITIONERS

The split between general practitioners and hospital doctors that emerged in the eighteenth and nineteenth centuries still exists, and general practice, although it has consistently attracted about 50% of qualifying doctors in the lifetime of the NHS, remains the less prestigious choice. Both the Royal College of General Practitioners and the General Medical Services Committee (GMSC) of the BMA have worked hard to improve the standing of general practice, and there is a growing recognition of the fact that general practice, as the key element of primary medical care, is the area where more planning of services and scrutiny of the outcome of treatment is able to alter the balance in the whole pattern of health care. The GMSC issued a booklet late in 1983 [25] reviewing the present state of general practice. It concluded that general practice remained a stable and widely appreciated part of the NHS providing the bulk of health care, and that that there was room for further development, particularly in reducing list size to allow doctors to spend more time with their patients.

Between 1949 and 1978 the number of GPs increased by 36%, compared with an increase of hospital doctors of well over 100%. The continued increase in GP numbers has allowed the average list size to decrease, so that in 1992 there were 30 020 principals (including around 2000 trainees and assistants) with an average list size of about 1900. It is the aim of the BMA to reduce the list size to 1700, although there are some doctors who feel that with appropriate organization, GPs could properly care for more patients. Within these figures there are important local variations. In order to secure an even distribution of GPs throughout the country, the National Health Service Act, 1946, established a nine-member independent body called the Medical Practices Committee (MPC), responsible for controlling the number of GPs operating in any one area. They did this by introducing four categories; designated areas, with an average list of over 2500; open areas, between 2101 and 2500; intermediate areas, between 1701 and 2100; restricted areas, 1700 or less. FHSAs are responsible for reporting vacancies to the MPC and making recommendations regarding the filling of posts, which will take into account population changes and other developments. FHSAs fill the vacancies once they have been authorized by the MPC. In a restricted area, the MPC cannot recommend approval, whereas financial inducements are offered to those wishing to practise in designated areas. The 1990 contract (discussed further below) encouraged GPs to undertake more primary care; some also continue with hospital work as clinical assistants or hospital practitioners, paid by the District rather than the FHSA.

Concern regarding deputizing arrangements, particularly in inner-city areas, led to government proposals in 1983 to eliminate the use of deputies in large practices and restrict their use for GPs working alone. It was estimated that if regulations were introduced only a fifth of GPs would still be allowed to use deputizing services. As the services are often provided by junior hospital medical staff, they would stand to lose valuable extra income. The 1990 GP contract restricted the use of locums further by introducing the requirement for GPs to take 24-hour responsibility for their patients.

PUBLIC HEALTH

Although, in the nineteenth century, major improvements in public health had been brought about by doctors whose standing was then high, a hundred years later this speciality is held in low esteem by the rest of the medical profession. Most of the successes in combating infectious diseases seemed to be over, and legislation has long since improved the environment to the point where clean air and water can be assumed. However, significant and repeated outbreaks of food poisoning, of diseases caused by new types of environmental hazards and newly identified viruses, have increased awareness that the public's health cannot be taken for granted; measures are still needed to protect the population.

The speciality of community medicine, meant to have been given impetus by the 1974 reorganization, has instead become increasingly demoralized and seriously understaffed (Table 9.3). The reasons for this decay are connected

184 *Doctors*

Table 9.3 Public health and medicine staff in England and Wales: 1985–92

Year	All Doctors	[Chief Officers]Consultants		Senior in Public Health Medicine	Senior Registrars and Registrars	House Officers
		Regional Directors of Public Health	District Directors of Public Health			
1985	871	14	180	338	239	–
1986	847	14	165	334	253	–
1987	800	11	140	343	250	–
1988	810	14	142	344	273	–
1989	818	13	142	344	288	–
1990	877	14	149	343	338	30
1991	910	14	151	351	363	24
1992	905	14	127	349	375	30

Source: *Health Trends*, Vol. 25, No. 4, 1993.

with the character of that reorganization, in which former Medical Officers of Health, autonomous public health specialists employed by the local authorities, found themselves transferred to District or Area Management Teams, where their often powerfully individualistic style of working was deemed inappropriate. Their role became ambiguous thereafter: were they to manage medical work, and if so, whose? Or were they primarily responsible for overseeing the care of the health of the community at large?

Despite the Hunter Report [26], which had called for the amalgamation of these doctors' managerial and clinical responsibilities, and the Royal Commission's opinion that community physicians should contribute to planning, health education, epidemiology and environmental health [27], their role and status diminished. In January 1986, Sir Donald Acheson, Chief Medical Officer to the Department of Health, was asked to make a special examination of the state of public health, and he reported two years later. In *Public Health in England* [28], he proposed that each District should have an appropriately trained Director of Public Health, together with at least one other consultant and a specialist in infection control, probably trained in microbiology.

Acheson's report completed what some regarded as the emasculation of their speciality by making the new Directors of Public Health (DPH) managerially accountable to the District General Manager. Slowly, however, particularly following the 1990 Act and the emphasis placed on epidemiologically based needs assessments to inform the contracting process (see Chapter 2), attitudes are changing, and the now obligatory annual report from the Director of Public Health is proving a useful instrument for heightening the consciousness of health authorities, the professions and the public to the broad challenges facing health care.

DOCTORS AND MANAGEMENT

The participation of hospital doctors in management and their contribution to the efficiency of the hospital service was a major theme of the 1974 reorganization, and stemmed from the fact that doctors were in a position to direct the use of costly resources with varying, but often considerable, degrees of autonomy. After discussions between the Minister of Health and the profession in 1965, the Joint Working Party on the Organization of Medical Work in Hospitals was set up to discuss the progress of the NHS, and particularly to review the hospital service. It produced three reports (1967 [29], 1972 [30], 1974 [31]), known as the Cogwheel reports because of the design printed on their covers. The first report recommended the creation of divisions of broadly linked specialities, with representatives from among consultants and junior medical staff which would constantly appraise the services and methods of provision within the division.

Such divisions were likely to be set up on a faculty or speciality basis, such as surgery, medicine, obstetrics, pathology, etc. Representatives of each division were to come together in each hospital as a medical executive committee, which would co-ordinate the work and views of the division and provide a link with nursing and administration. The sort of problems they might consider could include bed management and the organization of out-patient and in-patient resources. Most hospital groups gradually implemented this scheme, and, by 1972, the second report was able to identify the essential elements of an effective Cogwheel system and to report that, in large acute hospitals particularly, the system had been helpful in dealing with improved communications, reductions of in-patient waiting-lists and the progressive control of medical expenditure.

The third report clarified the role of Cogwheel systems in the newly reorganized NHS, because an emphasis of the 1974 reorganization was the part to be played by multi-disciplinary teams in integrated management, whereas Cogwheel had been set up as a doctor-dominated, hospital-based arrangement. The third report suggested that Cogwheel should continue to deal with issues where the agreement and action of hospital doctors was the main need, while problems requiring strong collaboration between all the professional groups, both within the hospitals and in community services, should be the province of the district management teams and their health care planning teams. It would still be appropriate for Cogwheel systems to concentrate on efficiency issues, and it would be helpful for hospital doctors to see their clinical freedom in the context of team work and the necessity of sharing resources.

Support for the Cogwheel concept was nevertheless fairly general, if at times somewhat grudging. Cogwheel divisions have not flourished everywhere, however, but, where they have, many have required a considerable amount of administrative support. The Royal Commission [32] noted an impatience among medical staff with the seemingly inevitable delays intrinsic to consensus management, and supported the idea of an executive team at hospital level which it thought would speed things up. The idea of unit management teams was endorsed in *Patients First* [33] and in circular HC(80)8 [34] on the new structure, but the involvement of doctors was somewhat ambiguously stated. It was not until HC(82)1 [35] that clear directions were given on how clinical members were to be appointed to the DMT following the 1982 reorganization; the consultant should be elected by the consultant body and the GP by all GPs in a District. This marked a change in some places, where previously the District Medical Committee, itself a representative body, had elected the DMT medical representatives.

Following the 1982 reorganization, Unit Management Teams were set up, usually as a triumvirate of doctor, nurse and administrator, although, in some cases, they included hospital doctors and GPs. The role of these teams was not altogether easy to determine, nor was their corporate relationship to the DMT. The 1983 Griffiths Report proposals [36] recommended modification to this type of team decision making. Ironically, it was hospital doctors' criticisms of consensus management which probably did most to encourage the Secretary of State to ask for the Griffiths Report in the first place. The resulting proposal, that there should be a general manager at District and Unit level, led the BMA to say that such a post should be held by a doctor, even though many doctors were doubtful that filling the role would be practicable, given their comparative or total lack of management training and their prime commitment to patient treatment, which would allow little time for the managerial role. In the event, 19% of Unit General Managers jobs in 1986 were held by doctors.

In the late 1980s, formal involvement of doctors in management was brought into focus again by the decision to appoint Clinical Directors (see Chapter 4). Under this system, which superseded the Cogwheel structures, one doctor heads a team of clinical colleagues, usually a single speciality, and is held responsible for the appropriate working of that speciality. Doctors need to be involved closely in the decisions about health care, but cannot spend too much time away from their patients. A study by the Institute of Health Services Management in 1990 [37] found that various approaches were being adopted for the appointment of Clinical Directors because the simple model, with one doctor in charge of all the other clinical staff of the team, had been seen as unacceptable. It would have challenged a doctor's clinical autonomy as well as the professional integrity of nurses and other workers. Whatever the local arrangements, the appointment of Clinical Directors does seem to be helping clinical staff to become more aware of the costs of care and the importance of setting priorities within cash limits [38]. These posts may also facilitate medical audit.

DOCTORS' PAY AND CONDITIONS

Doctors' pay has often been a difficult problem for governments to tackle. Doctors' negotiators are no less dedicated than those of other workers and industrial action is not unknown.

When the NHS began, systems for employing the services of doctors had to be carefully worked out and negotiated between the Government and the profession. Two committees, under the chairmanship of Sir Will Spens, reported in 1948 on the remuneration of general practitioners [39], and consultants and specialists respectively. They recommended pay scales for consultants and junior hospital doctors, arrangements for part-time contracts for consultants and a system of distinction awards which would provide for a significant minority the opportunity to earn incomes comparable with the highest that can be earned in other professions [40]. For GPs, the Spens committee recommended a graded scale of incomes, leading to an average net income for doctors at age 40 to 50, which would be paid out of a central pool. The income would be made up of a capitation fee for each patient on a GP's list, including a fixed allowance for practice expenses, plus payments for certain individual items of service. The figures for all doctors were quoted at 1939 money values, leaving to the Government the decision about which increases would establish and protect the status of these incomes relative to each other and to other professional incomes, in the context of rising inflation.

The adjustments fixed by the Government were not acceptable to the BMA in respect of GPs' incomes, and, after negotiations had broken down, the matter was referred to adjudication in 1953. Mr Justice Danckwerts awarded the GPs a substantial increase and said that the size of the central pool should be related to the total number of GPs and not to the population covered by the NHS, in order that required increases in the numbers of GPs would not be discouraged. The result was that some of the increased incomes were paid directly into a special fund from which GPs could draw if they spent money on improving or building new surgery premises.

The BMA again made a claim for increases in 1956, but this time on behalf of hospital doctors as well as GPs. The health ministers did not agree to it and the matter was referred to a Royal Commission under Sir Harry Pilkington, which sat from 1957 to 1960 [41]. It recommended new levels of remuneration, but also that a standing review body of 'eminent persons of experience in various fields of national life' [42] should keep medical and dental remuneration under review, making recommendations which were, on the whole, to be accepted without alteration, directly to the Prime Minister. The BMA refused to give evidence to this Royal Commission, but, when the Presidents of the Royal Colleges announced that they would co-operate by putting the view of hospital consultants and specialists, the BMA was left with no alternative but to submit a brief to the Commission if it wished the GPs to have a voice. The effect of setting up a review body in 1963 was to end the practice, initiated by Spens, of calculating doctors' pay increases in relation to the rate of inflation. However, at the same time, it left the pay settlements in the hands of a body, separate from the Ministry, that could be advised but not instructed by the Government. Chapter 12 will describe how the Whitley Council system for collective bargaining and determination of the pay of all NHS staff was set up, and how it has operated. In the case of doctors, the Royal Commission was persuaded to recommend the end of direct negotiations between representatives of the health departments and the profession on Whitley Councils through the creation of a permanent independent review body.

The Review Body

The Review Body on Doctors' and Dentists' Remuneration was duly set up, consisting of six members and the Chairman, Lord Kindersley. Its terms of reference were 'to advise the Prime Minister on the remuneration of doctors and dentists taking any part in the National Health Service'. Twelve reports were issued between 1963 and 1970, and these concerned the basic rates of pay for different grades of doctors and dentists as well as particular aspects of remuneration, including distinction awards. The Review Body constructed its recommendations after receiving evidence from doctors' and dentists' representatives, from the Ministry/DHSS, and factual information about changes in the cost of living, the movement of earnings in other professions and the state of recruitment in the profession.

However, general practitioners were not satisfied with the awards made to them by the Review Body, and, in 1965, BMA demands included direct reimbursement of practice expenses, of income from local authority and hospital sessional work and a system of seniority payments. The Review Body made an award of £5.5 million, on the condition that most of it would be used to reimburse those doctors employing ancillary help or spending above-average amounts in improving their services for patients. The BMA replied (through its General Medical Services Committee) that this award, and previous awards which maintained the pool system, could not enable GPs to secure 'just' remuneration. They demanded an immediate unconditional credit of the £5.5 million award to the pool – thus raising the value of the capitation fee – as an interim measure, and asked GPs throughout the country to sign undated resignation forms which would be used or not, depending on the outcome of negotiations with the Minister [43].

In March 1965, Kenneth Robinson (the Minister of Health since October 1964) agreed to add the £5.5 million unconditionally to the pool, and began discussing the GPs' suggestion for a completely new contract, as outlined in the BMA's publication 'A Charter for the Family Doctor Service' [44]. This set out a radically revised scheme of payments, including a five and a half-day working week, six weeks' paid annual holiday, payments for out-of-hours services, an independent corporation to make long-term loans to GPs for building or improving surgery premises, ending the pool system, direct reimbursement for practice expenses, ancillary help, and several other items.

Although the GPs did not get exactly what they had demanded, the gap between the incomes of GPs and hospital consultants was narrowed. A notable achievement of the whole dispute was, however, to encourage group practice from purpose-built or modified premises, through the setting up of the General Practice Finance Corporation, and the reimbursement of a greater proportion of practice expenses, which encouraged employment of ancillary staff. It also reduced the burden of signing National Insurance certificates, to which GPs had strongly objected.

In March 1970, the Twelfth Report of the Review Body [45] recommended a general increase of 30% for doctors and dentists to be introduced over two years, because their pay had been falling behind increases for other professions. The Government accepted this for the training grades of doctors and dentists, but only agreed to half the awards for career grades in hospital and general practice work, referring the balance to the National Board for Prices and Incomes. Lord Kindersley and the members of the Review Body resigned on the day after this announcement in June, and the BMA advised its members not to co-operate with the NHS administration. These sanctions were lifted after the general election in 1970, in return for assurances from the new Conservative Government that the reference to the National Board for Prices and Incomes would be withdrawn.

In November 1970, the Government set up three new review bodies to handle the pay negotiations for groups in the public sector where the negotiating machinery had been unsatisfactory – namely, doctors and dentists in the NHS, the chairmen and board members of the nationalized industries and the armed forces. These review bodies have interlocking membership and their secretariat is provided from the Office of Manpower Economics. The new terms of reference for the Doctors' and Dentists' Review Body (chaired by Lord Halsbury) laid down that their recommendations would not be referred to another body (this had been the reason for Lord Kindersley's resignation) and would not be rejected or modified unless it was unavoidable.

Lord Halsbury resigned as Chairman of the Review Body after the Fourth Report [46], published in July 1974, had been rejected by the profession who expressed their lack of confidence in him. The Review Body continued its work without a chairman, and published a supplement to the Fourth Report at the end of the year. This was accepted by the Government and the profession. Annual reports have been issued since then. By and large the recommendations of the Review Body each year have been accepted by governments.

The funding of pay awards over the last 10 or 12 years has not matched the actual awards however. Although governments have made up most of the difference between the pay award and funds already allocated to the NHS, from the 1980s onwards it increasingly left a deliberate funding gap, which had to be filled by Districts by funding the money through efficiency savings. In 1992, the Chancellor of the Exchequer, Norman Lamont, introduced a 1.5% pay ceiling for the public sector, in an attempt to curb government spending in the face of a huge deficit between tax revenues and expenditure. The ceiling affected the Review Body pay recommendations which were effectively ignored by the Government. In 1994, the Government stated its requirement to keep the rise in the public sector pay bill as close to zero as possible. Again, the Review Body's pay recommendations were ignored. With NHS

EARNING CAPACITY OF GP WITH 2000 PATIENTS (TYPICALLY AN URBAN GP WITH NO DEPRIVATION IN HIS AREA)

Income from existing fees and allowances	£	Income from new fees and allowances	£
Capitation		**Capitation**	
a. Standard capitation fees	17 625	1. Standard capitation fees	21 850
b. Supplementary capitation fees	1700		
Basic practice allowance		**Basic practice allowance**	
c. BPA	8560	2. BPA	6000
d. Supplementary BPA	1720		
Other fees and allowances		**Other fees and allowances**	
e. Seniority	5510	3. Seniority	3810
f. Group practice	1480	4. Registration fees[2]	750
g. Night visit fees	625	5. Night visit fees[3]	1440
h. Other payments (remaining unchanged)	4850	6. Other payments (remaining unchanged)	4850
TOTAL (A)	42 070	TOTAL (1)	38 700
		7. Postgraduate Education Allowance	1700
		8. Minor surgery sessions[4]	480
		9. Health promotion sessions[5]	540
		10. Child health surveillance fees (capitation)[6]	480
		TOTAL (2)	41 900
i. Cervical cytology[1]	310	11. Cervical cytology target[1]	1500
j. Childhood immunization[1]	480	12. Childhood immunization target[1]	2030
TOTAL (B)	42 855	TOTAL (3)	45 430

Assumptions:
1. Assumes 80% of eligible women on 5-year rolling programme are screened, and 90% of children are immunized. Assumes also GP screens/immunizes 2 out of every 3 patients in the target populations.
2. Assumes new registrations are 8% of list.
3. Less if GP uses deputizing service.
4. Assumes 1 session every month.
5. Assumes 3 sessions every two months.
6. Assumes GP earns fees for all children aged under 5.

Summary
This GP has a fairly busy urban practice, with a list size equivalent to the England and Wales national average. He is interested in achieving high coverage levels for cervical cancer screening and childhood immunization, and is keen to provide a wider range of services.

Under the new arrangements, this GP will benefit considerably. If he provides a full range of new services, he could increase his income by over £2,500.

By contrast, if the GP kept his workload to the minimum he would find his income would drop by over £3,000 – more if he uses a deputizing service, as he would then be paid night visit fees at a lower rate.

Figure 9.2 General practitioners' pay.

Source: *General Practice in the National Health Service; the 1990 Contract.*

trusts now having the power to negotiate pay and conditions for their clinical staff, it remains to be seen whether the Review Body has much of a role in future.

The 1990 GPs' contract

The next major change in GPs' pay was embodied in the new contract, implemented on 1 April 1990. The negotiations leading to this were protracted and, at times, bitter. The profession's own leaders in the BMA found the terms they had agreed with the Secretary of State were rejected by the majority of their membership. By August 1989 a revised contract was agreed and sent out to all GPs and, although it too was unpopular, the Secretary of State decided to impose it anyway. A vigorous campaign of opposition, involving patients, did not change his mind.

The new contract (Figure 9.2) gave greater emphasis to the core of the GPs' remuneration, the capitation fee. Better financial incentives were introduced to encourage more health promotion than before, and attaining targets for immunization and cervical smears is rewarded with cash. Since the implementation of the contract there does appear to have been a corresponding increase in activity in targeted areas (Figure 9.3), but there has been little evaluation of possible detrimental effects of the new target payments on other areas of GPs' work not attracting special payments. Special payments are

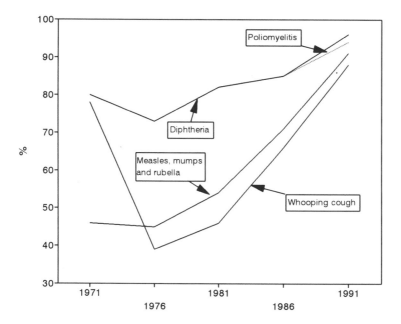

Figure 9.3 Immunization and vaccinations: 1980–1992.

Source: *Social Trends: 1994 Edition*, HMSO, London.

also made to encourage regular checks of children and the elderly, although recent evidence suggests that there may be few benefits for the elderly from their health checks.

GPs must be available to their patients for 26 hours per week, and they can no longer give up full responsibility to a deputy or locum. A new allowance was introduced for GPs who train medical students and who, themselves, take part in regular postgraduate activities. The overall intention was to reward doctors who provide a high quality of service, though many GPs expressed the worry that the contract would merely increase administrative procedures. There seems little doubt, however, that the new contract and the fundholding scheme has put more managerial and administrative pressure on GPs.

Hospital doctors

Relations between hospital doctors and the Government were not so troublesome until about 1972 when dissatisfactions with the form of consultants' contracts arose. The consultants' view, expressed mainly through the BMA, was that they had been required to take on several new responsibilities without adequate pay adjustments. At that time, their contracts specified the minimum number of hours to be worked, depending on whether the doctor had opted to work full-time for the NHS or part-time, in order to take on private work also. The system of distinction awards also made extra annual payments to a proportion of consultants (Figure 9.4).

Discussions between the consultants and the Department continued inconclusively, and in 1974 a general election replaced the Conservatives with a Labour Government. The new Secretary of State for Social Services, Barbara Castle, took up the consultants' problem by proposing to make full-time NHS work financially more attractive than part-time work. In addition, she proposed to recast the distinction awards system entirely by creating two new pay supplements: a medical progress supplement (to award valuable innovations in medical research or academic study, like the old awards) and a service supplement (to reward overburdened consultants in unpopular regions or unfashionable specialities, which the old awards neglected). Negotiations on these proposals were stormy, and took place in the context of the Review Body's deliberations on a claim from the consultants for a large interim backdated increase. At the beginning of 1975, the BMA called on consultants to 'work to contract', i.e. to do no more than the minimum they were required to do – to demonstrate their opposition to the Government's proposals and their rejection of the Review Body's decision not to grant them an interim award. The disruption caused by the consultants' action was quite widespread; it ceased late in 1975.

At about the same time, however, junior hospital doctors commenced 'work to contract', in support of their claims for a new contract to recognize the long hours and heavy responsibilities they had to shoulder. Again, the negotiations were acrimonious, but a settlement was reached later in 1975 when the Review

Figure 9.4 Meritorious and distinctive service awards: England and Wales: 1992

	Eligible practitioner/		Award holders											Non award holders	
			Total		A+		A		B		C				
	No.	%	No.	%	No.	%	No.	%	No.	%	No.	%	No.	%	
All specialties total	*17662*	*100.0*	*6058*	*34.3*	*203*	*1.1*	*703*	*4.0*	*1566*	*8.9*	*3586*	*20.3*	*11604*	*65.7*	
Accident and emergency	237	1.3	49	20.7	–	–	3	1.3	10	4.2	36	15.2	188	79.3	
Anaesthetics	2271	12.9	652	28.7	23	1.0	38	1.7	156	6.9	435	19.2	1619	71.3	
Cardiology	202	1.4	96	47.5	4	2.?	19	9.4	28	13.9	45	22.3	106	52.5	
Cardio-thoracic surgery	137	0.8	62	45.3	3	2.2	10	7.3	21	15.3	28	20.4	75	54.7	
Clinical neurological physiology	59	0.3	21	35.6	–	–	1	1.7	6	10.2	14	23.7	38	64.4	
Oral surgery	268	1.5	123	45.9	6	2.2	18	5.6	28	10.4	74	27.6	115	54.1	
Orthodontics	151	0.9	49	31.8	2	1.3	3	1.9	13	8.4	31	20.1	105	69.5	
Restorative dentistry	106	0.6	44	41.5	–	–	7	6.6	10	9.4	27	25.5	62	58.5	
Public health dentistry	10	0.1	5	50.0	–	–	1	10.0	1	10.0	3	30.0	5	50.0	
Dermatology	256	1.4	82	32.0	–	–	15	5.9	21	8.2	46	18.0	174	68.0	
Diseases of the chest	123	0.7	70	56.9	1	0.8	8	6.5	16	13.0	45	36.6	53	43.1	
General medicine	1567	8.9	772	49.3	35	2.2	129	8.2	210	13.4	398	25.4	795	50.7	
General surgery	1263	7.2	564	44.7	23	1.8	70	5.5	155	12.5	313	24.8	699	55.3	
Genito-urinary medicine	179	1.0	40	22.3	–	–	5	2.8	3	1.7	32	17.8	139	77.7	
Geriatric medicine	587	3.3	128	21.8	1	0.2	8	1.4	26	4.4	93	15.8	459	78.2	
Infectious diseases	42	0.2	21	50.0	1	2.4	2	4.8	6	14.3	12	28.6	21	50.0	
Mental illness	1344	7.6	374	27.8	14	1.0	37	2.8	95	7.1	228	17.0	970	72.2	
Child and adolescent psychiatry	387	2.2	81	20.9	3	0.8	4	1.0	18	4.7	36	14.5	306	70.1	
Forensic psychiatry	79	0.4	21	26.6	1	1.3	3	3.8	3	3.8	14	17.7	58	73.4	
Mental handicap	178	2.0	30	16.9	–	–	5	2.8	4	2.2	21	11.8	148	83.1	
Psychotherapy	111	0.6	28	25.2	–	–	–	–	9	8.1	19	17.1	83	74.8	
Neurology	219	1.2	110	50.2	4	1.8	22	10.0	39	17.8	45	20.5	109	49.8	
Neurosurgery	113	0.6	60	53.1	2	1.8	15	13.3	21	18.6	22	19.5	53	40.9	
Nuclear medicine	33	0.2	16	48.5	1	3.0	7	21.2	5	15.2	3	9.1	17	51.5	
Obstetrics and gynaecology	877	5.0	324	36.9	14	1.6	31	3.5	77	8.8	202	23.0	553	63.1	
Occupational medicine	30	0.2	6	20.0	–	–	–	–	1	3.3	5	16.7	24	80.0	
Ophthalmology	468	2.6	154	32.9	2	0.4	??	4.1	45	9.6	88	18.8	314	67.1	
Orthopaedic surgery	805	4.6	274	34.0	8	1.0	27	3.4	55	6.8	184	22.0	531	66.0	
Oeolaryngology	408	2.3	143	35.0	–	–	10	2.5	30	7.4	103	25.2	265	65.0	
Paediatrics	910	5.2	322	35.4	11	1.2	32	3.5	89	9.8	190	20.9	588	64.6	
Paediatric surgery	54	0.3	23	42.6	–	–	5	9.3	14	25.9	4	7.4	31	59.4	
Pathology: general	8	0.1	2	25.0	–	–	1	12.5	–	–	1	12.5	6	75.0	
Blood transfusion	35	0.2	11	31.4	1	2.9	1	2.9	4	11.4	5	14.3	24	68.6	
Chemical pathology	184	1.0	62	33.7	4	2.2	7	3.8	20	10.9	31	16.8	122	66.3	
Haematology	413	2.3	154	36.6	5	1.2	22	5.3	36	8.7	88	21.3	262	63.4	
Histopathology	655	3.7	205	31.3	6	0.9	23	3.5	56	8.5	120	18.3	450	68.7	
Immunopathology	47	0.3	30	63.8	2	4.3	8	17.0	11	23.4	9	19.1	17	36.2	
Medical microbiology	339	1.9	124	36.6	4	1.2	17	5.0	38	11.2	65	19.2	215	63.4	
Neuropathology	40	0.2	16	40.0	–	–	3	7.5	5	12.5	8	20.0	24	60.0	
Public Health Laboratory Service only	30	0.2	11	36.7	–	–	4	13.3	3	10.0	4	13.3	19	63.3	
Plastic surgery	131	0.7	45	34.4	–	–	5	3.8	16	12.2	54	18.3	86	65.6	
Public health medicine	543	3.1	155	28.5	9	1.7	16	2.9	37	6.8	93	17.1	388	71.5	
Radiology	1240	7.0	319	25.7	8	0.6	26	2.1	76	6.1	209	16.9	921	74.3	
Radiotherapy	227	1.3	97	42.7	4	1.8	10	4.4	22	9.7	61	26.9	130	57.3	
Rheumatology and rehabilitation	293	1.7	86	29.4	1	0.3	9	3.1	24	8.2	52	17.7	207	70.6	

Source: *Health Trends*, Vol. 25, No. 4, 1993.

Body priced two new types of supplement that junior doctors could receive if they worked extra hours over a newly defined basic working week of 40 hours. The cost of this settlement turned out to be more expensive than the Review Body had calculated, because of the way the Health Authorities awarded the new supplements. In addition, hospital work levels were significantly reduced as a result of the consultants and junior doctors 'working to contract', and this showed up as increased waiting-times for out-patient appointments and in-patient admissions.

The junior doctors' new contract took effect from February 1976, but, despite extensive discussion, a new contract for consultants has not materialized and there has been little development of local pay bargaining as a result of the freedoms conferred on NHS trusts. No significant further progress on changing the system of distinction awards has been made, except for changes introduced by the 1990 Act which allow managers to take part in the process of making recommendations for merit awards. The task of the Review Body, in the light of these disputes and under the constraints imposed by the Government's pay policy, has been made extremely difficult. The Review Body was, after all, set up to avoid recurrent disputes and to arrive at settlements which would be fair to the profession and to the taxpayer who foots the bill. In the event, the effect of increasing militancy among members of the medical profession, and Government attempts to control the rate of pay increases, has put great strains on the ability of both sides to negotiate acceptable pay and terms of work under the NHS.

Intrinsic problems persist with the negotiation of doctors' pay. When first set up, the Review Body seemed to be more sensitive and more influential than the Whitley Council, but it has also been politically more vulnerable to governments who can negotiate settlements on the assumption that doctors will not get any support from other groups of staff and their trade unions. As has been seen, the professional representatives of the Review Body are not always in accord, and at least twice in the last ten years the junior medical staff have had serious disagreements with their parent body, the BMA. Another problem with pay is that of relativities. Doctors have been able to demonstrate from time to time that they have done less well over time than other groups of staff.

In the changed managerial climate of the late 1980s, a more rigorous approach was taken to doctors' employment through the requirement that each consultant's work plan should be agreed with the local management to ensure these matched service needs. This was endorsed in one of the papers [47] accompanying *Working for Patients*, and led some consultants to fear that they could be expected to work more under non-medical direction than they considered compatible with their professional status. The substantial autonomy they enjoy has enabled them to practise with little or no enforceable accountability. Management's view, however, is that if there is to be greater efficiency, there must also be a clear contract with the consultants, specifying what is to be done, and when. It remains to be seen whether this will demotivate consultants, or whether the new authorities, through their providers, will thereby be able to increase consultants' efforts yet further and raise the standard of care, as there has been little change in the way trusts have handled consultants' contracts and their remuneration so far (1994).

CEPOD

Another initiative aimed at improving the quality of service was the White Paper's emphasis on the importance of medical audit. The Confidential Enquiry into Perioperative Deaths (CEPOD) [48] examined, in three Regions, all deaths within 30 days of surgical operation; this survey was later extended to the whole country. Every District is required to have clinical audit committees managed by the doctors themselves. The outcomes, reported anonymously, can be made available to local management. In due course, participating in medical audit could be made a contractual obligation. The medical profession's opposition to the 1989 White Paper was vociferous, but as had happened before, once the reforms were under way, doctors in hospitals and general practice decided it was simpler to accept change.

CONCLUSION

Despite the rise of the managerial class since the introduction of general management and the reforms of the 1990 Act, doctors remain the lead professional group in the NHS; and, although managers of the very largest trusts have seen their pay rise appreciably, doctors seem able to remain the best paid group of health care staff overall. This is partly because their contracts have advantageous elements not available to others: for example many consultants can do private work in addition to their NHS contract [49]. Doctors have also managed their own profession in ways that have reinforced their autonomous position at the top of the health care staff pyramid. This is not unique to the medical profession or to the UK, of course. Whether doctors can maintain their unique status in the future is questionable, given that virtually every other staff group has seen or is going through radical changes in their terms of employment – from short term contracts to performance-related pay.

NOTES

1. DHSS Circular HM(72)42 (1972) *Women Doctors' Retainer Scheme.*
2. DHSS Circular HM(69)6 (1969) *Redeployment of Women Doctors.*
3. Dowie, R. (February 1990) *Patterns of Hospital Medical Staffing. Junior Doctors' Hours, Interim Report,* British Postgraduate Medical Federation, London.
4. The 'New deal' for junior doctors set out various targets for average working hours for on-call rotas, partial shifts, etc., as well as targets for actual hours worked. Meeting these targets has been costly for small units or one-firm specialties.

5. Economic Research Unit, *Quarterly Bulletin*, Vol. 9, No. 1, March 1994, British Medical Association.
6. Further Medical Acts, passed in 1956 and 1969, consolidated amendments to the membership and powers of the Council.
7. *Report of the Committee of Enquiry into the Regulation of the Medical Profession* (Chairman, Dr A.W. Merrison), HMSO, London, 1975 (Cmnd. 6018). The GMC had decided to change the registration system to require doctors to pay an annual fee instead of the existing once-only payment. Doctors refused to comply with this, so, if the GMC had proceeded with the new system, the NHS would have been forced to employ non-registered doctors – an illegal arrangement. The inquiry into the GMC was announced to forestall the problem, and the committee itself decided to widen its brief to look at medical education and training as well as the membership and activities of the GMC.
8. Ministry of Reconstruction (1918) *Report of the Machinery of Government Committee* (Chairman, Viscount Haldane), HMSO, London (Cd. 9230).
9. Ministry of Health (1944) *Report of the Interdepartmental Committee on Medical Schools* (Chairman, Sir William Goodenough), HMSO, London.
10. *Royal Commission on Medical Education* (Chairman, Lord Todd), HMSO, London, 1968 (Cmnd. 3569).
11. Equivalent qualifications were also issued by the Conjoint Board of the Royal Colleges of Physicians and Surgeons (MRCS, LRCP) and by the Society of Apothecaries (LMSSA).
12. General Medical Council (1976) *Basic Medical Education in the British Isles*, Nuffield Provincial Hospitals Trust, London.
13. Department of Health, Department of Education and Science (June 1979) *Undergraduate Medical and Dental Education. Interim Report* (Chairman, Sir Christopher France), HMSO, London.
14. DHSS (1978) *Medical Manpower – The Next Twenty Years*, HMSO, London.
15. Ministry of Health and Department of Health for Scotland (1948) *Report of the InterDepartmental Committee on the Remuneration of Consultants and Specialists* (Chairman, Sir Will Spens), HMSO, London (Cmnd. 7420).
16. Ministry of Health and Department of Health for Scotland (1961) *Medical Staffing Structure in the Hospital Service: Report of the Joint Working Party* (Chairman, Sir Robert Platt), HMSO, London .
17. Op. cit., Todd Report.
18. *Royal Commission on the National Health Service*, HMSO, London, 1979 (Cmnd. 7615).
19. King's Fund Project, Paper No. 22 (1979) *The Organisation of Hospital Clinical Work*, King's Fund, London.
20. House of Commons. Social Services Committee, Session 1980–81, Fourth Report *Medical Education with Special Reference to the Number of Doctors and the Career Structure in Hospitals* (Chairman, Renée Short, MP).
21. DHSS (May 1983) *Health Trends*, Vol. 15, No. 2, p. 29, London.
22. DHSS Circular HC(82)4 (1982) *Hospital Medical Staff: Career Structure and Training*, HMSO, London.
23. Op. cit., Chapter 1, *Patients First*.
24. DHSS, BMA Joint Consultants' Committee, RHA Chairmen (July 1987) *Hospital Medical Staffing: Achieving a Balance*, London.
25. BMA (1983) *General Practice – A British Success*, General Medical Services

Committee, London.

26. DHSS (1972) *Report of the Working Party on Medical Administrators* (Hunter Report), HMSO, London.
27. Op. cit., Royal Commission (1979).
28. Department of Health (January 1988) *Public Health in England* (Acheson Report), HMSO, London (Cm. 289).
29. Ministry of Health (1967) *First Report of the Joint Working Party on the Organisation of Medical Work in Hospitals*, HMSO, London.
30. Department of Health and Social Security (1972) *Second Report of the Joint Working Party on the Organisation of Medical Work in Hospitals*, HMSO, London.
31. Department of Health and Social Security (1974) *Third Report of the Joint Working Party on the Organisation of Medical Work in Hospitals*, HMSO, London.
32. Op. cit., Royal Commission (1979).
33. Op. cit., *Patients First*.
34. DHSS Circular HC(80)8 (July 1980) *Health Service Development. Structure and Management*.
35. DHSS Circular HC(82)1 (January 1982) *Health Service Development. Professional Advisory Machinery*.
36. Op. cit., Chapter 1, Griffiths report.
37. Dixon, M. *et al.* (1990) *Models of Clinical Management*, Institute of Health Services Management, London.
38. See, for example, Audit Commission (1994) *Trusting in the Future: Towards an Audit Agenda for NHS Providers*, HMSO, London.
39. Ministry of Health and Department of Health for Scotland (1948) *Report of the InterDepartmental Committee on the Remuneration of General Practitioners* (Chairman, Sir Will Spens), HMSO, London.
40. Ibid., p. 10, para. 12.
41. *Royal Commission on Doctors' and Dentists' Remuneration* (Chairman, Sir Harry Pilkington), HMSO, London, 1960 (Cmnd. 939).
42. Ibid., p. 145, para. 428.
43. In fact, a total of 17 800 forms were eventually returned.
44. British Medical Association, A Charter for the Family Doctor Service. *British Medical Journal*, 18 March 1965, No. 3138, p. 89.
45. *Review Body on Doctors' and Dentists' Remuneration. Twelfth Report* (Chairman, Lord Kindersley), HMSO, London, 1970 (Cmnd. 4352).
46. *Review Body on Doctors' and Dentists' Remuneration. Fourth Report* (Chairman, Lord Halsbury), HMSO, London, 1974 (Cmnd. 5644).
47. Department of Health (1989) *Working for Patients: Working Paper 7*, HMSO, London, para. 2.5.
48. *Confidential Enquiry into Perioperative Deaths*, Nuffield Provincial Hospitals Trust, London, December 1987.
49. Yates, J. (1995) *Serving Two Masters*, Channel 4, London.

10

Nursing

The practice of nursing in its various forms aims to promote health, prevent illness, restore health and alleviate suffering. Nurses are by far the most numerous NHS staff (Figure 10.1) and, in an average acute services NHS trust, their salaries amount to over 40% of the total budget, a level of expenditure, therefore, that has to be managed particularly effectively. Since the 1974 reorganization, the nursing profession has undergone several fundamental changes in practice and organization. This chapter first provides a historical review of the origins of the various parts of nursing – united as one profession in 1979 by the Nurses, Midwives and Health Visitors Act – and then reviews recent events that have promoted nursing as an independent profession no longer subordinate to medicine.

HISTORY OF NURSING

Hospital nursing

Hospital nursing is rooted in the work of the nursing orders of the religious houses of the Middle Ages. Men and women who became monks and nuns were called by a sense of vocation to alleviate the sufferings of sick people. The oldest hospitals, St Bartholomew's (1123) and St Thomas's (1215), were founded to reflect this concern. By the time of the Reformation, in the sixteenth century, the pursuit of vocations was diminishing and, two centuries later, care available to sick people outside their immediate family was haphazard and unreliable. Although several of the great voluntary hospitals were founded in the eighteenth century, the standard of nursing within them was often poor, and undertaken by those who themselves were living barely above subsistence level.

In the mid-nineteenth century, attitudes began to change and the idea of nursing as a vocation started to revive. In 1840, Elizabeth Fry founded an Institute of Nursing at Guy's Hospital where women were trained under the influence of Quaker teaching. Florence Nightingale (1820–1910), traditionally the founder of modern nursing, turned her back on her cultured, idle upper-

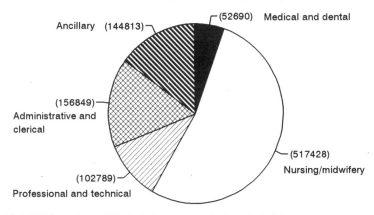

Figure 10.1 NHS staffing: UK (whole-time equivalents): 1992.

Source: *The Government's Expenditure Plans 1994/5 to 1996/7: Departmental Report*, HMSO, London (Cm. 2512).

class family, went to Paris and to Prussia to train as a nurse and returned with the intention of improving nursing in England. The outbreak of the Crimean War in 1854 gave her the opportunity to show her outstanding powers of organization as she redeemed the near hopeless care of the wounded with her 30 nurses. Returning from there, her reputation was secure and she devoted the remainder of her long life to public works and, in particular, to establishing nursing as a respectable profession [1] . The Nightingale Training School at St Thomas's was set up in 1860 and many others followed. In the hospitals, the hierarchy placed the ward sister as the agent of the doctor and the trainer of probationer nurses. Matrons were in charge of nursing, together with the whole range of domestic services required to run the hospital. The conditions of service for nurses remained restrictive for nearly a hundred years; they were expected to accept low wages in return for the privilege of looking after patients.

Voluntary hospitals were not the only institutions set aside for the sick; there were also poor law infirmaries, fever hospitals and lunatic asylums. Nursing training in these institutions took longer to be set up, and there was no recognized training for nursing mentally ill patients until 1891 when the Royal Medico-Psychological Society started to issue certificates. Statutory registration of nurses trained to an approved standard involved a long and complicated struggle, although one that was supported by doctors. Not until 1919 was the matter resolved with the passing of the Nursing Registration Acts, which established the General Nursing Council (GNC) as the registering authority. The GNC remained in this capacity until the establishment of the United Kingdom Central Council for Nursing, Midwifery and Health Visiting in 1983 (see below). The GNC maintained a register of nurses, trained in approved institutions, who had passed examinations after three years of study and supervised practice. The Nurses Act, 1943, recognized the scope for employing less highly qualified nurses and accordingly approved two-year training leading to enrolment. The Nurses Act, 1949, incorporated male nurses into the main register (they had been on their own register since 1919), but not until the Sex Discrimination Act, 1975, were men allowed to train as midwives. The 1949 Act also required money to be set aside specifically for nurse training administered by local nurse training committees.

A certain snobbery attached to where nurses trained or worked. Well-known voluntary and teaching hospitals could attract the best recruits, leaving other hospitals with the mediocre students. Male nurses were not trained in the 'best' hospitals until relatively recently. Local authority hospitals, elevated from their workhouse origins by the Local Government Act, 1929 [2], began to improve, and some new hospitals were built during the 1930s, giving nurses better training opportunities and conditions of work. The role of Matron, long seen as pre-eminent, began to change after the inception of the NHS in 1948, and by degrees, she (never males at that time) handed over most of the domestic duties to administrators. This emphasis on the professional nature of her work prepared the way for the major changes heralded by the Salmon Report in 1966 [3] (see below).

Community nursing

Community nurses, that is, district nurses, health visitors and midwives, unlike their hospital counterparts, always worked independently. The history of district nursing is closely associated with philanthropists such as William Rathbone in Liverpool and the Queen's Institute of District Nursing, set up with money given at Queen Victoria's silver and golden jubilees at the end of the nineteenth century. The Queen's Institute accepted nurses who were already registered and gave them further training to equip them to work in the community. Under the NHS Act, 1946, local authorities became responsible for organizing home nursing and, at first, tended to use Queen's Institute nurses on an agency basis until they began recruiting and training their own staff.

The title 'health visitor' probably first came into use in 1862 when a voluntary body, the Ladies' Sanitary Reform Association of Manchester and Salford, paid staff to visit people in those towns, concentrating on cleanliness, healing the sick and advising mothers on the care of their children. In 1875, the Royal Sanitary Institute (now the Royal Society of Health) was founded to promote the health of the people and began to set examinations for sanitary inspectors. In 1892, Florence Nightingale started a course at Buckinghamshire Technical College where 'health missionaries' were trained to meet the needs of 'home health-bringing', and the women thus trained were employed by the local council to visit people in need. The Royal Sanitary Institute set examinations for health visitors and school nurses from 1906, and, in 1908, the London County Council decreed that all health visitors should hold an accredited certificate approved by the Local Government Board.

The scope for improvements in health at that time is demonstrated by the infant mortality rate (deaths in the first year of life), which was 163 per 1000 live births at the turn of the century. Acts passed in 1907 and 1915 requiring births to be registered provided the means of identifying the problem, and from then health visitors have continued to concentrate on infant and maternal welfare. The Jamieson Report (1956) [4] endorsed this emphasis. The Royal Society of Health handed over responsibility for examining health visitors in 1962 to the Council for Training of Health Visitors.

Midwives

Midwives have been recognized from earliest times. Their long-standing acceptance as the women best able, in any community, to help deliver babies has only been challenged since the rise of modern obstetric medicine. Once, richer families preferred a doctor to deliver their babies; by the middle of the nineteenth century, the majority of midwives were said to be untrained, often ignorant and of 'very low character'. Their standards started improving again with the foundation of the Midwives Institute in 1881 by a group of women who wished to strengthen the status of the midwife. The Midwives Act was passed in 1902, and it established a Central Midwives Board to keep a roll of approved midwives and to ensure adequate training programmes and standards of good practice. The Ministry of Health, created in 1919, then took over supervision of the Board.

Midwifery was practised in hospital and in the community, and staff came initially from voluntary bodies. After 1948, local health authorities were given the statutory duty to provide a domiciliary midwifery service and to supervise standards of practice. Hospital management committees had to provide sufficient facilities for a mother to have her baby in hospital if she so wished. Following the recommendations of the Cranbrook Report (1959) [5] and the Peel Report (1970) [6], hospital confinement has become the norm, even though some mothers would still prefer to be delivered at home. This change has greatly affected the nature of the work midwives do, now that hospital obstetric services rely so much on medical expertise and sophisticated technical procedures for antenatal tests and monitoring. Those working only in hospital or only in the community may lose some of their skills, unless they are part of an integrated system which allows them experience in both settings. *Changing Childbirth* is a boost to their professionalism [7].

PRINCIPAL REFORMS

In 1963, shortages of trained nurses and the apparent decline in the status of nursing prompted the Government to set up a review of the profession under the chairmanship of Brian Salmon. Its report, published three years later [8], noted that the title 'matron' was applied equally to nursing heads of hospitals whether they had 10 beds or 1000, and that the distinction between their duties and functions had become increasingly unclear. It said that job titles were themselves anachronistic with more men holding 'sister' and 'matron' posts. The report, therefore, recommended a much clearer hierarchy to recognize that in nursing, as in other professions, there were intrinsic differences between top, middle and first line management. Policy was the responsibility of the top manager, the chief nursing officer; programming policies was what middle managers, principal and senior nursing officers were there to do; and the practical delivery of nursing remained with the first line nurse, nursing officer, charge nurse or sister, and staff nurse.

The recommendations were accepted and it was agreed that 16 pilot schemes should be set up and evaluated. As often happens, once the first schemes had been launched there was a clamour from everywhere else to follow suit, so the evaluation exercise was never seriously undertaken. This proved unfortunate. Doctors and administrators were always rather scornful of the idea of nurses as managers, caricaturing the new ranks as 'clipboard-carrying nurses' who would be at a loss if faced with a patient. Nurses themselves did not always implement the new structures wisely, and, by too slavishly following the Salmon Report's blueprint for several managerial levels, they created unnecessarily complicated local hierarchies. But the report did establish the professional head of nursing as an equal with his or her administrative and medical colleagues. This was later upheld through full-status membership of the management teams at District, Area and Region, following the 1974 reorganization.

There were also changes in the organization of community nursing. The 1968 report from the National Board for Prices and Incomes [9], as well as urging implementation of the Salmon structures to improve the pay prospects of more senior hospital nurses, also noted that the fragmentation of community nursing services should be counteracted by designating similar senior posts. Following this, the DHSS set up a working party, under the chairmanship of E.L. Mayston, to consider how far the Salmon management concepts were applicable to community nursing. Its report was published in 1969 [10] and commended by the Secretary of State to local authorities employing community nurses.

The Mayston Report noted that health visitors were concerned with the health of families as a whole, health education, the early detection of abnormalities in children and school health. It recognized that district nurses provided skilled care in people's homes under the clinical direction of GPs, and recommended that they be attached to GP practices more securely in order to facilitate integrated care. The Mayston Report proposed that:

- every local health authority should have a Chief Nursing Officer;
- the senior nursing structure should be immediately reviewed;
- there should be three levels of nursing management;
- management training should be given to senior community nurses.

Local health authorities restructured their nursing hierarchy accordingly, appointing a Director of Nursing Services accountable to the Medical Officer of Health for all nursing and midwifery services in the community. Because the

1974 reorganization then amalgamated the management of community and hospital services, the two nursing structures had to be brought together in each District under the District Nursing Officer. Some specialization remained, unlike in the social work services, where reorganization based on the Seebohm Report [11] had introduced the concept of the 'generic' social worker to respond to all types of client needs.

Community nursing was usually allocated to a community nursing division headed by its own divisional nursing officer. In some Area Health Authorities, community nursing remained in the control of the Areas rather than the Districts because, for instance, the organization of child health services benefited from a coterminous boundary with the local county education authority and was, therefore, thought to be better organized at Area level. There were also a few posts for nurses at Area and Regional level to participate in strategic planning. These opportunities away from practical nursing provided the more ambitious nurses, interested in management with a good career path similar to that of administrators and other senior specialists.

It was the reductions in these very opportunities that caused much of the resentment when, ten years later, general management was introduced. Nurses were potential candidates for the role of District General Manager but, in the event, few applied and even fewer were appointed. From holding the rank of a District Management Team member and the status of a chief officer accountable directly to the health authority, they became subordinates of the DGM. At unit level there was a similar effect, as the head nurse was made responsible to the Unit General Manager instead of the District Nursing Officer. The Royal College of Nursing campaigned vehemently through 1985, protesting at this loss of status, and stressing the indisputable fact that only nurses were with the patient 24 hours in the day; it said this gave them a position that had to be reflected in representation at the highest levels of decision making. But the concept of general management did not allow this. Where nurses did become general managers they quickly learnt that they could not wear two hats; the general manager function was paramount, whatever the incumbent's professional background.

By 1990, nurses had accepted the new position, probably encouraged by their experience that, in most Districts, the value given to nursing had not diminished even if there had been a slight loss in status. Indeed, in some cases, the middle manager and first line nursing staff expressed preference for the new arrangements, welcoming the opportunities they now had to convince general managers of the importance of their role, and eliciting much support in the process. For the displaced Chief Nursing Officers, the post-1984 period was difficult as they adapted to jobs with less managerial content, such as quality assurance and planning.

But these were not the only challenges to assail the nursing profession in the period following the 1974 reorganization. Practical nursing had traditionally been a task-orientated activity, with procedures carried out according to prescribed routines. Although this may have been efficient in some ways, it seemed to deny the patient's own identity and diminished the potential job satisfaction of the nurse herself. Following a report published in 1979, *The Extended Clinical Role of The Nurse* [12], the nursing process, as it came to be called, was required to concentrate on the patient as a whole. This led to the idea of a 'primary' nurse who was assigned to a group of patients on the ward and was primarily responsible for their care. Traditionalists complained that this led to less efficiency on the wards, but it has undoubtedly encouraged nurses to be more knowledgeable about those they care for.

In the community, the organization of nursing was still causing concern. The increasing number of nurses attached to GP practices had brought its own organizational problems, mainly because many GPs still had patients scattered around the locality and the overlap between neighbouring practices was considerable. This meant that nurses from several practices were working in the same area with a consequential waste of resources. The Cumberlege Report *Neighbourhood Nursing – A Focus for Care* [13] recommended that the advantages of having nurses attached to practices could be retained, and that better deployment would result if they were organized to serve communities of between 10 000 and 25 000 population. The report was disparaging about the practice nurses employed directly by GPs, saying they lacked the necessary skills and were professionally isolated. However, the 1990 GP contract ignored this criticism, giving emphasis to the continued employment of practice nurses and encouraging expansion of the role well beyond the competence of some individuals.

A pessimistic view of nursing might observe that the profession had a brief taste of power in the 1970s, while Chief Nursing Officers were on the Management Teams, until the 1984 general management reforms demoted them. Virtually no nurses were appointed as members of District Health Authorities in 1990. Following the reforms of the White Paper, *Working for Patients*, there has to be a non-executive nurse on FHSAs and an executive nurse member on the boards of management of trusts. At lower levels in the organization, the development of clinical directorates is seen by some nurses as a threat to their professional status, because ward nurses are obliged to be much more accountable to the clinical directors, who are invariably doctors. In the community, similarly, nurses are being pushed back under the closer control of GPs.

In an effort to rally morale, particularly of senior nurses, in 1989 the Chief Nursing Officer of the Department of Health published *A Strategy for Nursing* [14]. The document examined practice, manpower, education, leadership and management, and reviewed the changes taking place, or needed, to establish the profession as an equal partner with others involved in looking after the patient.

EDUCATION AND TRAINING

The General Nursing Council was set up in 1919 and survived, with various modifications, until 1 July 1983, when it was superseded by the United Kingdom Central Council for Nursing, Midwifery and Health Visiting (UKCC), which was established by the Nurses, Midwives and Health Visitors Act, 1979. The impetus for this change came from the report of the Committee on Nursing, known as the Briggs Report, published in 1972 [15]. As well as its more general concerns about nursing, it addressed the statutory framework controlling the professions of nursing and midwifery and their educational needs. The three branches of nursing had a different statutory history, and Briggs said this needed remedying so that a more coherent approach to education and training could be developed.

The 1979 Act repealed the Nurses' Acts of 1957, 1964 and 1969, as well as amending a large number of clauses of other Acts concerning nursing. The new Act required the UKCC to establish and improve standards of training and professional conduct, to determine rules for registration, for maintaining a single professional register and to protect the public from unsafe practitioners. The UKCC is supplemented by four national Boards for the four countries in the United Kingdom: England, Wales, Scotland and Northern Ireland. The Boards are responsible for implementing the policies and rules of the UKCC. In particular, they have to provide, or arrange for others to provide, courses of training leading to registration, and they have an important role in fostering post-registration courses developed by schools of nursing or other institutions of higher or further education such as universities, polytechnics and technical colleges.

The 1979 Act lowered the minimum age for entry to nursing training to 17½ and imposed a common standard of entry qualifications for all 'first level' entrants, which is five 'O' levels (or the GCSE equivalent) or passing a UKCC test. The term 'first level' requires some explanation. Shorter training for enrolled (or 'second level') nurses was first introduced by the Nurses Act, 1943. The Briggs Report discussed the concept of a 'common portal of entry' whereby instead of registered (first level) and enrolled nurses having to pursue different training schemes, all those intending to nurse would undertake a common core course of study, only specializing thereafter. This worried those who felt that the entry requirement would be too low to select nurses capable of high academic achievement, or so high it would deter the good practical nurse. This point was ultimately addressed by the proposals of Project 2000 published in 1986 [16] (see below). Meanwhile, the new register merged all previous registers maintained by nine separate bodies, combining first (registered nurse) and second (enrolled nurse) levels. It provides a single record of each nurse's details and qualifications. There are over half a million nurses in the UK, but not all are practising.

Project 2000

Project 2000 addressed the question of raising the status of nurse training, which had fallen far behind that of students in other disciplines. Since Florence Nightingale's day, nurses had been trained as apprentices are; they learned by doing. At first, academic work had to be done outside working hours. Then blocks of classroom work were scheduled and tied in with practical experience supervised not only by ward sisters but also by clinical tutors. Nevertheless, students, particularly in the later stages of training, risked being used as 'pairs of hands' and left alone in control of a ward, because of shortages of qualified staff. This led to intolerable pressure on individual students and was allegedly why significant numbers left before completing their training. Project 2000 aimed to exchange apprentice status for true student status, under which students are attached to a training school that may be away from the hospital, and attend the wards, departments or community settings as supernumeraries.

The initial core training course, adopted from the Briggs Report, lasts 18 months, after which the trainee proceeds to one of the branches of nursing: adult, children, mental health or learning disability. Midwifery remains somewhat outside the system as a result of rearguard action by the Royal College of Midwives, who insisted that midwifery is not an add-on to nursing but a profession in its own right. This hindered the intention behind the 1979 Act, which was designed to bring all aspects of nursing into a common profession. It is still, therefore, possible to train separately as a midwife.

Project 2000 was criticized for disregarding the problem of providing adequate numbers of nurses on the wards. If students were to be discounted from the workforce, others would have to take their place. The higher requirement for qualified staff would be expensive, even though the effect might benefit patients and students. The National Council for Vocational Qualifications was asked to recognize schemes of training for various health support workers, not only nursing auxiliaries, the unqualified members of the nursing team, but also supporting staff in other professions, such as physiotherapy and occupational therapy (see Chapter 11). This recalls some points made in the report of the Committee of Enquiry into Mental Handicap Nursing (the Jay Report) [17], which, in 1979, had challenged the assumption that the conventional training was an appropriate basis for looking after mentally handicapped people – it suggested a certificate in social work might be more suitable. The issue is still unresolved; perhaps the mental handicap branch of nursing proposed by Project 2000 could atrophy if alternative and perhaps less academic courses are found more appropriate for those choosing this area of work.

Project 2000 has been slow to be implemented for various reasons. The Government's enthusiasm has been tempered by the high costs of the changes. The report of Working Party 10 [18], associated with the 1990 NHS reforms, gave control of nurse education to the Regions, and schools of nursing have become larger in order to make the best use of teaching skills. It was suggested in a management consultants' report in 1989 [19] that the UKCC's National Boards should be reformed and streamlined because they had become too bureaucratic in their seven years' existence. In the absence of a clear government line, therefore, many authorities are doing what they can to adopt Project 2000, in the knowledge that the decline in numbers of young people on the labour market puts a premium on training and retaining well-qualified and skilled nurses during the next decade. Improving the status of nurse students is seen as imperative if recruitment is to be effective.

NURSES' PAY

Nurses are a powerful group because of their numbers in the NHS. They have always been able to command the sympathy of the general public. Despite this, nursing pay has not always compared well with rates in other countries. In the UK, nurses are usually assumed to be underpaid but, in fact, their position relative to other groups has varied. For most employees in the public sector, pay awards have seldom reflected the true costs of living; by degrees, the pay of NHS workers has fallen further behind the general level of settlements, which has provoked a crisis in relations with the Government and repeated calls from the staff for recognition of the justice of their claims. Nurses had not traditionally been militant but, in the late 1960s, a change in their approach was signalled by the Royal College of Nursing's 'Raise the Roof' campaign.

Discontent persisted until the Government commissioned Lord Halsbury to examine nurses' pay. His first report, in 1974 [20], gave substantial awards to most grades of nursing staff, and some increase in holiday allowances. The benefit was gradually eroded although a Review Body had been set up as an alternative to the Whitley Council (see Chapter 12) to determine nurses' pay. A new approach, agreed in 1987 [21], aimed to assess all the nursing responsibilities and allocate nursing grades according to agreed criteria. On the face of it this was a much fairer system than before, where some nurses had been undertaking more responsible work than others and yet had been receiving less pay. Unfortunately, this enquiry into clinical grading caused a storm of discontent. Many nurses disagreed with the assessments made by their managers, claiming that they took more responsibility than their manager said. In turn, the nurse managers would not agree to nurses claiming responsibilities that they regarded as superfluous or outside their competence. Doctors inflamed the situation by supporting the nurses' appeals against the managers, in pursuit of personal patronage and loyalty to the nursing staff they worked with.

Thousands of nurses lodged formal appeals and the hearings were only completed by 1994. What had begun as steps towards a rational and fair grading system ended by provoking more opposition among nurses to their employer than anything before. The experience was not all bad, however; at the end of the assessment exercise, management for the first time had a complete picture of what nurses were doing and to what standard of competence. There was now an explicit system for deciding the correct mix of skills for each type of clinical work.

Senior nursing staff, although dissatisfied over status, had held on to their advantageous pay rates and conditions of service throughout the 1980s. For example, the right to retire early with accelerated pension benefits continued, even when the original reason for such payments (living in and therefore being constantly on call) had long since ended. In 1991, a new pay scale for senior nurses was introduced to mirror that already in place for senior managers. The effect of this was to remove a long-standing difference between managers and nurse managers, which had caused considerable resentment of the nurses. It remains to be seen whether the shortages of staff expected during the 1990s transpire, and whether the creation of the single European market for employment [22] will increase nurses' bargaining power.

CONCLUSION

Although doctors may be seen traditionally as the most important group in the health service, nurses in fact provide the vast majority of care to patients in hospital and in the community. For most hospital patients, contact with doctors is small compared with the daily contact they have with nurses. For those receiving care from health visitors, district nurses and other community-based nurses, the nurse is the main health professional. As with many kinds of work, the history of nursing has been one of greater professionalization through the formation of national representative bodies, formalization of entry qualifications and increased training.

Along with this professionalization has come greater responsibility. For example, tasks once seen as the domain of doctors are now routinely carried out by nurses. More recently, the increased pressure on trusts, operating in a market, to examine the costs of providing care and treatment in the NHS has prompted close scrutiny of the appropriateness of tasks carried out by doctors and nurses, with a view to transferring some of the former to the latter. Such trends are likely to continue, stretching the umbrella title of 'nursing' to cover a wider and wider range of jobs and tasks with greater specialization.

NOTES

1. Woodham-Smith, C. (1950) *Florence Nightingale*, Constable, London. This is still the definitive biography.
2. *Local Government Act*, 1929, HMSO, London (Chapter 17).
3. Ministry of Health and Scottish Home and Health Department (1966) *Report of the Committee on Senior Nursing Staff Structure* (Salmon Report), HMSO, London.
4. *Report of a Working Party in the Field of Work, Training and Recruitment of Health Visitors* (1956) (Jamieson Report), HMSO, London.

5. Ministry of Health (1959) *Report of the Maternity Services Committee* (Cranbrook Report), HMSO, London.
6. Department of Health and Social Security, Central Health Services Council (1970) *Domiciliary Midwifery and Maternity Bed Needs* (Peel Report), HMSO, London.
7. Department of Health Expert Maternity Group (1993) *Changing Childbirth: Part 1: Report of the Expert Maternity Group*, HMSO, London.
8. Op. cit., Salmon report.
9. National Board for Prices and Incomes (1968) *Pay of Nurses and Midwives in the National Health Service*, Report No. 60, HMSO (Cmnd. 3585).
10. Department of Health and Social Security, Scottish Home and Health Department, Welsh Office (1969) *Report of the Working Party on Management Structures in the Local Authority Nursing Services* (Mayston Report), HMSO, London.
11. Home Office and others (1968) *Report of the Committee on Local Authority and Allied Social Services* (Seebohm Report), HMSO, London.
12. Royal College of Nursing (1979) *The Extended Clinical Role of the Nurse*, Royal College of Nursing, London.
13. Department of Health and Social Security (1986) *Neighbourhood Nursing – A Focus for Care* (Cumberlege Report), HMSO, London.
14. Department of Health, Nursing Division (April 1989) *A Strategy for Nursing*. A report of the Steering Committee chaired by Mrs Anne Poole, Chief Nursing Officer, Department of Health, London.
15. Department of Health and Social Security and others (1972) *Report of the Committee on Nursing* (Briggs Report), HMSO, London (Cmnd 5115).
16. UKCC (1986) *Project 2000: A New Preparation for Practice*, London.
17. Department of Health and Social Security (1979) *Report of the Committee of Enquiry into Mental Handicap Nursing and Care* (Jay Report), HMSO, London.
18. Department of Health (1989) *Working for Patients. Working Party 10: Education and Training*, HMSO, London.
19. DHSS, SHHD, WO, DHSS (NI) (August 1989) *Review of the United Kingdom Central Council and the Four National Boards*, Peat, Marwick McLintock, HMSO, London.
20. Department of Health and Social Security (1974) *Report of the Committee of Enquiry into Pay and Related Conditions of Service of Nurses and Midwives* (Halsbury Report), HMSO, London; Supplement, 1975.
21. DHSS (May 1988) Advance Letter NM1/88 *Clinical Nurse Grading Structure*, HMSO, London.
22. Britain's membership of the European Community made certain reforms necessary; the 1977 Directives specified that length of training should, in future, be counted in hours rather than years, and that all nursing recruits should have at least ten years' general education. No attempt was made to introduce a nursing qualification that was common throughout the Community.

11

Other staff

In addition to doctors and nurses, the NHS employs many other groups of staff (Table 11.1 shows the broad categories). Some of these are independent practitioners but most are directly employed by NHS trusts (since 1991). Both types are described in this chapter.

DENTAL SERVICES

In the seventeenth and eighteenth centuries there was no distinct profession of dentistry, but some barber-surgeons became known as 'operators for the teeth'. As scientific study of the teeth advanced, some practitioners were able to become very skilled specialists while others, who remained unskilled and unqualified, obtained their work through advertising. In 1878 the Dentists Act empowered the General Medical Council to examine and register suitable qualified dentists, but unqualified dentists continued to practise. The British Dental

Table 11.1 NHS staff: England: 1978–1992

(Figures in thousands)	1978	1982	1986	1989	1992
Medical and Dental	38	41	43	46	50
Nursing and Midwifery	351	397	403	405	382
Professional and Technical	57	67	76	80	90
Administrative and Clerical	100	109	111	117	135
Works (Professional)	6	6	6	6	⎫
Maintenance	20	21	19	17	⎬ 18
Ambulance	18	18	18	19	18
Ancillary	172	171	124	104	79
Total	762	831	802	793	796
Direct care staff	446	506	522	530	522
Direct care staff as % of total	58.6	60.9	65.1	66.9	65.6

Source: *The Government's Expenditure Plans 1994/5 to 1996/7: Departmental Report*, HMSO, London (Cm. 2512).

Association was founded in 1880 and dentistry became recognized as a profession. Unregistered practitioners continued to flourish, and many of them were inadequately trained. It was not until 1921, however, that a new Dentists Act dealt with this by effectively closing the profession to anyone who was not trained at a school of dentistry recognized by the newly created Dental Board. The Act made the Dental Board responsible for keeping a register and for investigating cases of misconduct, but the GMC retained control over disciplinary action and the power to license practitioners.

A further Dentists Act, in 1957, established the General Dental Council as the single statutory licensing and registering body, taking on the functions of the Dental Board and the GMC (in relation to dentistry). It supervises the standard of dental examinations and teaching, and keeps the register of dentists who have obtained the professional qualifications – either a degree (Bachelor of Dental Surgery, BDS) or a diploma (Licentiate in Dental Surgery, LDS) – from an approved school of dentistry. The training takes between four and six years, and dentists pay an entry and retention fee to have their name on the register. Practitioners' names can be erased if they commit a felony or if they are found guilty of professional misconduct by the Council's disciplinary committee.

The Dentists Act, 1983, revised the membership of the Council. There are now 29 members, of whom 18 are registered dentists elected from among themselves, four are the chief dental officers of England, Wales, Scotland and Northern Ireland, six are lay people nominated by the Queen on the advice of the Privy Council and one is a dental auxiliary. The President is elected from this membership. In addition three members of the General Medical Council can join discussions on dental education and examination issues. Those universities with dental schools can also send one member each (two for the University of London) who are additional to the 29 members and must themselves be dentists.

History of dental services

Before the NHS was founded, the general state of dental health was very poor, and, although dental benefits were available under the National Health Insurance scheme to 13 million of the working population, only about 6% made claims. After 1948, the NHS provided dental services in each arm of the tripartite structure. Hospital dentists specialized in dental surgery or orthodontics (the straightening of children's teeth) and were graded in the same way as hospital medical staff. Some worked in dental departments of general hospitals and others worked within specialist dental hospitals.

Local authorities were obliged by the 1944 Education Act to provide free dental inspection and treatment for all children in maintained schools, and they also cared for the dental health of expectant and nursing mothers. In fact, the School Medical Service, established in 1907, made provision for the dental care of mothers and children of pre-school age, but less than 2% of the eligible population made use of this. The explicit aim of the local authority dental services was to conserve teeth and to prevent premature loss of first teeth in children. The services were organized by a Principal School Dental Officer (responsible to the Medical Officer of Health) and his staff of School Dental Officers worked in the schools, clinics and treatment centres run by the local authority.

Then as now, the largest sector of the dental services was provided by dentists in general practice. These were qualified registered dentists who worked from their own homes or other premises, obtained their own equipment and supplies and employed ancillary staff. They held contracts with the executive councils which paid them for treating patients under the NHS. Many combined this with private practice, and they were not obliged to undertake any more NHS work than they wished.

In 1974, the reorganization changed only the administration of dental services; it did not alter this pattern of clinical work. Hospital dental surgeons (consultant oral surgeons and orthodontists) remained employees of the Regions (or, in the case of teaching Areas, the AHA(T)), and junior dental staff were employed by the Districts. Local authority dental staff were transferred to the new Areas which became responsible for community and school dental services throughout the Area. General dental practitioners remained in contract with the FPCs.

The 1982 reorganization fragmented these arrangements by devolving the Area responsibilities to each District, which appointed a District Dental Officer accountable to the DHA. Dental Advisory Committees ceased to be statutory in 1982, but most Districts have set one up. These committees exist to give expert opinion on the provision of dental services; they are not concerned with the relations between the profession and its employers or with the internal organization of the profession.

Dental care is provided by general dental practitioners to whom patients refer themselves for regular care; each episode of treatment is self-contained. The contract agreed in 1990 (see below) encourages patients and dentists to enter into a more continuous arrangement. Because nowadays children's teeth generally have a much lower incidence of caries, the community dentists mainly treat elderly people and the handicapped, particularly those who live in residential care. Specialist departments of dentistry in hospitals comprise the third branch of dental practice, where oral surgery, orthodontic and other restorative treatments are undertaken, the latter often with other surgeons in plastic surgery or ear, nose and throat departments.

Dentists' pay

As with doctors, dentists have one body to represent them professionally (the British Dental Association), one statutory body to regulate and control their practice (the General Dental Council) and separate bodies to negotiate their pay. Since 1960, their pay has been determined by the permanent Review Body which was established following the recommendations of the Royal Commission on Doctors' and Dentists' Remuneration [1]. Since 1974, community dentists have also become NHS employees and their pay has therefore also come within the scope of the Review Body. Hospital and community dental staff receive a salary from their trust, but the system for general dental practitioners is more complicated.

Before 1948, general dental practitioners received most of their income from private practice, and a committee [2] was appointed to work out a scheme for the average weekly chairside hours being worked, and the Health Departments and the profession jointly worked out fees for different items of service that should provide this level of income. However, the initial demand for dentures and dental treatment was enormous, so dentists worked more hours and received higher incomes than had been anticipated. The Government imposed limits on top earnings, and charges for dentures were introduced in 1951. Demand gradually declined, but because full information about dentists' total earnings (including private practice) and practice expenses was not available, the Health Departments and the BDA jointly discussed how to fix future levels of remuneration. The BDA demanded removal of the limit on top earnings, but the Department was insistent, although it suggested new rates for items of service which could raise the ceiling for top incomes. The BDA was not enthusiastic about this, but a survey of its members showed that a majority were not against this system of payment, so it accepted.

The Royal Commission on Doctors' and Dentists' Remuneration made some specific recommendations about the pay of dentists, and it confirmed that general dental practitioners' pay should be based on fees for items of service. The Doctors' and Dentists' Review Body advised the Government on the average net income that dentists should receive for working a specified number of chairside hours per year.

The Dental Rates Study Group (a committee of representatives from the profession and the DHSS under an independent chairman) assesses from time to time the level of dentists' practice expenses from information provided by the Inland Revenue, in order to determine average gross earnings, and hence draw up a scale of fees to produce average earnings of that level. The effect of this system was gradually to reduce the fee for a given treatment as more of those treatments were carried out faster or more efficiently. The system has been called 'the treadmill' because it rewarded dentists for doing a greater number of those treatments. It tended to reward restorative work (fillings) rather than preventive treatment. The costs of general dental services to the NHS were therefore controlled to some extent by the degree of accuracy of the Dental Rates Study Group's calculations.

The Dental Practice Board in Eastbourne has to give prior approval for discretionary fees which can be claimed for treatments where a range of possible costs exists. Its records indicate the number and range of different courses of treatment that are given under the NHS, but no comparable figures exist for the extent of private treatment and for the number of people who do not go to a dentist at all.

As with other services of the NHS, many patients are exempt from dental charges: young people under 18 (19 if they are still in full-time education), mothers during pregnancy and for a year thereafter and anyone receiving income support or family credit under the social security system. Other elderly people on low incomes may also be eligible, after a social security means test, to a certificate allowing them financial help. Dental charges for those who pay now amount to around 80% of the dentist's remuneration from the state.

The new dentists' contract

Introduction of a new contract for dentists in 1991 caused some dissension, as did that of the family doctors. Although most dentists soon endorsed what they agreed was in the interests of themselves and their patients, many dentists have reduced their NHS work to concentrate on their private practice because payments under the new contract were felt to be too low. The main elements of the new contract shift the emphasis away from self-contained episodes of treatment towards continuing care, giving an incentive to undertake preventive rather than solely restorative work. Dentists thus receive a capitation fee for each patient they agree to care for over a two-year period, renewable at any time by mutual agreement. Under this arrangement patients are entitled to emergency cover; this was formerly only available if the dentist voluntarily agreed to provide an emergency service. Dentists also receive capitation fees for children in their care, and about 20% of their monthly income is derived from capitation fees.

The system of obtaining approval from the Dental Practice Board before undertaking a particular treatment has been simplified. Combining private and NHS treatment is now permitted, although not on the same tooth. Dental practices are, like GPs, required to provide their patients with an information leaflet that lists the individual dentists and their qualifications as well as other facilities provided, surgery hours and access for disabled people. The contract also requires dentists to keep up to date with developments in research and practice, and entitles them to improved maternity, sickness and early retirement benefits.

Dental staffing

There are about 18 500 dentists in practice in the UK (1994). On average, each dentist will deal with 2000 episodes of dental care per year. There are considerable regional variations in the incidence of dental disease, with the industrial north of England and Scotland having poorer dental health than the south. A corresponding variation in the distribution of dentists shows there are proportionally more dentists in areas with proportionally more people in the higher social classes.

In order to strengthen the service, some observers favour greater use of dental auxiliaries. These staff work with general dental practitioners, dealing with all the administrative duties as well as preparing instruments, mixing filling materials and processing X-rays. Dental hygienists are trained in schools of dentistry to be able to clean, scale and polish teeth, and they also play an important part in giving advice to patients about dental hygiene. In the school dental service, dental therapists are trained to carry out simple fillings, extract milk teeth and clean, scale and polish the teeth of school children; they also teach them about the importance of proper oral hygiene. Although the number of auxiliary staff is small (their remuneration is negotiated through Professional and Technical Whitley Council B), they can clearly take on the routine work under supervision and allow the dentist to apply his specialist skills and knowledge more widely. The General Dental Council controls their professional conduct through a subcommittee, the Dental Auxiliaries Committee.

Dental technicians are needed to make dentures, crowns, inlays and other appliances. They serve an apprenticeship in a dental laboratory, a hospital or a commercial firm, or they can undergo full-time training. Many general dental practitioners use the services of a commercial laboratory, but, in hospital departments, technicians also do work in connection with the treatment of facial injuries.

OPHTHALMIC SERVICES

The Worshipful Company of Spectacle Makers was given a Royal Charter in 1629, and opticians date their professional origins back to this time. However, it was not until the mid-nineteenth century that instruments for examining the eye and investigating refractive errors were invented, thus enabling the scientific diagnosis and treatment of sight disorders to develop. Qualified doctors specializing in the study of the eye took on the work of sight testing as did the opticians who also sold spectacles. In 1895, the British Optical Association was founded, its aim being to achieve state registration for opticians, which would eliminate unqualified practitioners and establish professional status for the duly qualified. In 1923, a register of the Joint Council of Qualified Opticians was instituted, and the Council promoted a bill for state registration. But the BMA was against it, since it regarded doctors as being exclusively qualified to detect disease, and stated that all sight testing should be carried out under medical supervision. Most of the approved societies under the National Health Insurance scheme required the people they covered to go only to a practitioner on this register or to a doctor for sight testing.

In 1953, the Crook Report [3] recommended a General Optical Council should be established, to maintain a register of ophthalmic and dispensing opticians and to exercise governing and disciplinary powers over them. This was accepted by the Government, but it was not until 1958 that the Council was established under the Opticians Act, partly because of strong opposition by sections of the medical profession. The General Optical Council gave opticians their independent professional status and restricted legal prescribing and dispensing of spectacles to them (or registered medical practitioners). The necessary qualifications for registration of ophthalmic opticians after three years' full-time study are granted by the Worshipful Company, the British Optical Association and the Institute of Ophthalmic Science. Dispensing opticians obtain qualifications for registration after two years of full-time study, three years' day release or a four year correspondence course, from the Association of Dispensing Opticians or with the Dispensing Certificate of the British Optical Association. Most dispensing opticians are members of the National Ophthalmic Treatment Board (NOTB) Association, and practise from medical eye centres that this body monitors.

Opticians' pay is negotiated through the Optical Whitley Council, although most of them dispense non-NHS lenses and frames as well. An optician does not have a list of patients like a GP, but is paid a separate fee for each item of service, under the terms of his contract with the Family Health Services Authority. Patients also pay a charge for lenses and frames, and these payments virtually cover the cost of them to the optician.

The Health Services Act, 1984, removed the monopoly from opticians and allowed spectacles to be supplied by any retailer. This move was stimulated by the belief that the monopoly had kept the cost of non-NHS frames and lenses unduly high, particularly when compared to other countries. However, the proposal went much further and abolished the supply of NHS frames and lenses to all but children and certain people on low incomes. Although consumer representatives initially welcomed these reforms because of the opportunity to buy spectacles at a lower price, the ophthalmic profession was highly critical. They said it would mean that many people needing spectacles would obtain them without an eye test, thus endangering their sight and even their own and other people's safety.

This change in policy was one outcome of the government review of ophthalmic services set up in 1983. Until that time, the ophthalmic service had been very stable for a variety of reasons. First, apart from the development of plastic, multifocal and contact lenses, there have been no major technical advances in the production of spectacle lenses. Secondly, over the age of 45, an increasingly large section of the population needs to wear spectacles. Thirdly, the manufacturing process for NHS lenses is basically unchanged, so that increased production costs have been lower than increases in manufacturing costs in general. This stability has helped the NHS considerably, because the constant and wide demand for spectacles can be met by opticians who can extend their incomes through non-NHS work. The NHS has, therefore, been able to provide an adequate comprehensive service that is not fully integrated with the medical service, yet the existence of demand for private treatment has made it worthwhile for opticians to undertake NHS work as well.

The new FHSAs did not have an optician representative, but opticians have a representative body called the Local Optical Committee. The post-1974 Statutory Area Advisory Committee was superseded in 1982 by an optional District Optical Committee, with a membership of ophthalmic and dispensing opticians representative of both the general Ophthalmic Services and the Hospital Eye Service. DHSS advice also allowed for a Regional Optical Committee [4].

PHARMACEUTICAL SERVICES

The pharmacists' profession can also trace its origins back three or four hundred years, but it developed from two distinct lines. The Society of Apothecaries was founded in 1617, and its members dispensed medicines on the order of physicians as well as prescribing and dispensing medicines for patients themselves (see Chapter 9); the chemists and druggists were retail shopkeepers who did not prescribe, but prepared and sold medicines in competition with the apothecaries. The Apothecaries Act of 1815 allowed apothecaries to charge for their professional advice to patients as well as for the medicines they dispensed, and this encouraged them to become more like general medical practitioners. The chemists and druggists progressively took over as the dispensers of physicians' prescriptions.

The Pharmaceutical Society of Great Britain was formed in 1841, and the Pharmacy Acts of 1852 and 1868 gave it the statutory duty to register pharmaceutical chemists who had obtained its diploma after training and examination, and to prevent those who were not pharmaceutical chemists or chemists or druggists from dispensing medicines or selling poisons. Under the National Health Insurance scheme only registered pharmacists could dispense medicines prescribed for insured people (except in remote areas where the doctors themselves could dispense their prescriptions).

Under the National Health Service, separate arrangements are made for dispensing medicines in the hospitals and the community. The Hospital Pharmaceutical Service employs registered pharmacists and technicians to prepare and dispense medicines to hospital in-patients and out-patients as prescribed by hospital doctors. The General Pharmaceutical Service involves retail pharmacists in dispensing medicines prescribed by general practitioners, under contract with the FHSAs (previously FPCs). In 1974, AHAs appointed Area Pharmaceutical Officers to supervise the hospital pharmaceutical services, even though each District probably had a District Pharmacist. After 1982, DHSS advice left DHAs to decide on the status and role of the head of the hospital pharmaceutical services, but most, if not all, Districts appointed a District Pharmaceutical Officer who reported to a General Manager. Most Districts have a District Pharmaceutical Committee to advise on developments and on matters such as compliance with the Medicines Act and the formulation of drug use guidelines to ensure that money is not wasted on proprietary brands where a cheaper generic substitute would be as effective.

Pay negotiations for retail pharmacists are handled by the Pharmaceutical Whitley Council, and their central representative body is the Pharmaceutical Services Negotiating Committee. The National Pharmaceutical Union was founded in 1920 as a trade association for individual retail pharmacists. In recent years it has changed its brief to include the interests of employee pharmacists, and has also admitted company chemists to membership – this group now forms the majority of its members and it has changed its name to the National Pharmaceutical Association.

PARAMEDICAL STAFF

The work of the different types of paramedical staff is extremely varied, but overall it represents an identifiable and essential component in the whole programme of clinical care, without which medicine and nursing would be of limited effectiveness.

Many of the staff discussed in this section share the fact that their work is supervised directly or indirectly by doctors, and that most of them undergo training that is as long and thorough as nurses' training. Most of the occupations owe their development to the clinical and technical advances in medical science of the twentieth century. As medicine has become more sophisticated, specialization within the profession has increased, and with it has come the need for specialist supporting staff to provide the necessary backup services.

A number of landmarks should be mentioned before the individual professions are discussed. The first was in 1936, when the British Medical Association set up an independent Board of Registration of Medical Auxiliaries, incorporated under the Companies Act. Its object was to maintain and publish the National Register of Medical Auxiliary Services, listing those people who had satisfied the Board of their qualifications to practise. This arose because the doctors had become concerned that some of the techniques could involve risks if administered by untrained people. The result was that the professional organizations of dispensing opticians, dietitians, orthoptists, physiotherapists, speech therapists, chiropodists and radiographers became recognized by the Board, and their members were bound not to work except under the direction of a doctor, while the doctors undertook to refer patients only to duly qualified practitioners. This arrangement could not stop unqualified practitioners from working, since registration was entirely voluntary.

In this context, a committee was set up by the Minister of Health after the inception of the NHS, to consider 'the supply and demand, training and qualifications of certain medical auxiliaries employed in the NHS'. The result was the Cope report [5] which comprised separate analyses of the situation for almoners, chiropodists, dietitians, medical laboratory technicians, occupational therapists, physiotherapists and remedial gymnasts, radiographers and speech therapists. It recommended that statutory registration for medical auxiliaries working in the NHS should be necessary through separate registers. These registers and the recognition of approved training courses and examinations should be the responsibility of a single council with a number of constituent professional committees. Although these proposals were welcomed by the doctors and medical auxiliaries alike (but for different reasons), a long debate ensued between them over membership of the new bodies. In 1954, as an interim measure, regulations were introduced for the qualifications required for state registration of eight categories of staff by the NHS: chiropodists, dietitians, medical laboratory technicians, occupational therapists, physiotherapists, radiographers, remedial gymnasts and speech therapists.

Finally, in 1960, the Professions Supplementary to Medicine Act was passed. This established the Council for Professions Supplementary to Medicine (CPSM), and seven Boards, one for each of the professions mentioned above, excluding speech therapists. The Boards were made legally responsible for the preparation and maintenance of registers, for prescribing qualifications required for state registration, and for approving entrance requirements, training syllabuses and training institutions. They can remove practitioners from the register for professional misconduct and impose penalties for the improper use of the designation 'state registered'; they can also withdraw approval from training courses that fall below required standards. In 1966 the provisions of the Act were extended to include orthoptists. The Board of Registration of Medical Auxiliaries continued to provide for voluntary registration of chiropodists, orthoptists, dispensing opticians, operating theatre technicians, technicians in venereology, audiology technicians and certified ambulance personnel. The Council for Professions Supplementary to Medicine is itself composed of one member from each of the Boards, six nominees of the medical corporations and the General Medical Council, four nominees of the Privy Council (including the Chairman) and four nominees, giving a total of 21.

These paramedical and scientific occupations share problems of status and managerial authority in relation to other groups, particularly the doctors. It might be said that the move by the BMA to institute registration of medical auxiliaries was an attempt to exert control over other professions that it regarded more as a threat than an asset. Equally, these professions probably welcomed registration, since they saw it as an opportunity to expose charlatans and to close the ranks of truly qualified practitioners [6]. The wranglings over the constitutions of the boards recommended in the Cope Report [7] arose because the medical profession wanted to secure majority representation, but this did not eventually happen. The overall problem is that each of the occupations has to reconcile its desire for independent professional status with the inevitable fact that it serves the medical profession. They have to accept some degree of direction and control by the doctors, yet they regard themselves as competent specialists in their own right.

Chapter 7 of the Grey Book [8] on the organization of paramedical services did not meet with the agreement of the professions concerned when it was published in 1972. The disagreements centred on this problem of their accountability to doctors, particularly in the predominantly hospital-based professions. During the 1970s the debate continued. The Royal Commission [9] had little to say on the matter of status, directing its comments to the need to review of manpower and training needs of the professions. A DHSS circular in 1979 [10] was inconclusive, but the 1982 reorganization reopened the issue of status and accountability. Some professions, such as speech therapy and chiropody, had, since 1974, been organized on an Area basis; the devolution of their services to Districts was seen as a loss of status. Most Districts had District heads of services although these became the objects of criticism in the post-*Patients First* [11] discussions on the grounds that people who were trained to lay hands on patients were engaged in too much administration. Circular HC(80)8 [12] left DHAs to decide how best to organize these professions in the future but warned against filling posts at District level unless there was adequate work to justify such a post.

With the introduction of general management in 1984, the heads of these paramedical departments became managerially accountable to the District General Manager. The introduction of trusts following the 1991 reforms has led to fear that these professions might become fragmented as the individual specialists within them become more independent and geographically scattered.

Each profession is described below.

Chiropody

This is the treatment of superficial ailments of the feet, and the maintenance of the feet in good condition. In the eighteenth century chiropodists also cared for hands, but now they specialize in the treatment of existing deformities with appliances and special footwear, diagnosing and treating local infections, as well as preventive care, including the inspection of children's feet. Most chiropodists work in the community, holding clinics and making domiciliary visits. They work independently and do not require referral from a doctor, whereas those working in the hospitals work far more through referrals.

The Incorporated Society of Chiropodists was founded in 1912 to promote study and training and to improve services for poor people. In 1913, the London Foot Hospital was founded – the first specialist hospital of its kind. A number of other professional organizations grew up and, in 1937, five of these were recognized by the Board of Registration of Medical Auxiliaries. They amalgamated to form the Society of Chiropodists in 1945, but there continued to be a range of bodies examining and registering chiropodists. The 1954 regulations laid down conditions for state registration and employment in the NHS, and the Chiropodists Board of Council for Professions Supplementary to Medicine replaced these in 1963. In that year, it became the single body responsible for state registration, following a three-year full-time course at an approved training centre. By 1990 there were several degree courses available.

About one third of all NHS treatments, including those done at patients' homes, are carried out by private chiropodists who receive a fee from the NHS. The demand for chiropody outstrips supply, particularly for the priority groups – the elderly, the handicapped, expectant mothers, school children and some hospital patients. In 1977 the DHSS issued circular HC(77)9 [13] which recommended various measures to the Area Health Authorities to enable them to make better use of their existing resources. Of particular importance was the suggestion that 'foot care assistants' could be employed to carry out simple treatments such as basic foot care and hygiene, for which the skills of the fully trained chiropodist were not necessary.

Dietetics

A dietitian applies knowledge of nutrients contained in food, the effect of preparation and cooking of them and their use by the body, to advise on suitable diets as part of the treatment of illness, as well as constructing diets for people with chronic disorders (e.g. diabetes, kidney disease). Most dietitians work in hospitals, following up patients through out-patient clinics. In addition, there are some openings for them in the community services, for instance in advising mothers at antenatal and postnatal clinics on the balanced diets required for their babies, and in the nutritional values of meals on wheels.

The first training schools for dietitians were established in the United States in the 1920s, and their students were trained nurses. In 1925 special diet kitchens were opened at one or two hospitals in London, Edinburgh and Glasgow, and they accepted students who had pure science or domestic science qualifications. In 1933, a special training course for dietitians was started at the King's College of Household and Social Science in London, and the therapeutic work of these 'early' dietitians mostly involved the weighing and preparing of foods. Later, the development of drugs partly overtook the effect of dietetics in the treatment of certain conditions. The British Dietetic Association was founded in 1936 and joined the voluntary registration scheme before the institution of requirements for state registration in 1954. Since 1963, the Dietitians Board of the Council for Professions Supplementary to Medicine has been the responsible regulating body.

The District Dietitian was usually accountable to a General Manager for management tasks, while their colleagues worked in a service-giving relationship with doctors [14]. Since the reforms of *Working for Patients* in 1991, dietitians are employed by trusts.

Occupational therapy

In 1989, a commission of inquiry report from the College of Occupational Therapists [15] defined occupational therapy (OT) as the assessment and systematic treatment of people of any age who have physical or mental health problems, in order to restore independence. OTs usually specialize soon after qualifying, treating patients with either physical or mental disorders. In the NHS there are OT departments in general and mental illness hospitals, day hospitals, and units for mentally and physically handicapped children; other OTs are employed by local authority social services departments. Until the 1930s there were only untrained craft workers in mental hospitals. The Association of Occupational Therapists was formed in 1936, and from then on it registered OTs who had passed examinations after a three-year course. The Occupational Therapists Board of the Council for Professions Supplementary to Medicine was set up in 1963, making it necessary for OTs to be state registered in order to practise.

The number of OTs continues to increase: there was a rise of 173% between 1977 and 1987. Further expansion seems likely, with the current emphasis on care in the community. OTs employed by the NHS have different salary scales and terms of service from those working for Social Services Departments. This, and the division between those who specialize in mental as opposed to physical disorders, has impeded the emergence of a strong professional identity. Although the training syllabus for OTs overlaps in part with physiotherapy, experiments with joint training have not been successful, because there is insufficient common ground.

Physiotherapy

Physiotherapists use physical means to treat patients with injury or disease, and employing a wide range of methods including therapeutic movement, hydrotherapy, manipulation, electrotherapy, ultrasound and ice treatments. They treat most of their patients as hospital out-patients, and see people with bone injuries, chest disease or arthritis, pregnant women and handicapped children, and others referred to them by hospital doctors or directly by GPs. They assess the individual's needs and devise and implement treatment, reporting back to the referring doctor on completion or if problems arise. Long gone are the days when the doctor prescribed what treatment was to be administered. Private practice offers physiotherapists significant opportunities; here patients can refer themselves directly.

Physiotherapy's professional organization evolved from the Society of Trained Masseuses, founded in 1895. It was open only to women until 1920, when it became the Chartered Society of Massage and Medical Gymnastics and began to admit men. It changed its name to the Chartered Society of Physiotherapy in 1943, by which time it was the registering authority for practitioners, conducting examinations and approving training schools. There are now 16 schools, some affiliated to universities. All the training courses are being raised to degree standard. Remedial gymnasts used to be a separate professional group, using active exercise schemes to treat physical conditions. They merged with physiotherapy in 1986 and thus no longer have a separate Board within the CPSM.

Strong public demand for the services of osteopaths and chiropractors is viewed with concern by some physiotherapists who fear that professional standards might be undermined by unregistered or less well qualified practitioners. Gradually, however, training and registration arrangements of 'alternative' disciplines are becoming more exacting.

Orthoptics

This is the investigation of squints and other defects of binocular vision. Orthoptists work with medically qualified eye specialists and treat only patients referred to them by doctors. The majority of patients are children, and most orthoptists are women. The British Orthoptic Council was founded in 1930 and runs a full-time two-year course leading to a diploma. The Board of Registration of Medical Auxiliaries registered orthoptists until 1966, when the Orthoptists Board of the CPSM was set up to take this over.

Two other paramedical professions are concerned with therapy although they are not under the supervision of the CPSM. They are speech therapy and clinical psychology. A third profession, social work, while not paramedical, nevertheless provides support to medical and nursing staff.

Speech therapy

This is the treatment of defects and disorders of the voice and speech which may arise from a wide range of clinical or congenital disorders. Originally, the work concentrated on stammering, but, after about 1912, hospital departments and local authority clinics began to be set up to offer treatment for a range of disorders. The 1944 Education Act obliged local education authorities to provide treatment for children with speech disorders, so the profession became split between those working in the education and health services. There was a great demand for speech therapists as a result, and the College of Speech Therapists was formed in 1945 to press for independent status of the practitioners.

In 1972, the Quirk Report on speech therapy services was published [16], and it contained proposals for reorganizing and developing the profession so that it could cope with its expanding role in the NHS and the education service. It recommended that AHAs should be responsible for organizing the practitioners in a suitable career structure, and that training courses should be jointly arranged with universities so that the quality of the training might be enhanced. It also proposed a new central council to handle course assessment and registration of qualified practitioners, and that the College of Speech Therapists should remain as a professional body only, its present examining role being taken on by the central council. The Government approved the recommendations and, in April 1974, issued guidance to AHAs on how they might begin to integrate their speech therapy services along these lines through the appointment of Area Speech Therapists [17]. It was acknowledged that the transformation of the profession would take some time. Since 1982, speech therapy has usually been organized on a District basis.

The profession has faced serious problems for some time: the small numbers of fully trained members (some 3500 in employment in 1989); a small number of training places and a very wide choice of potential specialization. Statutory demands made on them by the Education Act, 1981 to provide services have put further pressures on their small numbers.

Clinical psychology

The role of the clinical psychologist has become increasingly important. Clinical psychologists have a crucial role in the treatment of mental illness, not only in assessment but also in devising appropriate treatment regimes. They formulate training plans for those people with learning disabilities who are being prepared to live in the community. They have a potential contribution to more clinical specialities and particularly family support, child health and rehabilitation. The Trethowan Report (1977) [18] emphasized the professional autonomy of clinical psychologists, but felt that, as they were used to working as part of a therapeutic team, that would not lead to relationship problems. Clinical psychologists have to possess a first degree in psychology, following which they undertake a further two years of specialist training. This extended training may be responsible for the relatively small numbers – just over 2000 (1990) working in the NHS.

Social work

Medical social work has its roots in the almoner's department of pre-NHS hospitals, which were principally concerned with the financial status of patients, a matter of significance in voluntary hospitals which relied on contributions from patients as well as donations from the general public. From this came a general concern for the patients' circumstances, so that social workers in hospital now have a particular responsibility for satisfactory discharge arrangements. In 1974, medical social workers ceased to be employed by health authorities and were transferred to local authority social services departments. This move was brought about by the Seebohm Report (1968) [19] which recommended a single social work service with full professional status. Medical social workers, often more highly qualified than social workers coming from the fields of residential care or mental welfare, were reluctant to make the change. In the event, most social service departments have maintained social workers in hospitals and honoured their specialism while enlarging their areas of concern. Social workers are also attached to primary health teams.

SCIENTIFIC AND TECHNICAL STAFF

The Zuckerman Report (1968) [20] proposed a reorganization of the scientific and technical services provided by medical laboratory technicians, some of the professions supplementary to medicine and others in the hospital service. The report included the professions shown in the box below.

The report recommended the creation of a National Hospital Scientific Council, to advise the Ministers on the organization of the hospital service, that might become one of the Standing Advisory Committees of the Central Health Services Council. Each Regional Hospital Board was to have an advisory committee and,

HOSPITAL SCIENTIFIC STAFF

Biochemists
Physicists
Other scientific officers
Audiology technicians
Audiology scientists
Cardiology technicians
Darkroom technicians
Dental technicians
Electroencephalography technicians
Medical laboratory technicians
Medical physics technicians
Radiographers
Animal technicians
Artificial kidney technicians
Contact lens technicians
Electronics technicians
Glaucoma technicians
Heart and lung machine technicians
Respiratory function technicians
Surgical instrument curators
Surgical and orthopaedic appliance technicians and fitters

at district general hospital level, the report recommended a Division of Scientific Services to include medical and scientific staff involved in clinical biochemistry, computer science and statistics, genetics, haematology and blood transfusion, immunology, medical microbiology, morbid anatomy and histopathology, physics with biomedical engineering, nuclear medicine and physiological measurement. Four classes of staff were proposed; scientific officer, technical officer, technical assistant and technical aide, to reflect different degrees of responsibility and knowledge and to provide an improved career structure.

These recommendations did not survive, and throughout the next 20 years piecemeal alterations to the organization of the services were made. Medical physics, a relatively new profession, developed with the encouragement of doctors, but medical laboratory sciences were not given similar recognition and, where some degree of autonomy was claimed, serious conflict developed.

As can be seen from the list, these staff are rather artificially classified under a single heading. They include some who have an extended training requirement (e.g. physicists), but also others who may have practically no formal training (e.g. darkroom technicians). Three groups need special note.

Medical laboratory sciences

This group of staff is concerned with facilities for the diagnosis and treatment of illness through examination of pathological specimens from out-patients and in-patients, and sent in from GP patients, under the supervision of consultant pathologists in the hospitals. The Pathological and Bacteriological Assistants' Association was founded in 1912 and in 1921 an examining council of the Pathological Society was set up to develop a system of certification. The Institute of Medical Laboratory Technology (now Sciences) was incorporated in 1942 as the single professional organization. It registered qualified technicians who had worked in approved laboratories and attended part-time courses. The 1954 regulations for medical auxiliaries laid down the requisites for state registration, and, in 1963, the Medical Laboratory Technicians Board of the Council for Professions Supplementary to Medicine became the regulating body.

Entrants to the profession need 'A' levels before proceeding to the Higher National Diploma (HND), and 25% of entrants now have degrees, which entitles them to two years' exemption from state registration as a Medical Laboratory Scientific Officer. Subsequent training, leading to Fellowship, is in one or more sub specialities, such as biochemistry and haematology, and by means of exams set by the Institute of Medical Laboratory Sciences.

Medical physics

The origins of medical physics were in radiotherapy. With the increasing need to give expert support to doctors using technical equipment, an independent profession developed, becoming recognized in the founding of the Hospital Physicists Association (HPA) in 1943. Hospital physicists need a minimum qualification of a degree in physics, engineering or associated subject. The HPA organized a two-year in-service training scheme, but advancement to the higher grades is unlikely without an M.Sc. or Ph.D. degree.

The 1200 or so members of the HPA are not required to be registered. Registration became a major issue in 1987 when a mistake in calibrating a radiotherapy machine in Exeter resulted in overdoses to patients and extensive litigation. It became clear that the professional accountability of physicists was ambiguous.

Radiography

X-rays were discovered in 1895 and they are used to help diagnose illness and injury, and to provide treatment for certain malignant and other conditions. Until 1920, non-medical assistants were employed, but, in that year, the Society of Radiographers was formed to organize training courses and examinations and to register qualified practitioners. Both diagnostic and therapeutic radiographers work under the direction of doctors, and there are standard protective and monitoring devices to ensure that they are not excessively exposed to radiation. Radiography is a hospital-based service.

In 1983, the training scheme was increased to three years, of which the first part is common to both diagnostic and therapeutic radiography students. After qualification, radiographers are required to register with the Radiographers Board at the CPSM. By 1990 there were 16 111 registered radiographers, the great majority working in diagnostic rather than radiotherapy departments. Computed Tomography (CT) scanning, nuclear magnetic resonance and ultrasound have enhanced diagnostic capability, and use techniques that are less invasive and less risky for patients. This has extended the complexity of the radiographer's work so that there is a need for degree-standard training and more postgraduate courses.

ANCILLARY STAFF

There are well over 310 000 patients in hospital on any one day in the year who have the sheets on their beds provided by the laundry staff, who eat three meals cooked and served by the catering staff in wards cleaned by the domestic staff. Equipment and sterile dressings are provided by the supplies staff, while porters fetch and carry specimens and equipment and conduct patients around the hospital. In addition, certain staff live in the hospital, so some of the 'hotel' services are required for them. Most of the ancillary functions are not exclusive to the NHS, and arise wherever meals and residential accommodation need to be provided. The community health services clearly require these services on a smaller scale since they are mostly concerned with non-residential care. Hostels and homes in the community are run by the social services departments unless they provide medically supervised care, in which case the ancillary staff would be employees of a trust.

In 1970, the DHSS issued advice aimed at improving the management of support services [21]. New posts of considerable seniority were set up in 1974 for District Catering, Domestic and Linen Service Managers. By 1982, however, functional management (as it was called) had been discredited largely because of the tension between local unit or hospital administrators and the District functional managers endeavouring to supervise services from a distance. A further change came in 1983 with the Government's campaign for privatization [22]. Districts were directed to check the efficiency of their support services in the open market. When an outside contractor for domestic, catering or laundry work could provide a cheaper service than in-service staff, the employment of such staff was terminated and the outside contractors employed. Money thus saved could be used to benefit patients in other ways. Figure 11.1 shows how the numbers of NHS employed ancillary staff has fallen since 1980 – mainly as a result of contracting out ancillary services.

Scant training and poor pay has led to high turnover in these grades – often as much as 50% in one year. In an effort to overcome this problem and to meet the needs of similar staff, known collectively as Health Care Support Workers (including nursing auxiliaries, physiotherapy aides, OT helpers and junior clerical staff), it was proposed in 1987 that a more structured national approach should provide a system whereby previously untrained staff could

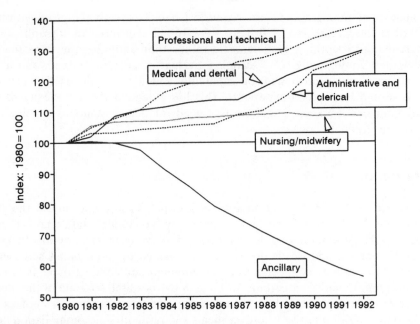

Figure 11.1 Staffing trends: UK NHS: 1980–92.

Source: *The Government's Expenditure Plans 1994/5 to 1996/7: Departmental Report*, HMSO, London (Cm. 2512).

acquire basic competencies. The initiative was adopted by the Care Sector Consortium, which comprises employee and employer representatives from the NHS, local government, the private health sector and voluntary bodies. The Consortium proposed that the National Council for Vocational Qualifications should approve appropriate training schemes, devised by further education colleges in conjunction with health authorities or organizations such as the City and Guilds Institute [23].

With the introduction of NHS trusts, responsible for their own staff and operating within a competitive market, the pressure to examine cheaper alternatives to in-house ancillary staff has grown. This will accelerate the already rapid decline in the numbers of ancillary staff directly employed by the NHS, which started in the early 1980s.

WORKS STAFF

This group of staff includes architects, quantity surveyors, engineers, building supervisors, electricians, painters, carpenters, ground maintenance staff and labourers. They deal with the planning, construction and maintenance of the buildings, plant and grounds of the health service and, as with the ancillary staff, they predominantly serve the hospitals. The senior works staff, who used to be based with the Regional Health Authorities, hold professional qualifications such as those of the Royal Institute of British Architects, the Royal Institution of Quantity Surveyors and the various engineering institutions. Senior works staff based in districts prior to the 1990 Act had technical qualifications, but the pattern among them and the skilled and other works staff is to belong to a trade union rather than a professional organization.

The stock of hospitals taken over by the NHS in 1948 included over 1200 (45%) that had been erected before 1891, and many were obsolete, poorly maintained or in unsuitable locations. In the late 1950s, money began to be specially earmarked for the development of hospital building, and, in 1962, the publication of *A Hospital Plan* for England and Wales [24] specified 90 new and 134 substantially remodelled hospitals to be started by 1970/71. It acknowledged the shortage of architects and engineers skilled in hospital planning, and in the same year the report of a study group investigating hospital engineering was published [25]. It recommended a number of steps to improve the training and quality of engineers, and suggested a minimum qualification requirement for employment in the NHS, as well as recognition of the group engineer as a chief officer.

The Woodbine Parish Report [26] published in 1970 made further recommendations for the improvement of building maintenance and the training of supervisory staff. When the Grey Book's [27] scheme for works staff in the reorganized NHS was published, it met with opposition from the professions concerned. Revised guidance was issued in 1974 [28] acknowledging some degree of autonomy for works staff, such that responsibility was shared between senior works officers and administrators for the execution of building and maintenance. This specified the new posts and their management arrangements (particularly the Area and District works and building officers and engineers), their departmental organization and degree of accountability to administrators.

Nevertheless, because these functions constitute such a costly element in spending by authorities, the Department of Health has always been concerned to monitor standards and local practices carefully, and it does this through a series of publications which give detailed advice and specifications about all aspects of health authorities' building, upgrading and maintenance work [29]. The Ceri Davies Report (1983) [30] felt that works departments were too concerned with capital building schemes and with engineering plant at the expense of the wider issue of estate management. The report suggested a change of title from Works Officer to Estates Officer.

Pressures to contract out works and estates functions in the same way as the ancillary services, and the introduction of trusts has effectively privatized the works function, although some trusts retain a small works and maintenance staff.

AMBULANCE STAFF

Ambulance staff in the 57 services in the UK have traditionally seen themselves as one of the three emergency services (with fire services and the police). Governments have disliked this link, as most of the work is for non-emergencies (in 1992/3, 3.1 million ambulance journeys were doctors' emergencies and '999' calls and 13.8 million were non-emergencies). The matter came to a head in 1989, when extended industrial action failed to promote the ambulance staff's position and, indeed, probably deepened the split between emergency and routine work.

By the end of 1995, the Department of Health hope to see one NHS Training Directorate-trained paramedic on every front line emergency ambulance. This extends the NHSTD basic training course for ambulance staff.

ADMINISTRATIVE AND CLERICAL STAFF

The early hospital administrators, called 'house governors' in voluntary hospitals and 'stewards' in local authority hospitals, were responsible to the board of governors or to the doctor in charge. With the introduction of the NHS in 1948, the new hospital management committees and regional hospital boards created a new pattern of administrative staffing, separating the senior staff (e.g. hospital secretary, group secretary, finance and supplies officers) from the junior grades (general administrators, clerical officers). All but the most junior of these designations have been superseded.

Two important reviews of administrative and clerical staff were conducted in the NHS's first 15 years, resulting in the Noel Hall (1957) [31] and Lycett Green (1963) [32] Reports. The latter proposed the setting up of a national staff committee to oversee the development of administrative staff. The Thwaites report (1977) [33] encouraged further systematic training and the Institute of Health Services Management was the first to offer a good foundation in professional hospital management through its diploma course. Now there are also other choices, such as the Diploma in Management Studies (DMS) and a Masters Degree in Business Administration (MBA). With the advent of general management, there is much more emphasis on training. It is also now accepted that anyone in a managerial position, whatever their professional discipline, needs management training.

Because the NHS is geared to patient care, it is perhaps inevitable that the supporting staff tend to be seen as less important than doctors and other clinical workers. Yet without them the direct care staff cannot function properly. This is all the more so now sophisticated analysis and planning of the use of NHS resources is crucial to success at improving the efficiency and effectiveness of health care. The administrative, clerical and managerial staff, always politically unpopular, have been the main agents for introducing the increasingly frequent organizational changes required by successive governments since 1974. The 1990 reforms, in particular, could not have been implemented without the positive support of administrative and general management staff, who were often left to resolve issues poorly formulated by the Secretary of State and his civil servants.

Managers' pay remained within the Whitley Council until the introduction of general management in 1984, since when, conditions of service for this new group are much less protective than had been the case in the NHS and other public services. Tenure is no longer assured and renewal of contracts depends explicitly on satisfactory performance. In return, salaries have risen quite rapidly for senior managers, paying rates for the first time comparable with well-paid jobs in the private sector. Total spending on general management staff remains relatively low, despite a substantial increase in the numbers of managers as a result of the 1990 reforms.

CONCLUSIONS

With around 1 million staff, the NHS is one of the largest employers in the world. For the majority of the professions described in this chapter, the NHS is the main or sole employer, and so their development is inextricably bound up with, and in turn influences, that of the NHS. The quality of the work carried out by the people described in this and previous chapters is **the** determinant of the effectiveness of health care – without the best from them the NHS cannot achieve its goals. Health policy, therefore, has to be seen by these people as something to which they must contribute, but also as something they need to adapt their goals to.

NOTES

1. *Royal Commission on Doctors' and Dentists' Remuneration* (1960) (Chairman, Sir Harry Pilkington), HMSO, London (Cmnd. 939).
2. Ministry of Health and Department of Health for Scotland (1948) *Report of the InterDepartmental Committee on the Remuneration of General Dental Practitioners* (Chairman, Sir Will Spens), HMSO, London (Cmnd. 7402).
3. Ministry of Health and Department of Health for Scotland (1953) *Statutory Registration of Opticians: Interdepartmental Report* (Chairman, Lord Crook), HMSO, London, (Cmnd. 8531).
4. DHSS (January 1982) *Health Service Development. Professional Advisory Machinery*, para. 26.
5. Ministry of Health. Department of Health for Scotland (1950) *Medical Auxiliaries, Reports of the Committees* (Chairman, Dr V. Zachary Cope), HMSO, London, (Cmnd. 8188).
6. The effect of making state registration a requirement of employment in the NHS is a valuable asset to these professions. It protects their name and educational standards, and also safeguards patients' interests.
7. Op. cit., Cope Report.
8. Department of Health and Social Security (1972) *Management Arrangements for the Reorganised National Health Service*, HMSO, London, p.84.
9. Op. cit., Royal Commission.

10. DHSS Circular HC(79)19 (October 1979) *Management of the Remedial Professions in the NHS.*
11 Op. cit., Chapter 1, *Patients First.*
12. DHSS Circular HC(80)8 (July 1980) *Health Service Development. Structure and Management.*
13. DHSS Circular HC(77)9 (1977) *Organisation and Development of NHS Chiropody Services.*
14. DHSS Circular HSC(IS)56 (July 1974) *The Organisation of the Dietetic Service within the National Health Service.*
15. College of Occupational Therapists (1989) *Occupational Therapy: An Emerging Profession.* A commission of enquiry chaired by Louis Blom-Cooper, Duckworth, London.
16. Department of Education and Science (1972) *Speech Therapy Services, Report of the Committee appointed by the Secretaries of State* (Chairman, Professor Randolph Quirk), HMSO, London.
17. Department of Health and Social Security (April 1974) *Speech Therapy Services: Interim Guidance*, Health Service Circular (Interim Series), HSC(IS)22, DHSS, London.
18. DHSS (1977) *The Role of Psychologists in the Health Services* (Trethowan Report), HMSO, London.
19. *Report of the Committee on Local Authority and Allied Personal Social Services* (1965) (Seebohm Report), HMSO, London (Cmnd. 3703).
20. Department of Health and Social Security, Scottish Home and Health Department (1968) *Hospital Scientific and Technical Services. Report of the Committee 1967–68* (Chairman, Sir Solly Zuckerman), HMSO, London.
21. DHSS Circular (May 1970). Advance Letter A/L4/70 *Administrative and Clerical Staffs Whitley Council.*
22. DHSS Circular HC(83)18 (1983) *Competitive Tendering in the Provision of Domestic, Catering and Laundry Services.*
23. DoH Executive Letter EL(MB)90/5 encouraged health authorities to review the roles and functions of support staff. EL(90)203 introduced the first National Vocational Qualification training schemes.
24. *A Hospital Plan for England and Wales* (1962), HMSO, London (Cmnd. 1604).
25. Ministry of Health, Scottish Home and Health Department (1962) *Report of the Study Group on the Grading, Training and Qualifications of Hospital Engineers* (Chairman, Major-General Sir Leslie Tyler), HMSO, London.
26. Department of Health and Social Security. Scottish Home and Health Department, Welsh Office (1970) *Hospital Building Maintenance: Report of the Committee 1968–70* (Chairman, D. Woodbine Parish), HMSO, London.
27. Op. cit., the Grey Book.
28. Department of Health and Social Security (October 1974) *Management Arrangements: Works Staff Organization and Preparation of Substantive Schemes*, NHS Reorganization Circular HRC(74)37, DHSS, London.
29. Hospital Building Notes: Hospital Technical Memoranda, Estmancode, Capricode, Data Sheets, Cost Allowance Guidance and Adapted Needleman Formula are some of the titles. They are prepared and revised by the DHSS which distributes most of them; others are available through HMSO.
30. DHSS (1983) *Underused and Surplus Property in the National Health Service. Report of the Enquiry* (Ceri Davies Report), HMSO, London.

31. Ministry of Health (1957) *Report on the Grading Structure of Administrative and Clerical Staff*, Sir Noel Hall, HMSO, London.
32. *Report of the Committee of Inquiry into the Recruitment, Training and Promotion of Administrative and Clerical Staff in the Hospital Service* (Chairman, Sir Stephen Lycett Green), HMSO, London, 1963.
33. King's Fund (1977) *The Education and Training of Senior Managers in the National Health Service* (Thwaites Report), King's Fund, London.

12

Human resources

The NHS is a labour-intensive service and its pay bill accounts for at least 75% of its total annual cost. This chapter looks at the management of the staff and the systems for negotiating pay with trade unions and other staff representatives.

PERSONNEL MANAGEMENT

The 1983 Griffiths Report [1] criticized, among other things, the paucity of good personnel management in the NHS. In a service so reliant on its staff, the status and number of specialist personnel officers were low; many of them were unqualified. The reason for this was rooted in the management arrangements of the past.

It had been customary for each departmental head to be responsible for the employment of staff. Thus nurses were recruited and managed entirely by other nurses, the administrator looked after administrative, clerical and ancillary staff, and so on, which resulted in a fragmented and often poor quality of personnel service. Not until the serious pay disputes of the early 1970s did the system begin to change, as specialist personnel officers were brought in. Reluctance to use specialists had not been entirely mistaken: managers regarded the employment of staff as too fundamental to be devolved to others. But they came to realize that the workload was too great, and that increasingly complex employment legislation required more expertise than a generalist could competently handle.

Personnel managers have several functions. First, they are involved in the process of recruiting new staff. Though this sounds simple, it requires care to match the recruit to the job while ensuring the process avoids bias. In this respect, the Race Relations Act, 1976, made it illegal for any employer to discriminate against an applicant on the grounds of ethnic origin. Despite this, it is still true that black and Asian people in Britain find it more difficult than whites to obtain any but the least skilled jobs. Women may also be discriminated against, and application forms should not ask details of marital status or number of children [2]. The NHS, like other employers, has yet to eliminate the baseless presumption that certain posts are only suitable for younger people. The rights of employees, beyond the recruitment process, are set out by all NHS employers in a compendium of personnel policies governing all aspects of employment, including disciplinary and grievance procedures as well as training, health and safety, and pay negotiations.

The personnel officer must be up to date with all employment legislation and help managers implement new requirements. He or she must acquire expertise in job evaluation and grading; this was particularly important in the large exercise to reassess the clinical work of nurses in 1989 (see Chapter 10). Deciding how many staff of which disciplines and with what levels of skill are required in order to run a particular ward or department at optimum efficiency demands specialist knowledge and expertise. Human resource planning helps managers to look ahead and estimate future changes in the demand for and supply of labour. With poor planning, there is a constant likelihood of scheduling too few or too many staff, thus risking failure to achieve minimum standards of care, as well as incurring unforecast financial costs. Shortages in the labour market mean that NHS employers have to adopt new strategies for recruiting and retaining the staff they need. Personnel managers can call on techniques for evaluating 'what if' scenarios, to model the alternatives facing them.

Some aspects of employees' rights have been protected by legislation since the nineteenth century, when laws were first passed in relation to industrial hazards. The Health and Safety at Work Act, 1974 (see Chapter 8), consolidated progress and has been supplemented by further regulations such as those concerning the control of hazardous substances [3]. Other guidance to protect the health of employees has been issued by the Health Service Advisory Committee, a joint consultative body set up by the Health and Safety Commission. Subjects include lifting patients and the disposal of clinical waste. Most NHS trusts have occupational health departments, some staffed by a full-time doctor, which provide care for people at the workplace, assess for management whether an applicant is fit to take on a particular task and make arrangements for employees whose ill-health is interfering with their capacity to fulfil their duties satisfactorily.

PAY

Until recently, in common with the rest of the public sector, the pay of NHS staff was mainly fixed through formal pay bargaining conducted at national level. In the NHS, this was originally through the Whitley Councils (see below). From 1959 onwards, certain professional staff had their pay determined by special national Review Bodies. By 1990, however, the shortcomings of centralized pay bargaining had become too great to ignore. It is important to examine how this elaborate system operated, to demonstrate that complex and time-consuming though central negotiating is, any successful substitute has to be able to overcome the problems it encountered.

Pay relativities need to be understood and addressed carefully if large-scale dissatisfaction is to be avoided. Cash limits always restrict NHS employers' discretion to award pay rises, all the more so in periods of significant inflation. The risk of allowing unrestrained local deals is that labour supply can become even more unpredictable as workers move to where they can do the same job for better rates. This exacerbates turnover, which is already about 23% annually on average, higher among ancillary staff.

Whitley Councils

Before the Second World War there had been little attempt to centralize pay bargaining for health workers. The Whitley system had originated in attempts to improve overall industrial relations during and after the First World War. J. H. Whitley (Deputy Speaker of the House of Commons) chaired a committee which recommended a three-tiered organization for voluntary improvement in relations within industries, consisting of a national joint industrial council, district councils and local works committees, as well as a permanent arbitration body.

During the Second World War, hospital labour was in short supply. The Government intervened by fixing minimum wages for student nurses prepared to work in hospitals where the shortages were particularly acute, and by guaranteeing higher wages for assistant and trained nurses working in hospitals that were part of the War Emergency scheme. In 1943 the Rushcliffe (England and Wales) [4] and Guthrie (Scotland) [5] Reports were published, recommending the wage rates for all ranks of hospital nurses and the committees remained in being to deal with revisions of their scales. In 1945, the Mowbray Committee [6] was set up to deal with domestic and similar hospital workers' pay, on a voluntary basis. It fixed national minimum rates and empowered provincial councils to fix higher local rates and to deal with local disputes.

During the war, the National Joint Council for Local Authority Administrative, Professional, Technical and Clerical Staff handled the negotiations for administrative and clerical staff of the local authority hospitals, while the British Hospitals Association and the Association of Hospital Officers (later the Institute of Health Services Management) held formal negotiations with the same groups of staff in the voluntary hospitals. In 1942, the Association of Clerks and Stewards of Mental Hospitals was wound up and members were advised to join the Association of Hospital Officers which then dealt with the administrative and clerical staffs' claims in the mental hospitals. In 1945, several of the paramedical professions arranged for joint negotiations with the employers through a voluntary committee, but the medical laboratory technicians (now scientific officers) remained outside this arrangement because their professional organization did not want to jeopardize its status by entering into formally negotiated arrangements. The hospital owners therefore had to deal with those trade unions which had medical laboratory technicians as members.

The 1946 NHS Act laid down that all employees of non-teaching hospitals would work under the instruction of their Hospital Management Committee, although their employer at law was the Regional Hospital Board. Schedule 66 of the Act empowered the Minister of Health to make regulations about the qualifications, remuneration and conditions of service of any employee of the NHS. In 1947, the Ministry and the Secretary of State for Scotland drew up a scheme for a central joint body covering the whole service, and for separate negotiating bodies for the main groups of staff.

The existing joint councils and committees naturally influenced the form of the new bodies, and all organizations with a claim to represent staff were appointed to the appropriate body. The result was one General Whitley Council and nine functional Whitley Councils. The functional councils determined pay and all those conditions of service requiring a national decision, affecting directly only those staff within its scope. The General Council's activities were, in practice, limited to matters of general application, e.g. determining travelling and subsistence allowances and the procedure for certain types of leave. The nine functional councils that were constituted were: Administrative and Clerical Staffs Council; Ancillary Staffs Council; Dental Whitley Council (Local Authorities); Medical and (Hospital) Dental Whitley Council; Nurses and Midwives Council; Optical Council; Pharmaceutical Council; Professional and Technical Staffs Council 'A'; Professional and Technical Staffs Council 'B'; and, in addition, there was a Scottish Advisory Committee to ensure that Scottish interests were properly represented. The General Council also had a staff side and a management side, the staff representatives being members of the functional councils.

The Mowbray Committee [7] became the Ancillary Staffs Council, the Rushcliffe and Guthrie Committees together became the Nurses and Midwives Council, and the staff members of the three bargaining bodies from the voluntary, local authority and mental hospitals amalgamated to form the Administrative and Clerical Staffs Council. There was unwillingness between the trade unions and professional associations to handle pay negotiations of paramedical, scientific and technical staff together, because these would involve the pay of professional workers who had paid for their own training, as well as technicians who had served an apprenticeship.

Many professional associations are registered as charities, and this legally restricts their freedom to act as bodies representing their members' interests in formal wage negotiations. Trade unions are limited by the fact that they cannot force an unwilling employer to arbitration. The result was that two councils were set up for paramedical, scientific and technological staff which broadly (but not entirely) separated the trade unions and professional associations. On Professional and Technical Staffs Council 'A' staff who deal directly with patients were represented predominantly through professional organizations, and on Professional and Technical Staff Council 'B', the rest (technicians, works staff, etc.) were represented mainly through trade unions. Separate councils were set up for those professional groups who could work as full-time employees in hospitals or for the local authorities, as well as being paid fees by the Executive Councils. Thus the Medical, Dental, Optical and Pharmaceutical Councils were set up.

By 1949 seven functional councils and the General Council were working, and, in 1950, the Medical Council and the (Local Authority) Dental Council were set up. Hospital dental staff were brought within the scope of the Medical Council in 1962, and its name was changed to Medical and (Hospital) Dental Council. However, the Doctors' and Dentists Review Body took over the work of the functional Whitley Councils in relation to doctors and dentists from 1963 (see Chapter 9). Following the transfer of responsibility for ambulance services to the health authorities in 1974, a new Ambulancemen's Council was created.

On most functional councils, staff organizations with relatively small membership claimed places alongside the major ones, and some trade unions with members in several branches of the health services gained places on more than one council. The composition of the management side reflected the curious position that the hospital authorities were in as a party to collective bargaining. Regional Hospital Boards and Boards of Governors were dependent on the government for all the money they spent. Clearly, they could not agree or grant concessions to their staff unless the Government was prepared to make money available, but, at the same time, the Ministry wanted to be involved in any discussions that might commit them to increased expenditure on wages. The management sides of the functional councils, therefore, consisted of officials from the Ministry of Health and Scottish Office, representatives from the Regional Hospital Boards, Hospital Management Committees and Boards of Governors, the Executive Councils (on Administrative and Clerical) and the local authorities (except on Administrative and Clerical).

The relative under-representation of the Regional Hospital Boards, Hospital Medical Committees and Boards of Governors in relation to the local authorities was perhaps surprising, but the hospital authorities were in no position to object. Following the 1974 reorganization, representatives from the Regional and Area Health Authorities and the Scottish and Welsh authorities became members of the management sides, and local authority membership ceased. Health Authority membership increased after the McCarthy Report, *Making Whitley Work* [8] (see below), but decreased again in January 1984 in an attempt to develop a more streamlined and better informed management side.

The way the Whitley Councils worked was for each side to meet separately to determine their attitudes and then, as a joint body, to discuss the issues together. Each side had a chairman and a secretary, the chair of the council alternating between the two sides from year to year while the secretaries were joint secretaries of the full council. The staff side secretary was elected from staff representatives, and the management side secretary was an official of the Department of Health. Regional and national appeals committees existed to hear the cases of employees who were aggrieved in any matter of their employment excluding disciplinary action or dismissal. Staff and management sides appointed equal numbers to the committees who jointly agreed on a decision by a majority of both sides. The appeal could only be made by a trade union or staff association, represented on a health service Whitley Council on behalf of the aggrieved employee. Staff also had access to industrial tribunals if they believed, for example, that they had been unfairly dismissed or discriminated against on the grounds of race or sex.

Increasingly, however, staff and employers alike became critical of the Whitley system. Why was this? First, it was very cumbersome. The large membership of each council was not an efficient way of conducting business. Secondly, and more seriously, the Whitley system failed to produce coherence or consistency in pay bargaining even within Councils and certainly not between Councils. There was no national Whitley strategy for NHS staff other than that contained within the Government of the day's pay policy. Effective negotiation was often not possible because the management side was given little discretion by the Government.

The limitations of the Whitley system led some groups of staff to seek a better arrangement, and as far back as 1963 a permanent Review Body on Doctors' and Dentists' Remuneration was set up. Electricians and other craftsmen also achieved special direct negotiation arrangements with the setting up of the DHSS Craftsmen's Committee. Finally, a Review Body for Nurses and Midwives and some professional and technical staff was set up in 1983 and the corresponding Whitley Councils were left to deal with conditions of service only.

Reforming Whitley: The McCarthy Inquiry

The McCarthy inquiry, set up in April 1975, published its findings late the following year. The report did not propose a radically new system for NHS wage negotiations, although most of the criticisms of the current arrangements were acknowledged. The report said that the Whitley Councils should be retained and strengthened, and that several important modifications should be made to ensure this. The major innovation suggested was that Regional Whitley Councils should be established as the forum for local negotiation, with the scope to fix specific details of settlements. As a consequence, the national Councils should negotiate more flexible agreements, which left room for interpretation and adaptation by the regional Councils. In addition, it was recommended that the DHSS loosen its grip over the management sides of the national Councils by restricting itself to concern with the overall cost to government of settlements, and with any effects of agreements on major aspects of government policy. The health authorities should, in turn, take greater care to select experienced and committed representatives who were well briefed and required to report back.

Lord McCarthy's other main finding was the lack of co-ordination between organizations representing staff. He recommended a reduction in the total number, through amalgamations, to produce more effective bodies with agreed areas of recruitment in the NHS. He said that NHS employees should be consulted on all important management decisions and that his proposed improvements in the negotiating machinery should dovetail with improvements in the consultative procedures at national, regional and local levels.

Although the Government accepted all McCarthy's recommendations, only one improvement was actually implemented – the management-side members were better trained and briefed. However, other initiatives have been taken, such as new efforts to train managers in industrial relations techniques and discussions about improving local disputes procedures. But, in its evidence to the Royal Commission on the National Health Service, ACAS (the Advisory, Conciliation and Arbitration Service, which has been called in to help resolve several disputes involving NHS workers) said, 'In our view the NHS has reached the stage where it should review its industrial relations policies and practices. Unless effective remedies are introduced urgently, we see little prospect of avoiding continued deterioration.'

The reform of the Whitley system made little progress. Discussions on an independent secretariat were prolonged but abortive. In 1983 a sub-group of regional chairmen, assisted by NHS officers, produced proposals aimed at simplifying the Whitley system by reducing the size of the management side. These proposals were warmly received by the Secretary of State and implemented on 1 January 1984. The new members spent much more time on Whitley affairs, gaining a greater degree of expertise. But by this time, as we have seen, over half the staff had opted out of the Whitley system. Despite the appointment of a personnel director on the NHS Executive, a lack of a coherent pay strategy still dominates the NHS's industrial relations.

Local bargaining

Current Government policy, following the creation of NHS trusts in 1991, is for more local bargaining to be undertaken by trusts, in line with the market discipline that informs relations between purchasers and providers. However, four years into the reforms, most trusts had not made any significant steps towards local pay bargaining – particularly on the clinical side. Performance-related pay (PRP) has gradually been introduced further down the managerial scales and is now appearing in other areas.

One of the problems, particularly in 1993 and 1994, with trusts' freedom to negotiate and set pay and conditions of service locally has been the Government's public sector pay policies. Although trusts are empowered to deal with their own personnel issues, trusts are still part of the NHS and hence their spending appears in the National Accounts. For governments concerned with the size of the Public Sector Borrowing Requirement (the shortfall between spending and tax revenues), NHS trusts' autonomy must be subordinated to macro-economic policy.

In 1993 the Chancellor of the Exchequer, Kenneth Clarke, imposed a wage freeze for 1994/5 across the public sector. The effect on trusts was that any pay rise had to be matched by rises in productivity. This provoked the need to define a measure of productivity. Most trusts settled on patient activity (the numbers of patients treated), although a quantifiable connection between the work of non-clinical staff and patient throughput is unreliable. In 1994, the new director of personnel on the NHS Executive indicated that trusts should proceed with caution with local bargaining, one of the fears being that it will lead to an inflationary spiral, as local trusts bid against each other for particular staff groups. It remains to be seen how this devolved function will develop in the future, although trusts will have to tackle it.

INDUSTRIAL RELATIONS

For many years after the introduction of the NHS, staff tolerated comparatively low pay because they felt rewarded by being part of a valued, caring service whose objectives were quite different from those of commercial industry. The NHS was characterized as one large happy family where everyone was content to know their place and work as a team. In the late 1960s, this idealized view was no longer tenable (if it ever had been) as the momentum of dissatisfaction grew. During the next decade disputes involved nearly every group of staff.

In 1965 general practitioners, increasingly frustrated at the lack of material recognition, threatened mass resignations from the NHS. Following this, in 1969, the Royal College of Nursing conducted a spirited campaign under the slogan 'Raise the Roof', through which they succeeded in obtaining a 22% wage rise. In the winter of 1973, ancillary staff completely withdrew their labour in many places and took action which had a direct and damaging effect on patient care. Despite the bitterness this dispute caused, the nurses were again campaigning in 1974, openly stating that they could not promise to safeguard patient care if the Government refused to listen. Consultants and junior hospital doctors took action in 1975 over their pay, limiting the work they were prepared to do. This caused a corresponding increase in waiting-lists. The 1979 'winter of discontent' [9] ancillary workers' dispute was worse than that of 1973, except that hospital managers, having encountered the unthinkable that year, were now much more prepared to deal with the emergency and less likely to concede points. Throughout the 1970s ambulancemen had taken sporadic action, sometimes withdrawing their labour.

Despite legislation introduced by Conservative Governments in the 1980s curbing the rights of trade unions and their members, the potential for unrest in the NHS was a constant factor. The reasons for militancy are complex, but three broad causes are government policy, the problem of pay relativities, and an increase in employment legislation.

Government policy

The 1974 Labour Government was ideologically opposed to private practice and, in particular, wanted to eliminate private beds from NHS hospitals. These had been a compromise in the negotiations with doctors over the setting up of the NHS in 1946. There were about 4500 private beds within NHS hospitals, which were seen as an anachronism in a service where medical need was the fundamental criterion for admission. Members of NUPE (the National Union of Public Employees, which represented many NHS workers and is now part of the union, Unison) took up the matter and tried to close down private beds in NHS hospitals by refusing to service them. Medical staff retaliated, and by 1976 only the setting up of the Health Services Board [10] broke the deadlock. The Board's task was to phase out private beds in a manner agreeable to both sides. The members of the board reflected the spirit of compromise, with half from the medical profession and half from trade unions and people sympathetic to their views. The case illustrates how the Government's pursuit of its own policy priorities rendered the health authorities themselves powerless to remedy the cause of the dispute, the local consequences of which they nevertheless had to bear.

A second case obliged Health Authorities to do more than cope with the consequences of industrial action; they were required to enact the Government's will. In 1983 the Government instructed Health Authorities to test the efficiency of their support services in the open market. The DHSS prepared specimen tender documents, and directives ensured that DHAs did not write specifications favouring themselves. Indeed, by not allowing DHAs to specify that all contractors should prepare their quotations on the basis that staff should be paid Whitley Council rates, the DHSS specifically put in-house tenders at a disadvantage. Industrial action was made less likely following the implementation of this policy because ancillary staff were cowed by the prospect of unemployment. 'Market testing' has led to many parts of the public service – including parts of the NHS – being provided either by existing private sector businesses or previously in-house groups setting up their own business.

Pay relativities

Pay relativities have been the root of much industrial unrest in the NHS for many years. It has already been shown how GPs and nurses threatened action when their pay negotiations seemed to be failing. The problem has affected all NHS staff in turn, and various attempts have been made to make these negotiations less volatile by introducing some guiding principles. One of these was to leave room for local negotiation.

In 1968, the National Board for Prices and Incomes produced a report (Number 29) [11] on manual workers in the NHS, local authorities, and the gas and water supply industries. The incomes of these workers were relatively low, but so was their productivity. What way could be found to improve productivity without necessarily increasing the public authority's wage bill? Incentive bonus schemes were suggested to meet this need. These productivity schemes had been common in many industries but had not been tried in the NHS before. Ancillary staff were offered the opportunity of a full, work-studied scheme, and, while they were waiting for that, could be given a bonus of up to 10% of their basic earnings on an agreed specification of work, providing the new productivity levels were self-financing. This could only be done by losing staff. Bonus schemes were also introduced for works staff in the early 1970s.

Bonus schemes remain, although they have provided a fertile ground for disputes. In some respects they have made matters worse by distorting relativities, so that shift workers earning bonus payments have been able to earn substantially more than their own supervisors. The negotiation of bonus schemes has required better local union organization, and the number of shop stewards has increased. With this has come an increased demand for facilities to conduct union affairs, such as time off and office space. Union rights were modified by the Employment Act, 1988, but these demands can still lead to friction with management.

For managerial staff, the bonus scheme principle has taken the form of performance related pay (PRP), which was part of the Individual Performance Review package introduced in 1986 [12]. Under this scheme, all managers and, in due course, other staff, are set annual objectives against which their performance is assessed. An annual pay supplement of an agreed percentage in any one year can be awarded to those who merit it. This payment has been criticized as an inappropriate inducement for the NHS, even though such awards are common in industry. By 1990, however, the total of PRP payments had become a significant element, and the Treasury realized the cost to public funds would be greater than it had estimated. Other inducements also common in private industry, such as company cars, cut-price health insurance and cheap holidays, are perhaps inappropriate in the context of a public service.

From time to time the deterioration in levels of health workers' pay has been examined by special enquiries. The Halsbury committee was set up in 1974 [13] in response to calls to remedy the hardship nurses had been forced to put up with. Though they and other paramedical workers were thereafter awarded large increases, five years later their relative position had again been allowed to worsen.

In 1979 the Prime Minister, James Callaghan, set up the Standing Commission on Pay Comparability, under Professor Hugh Clegg, to take a wider look at pay across a range of low-paid workers including NHS hospital ancillary staff, nurses, midwives, ambulance staff and the professions supplementary to medicine. The findings [14] pleased neither the incoming Conservative Government nor the staff themselves.

Another attempt at establishing comparability was undertaken by Jim Speakman [15] who examined the relative pay of chief officers in the NHS, but he was unable to suggest a definitive formula. A more general study was conducted by the Megaw enquiry into civil service pay in 1982 [16], which sought to find a way to facilitate collective bargaining within the constraints of government pay policy. The result was a pay spine with bands that could still accommodate discretionary variations, a concept that has not yet been adequately tried in practice. In the NHS, the pay spines for senior managers and senior nurses were made common in 1990. This diffused a longstanding cause of resentment among some managers who believed the nurses had, since 1975, been paid more for exercising less responsibility.

Employment legislation

All the above examples demonstrate a fundamental weakness in the NHS: the lack of a coherent strategy for pay and conditions of service. Most attempts to resolve anomalies between groups have been haphazard and opportunistic, perpetuating dissatisfaction. Now that more local bargaining is the Government's declared policy, mediated through the NHS Executive, it remains to be seen whether this will do anything to assist industrial relations.

Local personnel managers need considerable skill to handle the pay negotiations and, at the same time, prevent their trusts accepting inflationary settlements. Much employment legislation has been introduced in recent years aimed at enhancing and protecting the rights of employees. Although some of it has been repealed by subsequent governments, the acknowledgement of the need for effective representation of staff has remained. NHS employers, chiefly trusts, are required to give reasonable facilities for trade union members and their shop stewards (negotiating what is 'reasonable' has, however, proved far from straightforward).

In the case of intractable disputes between a group of trade union members and management, the Advisory Conciliation and Arbitration Service (ACAS) can be brought in. ACAS was set up by the Trade Union and Labour Relations Act, 1974. It has survived various changes in legislation, but it has not always been particularly successful in achieving reconciliation in major, nation-wide NHS disputes, partly because, as has been seen, local management have been constrained by government policy and instructions and have therefore been unable to negotiate freely.

Although the state of industrial relations remains volatile, and there is continuing dissatisfaction with pay and other conditions of employment, as well as a constant assertion that low morale prevails, most people who work in the NHS have done so all their working lives, including those who have transferable skills and could easily have left. Furthermore, a willingness to work beyond the obligations of their individual contracts is everywhere apparent. This customary loyalty is the paradox of the NHS: the service is generally alleged to be 'collapsing' and yet it goes on being sustained by highly motivated and hard working staff.

TRAINING

The NHS employs around one million staff of all kinds, including the most highly qualified and those without any formal skills. The importance of appropriate training is officially acknowledged, to ensure patients can rely on competent treatment in all aspects of their care. But, within the DHSS, training policy was administered by several departments, loosely co-ordinated and lacking any integrated strategic approach. This was changed in 1983 when the National Health Service Training Authority (later to become the NHS Training Directorate) was set up [17]. It replaced five national staff committees, the Training Aids Centre and the Educational Development Unit for Remedial Professions, and took over management of the training centres at Harrogate and at Falfield, Gloucestershire (used by engineering and works staff).

The NHS Training Authority

The NHSTA, based in Bristol, began work in 1985. It had four divisions: the first is responsible for developing strategic programmes for responding to the implications of change. For instance, it determined and organized advance training for the staff likely to be involved with introducing the 1990 reforms. The second division provide training resources. These could be national guidelines, for example on equal opportunities, or actual training materials for use on training courses throughout the NHS. The NHS has rarely evaluated with much rigour the training it does, so there is still little objective assessment of its effectiveness. The third NHSTA division was therefore concerned with setting standards to help trainers measure results. It also had a business division that runs the authority as an enterprise. The NHSTA's co-ordinating role brought more coherence into education and training in the NHS. Despite this, it was disbanded as a Special Health Authority in April 1991 and its functions restored to the Department of Health, under the NHSE's Director of Personnel as the NHS Training Directorate.

In 1986 the Department published *Better Management, Better Health* [18], which set out the importance of developing managerial skills. Until then, further education for managers had been patchy and had been concentrated on a small élite. Since the mid-1950s, a national General Management Training Scheme has been run for administrators (now managers). It recruits about 60 people a year, some of them graduates, some already working in the NHS, and provides a supervised programme lasting two years. An introduction to the service at all levels is followed by working experience in selected posts.

The training is supported by one of the associated academic departments: the King's Fund College in London or the universities at Manchester or Warwick. The trainees are expected to obtain a diploma or Master's degree in public sector management and may also acquire NVQ recognition of managerial competence. Following a review of the scheme [19], individuals are now encouraged to pursue further education throughout their managerial career. Continuing education is not confined to general managers: Districts and trusts are beginning to see its importance for all staff who have managerial responsibilities within their own disciplines and professions [20].

Turnover among those who do the less skilled work in the NHS tends to be much higher than in the professional groups. One way of stemming this is to provide more training for school leavers. Governments have experimented with various youth training schemes throughout the 1980s, while unemployment has been high, subsidizing short periods of training or initial work experience in conjunction with local employers, in order to improve young people's chances of finding permanent work and progressing their careers. The National Council for Vocational Qualifications was set up in 1986 to determine formal training objectives, particularly for those workers who had no specific qualifications. Within the NHS, this applies to health care support staff who are replacing nursing auxiliaries, assistants, aides and helpers (see Chapter 10), and to clerical and junior administrative staff, as well as more senior staff (see above). This initiative will go some way towards correcting the comparatively low priority formerly given to training NHS staff.

CONCLUSION

Despite considerable technological advance and the substitution of labour for capital over the last 50 years, the NHS remains a service reliant on its staff to a substantial degree. Although the numbers of staff directly employed by the NHS over the last decade has started to fall, the human resource will remain central to the service. Ideas about how this resource is managed, how its use is planned and how it is motivated have changed since the beginning of the NHS. In many areas, the notion of a 'command economy' – with centrally planned staff numbers and centrally negotiated pay and conditions of service – has started to break down. Devolution of many of the human resource functions has meant that trusts have to learn new personnel management skills and take on new responsibilities. The market pressures felt by trusts also mean that they have to start taking a more hard-headed approach to the way their most costly resource is used, and employees consequently have to live with greater job flexibility and its corollary, uncertainty.

NOTES

1. DHSS (October 1983) *The NHS Management Inquiry* (Griffiths Report), HMSO, London.
2. See Equal Pay Act, 1970, Sex Discrimination Acts, 1975–1986; the Equal Opportunities Commission gives guidance on measures that can be taken to achieve equality. See also General Whitley Council Section 51.
3. *Control of Substances Hazardous to Health Regulations 1988*, SI 1657; came into force 1 October 1989.
4. Nurses' Salaries Committee (1943) *First Report. Salaries and Emoluments of Female Nurses in Hospitals* (Chairman Lord Rushcliffe), HMSO, London (Cmnd. 6424).
5. *Scottish Nurses' Salaries Committee. Interim Report* (1943) (Chairman Professor T.M. Taylor, later Lord Guthrie), HMSO, London (Cmnd. 6425).

6. National Joint Council for Staffs of Hospitals and Allied Institutions in England and Wales (Chairman, Sir George Mowbray).
7. Ibid.
8. DHSS (1976) *Making Whitley Work* (McCarthy Report), HMSO, London.
9. Several people claimed credit for this description, including the General Secretary of NUPE, Rodney Bickerstaffe. The quotation comes from the opening lines of Shakespeare's Richard III: 'Now is the winter of our discontent made glorious summer . . .'. Significantly, the second phrase of the quotation was not used; nor did the ancillary staff obtain their demands.
10. The Health Services Board was set up under the Health Services Act, 1976, but abolished four years later.
11. National Board for Prices and Incomes. Report No. 29 (1968) *The Pay and Conditions of Manual Workers in Local Authorities, the National Health Service, Gas and Water Supply*, HMSO, London.
12. Individual Performance Review (IPR) was designed to be a nation-wide appraisal scheme. Later, performance related pay was added for more senior managers. Previous appraisal schemes, such as Staff Reporting in the 1960s, had decayed.
13. DHSS (1974) *Report of the Committee of Inquiry into Pay and Related Conditions of Service of Nurses and Midwives* (Halsbury Report), HMSO, London.
14. Standing Commission on Pay Comparability. Report 1 (1960) *Local Authority and University Manual Workers, NHS Ancillary Staff and Ambulancemen*, HMSO, London (Cmnd. 7641). Report 3 (1960) *Nurses and Midwives*, HMSO, London (Cmnd. 7795). Report 4 (1980) *Professions Supplementary to Medicine*, HMSO, London (Cmnd. 7850).
15. *Review of Top Posts in the National Health Service. A Report to the Nurses and Midwives, Administrative and Clerical and Professional and Technical (B) Whitley Councils*, prepared by A.J. Speakman, June 1977.
16. *Inquiry into Civil Service Pay* (1982) (Megaw Report), HMSO, London (Cmnd. 8590).
17. The NHSTA superseded various staff committees within the DHSS.
18. NHSTA (1986) *Better Management, Better Health* (Donne Report), Bristol.
19. Managing Health Services (MESOL), introduced in 1988, is a major course designed specifically for health service managers by the Institute of Health Services Management, the NHSTA and the Open University.
20. Similarly, the NHSTA designed another programme, 'Health Pickup', for the continuing education of professional staff.

13

The public and the National Health Service

This chapter is concerned with a range of issues that illustrate the relationship between ordinary people and the health services that are provided for them by the State. In the first section, statutory and other arrangements that relate directly to the general public rather than to people who have become patients are discussed. The next section goes on to consider selected health care issues on which sections of the public have expressed their view, particularly in criticism of prevailing NHS policies.

COMMUNITY HEALTH COUNCILS

Community Health Councils (CHCs), an innovation of the 1974 NHS reorganization, are bodies whose broad task is to represent the views of local users of the health services to the health authorities. The idea of setting them up arose principally because it was felt that health service users had exerted too little influence on the provision and planning of services in an organization that had become dominated by professionals. In the past, the tasks of managing the provision of services and monitoring their quality had been combined. Some members of the old hospital authorities and the former local authority health committees were specifically meant to represent the lay view, but their influence was felt to have been limited. On the AHAs, the lay members were appointed to shoulder managerial responsibilities, and the emphasis was to separate this from the responsibility for representing consumers' views. There is usually one CHC for each health District. They provide for over 6000 people to play an active part within the health service as members of statutory bodies for expressing consumer opinion, quite separate from the health authorities which take care of the day-to-day running of the services.

CHC membership has been worked out principally on the basis of the resident district population, and ranges from 18 in the smallest to 24 in the largest.

Half the members are nominated by the local authorities, one third by voluntary organizations and the remaining one sixth by the Regional Health Authorities. Regions have the job of officially appointing all the nominees, normally for a period of four years, and half the members retire every two years (although they are eligible for reappointment). A limited number of people can also be co-opted. Generally, each CHC has two full-time staff – the Chief Officer and his or her assistant – who work from offices chosen by the CHC. In some cases CHCs have obtained shop front accommodation, while others work from offices which may be rented from the health or local authorities. Administrative costs have been kept low. The money to pay staff salaries, office costs and all other expenses is made available by Regions. The staff of CHCs are employees of the Regions, who also arrange training opportunities for them.

To the majority of the population, questions of management in an organization as extensive as the NHS are not interesting. Individuals tend to have views about 'illness' rather than 'health', and find it difficult to consider questions which extend beyond their own personal experience. This is not a criticism but a reflection of the very low priority which governments and authorities have given to explaining issues of policy and management in a clear and honest way. Newspapers, radio and television are the principal sources of information about all aspects of national life for most people, but these are quite inadequate on the whole to enable people to develop a considered view of complex problems.

So, in order to be able to represent the views of their public to the NHS, CHCs are first faced with the task of providing a certain amount of information to interest people and activate awareness. Public meetings, advertisements, exhibitions as well as contact with many local groups and press briefings are some of the ways to do this. Through CHC members' own contacts with voluntary organizations and the local authorities, the work of the CHC can be further explained and developed, but this all requires time and effort, which may be in short supply. CHC members give their time voluntarily in addition to their other commitments, so the degree to which CHCs can become known and hence reflect the needs of local people is very dependent on the determination of the members and the staff.

The meetings of CHCs are open for members of the public to attend (as are those of the Regions and Districts) and perhaps given the opportunity to speak. People can also call at the CHC office for help and advice. If they have complaints about the NHS, the CHC can explain how to make best use of the official channels and procedures. Although it is not the responsibility of CHCs to judge or investigate individual complaints, by playing an active part they can support people through what may be complex and bewildering encounters with NHS management, and they can comment constructively on areas of complaint to the health authorities.

In terms of their overall influence in the NHS, it may appear that CHCs are relatively powerless – they certainly have no managerial responsibility for the provision of any services. But they do have the right to ask for and receive information; they have the right to send one of their members to Health Authority meetings; they have the right to visit NHS premises; they have the right to be consulted about development plans; consultation with them on hospital closures and substantial changes of use is required; they can give evidence to official committees; they can enlist the support of MPs; and, above all, they can use the press to articulate their views forcibly.

Most CHCs have divided into working groups, each concentrating on a defined sector of health care by meeting regularly to consider information, conduct investigations, make visits and reports. CHCs also have to prepare an annual report to their local Region, and there is a statutory annual public meeting with their local DHA. In relation to the family practitioner services, CHCs have more limited official powers. They only have observers at the meetings of those FHSAs who permit this and they do not have automatic access to GPs' surgeries. As a result, many councils have found it advantageous to make their own informal contacts with doctors and the Local Medical Committee in order to establish an atmosphere of mutual respect and to improve the exchange of information. In contrast, a number of CHCs send observers to the meetings of joint consultative committees; some have observer status or full membership of District planning teams.

In May 1974, the Secretary of State issued a consultative paper called *Democracy in the NHS* [1], which put forward ways in which the Government was prepared to strengthen the principle of delegated authority in the NHS. With reference to CHCs, the two main suggestions were that two members should be appointed to the Area Health Authority, and that a representative body should be created to advise and assist CHCs, with a budget drawn from central funds. The paper announced firm decisions to allow the posts of CHC secretaries to be filled by open competition (instead of being restricted to within the NHS); to oblige District Management Teams to send a spokesman to CHC meetings when invited, to answer questions in open session; to include CHCs among the bodies consulted by Regions before making appointments to the Areas; to make NHS employees and family practitioners eligible for CHC membership and to give CHCs a key role concerning hospital closures: CHCs, Health Authorities and other interested bodies were asked to submit their views on the paper's tentative proposals to the DHSS.

In July 1975, the Secretary of State announced that, in the light of these representations, each CHC would be allowed to send one member to attend AHA meetings with the right to speak but not to vote. In 1976, the DHSS amended its advice about appointing CHC members. It indicated that Regions should include a trades council representative and a disabled person among its own nominees, and pointed out that all members of CHCs should be 'prepared to devote a considerable amount of time and energy to their Council's work. It is important that appointing bodies should take account of this, and confirm with prospective members that they can undertake the necessary duties before putting forward nominations.'

By the end of the 1970s there was a feeling that CHCs were not worth their annual level of expenditure, small though that was. This attitude may have arisen as a result of too much CHC activity and too little. In a few cases, notably inner-city areas, some CHCs had spearheaded an attack on government policy and had disrupted Authority meetings. But in many other areas the CHCs were relatively ineffectual, duplicating some work done by health authority members themselves. The Royal Commission unequivocally supported the continuation of CHCs, but *Patients First* [2] was less sure and committed the Government only to a further review. In the event, Circular HC(80)8 [3] announced that CHCs would continue for the time being, and this was followed by a more detailed circular HC(81)15 [4] revising membership numbers to make most CHCs smaller, and clarifying other matters concerning the role of the CHC and the method of appointing members.

In many places CHCs have not been very successful in making their presence, felt partly because, being made up of many separate representative interests, it has been difficult to formulate a clear point of view, particularly one which may be critical of government policy. Even hospital closures have been difficult for CHCs to fight, conscious as they have to be that they will be expected to suggest alternatives if their opinion is to be considered seriously. CHCs are reliant on Districts and their staff for information, and this tends to reduce their power to do much more than give a second opinion on plans. In 1990, following the reconstitution of Districts, the role of CHCs in the NHS was confirmed, but more narrowly defined. They no longer have to be consulted whenever the health authority intends to introduce a substantial change to local services, but only if the District considers 'it would be expedient and in the interests of the health service to do so' [5]. CHCs do have access to trusts, but they are still excluded from examining GPs' services as of right.

The idea of a national body for CHCs was discussed for some time, until a meeting of CHC representatives decided, in November 1976, to proceed with its establishment. The first Annual General Meeting of the Association of Community Health Councils for England and Wales was held in June 1977, attended by representatives of more than 70% of CHCs who had decided to join. At the request of the DHSS, in 1975, a national information service for CHCs, including a regular publication called *CHC News*, was set up and sponsored by the King's Fund. This proved to be successful, and in 1976, the DHSS assumed responsibility for its costs. The withdrawal of financial support caused the end of publication in June 1984.

The reorganization of the NHS in 1974 and the creation of CHCs occurred at a turning point in the history of health service provision. Continued growth and expansion was for the first time seriously in doubt, and the public expenditure cuts of successive governments in the 1970s had a significant effect on the NHS. CHCs were not, therefore, in a position to expect demands for increased overall spending to be met, but they were in a position to pioneer attempts to encourage shifts in spending, particularly away from the hospital services towards the community services. Despite the reservations outlined above, they are, through their knowledge of the way the NHS works and through their involvement in the planning cycle, potentially able to promote the more effective use of limited resources, particularly in relation to the needs of the local community.

PUBLIC OPINION

CHCs provide only one of several sources of feedback to Health Authorities on the services they provide. A number of surveys are conducted to record what the public thinks of aspects of the NHS. Every year the National Association of Health Authorities and Trusts (NAHAT), together with the *Health Service Journal*, publishes the findings of a wide-ranging opinion poll. The British Attitudes Survey also asks the public's opinion of the NHS. Since the beginning of the 1980s (when these polls were first conducted) there has tended to be a decline in satisfaction up to 1990. Whether this is because the quality of the service is falling or expectations are rising is a matter of debate. Figures for 1991 and 1992 [6] suggest that satisfaction has increased slightly (Figure 13.1).

Locally, Health Authorities commission opinion polls, host open meetings about local health care provision and conduct consumer surveys. All these are

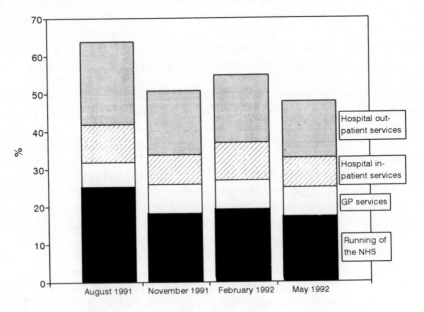

Figure 13.1 Public opinion of the NHS: percentage quite or very dissatisfied with the NHS.

Source: *Omnibus Surveys*, 1991 and 1992, OPCS.

important in assessing how far local people obtain what they expect from the service. The media can be helpful in explaining issues, but can also foster negative attitudes by sensationalizing shortcomings, and NHS managers can no longer afford to disregard public relations. Although using the methods of commerce to promote a falsely positive image would court accusations of the misuse of public money, failure to address the declining regard for the NHS permits an accelerating loss of public confidence. This faces management with an acute dilemma.

Since the reforms of the NHS in 1990, there has been an increase in the number of locally conducted opinion polls and a surge of interest in trying to make the whole process more scientific. Three factors are responsible. First, with the abolition of health authority members – which included the loss of trade union and local authority representatives – the reforms have diminished public accountability of health authorities. Seeking the public's opinion was seen, in a small way, as helping to redress this loss.

Secondly, and more importantly, the new purchasing role given to Districts has exposed the hitherto implicit priority setting and rationing process which has always existed in the NHS, and this has perhaps prompted Districts to spread the burden of making difficult decisions through public consultation and opinion surveys. One example many Districts have followed with interest was an experiment in the US state of Oregon, where public meetings and surveys were used extensively as part of a process to try and elicit a priority ranking for services to be provided within a limited Medicaid budget (see Chapter 14). In essence this is exactly the same problem facing British health authorities. Analysis of these types of surveys has revealed considerable shortcomings: it would seem that any answer can be obtained if the right question is asked.

Thirdly, to obtain additional information to help purchasers respond to the wishes of their local populations, Districts have carried out surveys of the attitudes of patients and the public to local services. Some providers have been inundated with patient satisfaction surveys, and many now carry out their own in order to acquire evidence for their purchasers about patients' opinions of services they have received. These surveys have also been used to impress potential purchasers.

Finally, the implementation of the *Patient's Charter* and the political importance attached to it (see below) have probably given an impetus to the process of finding out what the public think, what they want and what patients feel about their services.

COMPLAINTS

One aspect of consumer relations that has received considerable attention is the complaints procedure. The first official advice from the Ministry of Health on how to handle complaints about hospital care was set out in Circular HM(66)15 [7]. It differentiated between minor complaints that could be dealt with on the spot and more substantial cases of dissatisfaction. However, health service staff were generally unsympathetic to complaints and were inclined to dismiss them. The Davies Committee was set up to examine hospital complaints procedures. Its report (1973) [8] suggested a detailed code of practice and the establishment of investigating panels.

Although the Government welcomed the report, only in 1976 did it announce that a uniform code of practice would be implemented for hospital and community services. This did not cover complaints about GP services, where patients encounter the greatest obstacles to being given a fair hearing when they feel aggrieved. The problem is not just that GPs are highly defensive about their professional judgement and practices and resent any challenge from lay people, but that the formal procedures for making complaints are excessively rigid (see below). For instance, complaints more than three months old were not usually accepted by the FHSA. Districts, in comparison, did not normally set such time limits, recognizing that an ill person may not feel able to proceed with the official complaints procedures until they are better and the episode of care in question is completed.

Clinical complaints

In 1981 further guidance was issued, and it included an important new procedure for handling complaints about hospital clinical matters. This had always been difficult for patients and their relatives because they had only two choices: either accept the management's explanation or sue. The new procedure, negotiated with considerable difficulty with the BMA, provides three stages for handling the complaint. Stage one is the same as for any complaint: the matter is drawn to the attention of the consultant (consultants are responsible for the actions of their juniors) and to the health authority managers. If their answer is unsatisfactory to the complainant, he or she then renews the complaint and asks for the Regional Medical Adviser to be involved. An informal reconciliation is attempted, but if this fails the matter then passes to the third stage, the setting up of an independent professional review panel. Doctors appointed to this panel are paid.

The new procedure was set up in September 1981 and after 16 months a report was presented to the Secretary of State [9] who concluded that the new arrangements were working well. Overall the procedure was welcomed, as it dealt more satisfactorily with complaints arising from diagnosis and treatment. The total number of complaints remained very small, given the millions of patient contacts each year. However, the new arrangements did not ensure all health authorities dealt with complaints adequately. The Hospital Complaints Procedure Act, 1985, required health authorities to establish a designated complaints officer who prepares regular reports for the health authority [10].

By 1993, the Secretary of State had responded to mounting criticism by setting up a new inquiry into complaints procedures (see below – The Wilson Report

[11]). In the case of complaints made against GPs, general dental practitioners, opticians and pharmacists providing NHS services, the complaint has to be made in writing to the FHSA general manager, normally within three months of the event which gave rise to it. It has to allege a breach in the practitioner's terms of service, i.e. his contract with the FHSA. The general manager initially tries to settle informally, with the complainant, all those complaints that are relatively minor, but, if it is a more serious matter, he refers it to one of the Service Committees of the FHSA.

The Service Committees are small bodies appointed by the FHSA, with professional and lay members who hear the complaint and give the complainant and the practitioner the opportunity to present their cases and call witnesses. The Service Committee's decision can be appealed against by either party if it is adverse to them, in which case the Secretary of State can arrange for a small committee to consider the case again, sometimes with an oral hearing, both parties having the right to be legally represented.

Various penalties can be imposed on a practitioner who is found to have breached his terms of service, and can involve a warning or a withholding of remuneration. In exceptional cases, a practitioner can be referred by the FHSA to the National Health Service Tribunal. This body has the power to remove a person from the FHSA's list if continued inclusion would 'be prejudicial to the efficiency of the services'. The practitioner then has the right to appeal to the Secretary of State who may confirm or revoke the Tribunal's decision. This procedure is distinct from the profession's own disciplinary powers to erase the name of a practitioner from the professional register, and hence to disqualify that person from practising at all. A practitioner who has had his or her name removed from an FHSA list by a decision of the NHS Tribunal is still free to practise privately or as a salaried employee of the NHS.

Until the implementation of the Wilson Report [12], arrangements for investigating complaints were governed by the National Health Service (Service Committees and Tribunal) Amendment (No. 2) Regulations, 1990 [13], which came into operation on 17 September 1990. In 1976, the DHSS initiated a review, and invited interested parties to submit views on those suggestions and on any other improvements. In particular, the Council on Tribunals said that the Service Committee procedure could be criticized for being insufficiently independent, since the FPC was responsible both for providing services and for deciding whether a complaint about them is justified. The machinery for hearing complaints rests entirely with the administering authorities and the professions, which are the parties to the contractual arrangements. Furthermore, at Service Committee hearings, both parties can be assisted by a person of their choice, provided that person is not a 'paid advocate'. The position of CHC secretaries as active helpers to patients under the regulations led to some controversy, and the Council on Tribunals suggested that the term 'paid advocate' should be clarified in order to resolve the position of MPs, paid officials of trade unions and professional associations and CHCs.

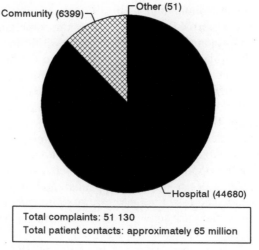

Figure 13.2 Written complaints by or on behalf of patients: England: 1991–2.
Source: Department of Health.

In 1978 the DHSS issued proposals for improving the procedures. These covered extension of the informal procedure, service committee chairmen to be drawn from a panel of legally qualified people, changes in membership, role of the administrator, representation of parties by unpaid advocates, access to medical records, time limits, oral complaints and other points. Under the 1990 amendments, the chairman of the complaints committee has to be legally qualified if possible [14].

The Wilson Committee

There was no doubt that even with the 1990 reforms of the complaints procedure and previous changes, the system was not user-friendly. Historically, the NHS had had a very low rate of complaints, given the enormous number of contacts patients had with the health service and its staff (Figure 13.2). But in all likelihood, this low rate is due less to the overwhelming satisfaction of patients with their care, or to a natural unwillingness to complain or make a fuss, than to the difficulty of actually making a complaint [15].

In 1994 Professor Alan Wilson, chair of an independent committee appointed by the Secretary of State, published his recommendations for streamlining the complaints procedure in the NHS. The report, *Being Heard* [16], envisaged a two-stage procedure. First, complainants would be offered immediate access to and response from front-line staff, followed by investigation, conciliation and, if necessary, action by the FHSA or trusts involved. Stage two would be for complaints not adequately dealt with internally, and would involve an independent panel with a majority of lay members who would further investigate difficult cases. The report also recommended that all trusts and FHSAs should employ a complaints officer (a number of trusts already did so), and envisaged that the time taken to deal with complaints would be speeded up, so that most would be dealt with within days. If further investigation were necessary, then this should not take more than a few weeks, and all complaints should be seen to within three months. Although the Wilson Report dealt with the rather fragmented complaints procedure, it did not tackle the issue of medical negligence, which is still the domain of the General Medical Council.

The Health Service Commissioner

A further channel for the consideration of complaints was created by the appointment of the Health Service Commissioner, under the 1973 Act. The Commissioner took up office on 1 October 1973, and is empowered to investigate complaints received directly from members of the public concerning failures in provision of services or incidents of maladministration by the Health Authorities in England, Wales and Scotland. These mainly concern grievances about the treatment and care of patients and the failures in communication between patients and the hospital staff.

Specific examples quoted in the Commissioner's reports include complaints about the length of time patients have had to wait for hospital treatment, the repeated postponement of a major operation and performing an operation without a patient's consent. The Health Service Commissioner was specifically excluded from investigating actions taken solely in consequence of the exercise of clinical judgement, personnel matters or any action taken by a person providing general medical, dental, pharmaceutical or ophthalmic services for which the FHSA is responsible. However, the Wilson Report recommended that the Ombudsman's role should be widened to include the power to investigate complaints about GPs and about doctors' clinical judgement. Health authorities may also refer matters to him if they have been unable to resolve them satisfactorily.

The Commissioner is based in London and has a small staff of civil servants and staff seconded from NHS work. There are also investigating units in Cardiff and Edinburgh, 13 members of the medical profession are available to provide advice in deciding whether a particular complaint from a patient involves clinical judgement. In 1989/90, the Commissioner received 794 complaints, 486 (61%) of which had to be rejected as outside his jurisdiction – mainly because the body complained against had not been given the opportunity to consider the complaint first, a step required by the Act before the Commissioner can take up the complaint. In the first 17 years, 11 789 complaints were received. Of these, 7118 (60%) were rejected, 2476 (21%) referred back to the complainant and 1930 (16%) investigated and reported on [17].

THE *PATIENT'S CHARTER*

In July 1991, the Government published the *Citizen's Charter* [18]. The idea behind the White Paper was to improve quality and standards in all public services through such mechanisms as privatization, contracting out services, greater competition, performance-related pay for public servants, published performance targets, more effective complaints procedures and so on. With the emphasis on privatization and contracting out, the Charter summed up the Conservative Government's attitude to public services as inherently (almost unreformably) inefficient and unresponsive to users' needs and demands. While the *Citizen's Charter* set out the overall framework of the Charter idea and gave examples of targets and policies for different public services, such as British Rail, the police and the Inland Revenue, it was up to each service to produce its own Charter.

In 1991 the NHS published the *Patient's Charter* [19], which set out seven existing rights for patients: to receive health care on the basis of clinical need; to be registered with a GP; to receive emergency medical care at any time; to be referred to a consultant if thought necessary by a GP; to be given a clear explanation of any treatment proposed; to have access to health records; to choose whether or not to take part in medical research. Three further rights were to be implemented by 1 April 1992: the right to detailed information about available local services, quality standards and maximum waiting times; guaranteed admission to hospital no later than two years from the day a patient joined a waiting-list (subsequently reduced to 18 months and then a target of a year); the right to have any complaint investigated and to receive a full and prompt written reply from the chief executive of a trust or District or FHSA. More general standards of service outlined in the *Citizen's Charter* also apply to the NHS. From April 1992, local Charter standards were also introduced requiring trusts and health authorities to minimize out-patient waiting-times and all front-line staff to wear name badges.

THE WORK OF VOLUNTARY ORGANISATIONS

As the historical summaries in earlier chapters have shown, many of the existing health services have their origins in the work of volunteers and voluntary organizations. Outstanding examples are the voluntary hospitals themselves, district nursing and health visiting, the blood transfusion service, occupational therapy and family planning services, and there are many others.

The term 'voluntary organization' covers those non-profit-making associations of individuals (or organizations) which are not created by statute. Depending on their constitution or statement of objective, they may be registered charities, registered companies, chartered bodies or have some other legal status. The contribution of voluntary organizations alongside the statutory provision of health and social services is considerable. Governments continue to recognize that this co-operation is mutually beneficial, since in some cases the work of the voluntary organizations supplements that provided by the State, while in other cases the voluntary organizations fill in the gaps of State provision.

There is, however, an important distinction between voluntary and statutory services. Voluntary organizations often identify particular areas of need and specialize in educating public opinion on the deficiencies and potential improvements in statutory services, and they can often do this more flexibly and experimentally than a statutorily prescribed organization.

Those organizations registered under the Charities Act, 1960 (probably the majority in the health and welfare area), enjoy a number of financial benefits. Much of their income is derived from donations, legacies, government grants and fund-raising activities. They are entitled to direct relief of tax payable on this, as well as being able to reclaim the tax paid by individuals on donations given as a covenant and being allowed considerable relief on the local tax payable on their premises. Some of the larger charities also derive a part of their income from their capital assets. Money is required to cover staff wages and administrative costs, advertising campaigns, research support and direct grants. The increasing inflation of recent years has put considerable financial pressure on many charities, particularly those whose income from year to year is less predictable. *Care in Action* [20] encouraged the use of voluntary organizations as agents of the health authorities, because they could be more sensitive to new demands. Many existing voluntary bodies could not exist, however, without money from health and local authorities. The voluntary and statutory services are mutually dependent – many hospitals employ a co-ordinator of voluntary work.

The role of the voluntary sector has been debated a good deal, especially since the Conservative Party came to power in 1979. Circular HC(80)11 [21] encouraged health authorities to involve themselves in fund raising if this seemed beneficial: previously, direct fund raising had not been allowed. In the discussions leading up to the 1982 reorganization, the Secretary of State, Patrick Jenkin, suggested that much more could be provided by the voluntary sector, leaving the statutory bodies as a 'safety net' to ensure no one was left without support [22]. Such a view was anathema to the Labour Party. Even less acceptable was the idea that voluntary work was a suitable alternative for paid work at times of unemployment. Indeed, despite a sharp rise in unemployment, volunteers have not always been easy to recruit. Health services have long been supported by leagues of hospital friends and numerous other bodies, but they cannot rely on raising large sums of money on a recurring basis to become a sufficient, realistic alternative to central funding.

As well as voluntary bodies and CHCs, pressure groups enable the public to influence the NHS. They are set up with a specific purpose, such as saving a hospital from closure or campaigning for services for a particular group of patients or for a new facility. The newspapers, radio and television have become increasingly interested in health matters, notably aspects of high technology medicine and hospital life. Informed radio and television programmes involve and educate the public about medical research and new treatments. Popular television series such as *Casualty* cover many areas of concern, from how best to care for the elderly to epilepsy and solvent abuse.

Since the 1974 reorganization, health authorities and their staff have become more responsive to their role as agents of the public they serve and a more open attitude to the media has resulted. The media, in their turn, can do much to protect the rights of the public. This is particularly important in matters of research and to ensure patients' rights are not abused in other ways.

MEDICAL RESEARCH AND INTERVENTION

Research into new and more effective forms of treatment is a necessary and expected activity, and the benefits of its results are well known. However, a strong body of opinion is opposed to the conduct of certain techniques and experiments on animal and human subjects. The State finances research directly through the Medical Research Council and through grants to individuals, and indirectly through its funding of academic institutions which carry out research. Most of this work is carefully done, but concern has arisen over cases where the rights of the subjects may appear to have been disregarded. To overcome this, ethical committees were set up to vet all new proposals for clinical research. This acknowledged that the responsibility for deciding on the ethics of an experiment should not rest with the investigator alone. Yet review of ethical committees sponsored by the King's Fund and undertaken by Rabbi Julia Neuberger in 1991 demonstrated that not all such committees worked satisfactorily.

In the development of new drugs, the Medicines Commission scrutinizes methods of testing, but it still remains true that animal and human subjects have to be used at an early stage, before a medicine can be known to be safe and effective or not. The case of thalidomide illustrates a possible outcome of insufficient preparatory research. The drug thalidomide was first synthesized in Germany in 1956 and marketed as a sedative and hypnotic. In 1958 it was manufactured and marketed in Britain, under licence to Distillers Company Biochemicals Ltd, under several brand names including 'Distavel'. It was found to be a particularly effective sedative which did not have some of the disadvantages of the barbiturates, and was prescribed for pregnant women to reduce feelings of tension. In November 1961, a German paediatrician reported the suspected connection between congenital deformities in babies and the use of thalidomide in early pregnancy. On 2 December 1961, Distillers announced withdrawal of the drug. About 8000 deformed children were born as a result of the use of thalidomide, over 400 of them in Britain [23]. Legal actions against Distillers were pursued by a number of the children and settlements were made in other cases, some following an investigation by Sir Alan Marre, largely completed in 1978.

This affair was one of the factors contributing to the revised legislation on the testing of new drugs and the advertising of their properties. Even so, there have been other cases where significant numbers of patients have been adversely affected by a drug. Furthermore, when drugs have been declared suitable for use, doubts about their safety can remain, as for example with certain steroid preparations and the contraceptive pill.

ETHICS

A related problem is the ethics of medical intervention, either in terms of keeping people alive by artificial means or withdrawing treatment because of a patient's inability to benefit – often affecting elderly people. When heart transplants were first performed in the 1960s they captured the interest of the press, but the success rate remained relatively disappointing. The high cost of the procedure and the problems of finding suitable donors at the right time limited what can be achieved in this area.

However, despite improvements in the survival rates for heart transplant patients, kidney transplantation has proved more successful. Many people with chronic renal failure are kept alive by being attached to a kidney machine for intermittent dialysis, but the demand for treatment far exceeds the availability of resources. The transplant operation, itself, is technically less difficult than for the heart, and, if a suitable donor can be found and the considerable problems of tissue rejection managed, a patient with a transplant can recover to lead a fully active and normal life. The untreated disease is fatal, and life with a kidney machine is far from easy, so transplantation can offer the best solution for many sufferers. In 1972 the DHSS launched a public campaign to encourage people to decide to allow their kidneys to be used for transplantation if they died. Response to further campaigns remained disappointing and, although many hospitals were fully equipped to perform the operation (except for shortages of technical staff in some places), people with the disease are still dying prematurely because there are insufficient donors.

The decision whether to prolong a patient's life or not can be extremely difficult to make, especially when facilities for their continuing care are in short supply. The increasing incidence of degenerative and terminal illnesses in old people bears witness to considerable mastery over the infectious and damaging diseases and the poor social conditions that limited life expectancy for earlier generations, but this brings its own problems. One observer has written: 'It is clearly pointless to keep a patient with an inoperable brain tumour breathing when a fatal outcome is certain, and in the case of recurrent chest infections in the elderly respiratory cripple there may come a time when it is unkind to rescue the patient yet again from an acute episode only to restore him to distressing permanent disablement. The decision to submit a patient to resuscitation or intensive therapy must be informed, deliberate and responsible' [24].

A report from the Royal College of Physicians in May 1994 accused Health

Authorities and providers of discriminating against elderly patients, on the assumption that the elderly should be at the back of the queue because they had less time to live [25], [26]. The Royal College of Physicians recommended that 'The guiding principle upon which the provision of acute medical care to elderly people is based must be that there is no distinction or negative discrimination on grounds of age.' Whether this means that it is justifiable to discriminate on the grounds of life expectancy – which would tend to mean preference given to younger rather than older people – is unclear. Or should every patient receive maximum treatment even if this prolongs their life by only a few days and deprives someone else of resources which would prolong their life by years? The ethics are extremely difficult and the rigid application of any one set of principles may be costly in terms of human lives.

Cases of serious and possibly irreversible brain damage following road accidents, or the birth of babies with congenital abnormalities exercise the judgement of doctors and families to the extreme, and the definition of meaningful survival and the cost of intervention, both financial and emotional, have to be made somehow. Ever since the Helsinki Agreement on guidelines for research in 1964, there has been concern about the ethical aspects of health care. Doing what is right is not now seen as a matter only for clinical staff; managers and the population at large need to contribute to the ethical debate [27], [28].

CONCLUSION

Matters raised in this chapter lead to the question; Is the NHS sensitive enough to the public it serves? Health Authorities themselves, the CHCs, voluntary bodies, pressure groups and the media all help to protect the public interest. Unlike some countries, in the UK litigation is a relatively insignificant factor in bringing about changes. In the early 1980s, the Government took the view that subjecting the NHS to more competition might improve standards, so private hospitals were enabled to develop more rapidly. But the private sector still provides only a small part of total patient care. Such provision did draw to health authorities' attention the scant concern most hospitals and community units had shown for fostering better staff attitudes towards patients, and the widespread complacency about waiting-times in out-patient departments and waiting-lists for admissions.

Policy statements by government ministers have emphasized the pressing need for the NHS to show it really is concerned about the consumer. Special funds have been earmarked for promoting improvements in quality, for example to reduce waiting-lists and to make out-patient departments more acceptable places to be in. The very titles of White Papers – *Patients First*, *Working for Patients*, *Caring for People* and the NHS version of the *Citizen's Charter*, the *Patient's Charter* – underline this desire to portray the NHS more in the image of a commercial concern committed to pleasing its customers, and less like a welfare institution where the recipients of care are expected to be grateful for whatever they are fortunate enough to receive. Health Authorities and their providers of health care have been set a challenge by the 1990 Act; it remains to be seen whether in an equally challenging economic environment, the confidence of the public in the NHS can be secured.

NOTES

1. Department of Health and Social Security (1974) *Democracy in the National Health Service*, HMSO, London.
2. Op. cit., Chapter 1, *Patients First*.
3. DHSS Circular HC(80)8 (July 1980) *Health Service Development: Structure and Management.*
4. DHSS Circular HC(81)15 (December 1981) *Health Service Development: Community Health Councils.*
5. DoH. The NHS Management Executive issued guidance in December 1990 entitled, *Consultation and Involving the Consumer.*
6. For a useful collation of a number of opinion surveys and a discussion of their interpretation, see Judge, K. and Soloman, M. (1993) Public Opinion and the National Health Service: Patterns and Perspectives in Consumer Satisfaction. *Journal of Social Policy*, **22**(3), 299–327.
7. Ministry of Health Circular HM(66)15 (1966) *Methods of Dealing with Complaints by Patients*, HMSO, London.
8. Department of Health and Social Security, Welsh Office (1973) *Report of the Committee on Hospital Complaints Procedure* (Chairman, Sir Michael Davies), HMSO, London.
9. DHSS, SHHD, Welsh Office (November 1983) *Report on Operation of Procedure for Independent Review of Complaints Involving the Clinical Judgement of Hospital Doctors and Dentists.*
10. DHSS Circular HC(88)37 *Hospital Complaints Procedure Act, 1985*, HMSO, June 1988.
11. Department of Health (1994) *Being Heard* (The Wilson Report), HMSO, London.
12. Ibid.
13. DoH Circular FPCL 190/90 *Family Health Services Complaints*, HMSO, September 1990.
14. Ibid., para. 3.
15. Between 1991 and 1993 the number of complaints rose by 50%. This may be partly due to a higher profile given to patients' rights as a result of initiatives such as the *Patient's Charter.*
16. Op. cit., *Being Heard.*
17. House of Commons (1990) *Health Service Commissioner Annual Report for 1989–90*, HMSO, London (HC 538).
18. Cabinet Office (1991) *The Citizen's Charter*, HMSO, London (Cmnd. 1599).
19. Department of Health (1991) *The Patient's Charter*, HMSO, London.
20. DHSS (1981) *Care in Action. A Handbook of Policies and Priorities for the Health and Personal Social Services in England*, HMSO, London.
21. DHSS Circular HC(80)11 (December 1980) *Health Service Management. Health*

Services Act 1980: Fund Raising by NHS Authorities.
22. Patrick Jenkin, article in *The Guardian*, 26 January, 1981.
23. Ministry of Health (1964) *Deformities Caused by Thalidomide, Reports on Public Health and Medical Subjects No. 112*, HMSO, London.
24. Miller, H. (1973) *Medicine and Society*, Oxford University Press, p. 2.
25. Royal College of Physicians (1994) *Ensuring Equity and Equality of Care for Elderly People*, RCP.
26. In fact, when asked, members of the public tend to express opinions and values which imply discrimination against the elderly (given the need to make choices as a result of scarce resources). For example, in the Oregon experiment, preferences emerged for services for babies and children rather more than for services for the benefit of the elderly. The extent to which housebound elderly were able to get to the public meetings on which this opinion was based has, however, been criticized.
27. Wall, A. (1989) *Ethics and the Health Services Manager*, King's Fund, London.
28. Wall, A. (1993) *Values and the NHS*, Institute of Health Services Management (IHSM), London.

14

The NHS in an international context

The health services in the UK are in many ways specific to this group of countries, and have not only emerged from a particular history and set of circumstances but have also had to deal with particular health needs. Nevertheless, while every health service could claim such uniqueness, all countries' health services often face a number of similar problems and issues. Setting priorities within a limited budget is the same in Mozambique as it is in Germany or the UK. The order of magnitude and the choices involved may be different – malaria control versus a TB vaccination programme compared with the latest portable bone scanner versus a community psychiatric nurse – but the need to make a choice is the same. Different countries also share a considerable unity in the aims and objectives of their respective health care systems and institutions; equity of access, efficiency and effectiveness are, for instance, often cited as health care aims by different countries.

Recognizing such similarities is not to ignore the existence of obvious differences, but all health care services have much to learn from each other about good and bad practice. The flow of managers, clinicians and academics has been significant over recent years as more and more countries have looked abroad to see how others do it, whether it works and whether it would still work back home. As health care systems in many countries are currently tackling similar changes and reforms, this chapter looks abroad to examine the way other countries organize and fund their health care services, and to assess their relative success in achieving equitable, high quality and efficient services for their populations.

EQUITY OF PROVISION

There are many ways to define equity of provision of health care. At one extreme, equity could refer to equality of outcome of medical intervention. However, some notion of fairness concerning access to health care services is a commonly accepted definition. The fundamental belief underlying this is that people in equal need of care should have equal access to care, and this means minimizing barriers to care and treatment. This belief is common to all health care systems [1].

In the UK, except for certain notable exceptions such as prescriptions and dentistry, health care is free at the time of use. In the US, although health care is more like a conventional economic commodity, the Government spends billions of dollars every year to underwrite a degree of equity of access for those on low incomes and the elderly. However, even in countries such as the UK, Canada, New Zealand, Sweden, Denmark, Spain and Germany with few, if any, payment requirements at the time of use, fully equitable access to health care has never been achieved.

Studies of a number of European countries have shown that inequitable access (defined in terms of the shares of health care spending devoted to different income groups) is not uncommon [2]. In the UK, inequity favours the well-off, but the UK is not unique in this. Interestingly, differences between countries in access to health care appear to be unrelated to the existence of universal public health care coverage. A pan-European study [3] suggested that in the Netherlands and Switzerland, where comprehensive public cover is limited, there is little income-related inequity.

But what is 'need'?

Health economists define 'need' in the context of equity as the ability or capacity to benefit from medical intervention. From this perspective, equality of access for those in equal need can give rise to discrimination between people experiencing exactly the same health problem but a different capacity to benefit. The health economists' argument is that while two people may have the same poor health status, if choices have to be made between competing scarce resources, then the aim to use those resources efficiently should not be completely dominated by the goal of equality of access. In other words, a person with poor prospects of survival from an operation to remove a malignant tumour should, given the necessity to make a choice, receive less care (or perhaps no care) compared with someone with the same problem but with better prospects of recovery.

Despite some vehement critiques of the health economists' position [4], their view hardly differs from actual medical practice [5]. In formalizing what actually happens, the economists thereby expose some of the extremely difficult (and, to many, unpalatable) ethical decisions being taken by clinicians every day in the NHS. Opponents of the economists' view of need argue that every human life is equally valuable, and that it is therefore immoral to discriminate using the criterion of the capacity to benefit from medical treatment (just as it is wrong to discriminate on the grounds of income). Economists argue that if followed rigidly, such a decision rule would entail an enormous waste of resources and hence unnecessary loss of life and additional suffering.

Most economists recognize that both stands, if taken to their extremes, are undesirable and would produce irreconcilable ethical disputes.

One answer is to leave matters as they are, with doctors and others muddling through, and simply accept the inconsistencies and potential loss of equity/efficiency that inevitably arises [6]. This position distinguishes between access to the system as a whole and access to a particular amount or level of care once inside the system. Discrimination with regard to the former is then highly discouraged but, with regard to the latter, is accepted as unfortunate but necessary (and should be left largely to doctors to sort out). Whether, in the light of the greater transparency of decision making and the need to make choices following the 1990 reforms in the UK, this is a tenable resolution of the issue remains to be seen. The ethical dilemmas inherent in concepts such as need and equity are universal; all countries continuously grapple with competing judgements and views in these matters.

Social class, income and equity

In practice, inequitable access to the health care system as a whole generally arises for three reasons: social or racial standing, financial status and geography. First, with regard to social or racial standing, the Black Report [7] and numerous previous and subsequent research studies, established that people in the UK belonging to lower occupational classes suffer more ill-health. The evidence from the Black Report suggested that if the mortality rates of class I (professional people and their families) were applied to classes IV and V (manual workers and their families) during 1970–72, as many as 74 000 lives would not have been prematurely lost. The association of poor health with low social status persists, and this is largely outside the scope of the health services because it includes low income, poor housing, less education and, consequently, a comparatively deprived lifestyle.

How far are these findings applicable in other countries? The Black Report wrestled with the inherent difficulties of making international comparisons [8] where the statistics do not have a common base, but nevertheless concluded, in its study of infant mortality, that socio-economic factors were usually influential, although different rates between countries stimulate more questions than answers. It is still not clear why the results are so much better in Sweden and Norway than in England. How has France improved its position so markedly in a relatively short period?

In the UK, the NHS is in theory available to all, irrespective of their social class. In practice, different classes have different patterns of use and consumption of health care from the NHS which cannot be completely explained by differences in their health status. Some other countries demonstrate more entrenched or formalized class-related services. In the USA, middle-class people widely use private sources of care based on a fee for services system. But the poor, estimated at over 30 million people, racial minorities and those living in inadequate conditions in inner cities have to rely on a public system, mostly based on the local county or city hospital. Unlike the middle-class middle-income patients who have potentially limitless choice, the disadvantaged have little or no choice. Germany has a tiered hospital system in which paying more money buys a better level of service and access to more experienced and senior doctors. This is reminiscent of pre-1948 Britain, where access to the voluntary hospital often required a member of the management board to sponsor the individual, while patients could be admitted to municipal hospitals directly.

A fundamental principle embodied in the creation of the NHS was that patients should be treated equally, entirely irrespective of their financial means. Despite the increase in private medicine, which allows people to buy themselves prompt treatment instead of having to queue on the waiting-list, this principle has remained largely intact. But, as mentioned above, there still remains a hidden discriminator. Studies have shown that middle-class people use the NHS more, as well as more effectively, than working class people [9]. This is true in the preventive field too, where voluntary screening programmes fail to reach those most at risk. High socio-economic status is associated with more knowledgeable individuals who are more able to make better use of the services available. The same effect is observed in other countries. In America, those with money can afford as much health care as they like, those without have limited choice, but are also restricted to more stringently controlled services where even the number of consultations or referrals to hospitals are regulated.

Geography and equity

Does distance from a hospital lead to poorer levels of health care? Apparently not. Sweden achieves some of the best results in the world with, for instance, an infant mortality rate of under 5 per 1000 births compared with the UK's figure of 6.6 per 1000 births (1992). Furthermore, the most remote county in Sweden has the lowest rate in Sweden itself.

The Royal Commission on the NHS undertook a study, in 1978, to examine whether location within the UK was a significant influence on people's view of their access to health care [10]. This study looked at a rural community in Cumbria and a London borough, and found that patients in both places were satisfied with their access to care, at least at the primary level. The public support for retaining local hospitals in the UK suggests that physical proximity is an important consideration. But how do other countries manage where distances are much greater?

The actual distribution of hospitals tends to be determined by the population distribution characteristic of that country. In the United Kingdom, 10 miles may be regarded as too far from the nearest hospital, while in rural Sweden 100 miles might be considered reasonable. Sweden's population is only 8.2 million, of which 3 million live in three cities, and the remainder are spread thinly over an area bigger than Italy, Austria and Switzerland combined. As in Canada, health facilities in Sweden have to be widely spaced. In France, legislation between 1958 and 1968 developed a three-tiered system of university hospitals, general hospitals and local hospitals. Other countries such as Germany, the Netherlands and the USA have a less structured system, but through planning regulations they are attempting to rationalize hospital provision and reduce maldistribution.

Availability of health care services

The variations in access to health care associated with class, financial and geographical factors are important, but equally significant is the actual availability of health services: the policies controlling distribution of doctors and other health care workers, hospitals and clinics is crucial. Access to treatment is principally determined by doctors. There are marked differences between Western countries. One of the successes of the NHS is the much more even distribution of family doctors than before. GPs have an average of around 1800 patients on their lists and, because of the system of regulation (see Chapter 9), the number of doctors working in each area is controlled. In Germany, a system of incentives was introduced in 1976 to encourage doctors to practise in unpopular areas, but these doctors were not general practitioners in the English sense. Indeed, only Denmark and the Netherlands have a system of general practice remotely comparable to the English system. In other countries, there is no difference between general practitioners and hospital doctors. A doctor will first see a patient in the surgery and then, if hospital care is needed, will treat the patient in hospital or refer the patient a colleague.

Out-patient departments are not found in some countries. In Germany, out-patient departments have only recently been established, and then only in university hospitals. In Sweden, community health centres, covering a population of between 20 000 and 50 000, provide both primary care and out-patient consultation. Norway has smaller health centres, so the out-patient element is less significant, but the Municipal Health Act of 1984 has promoted locally controlled primary care services.

The most common system, found for example in Germany, the USA and France, allows patients to attend surgeries of their chosen specialist doctor or, in some cases, as referred by their employer. The doctor then decides how best to treat the patient. This system is often criticized in these countries because it has several disadvantages. First, patients may make the wrong choice and consequently be at risk from inappropriate treatment from a doctor not in an appropriate speciality. Secondly, their care consists of uncoordinated treatments for single episodes of illness. Thirdly, this encourages waste, as the more affluent patients may go to more than one doctor for the same symptoms. In Germany and Sweden, where the number of hospital beds per population is generous, patients may be admitted to hospital unnecessarily, but they will not wait. Nowhere else has the UK's problem with waiting-lists.

The total number of doctors affects the situation too, and there are wide variations; 1990 figures suggest that Germany and Sweden are well provided, with one doctor for approximately 370 members of the population. Australia has 560 and New Zealand 645 per doctor. The USA has about 420. The UK has about 1 doctor for every 700 people. In France, where there are roughly 350 people per doctor, maldistribution is a problem the Government has been trying to tackle; 35 000 of the 46 000 doctors are private practitioners and the regulation of these has brought about major conflicts.

Paying doctors

Doctors are paid differently from country to country. In the Netherlands there is increasing pressure to employ doctors on a direct salary. As in Sweden, where 85% of doctors are publicly employed, this seems likely to gain support, even from doctors themselves, because it would eradicate major differences in earning power between doctors. In this respect, Sweden is the most radical of all Western countries: it abolished fees in 1959 for hospital care and in 1970 for ambulatory (out-patient or community) care. Recent reform proposals for the Swedish health care system, which involved changes in payment methods and employment terms for doctors, encountered widespread opposition. In the NHS, the original NHS Act and the 1966 GP Charter were a political trade-off for improving general practice primary care. Following the 1990 contract, GPs continue to be paid by basic capitation fees, together with certain incentive payments.

In the USA, various attempts are being made to curb the increasing level of doctors' fees; for instance Health Maintenance Organizations (HMOs), introduced in 1973, enable doctors to set up pre-payment group practice. In this way, they can provide more comprehensive care with less reliance on hospitals and at correspondingly lower cost. The recent reforms in the US were led by Hilary Rodham Clinton and were designed to address many of the criticisms of inequity, inefficiency and expensiveness levelled at the US health care system. 'Managed health care', building on the apparent success of the HMO movement, was central to these reforms, but, by 1994, it seems the reforms are unlikely to be implemented.

In the countries mentioned, the number of doctors has increased and often doubled in the last 30 years, to the point where some countries believe they have too many doctors. In the UK, numbers entering medical schools have been regulated, although in the 1960s the Government expanded the number of medical schools, thinking there might otherwise be too few doctors. Recent regulation of medical student numbers intake in France has been unpopular. In the USA, regulation of medical schools started in 1910, and current estimates suggest that the country as a whole is becoming over-doctored, but distribution continues to be uneven.

The work of doctors is determined not only by the needs and demands of the public, but also by the availability of hospital beds and other facilities and the medical profession's attitudes to treatments. In the UK, a shortage of beds is often cited as the reason for long waiting-lists, whereas it is the throughput of cases for these beds that compares unfavourably with some other countries. The USA and other countries which rely on a payment system for occupied beds per day have a vested interest in maximizing the use of beds, and management of the beds tends to be affected by these considerations. Whether the patient needs to be in the bed is a separate issue. Operation rates vary widely between England and the USA because some surgical procedures are much more readily undertaken in the USA. Continental European countries also have a higher level of bed provision than the UK. The Netherlands has about 5.5 beds per 1000 population for short-term care (comparable to what the UK calls acute), Germany has 7.7 beds, whereas Department of Health guidance allows only 2.8. The allocation of beds for the elderly in England, 8.5 to 10 per 1000 population over 65, is eight times lower than in Sweden. Since the mid-1970s, admissions have increased in all countries at the same time as the length of stay has shortened dramatically. Yet there are still wide discrepancies in throughput which are difficult to explain; no one knows how to define the 'correct' number of beds. Influential factors are the supply of community and primary care, the availability of out-patient facilities, the extent of market competition between hospitals, the historical distribution of beds and variations in medical practice.

The number of beds has a major effect on the cost of the service. The UK's relatively low annual cost as reflected in its proportion of the GNP is the consequence of its relatively low number of beds. Most countries are worried about the high cost of hospital services and acknowledge that they have too many beds or that these tend to be wastefully used. To a certain extent this is due to the way doctors exercise control over hospital resources.

QUALITY OF SERVICE

The subject of quality in health care is problematic. What do we actually mean by a 'quality' service? Ultimately, of course, the quality of a service is reflected in the outcome of treatment. In this sense, quality really means (medical) effectiveness and appropriateness (that is, a patient not only receives a treatment that works, but one from which they benefit). However, quality standards, controls and assurance are essentially instruments: important for what they achieve (i.e. improvements in health status) rather than for any inherent self-worth. Methods for improving quality and hence the outcomes of services range from hospital and doctor accreditation to organizational and managerial 'quality' marks, guaranteeing that a particular process, shown to deliver good outcomes, is always used.

Table 14.1 Public attitudes to health care services

	Minor changes needed (%)	Fundamental changes needed (%)	Completely re-build system (%)
Canada	56	38	5
Netherlands	47	46	5
West Germany	41	35	13
France	41	42	10
Australia	34	43	17
Sweden	32	58	6
Japan	29	47	6
United Kingdom	27	52	17
Italy	12	46	40
United States	10	60	29

Source: Harvard-Harris-ITF, 1990 Ten-Nation Survey. In, Blendon, R. *et al.* DataWatch: Satisfaction with health systems in ten countries. *Health Affairs*, **10**(2), 185–92.

What does the public think of the health services? Are they confident that the expenditure and the organization of health care provides appropriate benefits? Table 14.1 shows the considerable differences in public attitudes between ten developed countries. By monitoring the quality of the services provided and, in particular, the work of doctors themselves, it is possible to see where there is specific scope for reform.

The quality of doctors

Countries vary in their attempts to control the quality of doctors' work. The NHS has lagged behind in this respect. It is a public service under the scrutiny of health authorities within the framework set by the Government, but the attempts at quality control until recently had been limited to advisory systems such as the Health Advisory Service, the Development Team for the Handicapped and Community Health Councils. What also has been missing until recently was the systematic review of clinical performance.

Medical audit, for a long time regarded as a management tool rather than a potentially useful process for improving clinical performance, has only received general support from doctors since the White Paper, in 1989, insisted on its importance [11]. Historically, the Royal Colleges exerted some sanctions, where they judged standards too low, by withholding recognition of junior doctor posts for training. General practitioners are subject only to scrutiny of the costs of their drug prescribing. It is noteworthy that until recently the State had allowed control of standards of performance and quality of care to receive so little emphasis.

Although District and GP fundholder purchasers have stipulated strong commitments to the provision of high quality services in their contracts with providers, there is little evidence that purchasers or providers have found reliable ways to measure and monitor quality. Recent initiatives such as the Patient's Charter [12], the Confidential Enquiry into Perioperative Deaths (CEPOD) [13] and the limited use of the quality standard BS 5750 by providers [14] are a step forward with regard to quality, although whether waiting-time targets are an adequate reflection of service quality is debatable. Other countries have done more, for example the USA and France.

Accreditation

Although health services in the USA are apparently allowed to flourish in the open market of free enterprise, hospitals and doctors are in fact closely regulated. All doctors have to be licensed practitioners, and beyond this there is a system for further professional accreditation after postgraduate training. Hospitals themselves are also subjected to accreditation procedures.

The Joint Commission on the Accreditation of Hospitals (JCAH) assesses hospitals every two years on their organizational structure, physical environment and the staffing levels. More recently JCAH has started to examine medical audits undertaken within hospitals by their own staff. Hospitals appoint specialist staff to carry out the accreditation, and those failing to meet the standards face withdrawal of federal or state funds and a consequent loss of financial viability. In 1972, the US Department of Health Education and Welfare introduced Professional Standards Review Organizations (PSROs) to undertake reviews of the use of facilities. These are conducted by physicians and examine individual medical practice in detail. PSROs have been unpopular, and some critics doubt whether they have materially controlled the inflation in hospital costs [15].

France has a well articulated system of inspection. About 4000 physicians, employed by the social security administration, have to authorize costly procedures and scrutinize lengthy stays in hospital. The system is bureaucratic and resented, but the inspectors are well paid and there is no difficulty in recruitment. Hospitals themselves are inspected by a smaller body of civil servants at Département level. At national level, a further body, usually staffed by administrators, undertakes special studies and issues an annual report. Auditors have the right to examine any aspect of the country's administration, and recent reports from them have drawn attention to poor standards in some French hospitals, particularly for longer-stay patients.

FINANCING HEALTH CARE

Methods of financing health care vary considerably, but in all developed countries there is a mix of state funding, insurance and direct payments. Table 14.2 shows the variations in funding sources in nine European countries.

A major concern of all governments is to control costs whatever their methods of financing health care. In the UK, the NHS Review leading to *Working for Patients* [16] studied the various systems for financing health care. After some interest in switching to an insurance based scheme, it was concluded that the present method, largely dependent on taxation (see Chapter 7), was probably better than any other. Certainly the British system is simpler, and this is reflected in the lower administrative costs of the service. It is said that administrative costs in the USA are over 20%, in France 10%, but in the United Kingdom less than 5%.

Equity in financing

All countries profess to be committed to equity in both the provision and financing of health care. In fact these commitments vary considerably. Given that health care consumes resources, what is the fairest way of paying for health care? Because the British NHS is funded largely from general taxation, and because the (direct) tax system is mildly progressive (that is, the rich pay proportionately slightly more in tax than their total share of pre-tax income), NHS funding is also mildly progressive. The Dutch and US systems, in contrast, tend to be regressive – lower income groups contribute proportionally more to health care spending than their share of pre-tax income [17].

Although Sweden and the UK have state-financed systems, the Swedish health service allows for 23 county councils (average population 350 000) and three county boroughs to raise 75% of the total finance through local taxation. Recently there has been a move towards greater central control, particularly vetting new capital building and manpower developments. The Federation of County Councils negotiates with the National Board of Health and Welfare. Around the 1960s, the high standard of living and relative social equality in Sweden led to an explosion in health care facilities and expenditure, but subsequent slower economic growth rates have required costs to be controlled more rigorously. There is some interest in fixing costs through the use of Diagnostic Related Groups (DRGs) and introducing some competition into the system. In common with other countries, the number of elderly in Sweden has increased, as have demands for high technology medicine.

The system in the Netherlands is markedly different from the NHS, (at least before the 1990 Dekker reforms) in that a large proportion of health care is provided by the private sector, but controlled through a series of Acts of Parliament, such as the two Hospital Facilities Acts of 1972 and 1979 and the Health Charges Act 1984. Private fees account for 25% of the total budget of health care, and the rest comes from the Sickness Fund Insurance Scheme set up in 1964 (43%), the Special Sickness Expenses provisions (27%) and a small proportion of direct state funding. The German system is acknowledged to be complicated. Insurance covers over 90% of the population, of whom 57% are compulsorily insured, 13% voluntarily insured and 30%

retired but insured. State employees claim 50% to 70% refunds for services received, but many take out private insurance to cover the cost not reimbursed by the State.

Under the French system, patients first pay in full and then claim back about 75% of the cost. Within that, 80% of in-patient costs are charged direct to the patient's insurance fund, leaving the remainder to be met by the patient. The costs themselves vary geographically and are related to doctors' fees. Insurance cover is by no means universal, and in the early 1970s it was estimated that 80% of the population under the age of 35 was covered, but of the over 80s only 51% of men and 29% of women were covered. A social aid programme, therefore, exists to support those not covered, and those suffering from such chronic illness as tuberculosis or mental disorder.

In the USA, health care is predominantly an insurance-based system, financed in four different ways. First, from private practice on a fee-for-service basis; secondly, by local government, particularly for the poor inner-city and minority groups; thirdly, through the Veterans Administration system and fourthly by the military authorities. Only the last of these could be said to be well organized and integrated, because it deals with a finite population and the organization is susceptible to clear procedures. The Veterans Administration is mainly a hospital service and looks after retired and disabled people who previously served in the forces; it is therefore largely for men, and is exposed to considerable consumer and political pressure.

The local government programme in the USA is heavily supported by federal funds in the form of Medicaid, set up in 1965 to provide a safety net for those too poor to be eligible for private health care insurance schemes. Medicare is also funded by federal government and provides cover for all people over 65. County and city hospitals, private hospitals and many nursing homes recover the daily cost of treating patients under these two schemes. The system allows quality of service standards in these institutions to be scrutinized and, if they are found unsatisfactory, funds may be withdrawn. For instance, a South Carolina hospital, slow to integrate black and white patients, was threatened with the withdrawal of federal funds, which, if implemented, would have closed the hospital. Integration therefore took place [18].

Private care in the USA is available for anyone capable of paying or who has private insurance. The heavy reliance on this system and inadequate financial control of health care charges has inflated costs, so that by 1994 over 15% of GNP was being spent on health care in the USA, and yet the services remained ill-coordinated and underplanned. This is despite the National Health Planning and Resources Development Act which, in 1974, had provided a major impetus to efforts to cut some of the waste inherent in the multiplicity of health care systems. Up to the mid-1960s, government funds contributed only about 25% of the total health care budget, but by the mid-1980s this had increased to 40%. The Reagan administration, in the early 1980s, became increasingly unhappy with this commitment and endeavoured to shift expenditure from federal government to the states, and to encourage more cost sharing with the

Table 14.2 Sources of health care funding: selected countries

Country		Taxation	Social insurance	Private insurance	Out-of pocket payments
Denmark	1981	General central and local government tax revenues used to fund public health care.	None.	Usually provides cover only for public sector copayments.	Copayments for prescription drugs, dental care, physiotherapy.
France	1985	Some revenues from tax on car insurance used to cover social insurance fund deficit.	Three separate occupational health insurance funds covering 98% of population. Contributions related to earnings but vary across schemes. Compulsory in case of employees and split between employee and employer. Ceiling on contributions recently removed for *Régime Général*.	Supplementary insurance paid to mutuelles and private insurance companies. Premiums to *mutuelles* related to earnings and provide cover for *ticket modérateur*. Premiums to private insurees related to risk.	*Ticket modérateur* covers 25% of cost of GP visits and 30% of cost of medicines. Private and *mutuelle* policy-holders can obtain at least partial reimbursement except for some medicines. Some groups and some medicines exempt from *ticket modérateur*. Some small copayments for inpatient care.
Ireland	1987	General central government tax revenues used to fund public health care. Tax deductability of private insurance.	Small health-specific social insurance contribution goes towards funding of public health care.	Mainly taken out by persons in middle and upper income groups whose public cover is limited. Private insurance tax deductible.	Middle income group liable for copayments for inpatient and outpatient treatment, and payment in full for GP visits and prescription medicines.

Table 14.2 cont.

Country	Year	Taxation	Social insurance	Private insurance	Out-of pocket payments
					Top income group liable for copayment for inpatient hotel facilities, and payment in full for consultant services, outpatient and primary care, and prescription medicines.
Italy	1987	General central government tax revenues paid into national health service fund in respect of fiscalization and under other headings. Taxes also used ex-post to cover health services fund deficit.	Compulsory earnings-related contributions to social health insurance fund. Some general social insurance contributions also used to fund public health care. In both cases, contributions schedules vary across professional groups.	Taken out as supplementary cover to health service cover. Includes compulsory scheme for managers.	*Ticket modérateur* payable for prescription drugs, with disabled, etc., exempt. Direct payments to private sector by persons with and without private insurance.
Netherlands	1987	General central government tax revenues used to subsidize sick funds and to finance preventive care.	Compulsory contributions payable by all to AWBZ scheme for catastrophic expenses. Additional insurance contributions payable to sickness funds by	Taken out by persons with income in excess of Dfl49 150 to cover non-catastrophic expenses.	Copayments deductibles paid by persons with private insurance. Direct payments by persons without insurance cover for non-catastrophic

Table 14.2 cont.

Country	Year	Taxation	Social insurance	Private insurance	Out-of pocket payments
			persons with income less than Dfl49 150 for non-catastrophic expenses. In both cases contributions proportional to earnings but subject to ceiling.		expenses. Copayments by sickness fund-insured.
Portugal	1981	General central government tax revenues used to fund public health care and subsidize occupational health insurance schemes operating in public sector.	Some compulsory occupational schemes providing double cover to public sector employees. Contributions related to earnings.	Taken out as supplementary cover to public sector cover.	Copayments to public sector for consultations, diagnostic tests, and medicines. Direct payments to private sector by those with and without private/occupational insurance.
Spain	1980	General central government tax revenues used to cover social insurance deficit and to fund some public care.	Compulsory contributions to social health insurance fund. Contributions proportional to earnings but subject to ceiling which varies across professional groups.	Taken out by persons without public cover and as supplementary cover by persons with public cover.	40% *ticket modérateur* for prescription medicines, but pensioners exempt. Payments to private sector for some services available in public sector and for other services.

Table 14.2 cont.

Country	Year	Taxation	Social insurance	Private insurance	Out-of pocket payments
Switzerland	1981	General federal, cantonal, and communal government tax revenues used to subsidize basic cover provided by sickness funds and to fund public hospitals.	Compulsory contributions to the national accident and disability insurance.	Non-compulsory health insurance premiums paid to sickness funds. Premiums not related to earnings, but vary according to age at time of entry into sickness fund, gender, and (mainly) comfort of inpatient care. Sickness funds are private but subsidized and regulated by the federal government.	
UK	1985	General central government tax revenues used to fund NHS.	Some general social insurance contributions used to fund NHS.	Taken out as supplementary cover to NHS cover.	Charges for prescribed medicines, dental care, and opthalmic care.
US	1981	Federal and state general revenues used to fund Medicaid and some Medicare, and general assistance. Some state and local revenues used to support public hospitals.	Some social insurance contributions go towards funding of Medicare.	Provided mostly as fringe benefit to employees. Participants in Medicare also purchase supplementary cover.	Copayments for inpatient and primary care payable by the privately insured and Medicare enrollees.

Source: van Doorslaer, E., Wagstaff, A. and Rutten, F. (eds) (1993) *Equity in the Finance and Delivery of Health Care: an International Perspective*, Oxford Medical Publications, OUP, Oxford.

consumer while preserving a basic minimum level of service. For the poor, inner-city dweller, the minimum standard may be very low indeed, even in a highly developed country.

As already mentioned, in 1993/4 the Clinton administration attempted to tackle some of the inefficiencies, high costs and inequalities in the US health care system.

Financing health care is a problem in all countries. All governments find themselves spending more than they wish, all complain of waste and poor control, all are worried for the future. Significantly, since the 1980s most have introduced major legislation to control health care costs and financial allocations. It seems that whatever the ideological stance of the government, more state involvement and more state control is inevitable in financing health care.

In the UK, the increasing interest in cost-sharing through privatization and the introduction of a limited form of provider competition to promote the more efficient use of resources, together with the determination to hold management more accountable, all echo the concern of other countries and their governments. Despite the problems facing the NHS, the services produced for the resources provided still make it relatively cost effective.

DEVELOPING COUNTRIES AND EASTERN EUROPE

Although there are fundamental similarities between the health care systems of developing countries and developed countries, there are also basic differences which make direct comparisons difficult, because, for example, so much of the ill-health in developing countries is due to infectious diseases and malnutrition brought about by climate, war and poverty. The work of the World Health Organization (WHO) has been significant in reducing and, in the case of smallpox, eliminating infectious diseases, but poor water supplies remain the most significant source of disease in many countries. AIDS has now become a major threat, particularly in parts of Africa. Some states, especially those which have become rich from oil revenues during the last 30 years, have superimposed Western-style hospitals on a relatively under-developed society. Where this prosperity subsequently collapses, the sophisticated Western-style medicine is likely to wane, exposing the underlying public health problems again.

Momentous recent political and economic upheavals in the former Soviet Union and many of the countries of Eastern Europe have deeply affected health care services in these areas. Converting command economies into ones driven primarily by market forces has created enormous economic and social problems which remain largely unresolved. This has provided an unstable environment for the implementation of health services reforms. Many former Soviet bloc countries exhibit an uneasy mix of the sophistication of industrialized countries alongside basic problems still common in the Third

World. As all countries strive to improve their economies and raise the standard of living of their citizens, they face difficult dilemmas about the amount of health services to provide and the way to pay for these.

International financial institutions

The influence of the World Bank and the International Monetary Fund (IMF) in the economies of many developing and Eastern European countries has expanded in the 1980s and 1990s, to the point where the Bank has developed a loan strategy which embraces social and political as well as economic goals. Because the effects of structural adjustment policies [19] have, controversially, spilled over into other areas such as health and education, the World Bank has increasingly taken an interest in how countries accepting loans organize and fund their public services. In its *World Development Report* for 1993 [20], devoted to health and health care, the World Bank set out detailed policies for the organization of health care services in developing countries.

Many of these policy ideas, such as the promotion of a diversity of competing health care providers and greater use and development of information on cost-effectiveness and provider performance, are familiar to those working in the NHS in the UK. But the Bank's ideas also raise issues which the NHS have only more recently begun to consider. One of these is that governments should specify in detail, and fund, a basic package of health care which is available to all. The question of what particular services the NHS should provide and what it should not has never been overtly or systematically addressed. The greater explicitness in purchasing arising from the reforms of *Working for Patients* [21] will increasingly force purchasers to tackle this decision.

CONCLUSION

This chapter has been, of necessity, a selection of 'snapshots' of health care systems. No two systems are exactly the same (although all have elements in common), and nearly all are experiencing change. Getting the best health care out of a finite budget is a universal concern, as are notions of justice and fairness in terms of access to, and financing of, health care. A policy theme common to many countries is the idea of a mixed economy of health care, and limited or controlled forms of market or managed competition.

NOTES

1. See, for example, van Doorslaer, E. and Wagstaff, A. (1992) Equity in the delivery of health care: some international comparisons. *Journal of Health Economics*, **11**(4), 389–411.
2. See note 1. Empirical work to test the existence and degree of inequity of health care delivery can be very sensitive to the variables chosen to represent health (i.e. need).
3. Op. cit., van Doorslaer and Wagstaff.
4. Harris, J. (1987) QALYfying the value of life. *Journal of Medical Ethics*, **13**, 117–23.
5. One or two examples of patient selection on the grounds of their capacity to benefit hit the headlines every year. In 1993, for example, surgeons at a hospital in the north of England refused a heart operation to a patient who smoked. The clinicians involved justified their refusal on the grounds that the patient would not benefit from treatment as he refused to give up smoking, and that the resources involved could be better spent on someone else.
6. Hunter, D. (1993) *Rationing Dilemmas in Health Care*, Research Paper No. 8, NAHAT, Birmingham.
7. DHSS (1980) *Report of the Working Group on Inequalities in Health* (Black Report), HMSO, London.
8. This chapter faces the same difficulties, but the literature of international comparisons is expanding. Useful books are McLachlan and Maynard, *The Public/Private Mix for Health*, Nuffield Provincial Hospitals Trust, London 1982; Maxwell, *Health Care: the Growing Dilemma*, 2nd edn., McKinsey & Co., 1976, *Health and Wealth: an International Study of Healthcare Spending*, Clexington Books, 1981; Mizrahi, Mizrahi and Sandier *Medical Care, Mobility and Costs*, Pergamon, Oxford, 1983; and Ham, Robinson, Benzeval *Health Check* Kings Fund, London 1990.
9. See, for example, Le Grand, J. (1982) *The Strategy of Equality: Redistribution and the Social Services*, Allen and Unwin, London.
10. Simpson, R. (1978) *Access to Primary Care*, Research Paper No. 6, Royal Commission on the National Health Service, HMSO, London.
11. See, for example, Kerrison, S. *et al.* (1994) Monitoring Medical Audit, in, Robinson, R. and Le Grand, J. (eds), *Evaluating the NHS Reforms*, King's Fund Institute, London.
12. DoH (1991) *The Patient's Charter*, HMSO, London.
13. CEPOD was launched in 1988 and has published the results of three national surveys (completed on a voluntary basis by clinicians) concerned with the quality of the delivery of anaesthesia and surgery and the perioperative care of patients.
14. BS 5750 on Quality Systems is a 'kitemark' of the independent British Standards Institute which is awarded to businesses and organizations to indicate that they follow a predetermined set of standards and processes. It does not necessarily give an indication of the quality of the eventual outcome of the process.
15. For an account of PSROs see Williams and Towers (1980) *Introduction to Health Services*, John Wiley & Sons, New York, pp. 345–6.
16. DoH (January 1989) *Working for Patients*, HMSO, London (Cm. 555).
17. Wagstaff, A. and van Doorslaer, E. (1992) Equity in the finance of health care: Some international comparisons. *Journal of Health Economics*, **11**(4), 361–87.
18. For a full account of this, see Hepner, James O. (ed.) (1980) *Hospital Administrator–Physician Relationships*, C.V. Mosby, St Louis.

19. The term 'structural adjustment' has been used to describe a clutch of economic policies promoted by the World Bank and the IMF in return for loans. These policies include relaxation of exchange rates and reductions in public spending and are designed to liberalize the economies of 'borrower' countries'. Although associated mainly with African countries, the UK was subject to IMF adjustment policies when the British Government took out a loan in the late 1970s. For a clear exposition of structural adjustment, see Melamed, C. (1994) *Adjusting Africa*, Worldview, Oxford.

20. World Bank (1993) *World Development Report 1993: Investing in Health*, Oxford University Press, Oxford.

21. Op. cit., *Working for Patients*.

15

The NHS and the future

The NHS, now approaching its half century, has been the proud epitome of the welfare state. But the principles upon which it was founded are increasingly being challenged. Some people think it is no longer appropriate for the State to act in this way because, they say, it robs people of their personal autonomy and provides no incentive for them to take charge of their own lives. Furthermore, they believe that monolithic state organizations are intrinsically bureaucratic and, therefore, inefficient and insensitive to the people they are set up to serve. In addition to these political criticisms, the NHS also faces changes arising from advances in medical technology, changes in expectations, patterns of disease and illness and external economic forces.

This chapter discusses key issues now facing the NHS, and explores the likely effects of the changes brought about by the National Health Service and Community Care Act, 1990. First, the issue of priority setting is examined, then there is a discussion on resources, and, finally, an examination of the organizational and political responses to views on how the NHS should be run in the light of all the forces which together shape the nation's health services.

PRIORITY SETTING

In looking at other countries' health care systems, Chapter 14 noted that while there are obvious differences between systems there are also universally shared themes, issues and problems. One such is the inevitable need to make choices in health care, to set priorities. At the national level, choices are between health care and education, or defence, or roads, or any other service or good (public or private) that consumes resources (land, labour, etc.) which we would like to enjoy.

The need to choose arises from the impossibility of completely satisfying all demands, wants or needs. In the rather dismal words of economics, sacrifices have to be made and opportunities forgone. This represents a particular view of human beings and their (implicitly greedy) desires; it could be argued that while, in theory, demands and needs are infinite and insatiable in total, in practice this is not how people do, or should, behave. Experience suggests that by and large (and given the opportunity) there is a tendency to express demands beyond the total resources available (however much these are). Whether people should behave like this is another matter. Things would be easier if everyone were completely satisfied with their lot in life, whatever that amounted to. One consequence would be mass redundancies among economists and no need for politicians or, indeed, a political system. Economists and politicians of all persuasions have predicted that the ultimate outcome of both capitalism and socialism would be a withering of the state to a form of anarchy [1]. Whether this is a reliable prediction is open to doubt, however. For the foreseeable future the need to make choices appears inescapable, not only at a national level but within health care systems as well.

Nevertheless, it is important to be aware of the role of behaviour and expectations in relation to priority setting, and not assume that these are either totally malleable or carved in stone. For the NHS, the issue of needs, demands (what we want our health services to do) and the role of expectations are intrinsic factors which exert an enormous influence, not only over the services and treatments provided by the NHS but also over the way it is organized, the way services are delivered, to whom and in what way. It is impossible to ignore these fundamental issues in looking at the future of the NHS and the way it may set priorities.

Need, demand and expectations

Need and demand are interrelated, not the same. Need is based on an objective assessment against known criteria. So, for example, the needs of very elderly people can be gauged by assessing their level of physical disablement and social isolation. From this, appropriate ways of reducing the effects of disability and loneliness can be planned. Demand, on the other hand, is more volatile and is based on expectations, realistic or not.

The increasingly sophisticated knowledge of the population in matters of health and illness, fuelled in part by coverage in the media, excites expectations that may be unreasonable because of uncertain outcome or excessive cost. Heart transplants for babies attract great popular interest, even though this expensive procedure is rare and has, as yet, a relatively poor success rate. On the other hand, the growing understanding of the causes of heart disease ought not to lull people into thinking that the risk of avoidable illness or premature death has thereby been eliminated. Many screening programmes have proved to be surprisingly costly and sometimes ethically dubious. These schemes, which may identify only one positive in many thousands of negatives, prompt the question, how much money can justifiably be spent on finding those at risk? Also, if screening reveals disease that is then untreatable for medical or financial reasons, is it right to have put the individual under that degree of distress? The incidence of AIDS pinpoints this dilemma: what benefit does a test that establishes a patient as HIV positive have on that person if nothing can yet be done to cure him or her, or relatively little done to alleviate symptoms? The mass screening of women for cervical cancer finds proportionately few positive cases. The cost, estimated at over £300 000 per positive result, may be thought unreasonably high if that money could be more effectively used on other services with unequivocally beneficial outcomes.

Health service objectives

The public has not yet grappled with the full implications of these difficult issues and, until it does, demand, as enshrined in the now fashionable concept of consumerism, will dominate the debate about health care. But it would be extremely unwise to allow demand to overrule need, so how should the NHS decide what to do? Should it target disadvantaged groups? Should it ignore accusations that it interferes in the rights of individuals? Can it justify spending large sums to screen the population in order to identify only small amounts of disease? In 1979, the Royal Commission on the NHS [2] listed seven main objectives of the service, and they are still appropriate:

1 Encourage and assist individuals to remain healthy.
2 Provide equality of entitlement to health services.
3 Provide a broad range of services of high standard.
4 Provide equality of access to these services.
5 Provide a service free at time of use.
6 Satisfy the reasonable expectations of its users.
7 Remain a national service responsive to local needs.

The policies and actions of successive governments clearly have not always honoured these. Health promotion was shown, in Chapter 8, often to have elicited half-hearted responses, compromised by conflicting interests. Certainly the NHS generally provides a wide range of care and treatment for all, but long waiting-lists have been allowed to become an endemic problem: in 1994 there were over one million people waiting for admission to hospital, 6% of them obliged to wait well over 12 months for treatment. This has become an embarrassment for the Government by so obviously displaying one way in which the NHS has failed, particularly when other countries have avoided the problem.

Equality of access to care is a more complicated objective: who should have priority? The Black Report [3] (and many others since) produced a detailed description of social inequality and related this to ill-health. The report's finding, that there is a much higher incidence of disease among the poorest and most deprived, may now seem unsurprising, but it still poses challenges for any government wishing to correct the inequality. At a time when the welfare state is criticized for supposedly weakening individuals' self-reliance, it may be politically inappropriate for governments to direct the NHS to single out disadvantaged groups for special favour, even though failure to do so increases the prevalence of avoidable ill-health. Similarly, immunization is a successful and simple way of eliminating certain diseases and is now, on the whole, accepted as a voluntary duty, while other preventive measures remain controversial. Official steps to combat poor diet, reduce alcohol intake and cigarette smoking and enforce the wearing of car seat belts are regarded by some as improper trespasses upon the liberty of the individual.

Very few copies of the Black Report were printed when it was published in 1980 and discussion was effectively suppressed by the Conservative Government, even though the report had been officially commissioned in 1977 and was conducted by an eminent senior figure in the medical profession. He presented his findings in careful, sober terms. In the mid-1990s, there are few signs of a coherent national approach to addressing the inequalities he identified. Certainly the resource implications are enormous, but so are the social and ethical consequences of continued wilful neglect.

Demands for health services come not only from patients; doctors have been the most powerful claimants for NHS resources. Technological advances now permit them to make highly complicated interventions. These include such sophisticated diagnostic techniques as computerized tomography (CT) scanning and nuclear magnetic resonance, both of which are real improvements on the older, more invasive forms of radiological investigation. Joint-replacement surgery and microsurgical techniques have greatly increased the range of possible treatments. New drugs, too, though often extremely expensive, have unquestionably alleviated hitherto medically untreatable conditions. Doctors have not been slow to share their successes with the public and this, in turn, has boosted expectations. At the same time, the rising number of infirm elderly in the population is currently accompanied by a shortage of those most likely to look after them. Elderly people's use of health services in general is relatively high, although only about 10% of them actually need residential or hospital care at any one time. The types of community-based services they need compete unequally for resources with glamorous, headline-making high technology hospital medicine.

Future choices

If one thing is certain in the future, it is the necessity to make choices between competing demands on scarce resources. This remains true with or without the NHS. If the NHS did not exist, then choices would transfer to individuals, who would then have to engage in trade-offs between different health-giving activities and commodities, subject to limits on their personal resources, such as time and money.

Traditionally, the NHS has tackled the question of priority-setting through a combination of political and administrative processes. At the level of choice for individual patients, it has relied on doctors to shoulder the ethical and moral burden of selecting who should receive treatment (and how much) and who should not. Generally, this arrangement (particularly the doctors' role) has been covert. This is changing, now that questions about priority-setting and its related activity of rationing become much more public. The separation of purchasers – whose main role is to maximize health gain or, put another way, choose whom not to buy care for – and providers has highlighted the essential priority-setting task and more clearly identified purchasers as responsible for undertaking it.

How are purchasers best able to tackle this? One possibility is to adopt the health economists' technical answer to the problem, that is to redefine the objectives of health care in terms that allow them to make rational (and justifiable) purchasing decisions. Although appealing in its logical simplicity, this priority-setting method not only requires the resolution of complex value judgements and trade-offs with other objectives, but also implies a huge data collection and research exercise to establish the outcomes of medical interventions.

An alternative course, mentioned in Chapter 4, would be to pursue the traditional method of 'muddling through' in a way that maximizes society's agreement rather than maximizing the health care outcomes, however measured. In return, this will produce (as it has done in the past) numerous examples of inconsistency and variation between clinicians, geographical areas and over time.

The dilemma for the NHS is that there is no agreed rule for opting between different ways of choosing. In these circumstances, an important role for the NHS is to educate the public about the issues involved and to be open about the costs as well as the benefits of whatever methods are used to make the choices.

THE RESOURCE QUESTION

The NHS is mainly financed from general taxation, with National Insurance contributions and charges contributing under 20% of the total budget. It is, therefore, inextricably linked with the state of the economy. Chapter 7 showed that the proportion of the gross national product (GNP) spent on health services was lower than in most other comparable countries, but that, despite this, value for money was relatively high. One reason for the 'low' level of expenditure is the fact that doctors and other professional workers are paid comparatively less than their counterparts in other countries. Yet it is still broadly true that most patients who are acutely ill will be able to receive the treatment they require.

Why then should so many UK governments have investigated other ways of paying for the resources the NHS consumes? Their first concern is control: the pressure from unrestrained demand would soon become intolerable. Experience in other countries demonstrates that however much money is invested in health care, the trend is always for it to require more. In the UK, the method of financing (general taxation) and the system for determining the level of financing (imposition of an overall budget determined by the Government) have remained largely unchanged over the years and though alternatives have been canvassed and explored, the costs of change and the new disadvantages they bring have never been deemed worth the benefits of solving other problems. For example, insurance-based schemes inflate costs and exclude those who are likely to be bad financial risks. Chapter 14 showed that millions of people in the USA are uninsured and, according to the criteria adopted by the insurance companies, uninsurable. Voucher schemes are an imperfect method because, while they equalize the potential for access, they do nothing to ensure actual needs are met. A patient requiring extended care may run out of entitlement, while a healthy person could choose to spend his or her vouchers on inessential treatment.

However, within the NHS itself, various initiatives have been explored to address the resourcing issue. One is to control wasteful use within the system. In the case of hospital ancillary services, this was coupled with an attempt to curb union power to bias the labour market through restrictive practices. The introduction of competitive tendering caused a fall in the number of staff required and in the cost of the service (Chapter 11). Bonus schemes and industrial action in 1979 promoted savings in the hotel services and gave better results. But these were marginal gains that did not address the core activity, clinical patient care. The introduction of local professional clinical and management audit and studies by such government agencies as the Audit Commission and the National Audit Office have put specific health services and activities in the spotlight. No longer can wide variations in the costs of clinical procedures be explained away as permissable manifestations of doctors' clinical autonomy. Why should the same operation in one hospital cost double in another?

The introduction of the internal market following the 1990 reforms of the NHS is meant to promote efficiency and make available resources go further. In theory, high cost hospitals will suffer financial penalties because patients will be referred to competing units, where the same treatment can be obtained for a lower price. In practice, the extent to which this basic market principle actually operates in the NHS is unknown and will depend on whether prices will (or can ever) properly reflect or transmit all the characteristics of a provider's services. Another problem with the price signal is that purchasers are likely to use other criteria in choosing providers, such as how close they are situated to the populations they will serve [4].

Although some changes that seem to have been brought about by the market (see Chapter 2 on London's health services, for example), it is difficult to see how this will develop in the future or its implications for resources. Ironically, given that the genesis of the reforms lay in calls to tackle underfunding, the answer – a competitive market – may do more to expose the extent of this underfunding than any other approach.

ORGANIZATIONAL STRUCTURE

The NHS is one of the largest employers in the world, with a staff of nearly 1 million people. An organization as big as this is likely to concern governments, not only because of the huge resources it requires, but because its day-to-day business is ultimately beyond a government's grasp.

If Health Authorities were to challenge government policy en masse, the political consequences could be immense. Recent reorganizations and reforms have been designed partly to reduce the risk of organizational anarchy by strengthening lines of accountability and imposing stringent checks and balances. The new duality of purchasers and providers has established counter-vailing forces which will quite quickly render the previous monolithic structure obsolete. The theory of the new market now developing in the NHS is that neither the purchasers nor the providers can dominate, because they are locked into mutual dependency and are obliged to negotiate with one another.

However, experience from private sector markets should sound a note of caution about this apparently reliable, neat symmetry of market forces. Only under the most idealized of conditions do markets reach a state of competitive equilibrium, in which demand equals supply and no one can be made better off without making someone else worse off [5]. Even a small deviation from the ideal, perfect market means that not only will equilibrium not be reached, it can be missed completely. In other words, the market fails to allocate resources efficiently. This has been known by economists for years [6].

The latest reorganization of the NHS Executive and the Regions was meant to set up a regulatory framework to manage the market so that it would not fail. By the mid-1990s it is unclear exactly how such regulation will be achieved. The Department of Health does not even have adequate measures to identify readily even the most blatant of (potential) market failures as monopoly providers. The publication of *Local Freedoms, National Responsibilities* in 1994 went some way to addressing problems of market regulation, however [7].

The introduction of trusts and the extent of their freedoms add an uncertain element. If several of them all concluded, for sound financial reasons, that they would not offer all the basic services the conveniently situated health author-ities wished to buy from them, would that signal the end of comprehensive local care under the NHS? Or would the market regulators, in the form of the Regional Offices, have the power to force providers to comply with the wishes of purchasers?

On the purchaser side, merging Districts with FHSAs is creating around 90 health commissions in England. But with local government boundary changes coterminosity still has not been achieved and this may make it difficult to deal properly with the predicted shift to community-based care. However, will this also resolve the conflicting roles of GP fundholders (who only are responsible for the people on their lists) and Districts (who are responsible for all the resi-dents in their area)? New models and groupings in purchasing are emerging all the time, on a spectrum from 'total fundholding', in which GPs control the entire health care budget for their patients, through to multifunds and Districts working on the basis of locality purchasing, which more closely involve the views and decisions of their local GPs. Further difficulties arise from the fact that health care is free at the time of use but social services are largely means-tested [8]. This puts a premium on good relationships and the need for agreed protocols working across the range of NHS and local government purchasers.

CONCLUSION

Whatever the organizational solutions, the NHS seems likely to remain, in most respects, a public, government-financed service for the time being. The 1990 reforms provide opportunities for greater innovation and enterprise, but also for more local regulation through accreditation and monitoring. The increased emphasis on standards, on quality, on evaluating outcomes and ensuring greater efficiency and effectiveness present important challenges to the managers and professionals on whom the service depends. By the end of the century it will be time to judge whether, after 50 years of the NHS and 30 years of virtually continuous reorganization, the NHS is still able to honour its prime objective of providing a comprehensive service aimed at improving the overall health of the nation.

NOTES

1. In an ideal free market all markets would 'clear', i.e. demand would equal supply; there would be no unemployment and no need for intervention by government. A government's role would be reduced perhaps to maintaining national defence. In his political and economic writings, Karl Marx came to similar conclusions about the eventual outcome of socialism.
2. *Royal Commission on the National Health Service* (1979), HMSO, London (Cmnd. 7615), para. 2.6, p. 9.
3. *DHSS Report of the Working Party on Inequalities in Health* (Black Report) (1980), HMSO, London. Also published in amended form by Pelican Books, London, in 1982.
4. In 1994 there was an example of the provider travelling to the patient, when Bradford Hospitals trust won a contract to run some services in Surrey, over 200 miles away.
5. This is known as a 'Pareto optimum' after the economist Vilfredo Pareto.
6. There are many somewhat technical papers by economists dealing with the inherent weaknesses of the competitive equilibrium theory (e.g. Radner, R. (1968) Competitive Equilibrium under Uncertainty. *Econometrica*, 36; Lancaster, K. and Lipsey, R. (December 1956) The General Theory of the Second Best. *Review of Economic Studies*).
7. NHSE (1994) *Local Freedoms, National Responsibilities.*
8. DoH (1995) Circular HSG (95)8, LAC (95)5, *NHS Responsibilities for Meeting Continuing Health Care Needs.*

Index